T0328139

Accounting Thought and Practice Reform

This book is a sympathetic portrait of one of the outstanding accounting thinkers of the twentieth century, offering new insights, from original sources, into his astonishingly varied interests and activities.
—**Professor Geoffrey Whittington**, *Cambridge University, U.K.*

Raymond John Chambers was born just over a century ago on 16 November 1917. It has been more than fifty years since his first classic, *Accounting, Evaluation and Economic Behavior*, was published, more than forty since *Securities and Obscurities: Reform of the Law of Company Accounts* (republished in 1980 as Accounting in Disarray), and over twenty since the unique *An Accounting Thesaurus: Five Hundred Years of Accounting*. They are drawn upon extensively in this biography of Chambers' intellectual contributions, as are other of his published works. Importantly, we also analyse archival correspondence not previously examined.

While Chambers provided several bibliographical summaries of his work, without the benefits of reviewing and interspersing the text with correspondence materials from the Chambers Archive, this study would lack an appreciation of the impact of his early childhood and nuances related to his practical (including numerous consultancies) and academic experiences. The 'semi-biographical narrative' codifies article and editorial length exercises by the authors drawing on parts of the archive related to theory development, measurement, and communication. Other parts are also examined. This allows us to respond to those critics who claim his reforms were naive. They further reveal a man of theory and practice, whose theoretical ideas were solidly grounded on observations from his myriad interests and experiences. Many of his practical experiences have not been examined previously. This approach and the first book-length biography differentiate this work from earlier analyses of Chambers' contribution to the accounting literature.

We provide evidence to support the continued push for the reforms he proposed to accepted accounting thought and practice to ensure accounting is the serviceable technology so admired by Pacioli, Da Vinci, and many other Renaissance pioneers. It will be of interest to researchers, educators, practitioners, and regulators alike.

Frank Clarke is Emeritus Professor of Accounting at The University of Newcastle and Honorary Professor of Accounting at The University of Sydney, Australia.

Graeme Dean is Emeritus Professor at The University of Sydney, Australia.

Martin Persson is the J. J. Wettlaufer Faculty Fellow and an Assistant Professor of Managerial Accounting and Control at the Ivey Business School, Canada.

Routledge New Works in Accounting History

Series Editor: John Richard Edwards, Richard Fleischman, Garry Carnegie, Salvador Carmona

This innovative series contains volumes on accounting history, auditing, bibliography, development of accounting principles and standards, education and ethics, financial reporting, law and regulations, management accounting and the theoretical works of leading scholars. Providing students, teachers and researchers with the opportunity to learn more about the discipline of accountancy and its past, this series is a vital addition to any accounting library.

Accounting and Food: Some Italian Experiences
Edited by Massimo Sargiacomo, Luciano D'Amico, & Roberto Di Pietra

**Memorial Articles for 20th Century
American Accounting Leaders**
Edited by Stephen A. Zeff

The Italian and Iberian Influence in Accounting History
The Imperative of Power
Edited by Michele Bigoni and Warwick Funnell

The Origins of Accounting Culture
The Venetian Connection
*Edited by Massimo Sargiacomo, Stefano Coronella, Chiara Mio,
Ugo Sostero, and Roberto Di Pietra*

Accounting for Alcohol
An Accounting History of Brewing, Distilling and Viniculture
Edited by Martin Quinn and João Oliveira

Accounting Thought and Practice Reform
Ray Chambers' Odyssey
Frank Clarke, Graeme Dean and Martin Persson

For a full list of titles in this series, please visit www.routledge.com

Accounting Thought and Practice Reform

Ray Chambers' Odyssey

Frank Clarke, Graeme Dean and Martin Persson

 Routledge
Taylor & Francis Group

NEW YORK AND LONDON

First published 2019
by Routledge
605 Third Avenue, New York, NY 10017

and by Routledge
2 Park Square, Milton Park, Abingdon, Oxon, OX14 4RN

First issued in paperback 2020

Routledge is an imprint of the Taylor & Francis Group, an informa business

Library of Congress Cataloging-in-Publication Data
Names: Clarke, Frank L., 1933– author. | Dean, G. W., 1951–
author. | Persson, Martin E., author.
Title: Accounting thought and practice reform : Ray Chambers'
odyssey / Frank Clarke, Graeme Dean, and Martin Persson.
Description: New York, NY : Routledge, 2018. | Series: Routledge
new works in accounting history | Includes bibliographical
references and index.
Identifiers: LCCN 2018034643 | ISBN 9781138337596 (hardback) |
ISBN 9780429442278 (ebook)
Subjects: LCSH: Chambers, R. J. (Raymond J.), 1917–1999. |
Accounting teachers—Australia—Biography. | Accounting. |
LCGFT: Biographies.
Classification: LCC HF5604.5.C49 C58 2018 | DDC 657.092
[B]—dc23
LC record available at https://lccn.loc.gov/2018034643

ISBN 13: 978-0-367-73307-0 (pbk)
ISBN 13: 978-1-138-33759-6 (hbk)

Typeset in Sabon
by Apex CoVantage, LLC

Figure 0.1 Ray Chambers

Contents

Tables

Figures

Illustrations

Contributors

Frank Clarke is Emeritus Professor of Accounting at The University of Newcastle, Honorary Professor of Accounting at The University of Sydney; visiting appointments also at the Universities of Sydney, Glasgow, Canterbury (NZ), and Lancaster; a past editor of *Abacus*, currently a consulting editor; author or joint author of nine books and over 100 refereed journal articles.

Graeme Dean is Emeritus Professor at The University of Sydney; has held visiting appointments also at several overseas universities, Canterbury (NZ), Cardiff, Glasgow, Hohenheim, Munich, Stuttgart, and Graz. Editor (1994–2009), currently consulting editor of *Abacus*, the fourth oldest and one of the leading Anglo-American accounting academic journals; published over a dozen books and books of readings, as well as more than sixty-five refereed journal articles.

Martin Persson is the J. J. Wettlaufer Faculty Fellow and an Assistant Professor of Managerial Accounting and Control at the Ivey Business School and his research is focused on the development of accounting thought. He is particularly interested in people, ideas, and institutions from the 1900s as well as classical accounting theory and measurement issues. His research has been published in Emerald's book series *Development of Accounting Thought* and in journals such as *Abacus*, *Accounting Historians Journal*, *Accounting History*, and *Accounting History Review*.

Abbreviations

AAA	American Accounting Association
AAHoF	Australian Accounting Hall of Fame (University of Melbourne)
AARF	Australian Accounting Research Foundation
AASC	Australian Administrative Staff College
AAT	*An Accounting Thesaurus: Five Hundred Years of Accounting*
AAUTA	Australasian Association of University Teachers of Accounting; forerunner of AAANZ and AFAANZ
ABR	*Accounting and Business Research*
Abacus	*Abacus: A journal of accounting and business studies*
AE&EB	*Accounting, Evaluation and Economic Behavior*
AAANZ	Accounting Association of Australia and New Zealand
AFAANZ	Accounting and Finance Association of Australia and New Zealand
AFR	*Australian Financial Review*
AHF	Accounting Hall of Fame (U.S. Ohio State University)
AIA	American Institute of Accountants
AICPA	American Institute of Certified Public Accountants
AIFRS	Australian International Financial Reporting Standard
AIM	Australian Institute of Management
APB	Accounting Principles Board (U.S.A.), antecedent body of the FASB
APESB	Accounting Professional and Ethical Standards Board
ARB	Accounting Research Bulletin (published by AICPA)
ARB33	'Depreciation and High Costs,' issued by AIA (December, 1947)
ARB51	'Consolidated Financial Statements,' AICPA (issued by Committee on Accounting Procedure, August 1959)
ARIA	Accounting Researchers International Association
ARS	Accounting Research Study (commissioned by AICPA)
ARS1	'The Basic Postulates of Accounting,' Moonitz (1961)
ARS3	'A Tentative Set of Broad Accounting Principles,' Sprouse and Moonitz (1962)
ARS6	'Reporting the Financial Effects of Price-Level Changes,' Staff of the Research Division of AICPA (1963)

ASA	Australian Society of Accountants (or 'Society'), antecedent of CPAA
ASC	Australian Securities Commission (1991–98), antecedent of ASIC
ASIC	Australian Securities and Investments Commission (1998–)
ASX	Australian Stock Exchange
ASRC	Accounting Standards Review Committee
ASR190	Accounting Series Release 190, 'Amendments to Regulation S-X Requiring Disclosure of Certain Replacement Cost Data,' SEC (1976)
BACA	Business Archives Council of Australia
BHP	The Broken Hill Proprietary Company Limited
BIS	Bank for International Settlements
'Blueprint. . .'	Blueprint for a Theory of Accounting
CBD	Central Business District
CCAB	Consultative Committee of Accounting Bodies (U.K.)
CCA	Current Cost Accounting
CCE	Current Cash Equivalent
CICA	Canadian Institute of Chartered Accountants
CLERP	Company Law Economic Reform Program
CoCoA	Continuously Contemporary Accounting; originally written as COCOA
CPAA	Certified Practising Accountants of Australia
CPP	Constant Purchasing Power
ED	Exposure Draft
ED8	U.K. Exposure Draft 8, 'Accounting for Changes in the Purchasing Power of Money,' Accounting Standards Steering Committee, ICAEW (January 1973)
ED18	U.K. Exposure Draft 18, 'Current Cost accounting,' Inflation Accounting Steering Group, ICAEW (May 1978)
EU	European Union
FAS	Financial Accounting Standards (issued by the FASB)
FASB	Financial Accounting Standards Board (U.S.A.)
FITB	Future Income Tax Benefit
FSB	Financial Stability Board (from April 2009 until present; formerly the FSF)
FSF	Financial Stability Forum (1999 until April 2009 when reconfigured as the FSB)
GAAP	Generally Accepted Accounting Principles
GFC	Global Financial Crisis
GPP	General Purchasing Power
HCA	Historical Cost Accounting
IAAER	International Association for Accounting Education and Research
IAS	International Accounting Standards

IASB	International Accounting Standards Board
IASC	International Accounting Standards Committee
ICAA	The Institute of Chartered Accountants in Australia (or 'The Institute')
ICRA	International Centre for Research in Accounting (Lancaster University)
ICAEW	The Institute of Chartered Accountants in England and Wales
ICWA	The Institute of Cost and Works Accountants
IFAC	International Federation of Accountants
IFRS	International Financial Reporting Standards
IMF	International Monetary Fund
INFORMS	Institute for Operations Research and the Management Sciences
JAR	*Journal of Accounting Research*
LIFO	Last-in-first-out inventory method
MAT or *Modern. . .*	*Modern Accounting Thought* (a proposed book by Chambers)
NAO	National Audit Office (Australia)
NCSC	National Companies and Securities Commission (1978–83)
N.S.W. CAC	New South Wales Corporate Affairs Commission (1974–83)
PAC	Pacific Acceptance Corporation Pty Ltd.
PAT	Positive Accounting Theory
PARB	Public Accountants' Registration Board (N.S.W.)
PE	Private Equity
PJT	Prices Justification Tribunal
Probus	Branch of Rotary in Australia that deals with business issues
PwC	PricewaterhouseCoopers
RBA	Reserve Bank of Australia
Sandilands	U.K. *Inflation Accounting: Report of the Inflation Accounting Committee* (Chairman F.E.P. Sandilands)
SAR	Studies in Accounting Research (commissioned by the AAA)
SATTA	Statement on Theory and Theory Acceptance (AAA publication)
SEC	Securities and Exchange Commission (U.S.A.)
SFAS	Statement of Financial Accounting Standards (SFAS)
SIV	Special investment vehicle
SMH	*Sydney Morning Herald*
S&O	*Securities & Obscurities: A Case for Reform of the Law of Company Accounts*
SPE	Special purpose entity
SSA	*Sydney School of Accounting: The Chambers Years*
SSAP7	U.K. Statement of Standard Accounting Practice No. 7, 'Accounting for Changes in the Purchasing Power of Money,' Accounting Standards Steering Committee, ICAEW (May 1974)

TAR	*The Accounting Review*
TIMS	The Institute of Management Sciences
UNSW	University of New South Wales
U.S.	United States
U.S.A.	United States of America
USA P202	University of Sydney Archives, Personal Collection #202 (Ray Chambers)
Wisdom . . .	*Wisdom of Accounting* (a proposed book by Chambers)

Prologue

[W]hy is it that accounting is so clumsy, graceless, discordant, undisciplined?
—Chambers, letter to Maurice Moonitz, 1991

We can study the graphic, the literary and the musical arts scientifically without calling them sciences. I believe that flirtations with science (most of them ignorant or arrogant) have given rise to the errant and vagrant movements that are the butt of your shafts [referring to criticisms of positive accounting in William Cooper and Steve Zeff, 1987]. . . . It may not be easy to stem the tide; but easy things are only for the indifferent, the delinquent or the indolent.
—Chambers, letter to Cooper, 1987

We sit [in the Great Hall of the University of Sydney] beneath a set of seraphs holding books which signify study of the liberal arts, the mathematical arts, the sciences and ethics, the corpus of ideas and ideals for which the University stands. I have always felt comfortable under these symbols, for accounting is in essence a language of verbal and mathematical signs dedicated ideally to the service of trust between men.
—Response by Chambers to Baxt's address, 1991[1]

An Intellectual Biography

Raymond John Chambers (1917–99) was one of the twentieth-century accounting reformers with varied interests and activities. He was a first-class *educator, researcher,* and *mentor*. He has been described by his peers as an 'accounting pioneer' (Maurice Moonitz, 1982), an 'intellectual giant' of the twentieth century (George Staubus, 2003)—truly a 'Renaissance man' (Giuseppe Galassi, private correspondence with Graeme Dean, 2000) and an 'intellectual leader and an always stimulating presence: a rigorous theorist and prolific author whose impact was felt around the world' (Zeff, 2011). One pre-publication reviewer likened the importance to accounting of Chambers' accounting theory to that of Keynes' 'General Theory. . .' to economics. Chambers was selected by Dick Edwards (1994) as one of his *Twentieth Century Accounting Thinkers*. Additionally, he was the first academic outside of North America to be inducted into the Ohio State University Accounting Hall of Fame. He received many other awards, such as in 1958 being the first recipient of the ASA's Citation for Meritorious Contribution to the Literature of Accounting, *Accounting and Action*, and in 1967 the AICPA's Gold Medal for outstanding contribution to accounting literature, *Accounting, Evaluation and Economic Behavior*. In 1978 he was awarded the Order of Australia for services to commerce and education, particularly in accounting and business management. These, and other recognitions, are listed in his 'Aide Memoire.'[2]

Chambers' accounting odyssey was driven by the search for order in commercial dealings. He concluded this would only be achieved if, through a theoretically based set of reforms, accounting could be shown to be an effective form of instrumentation. Its readings would provide generally relevant information, facilitating investment and financing decisions. To achieve this accounting educators needed to be educated.

Our approach in describing his life is similar to that taken in *Mad World: Evelyn Waugh and the Secrets of Brideshead*, where Paula Byrne observed that: 'As a literary genre, the heavily footnoted biographical doorstopper had its heyday in the second-half of the twentieth century,' and following an accepted alternative path she instead sought to unravel matters related to Waugh's life through his major novel, *Brideshead Revisited*.

We consider Chambers' life and experiences, examining his intellectual contributions to the reform of accounting thought and practice, through published and unpublished correspondence from the *R.J. Chambers Collection* (hereafter the Chambers Archive).[3] As well, we analyse his three classic books and several of Chambers' published works collected by the Chambers and Dean (1986a-e, 2000) six-volume *Chambers on Accounting*.[4]

Also examined are responses from family members to our questions. These sources allow us to explore more deeply the many forces that forged Chambers' thinking about accounting as a purposive technology.

Importantly, this account is presented to an audience, many of whom are likely to be unfamiliar with much accounting thought and practice from the twentieth century. Some things have changed: the advent of globalization and securitization with the associated internationalization of accounting, and many financial service institutions have morphed from partnerships to limited liability companies with reduced personal customer/financier relationships and reduced trust generally in the financial services sector. The early part of that century saw accounting practices relatively unregulated. By the middle there were profession-recommended principles of accounting practice, and by the end national and international standards were prescribed, some even by legislation.

However, it might be a surprise to many that, while some tweaking of business structures and financing practices has accompanied accounting regulatory changes, the financial and management fundamentals of business have not changed. But the role of accounting in facilitating trust, by informing the risk- and reward-based negotiations of interested parties in all organizations, is even more critical now as the lack of trust in the financial sector grows. Fairness in those negotiations, which requires a level reporting field, persists as the lynchpin.

Chambers entered accounting at a time when there was little in the way of theory, or indeed grounded research. Much was achieved along the way. Importantly, after graduating from university, his practical experiences during World War II in industry and the Prices Commission, coupled to his post-war development of management education programs at Sydney Technical College, the Australian Institute of Management, and the Australian Administrative Staff College, Mount Eliza, saw him immersed in the consideration of accounting's role in resolving practical problems. An early address in this area was titled 'Management in Wonderland' captured concerns that accounting failed to fulfil that role.[5]

Those experiences also pushed him to the forefront of the movement by educators, practitioners, and regulators for improved education programs for managers and commerce programs for accountants. Considerable practitioner connections resulted in significant consultancies throughout the 1950s–1970s and his participation from the mid-1960s in what became known as the Sydney General Management Group. This coincided with the formulation of his theory of Continuously Contemporary Accounting (CoCoA).

Evidence of these contiguous theory and practitioner pathways has not previously been discussed.

While much was achieved along the way, because of the challenges posed several matters remain 'unfinished business.' The reflections of Chambers and others throughout the biography show that the reform work continues— with several works being undertaken by members of what is now termed the 'Sydney School.' They cover areas of accounting as a measurement and communication system—in particular related to fair value accounting, said to underpin the post-2005 IFRSs regime.[6]

The biography is very much a tribute to Chambers' efforts in acting as an irritant to his beloved profession, to rid it of the infelicities that he had long noted. The reproduced materials in the 'Unfinished Business' chapter relating to his proposed *Wisdom of Accounting* monograph show a determination to continue his reform efforts, to make accounting a serviceable technology, an effective instrumentation. While his observations are forcefully expressed, this was deemed necessary to prod significant responses from practitioners, regulators, and academics who he felt were all too happy to continue doing what they were presently doing. He experienced several setbacks, and his prodding upset some.

Born in 1917, Chambers had a difficult childhood. Experiences growing up in Newcastle, Australia, just prior to and during the Depression affected him in several ways. The death of his mother, Louisa, when he was four and his brother, Albert Cyril (Bert)- was two, meant their childhood was spent separately with relatives. During the latter part of the 1920s and early '30s, both boys shouldered a lot of work in the milk-vending and newspaper businesses run by their father. This was while they attempted to complete their schooling. The pressures presumably hardened both to confront future life experiences, especially the inevitable setbacks. Joseph Chambers' loss of around 90 per cent of the purchased goodwill (i.e., that part of the Sydney newspaper franchise purchase price due to maintaining income from existing clients), when he sold the franchise after the Depression hit, significantly influenced Chambers' thoughts about the goodwill concept and how to account for it (chapters 5 and 6).

Regarding Chambers' religious influences and desire to achieve social justice, we show that, in his writings and through the observations of his children, Chambers strove to ensure fairness in dealings generally, and in his academic life his preferred system of accounting was premised on the need for a level playing field through the provision of up-to-date disclosures. This would, he felt, go a long way in achieving the goal of commercial order.

The early chapters also show that from the initial stages of his academic career, he found solace in music and the arts more generally. He was fascinated in artistic achievements, whose excellence, simplicity, and concord at their greatest generally contrasted with what he saw all around in his accounting domain. Discord and complexity and the acceptance by the masses of these features were anathema to him.

Chambers' primary and secondary school education was in Newcastle. With the benefit of a tertiary scholarship to study economics at the University of Sydney, he graduated in 1939. Following practical stints in business and the government, he began teaching at Sydney Technical College. This was followed after several years with appointment as the first full-time senior lecturer, then the first full-time associate professor, in accounting (1953 and 1955), at the University of Sydney. He was appointed to the university's foundation Chair of Accounting in 1960, a position held till his retirement in 1983.

After formally retiring, Chambers continued to work and publish at a prodigious rate until his untimely death in 1999. A brief account by two of the current authors (Clarke and Dean) and their Sydney colleague Murray Wells, *The Sydney School of Accounting: The Chambers Years* (*SSA*), records aspects of life in the Sydney School during those years.[7] It made no pretence of being a complete history, but it captured the spirit of enquiry and experimentation, the excitement of discovery and the joy of teaching within the school. Chambers' teaching skills had much to do with this.

Chambers is especially known for a proposed alternative to the conventional historic cost accounting system, CoCoA. A market-based system, it supplants historic costs as the primary valuation basis for reporting an entity's assets and liabilities. Determining income for a period under CoCoA has three components: net revenues—all receipts less all payments made in the ordinary course of business; a price variation adjustment—the net amount of all changes in the cash equivalents of physical assets (namely, plant and equipment, buildings, and stock in trade); and the capital maintenance adjustment—the scale adjustment necessary to restate net wealth at the period's commencement in terms of the general purchasing power of the currency at its end.

A letter to the editor of *The Australian* newspaper in 1966 shows he had long felt that, as a practising art, accounting was a deeply flawed instrumentation system, being unserviceable for the decision making and control uses ordinarily made of it. He suggested 'accounting should move into the space age . . . with much finer instrument systems.'[8] His posthumously published article, 'Life on the Fringe—an Accounting Odyssey,' succinctly indicates those concerns endure:

> That its practice was fundamentally faulty was illustrated abundantly in the post-war inflation in the 1950s, '60s and later, by the spate of take-over bids covering the same period, and by the disparity between what companies—or what company accounts—said their properties [assets] were worth and what they were really worth. Company accounts were false though they were said by company officers and auditors to be true. And what was false could be of no use to managers, investors or creditors. The flaws were universal—and if they could be excused or papered over in practice, that was no safe or serviceable ground for an extensively influential profession. I determined to try to set things right—by reworking basic ideas, challenging conventional practices or habits, and teaching a set of ideas to the rising generation of practitioners.[9]

Developed as part of repeated attempts to reform the law of company accounts, CoCoA is based on theoretical footings that are grounded in Chambers' observations of commerce and the role of accounting in it. This grounded theory aspect is little known, or certainly rarely acknowledged. To undertake those reforms, Chambers pursued many matters—in particular, the desire for, and pursuit of, general public awareness that there could be a better corporate reporting system. The *SSA* monograph observed that he wanted to establish:

> a system based not on custom and dogma, but one that was rigorously, scientifically based. This meant the need for greater recourse to research, to theoretical explorations, to the history of its underpinning ideas, and to the empirical findings and testing of reform proposals.[10]

And consistent with his view, that accounting was 'a language of verbal and mathematical signs dedicated ideally to the service of trust between men,' he initially searched for a definitive function of accounting as an instrumentation before settling on his preferred measurement attribute for reporting assets and liabilities.

Being a polymath, he was convinced that accounting was like any communication system, he drew also on contemporary ideas in that wider field. A leading, if not the leading 1960s U.S. accounting academic, Maurice Moonitz suggested that Chambers' understanding and ability to summarize the relatively new communications literature and related fields, as evidenced in *Accounting, Evaluation and Economic Behavior*,

> probes more deeply the "foundations" of accounting than any other similar work . . . explores the contributions of related fields in a manner that if not unique, is certainly not equalled by any other work with which I am familiar . . . I found his Chapter 7, "Information and Information Processing," Chapter 8, "Communication" and Chapter 12, "Financial Communication Within Organizations," to be lucid summaries of the work done recently in those fields, summaries . . . superior in many respects to those prepared by scholars in the fields themselves.[11]

But as the Sydney School history further noted:

> At a time when others were concentrating on accounting from an "earnings viewpoint"—especially having recourse to the matching principle—he adopted a "balance sheet" viewpoint in the calculation of income, and the need to articulate definitions of asset, liability, revenue, and expense, distributions, and contributions—and of course the property of assets and liabilities to be measured. In this regard, he anticipated what is now widely known as the "conceptual framework" of accounting and the real (in an economics sense) exit price form of fair value accounting.[12]

Little discussed is Chambers' role in lifting the status of accounting to that of an equal among other university disciplines, such as mathematics, philosophy, law, economics, engineering, medicine, and physics. Whittington and Zeff[13] noted that, with Australian confreres (like Russell Mathews, Lou Goldberg and Reg Gynther), he advocated this for half a century. Success began in 1960 with his appointment as the foundation professor of accounting at the University of Sydney, thereby having accounting recognized at his home university as an academic discipline.

For many more years he continued arguing the case for that recognition to be justified. Part of this entailed the profession accepting graduate entry to it, but noting the need for a 'Professional Year' that contrasted with what the graduate student had been exposed to. In 1979 together with his University of Sydney colleague, Murray Wells, a joint submission was sent to

Mr Bill Burgess, Chairman of the ICAA's Education Review Committee, detailing their concerns about the proliferation of institutions delivering accounting education programmes over the last decade. They concluded, *inter alia*, that:

> the Professional Year should 'extend the [graduate] student's understanding of professional accountancy . . . [and provide] the means of applying his knowledge to the needs of practice.' Further, they suggest: 'the Professional Year should be more concentrated and less diffuse in its contents . . . [examining] matters not generally dealt with in academic institutions, and with such matters as professionalism, ethics, conflicts of interest, independence, legal liabilities, obligations to the profession and the community at large, the organisation of work assignments and their supervision . . ., and so on.[14]

Interestingly, those matters were integral in developing his theory of accounting, and later in the compilation of his *Thesaurus*. His ongoing interest in them is evident especially in articles, addresses, and miscellaneous works reproduced in volumes 3 and 6 of *Chambers on Accounting* and in his monograph *Foundations of Accounting*.

There are many sources detailing various aspects of Chambers' life, including two Festschrift issues of *Abacus*, a major work by Michael Gaffikin, and several articles.[15] As well, useful personal summaries by Chambers include: the 1991 'An Academic Apprenticeship' and the introductory preface to the rerelease in 1984 of *Accounting, Evaluation and Economic Behavior*. Those accounts are augmented here with analyses of correspondence from the Chambers Archive. One with friend and colleague Tom Lee that is especially pertinent discusses Chambers' recourse to relevance and reliability as the two critical accounting criteria.[16]

Chapters 7 and 8 not only reveal a man who was aware that, to be credible, reliable, and relevant, an applied discipline needed a theoretical grounding, but someone totally immersed in the particulars of the practice of accounting. This latter feature is another aspect of his life that previously has been little acknowledged. The correspondence provides insights into those experiences and the observations made, which were critical in the development of his new theory of accounting. Chambers and Dean described the period to which those letters relate as:

> perhaps the most eventful period in the history of accounting up to the terminal date [1985]. It was a period of substantial growth, of conglomeration on a large scale by mergers and takeovers, of intense multinational corporate development, of increasing use of modes of organization and methods of financing that were novel at the beginning of the interval [1946].[17]

Significantly, many letters drawn upon here have not previously been examined in any systematic way. In each of the chapters, but in chapter 2 in particular, we draw on them to put flesh on the bones of many aspects of 'Chambers the man.' Additional evidence is adduced from observations of family members, academic and practitioner colleagues, as well as recollections of the authors, to show that he was a man of candour, humour, great diligence, at times a loner, while always a very social person. Many colleagues wrote to Chambers upon his retirement and, like Allan Barton, commented on his excellent writing skills.[18] He was a wordsmith who, in the drawn-out debates over CCA in the 1970s, resorted to publishing his ideas in verse under the pseudonyms, L.O.M. Bard and Ern Malley.[19] In the former nom de plume, Chambers playfully calls on images of both Shakespeare (the Bard of Avon) and the London's finance sector, Lombard Street. The latter was the name used in 1943 by two Australian poets in a literary hoax that attracted international attention. Their aim was to deride modernist poetry. Chambers sought to deride CCA's alleged virtues through verse.

Chambers could also be acerbic, both in written and verbal debates. His several personas, for example, led his daughter, Rosemary Pearce, to describe her father as enigmatic—while his academic and practitioner opponents have described him, at times, as both arrogant and charming.[20]

But above all, chapter 2 reveals he was a committed family man. On several occasions in the 1960s and '70s he turned down offers of overseas chairs and visiting professorial appointments in major universities so he could remain close to his devoted wife, Margaret, his daughters, Rosemary and Margaret, son, Kevin, and grandchildren. He acknowledged in the letters of refusal that he was spending many of the available daily hours dedicated to the mission of seeking a better accounting. Those hours away from his family were already regarded by him as too many.

Chapter 5 discusses the early management lectures and ideas that underpinned, among other things his first book, *Financial Management*. Published in 1947, it went through three later editions, the last one in 1986. Articles on the practice and teaching of accounting soon followed. Education and vocational training were differentiated, something not previously stressed in the accounting literature. But accounting (he did not differentiate internal from external accounting) was considered together with finance and management. These areas were viewed as integrals, not isolates.

Chambers' theoretical developments arose from attempts to resolve simultaneously recurring accounting problems—asset valuation issues generally, but specifically in takeovers with related asset-stripping sagas and in unexpected company failures, how to account for price and price level changes, and removing the legal anomalies in corporate financial reporting. This contrasted with what conventionally had been the case, treating them as isolated problems. Regarding Chambers' 1960s and '70s articles on price and price level accounting, Gaffikin said these were a way of 'selling'

CoCoA. This claim has been reconsidered more recently by Persson and Napier.[21] The analysis in chapters 6 and 8 provides counter evidence to support the claim that, since the late 1940s, price and price level changes were integral in honing his thinking about accounting, finance, and management. Any 'selling' aspect was incidental.

To begin a theoretical breakthrough in the mid-to-late 1950s, he sought to delineate the function (part of a conceptual framework) of accounting, with major contributions in 1955 and 1957—'Blueprint for a Theory of Accounting' and 'Detail for a Blueprint.' Both proved seminal works in this regard. In contrast with the professional accounting standards setters' view of what a conceptual framework entails, Chambers saw it as the commercial setting within which accounting sits.[22] He articulated the function of accounting in *Accounting, Evaluation and Economic Behavior*, namely: 'to provide detailed and aggregate financial information as a guide to future action.'[23] This was embellished later with the statement that:

> the discovery of the facts which at any time predict the limits of action, is thus strictly a scientific function, a continuous research function, inasmuch as the facts are continually changing. Its processes will necessarily be carried out with the same detachment from the facts, and the same pertinacity in seeking the facts, as any other scientific inquiry.[24]

Hence, accounting needed to satisfy a 'decision usefulness' criterion. Capturing this feature are the titles of two of his major early works, *Accounting and Action* and *Accounting, Evaluation and Economic Behavior*, as well as in the first collection of his articles, *Accounting, Finance and Management*.

The theoretical and empirical work embodied in *Accounting, Evaluation and Economic Behavior* both presaged CoCoA and conflicted with many contemporary conventions in accounting practice. Yet it was consistent with a large body of economics literature on money, prices, price changes, price level changes and price structures, the tenets of measurement theory, new insights in communication theory,[25] and the common sense rules of financial calculation and adheres to legal and ethical principles.

Specifically, CoCoA provides data that are generally relevant for all uses by parties interested in business decision making. It requires that a business's wealth be measured by the unencumbered current general purchasing power it commands: over some time period, income arises if there is an increase in the entity's net wealth; and a loss, when there is a decrease. Net wealth is the aggregate of the face values of its cash and other liquid assets plus the cash equivalents of its severable physical assets, less the contractual amount of its liabilities. The cash (or monetary) equivalent of separable physical assets is taken to be best indicated by their current selling prices. Transactions are accounted for in a manner consistent with traditional double-entry bookkeeping and the matching principle is used systematically.[26]

Chambers' theoretical exploits and the relationships with practitioners and regulators are the foci of several chapters. In these, developing relationships with academics, practitioners, and regulatory colleagues are shown to be crucial. Also, globalization of commerce and the attendant internationalization of accounting and finance, as well as related political factors, are revealed as parts of the turbulence and constraints he faced in developing reforms. In seeking reforms, he recognized the importance of attracting like-minded academics across many countries. He advocated on many occasions the need to form an international think-tank of academics during the late 1950s and the 1960s. This underpinned an involvement in the failed elite academic society, Accounting Researchers International Association (ARIA,1973–92).[27] He was more successful in advocating an early version of what became known as the International Association for Accounting Education and Research (IAAER).

Insights into his approach to regulatory reform are pursued, especially in chapter 8. For many decades a missionary-style pursuit of a holistic, rigorous (in a logical and empirical-based sense) change to the conventional (traditional) reporting system characterized his approach. He promoted this by attempting to educate practitioners, regulators, academics, and students. This has been described by some commentators as being politically naive. However, it is little known that Chambers also sought change over many decades through private correspondence and personal meetings with regulators in many jurisdictions. This was undertaken to understand their regulatory responses to numerous unexpected company failures and associated investor losses and company takeover imbroglios. He identified that those responses had entailed increased, but more of the same type of, publicity obligations of corporations. He also sought through these meetings to influence their views.

Ongoing correspondence augmented his continuing analytical and empirical efforts in providing evidence to support his reforms. For example, consider, *inter alia*, the 1965 *Abacus* article 'Financial Information and the Securities Market,' the 1967 Berkeley Symposium paper,[28] the 1973 *Securities and Obscurities*, commissioned work at the APB with Moonitz in 1961–62 on the postulates and principles series, contacts with politicians and regulators (at the SEC in the early and middle 1970s, ongoing discussions for many years with local regulators, like the 1970s N.S.W. Corporate Affairs Commissioner Frank Ryan and the National Companies and Securities Commission chairmen during the 1980s and 1990s, Leigh Masel and Henry Bosch), submissions to various state attorneys-general[29] and his work as chairman on the 1978 N.S.W. Accounting Standards Review Committee (ASRC), following appointment by the Attorney-General Frank Walker.

Chapter 6 shows that consideration by the press and others of unexpected company losses and the role of corporate accounting misinformation in the early 1960s occurred as Chambers honed his theory of CoCoA that would eventually appear in *Accounting, Evaluation and Economic Behavior*. Several years later those aspects would form the evidence documented in

Securities and Obscurities. Information needed to conduct a fair securities market was integral to the development more generally of his theoretical ideas. Drawing on his strong religious beliefs and innate desire for fairness in commerce, he prescribed a level playing field in commercial negotiations. This meant that changes were required to the existing company financial publicity obligations.

As chapters 6 and 8 reveal, Chambers' pre-and-post-1960s analyses of accounting for price and price level changes reinforced his view that the main purpose of corporate accounting was to provide for myriad decision *uses* verifiable, up-to-date, market-related information about an entity's financial position and performance. Reliable information was deemed critical for the uses ordinarily made by managers, investors, and other interested parties. It was something sadly lacking in the conventional historical cost-based accounting regime of the time. In this respect, the post-1972 'Trueblood era,' which gave primacy to one user group, namely investors (shareholders and creditors), was deemed inappropriate. Chambers preferred to focus on the uses of the accounting technology, not its users. He argued that accounting could never address all the specific decision needs of any or all users—but it could address the necessary, *generally* relevant information for all uses of accounting data. He addressed this in *Accounting, Evaluation and Economic Behavior*, again in two 1976 articles and (as chairman) in the 1978 N.S.W. ASRC Report.[30]

Chambers was in the thick of professional moves worldwide to respond to changing prices and price levels. This was so from his initial post-war thoughts through the years to the professional, business, and regulatory brouhaha during the 1970s and early '80s. In the later period, formal suggestions to supplant historic cost accounting increased dramatically with the profession's CPP and CCA exposure draft reform proposals, initially in the U.K., Australia, and then elsewhere. Table 7.5 details Chambers' submissions to those inquiries. The push for change resulted in mid-1975, with Chambers, frustrated by his profession's prevarication, producing his own exposure draft describing the features of CoCoA.

While he often in his later years lamented the failure to achieve effective reforms, this 'man for all seasons' had achieved much. This included: in the 1940s and '50s he was a leader of a group of Australian accounting academics and practitioners who argued strongly for accounting to be accorded university status alongside the traditional applied disciplines, and the related push for a graduate entry to the accounting profession; he advocated the need for accounting to profess the truth and for academics to expose false doctrines;[31] he also advocated gradual movement toward a professionally endorsed conceptual framework that entailed a decision usefulness based approach to accounting and the concomitant recourse to a partial form of market price accounting (including fair value accounting for financial instruments); as well as pursuing general acceptance of the annual rather than ad hoc revaluation of fixed assets.

These and other achievements are testimony to the reform efforts of Chambers and the coterie of like-minded Sydney School colleagues. His 'Aide Memoire' details the recognition by many overseas professional accounting bodies, multiple awards from accounting associations in Italy, the 1976 appointment as the inaugural American Accounting Association's Distinguished International Visiting Lecturer and his induction in 1991 to The Ohio State University's U.S. Accounting Hall of Fame. Posthumously, he was in 2010 in the first round of inductees to the University of Melbourne's Australian Accounting Hall of Fame.

Achieving such things did not, however, satisfy Chambers—for there was still unfinished business on his agenda when a fall in the city led to his death.

Our account shows that inertia by practitioners, regulators, and educators continues to be a major obstacle to change, as are the continued belief in conservatism in reporting and the use of committees to provide professional prescriptions. Other obstacles include: whether market prices are relevant, the 'cost' of their provision is understood, earnings management is really the problem that Chambers suggested; or whether his reform approach is appropriate. Many of the works and correspondence discussed here entail responses to such concerns.

Chapter 9 picks up on that 'challenged, and hence unfinished, business' theme. Chambers' epigraphs to the prologue are brief examples of what he described elsewhere as 'jottings' and 'scribblings with rigour.' They show considered thinking about a wide range of accounting matters. Present standards-based accounting is shown to be a flawed technology, more the product of political compromise between business and regulators than a proper functioning instrumentation system. Chambers regarded this as folly, bereft of wisdom, unbecoming of an enduring device that was formalized and distributed through publication over 500 years ago in the Renaissance to provide mathematical order to commerce.

One major piece of unfinished business was a proposed monograph. Chambers had begun *Wisdom of Accounting*, a play on Hanbury Brown's 1986 *Wisdom of Science*,[32] that had shown how progress since the sixteenth century had much to do with better appreciating through a scientific analysis how practical things worked. This was largely brought about by the advent of printing and the divorce of church and science. Similar events had influenced accounting. Material in the Archive reveals he had scoped the book, but made only minimal inroads. He had confided to the present authors and other Sydney colleagues that much of the evidence for the book was his *Thesaurus. Wisdom* was to address further his perceived need to fix the disarray of accounting. While some reforms had occurred, many major problems with accounting remained virtually as they were when he began his business career in the late 1930s and academic career in the 1940s. *Wisdom* would show what academics and others still needed to do more than half a century later.

Ten years after Chambers' death the disarray manifested itself in the accounting criticisms emanating from the aftermath of the GFC[33]—primarily in the areas of fair value accounting, loan loss provisioning and accounting for groups, especially inadequate group reporting of the activities of financial institutions' off-balance sheet 'shadow banks.' That disarray underpins chapter 9's summary of what he felt still needed to be done to produce a system of accounting that is relevant and reliable. This includes a call for his ideas, which had been partially implemented (namely, the market price elements of the more recent 'fair value'-based standards) by accounting standards setters, to be further tested.

A related unfinished business is the need for accounting education reform. Chambers observed that any effective change to practice required concomitant changes in the way accountants were educated. Chambers had alerted the academic community to this in several works in the early to mid-1960s and again in the 1980s and '90s.

Chambers promoted his reform ideas with enthusiasm over approximately fifty years. They are the product of an informed all-rounder, whose life involved the continual search for ways to instil order in what he and many others perceived as commercial chaos. Our account reveals he was a maverick who experienced a full, albeit at times frustrated, life.

Notes

Many of the following notes refer to correspondence extracts retrieved from the R.J. Chambers University of Sydney Personal Archive P202, part of the Archives of the University of Sydney. They are referred to as: P202, #000, date. The history of the Chambers Archive is described in Dean, Clarke and Wolnizer (2006).

Also included in the notes are reference details of items cited in the text.

PROLOGUE

1. Chapter epigraphs:
   Chambers letter to 1950s and '60s U.S. accounting professor, Maurice Moonitz, P202, #7345, 21/03/1991.
   Chambers letter to U.S. operations research Professor William Cooper, P202, #7577, 17/06/1987.
   Response by Chambers to Professor Bob Baxt's Address at a Sydney University Dinner to recognize his Induction into the Ohio State University Accounting Hall of Fame, P202, #7336, 27/07/1991.
2. Aspects of those achievements have been discussed by, among others, Chambers and Dean (Vols 1–5, 1986a-e, and Vol. 6, 2000, which includes Chambers' 'Aide Memoire'), Gaffikin (1988, 2000, 2012), Al-Hogail and Previts (2001), Whittington and Zeff (2000), Zeff (2011) and Wolnizer and Dean (2000).
3. The Chambers Archive was officially launched by the University of Sydney Vice-Chancellor, Gavin Brown, and made available to the public in November 2004. It was initially accessible at http://chamberslibrary.econ.usyd.edu. au, and also indirectly, along with several digitized accounting databases, through the auspices of a joint EAA/AAA project, known as GADAN at www. https://aaahq.org/pubs/GADAN.htm; see also: http://accountingarchive.org/. The digitized archive version appeared on the University of Sydney Business School website until the end of 2012. From then it became accessible

from the University of Sydney Archives website handling personal archives groups; as this monograph goes to press, the P202 Chambers Archive is accessible at http://sydney.edu.au/arms/ archives/chambers_items871.shtml. A discussion of some aspects of these collections appears in Potter (2003) and Cobbin *et al.* (2013).

4. Chambers' 'Aide Memoire' reveals he wrote a dozen monographs, books and more than 300 articles, discussion papers, expert witness opinions and newspaper op eds.

5. Chambers' 'Aide Memoire' states that 'Management in Wonderland' entails 'rhymed reflections' on management at the close of a 'School for Executives,' Geelong, May 1950.

6. Chambers (2000b, 322).

7. Clarke *et al.* (2012).

8. Chambers letter to the editor of *The Australian* newspaper, P202, #8659, 28/03/1966. Often he used the space age instrumentation analogy in press and seminar presentations in the late 1960s.

9. Chambers (2000b, 322).

10. Clarke, Dean and Edwards (2010, 2012, 12).

11. Letter of support by Moonitz submitted to the Registrar of the University of Sydney, in respect of Chambers' nomination for a DSc Econ. at Sydney University, November 1971. It is an unnumbered entry in the Archive.

12. Reference to a 'real' exit price system is recognition that Chambers' preferred accounting included a one-off measurement scale adjustment to incorporate in the accounts and financial statements the effects of changes in the general level of prices. This aspect is often ignored by commentators on Chambers' ideas.

13. Whittington and Zeff (2001).

14. Chambers and Wells letter to Burgess, P202, #5219, 17/01/1978.

15. *Abacus* (December 1982 and October 2000), Gaffikin (1988), Whittington and Zeff (2001), Previts (1996), Al-Hogail and Previts (2003) and Gaffikin (2000, 2012).

16. Analyses of correspondence from the Chambers Archive, namely: P202, #7402, 13/01/1993, #7403, 27/01/1993. Chambers condensed these two criteria into what he defined as 'usefulness' or 'serviceability.' He discussed this in a major article 'Usefulness—the vanishing premise in accounting standard setting' (Chambers, 1979). This is discussed more in chapter 6.

17. Chambers and Dean (1986a, Vol. 1).

18. Barton letter to Chambers, P202, #6549, 01/02/1983. Barton also commented in that letter: 'Your contributions to the advancement of the accounting discipline have been truly outstanding and it is difficult to think of anyone who has done more. I am sure your works will be the subject of much historical study in the future and your name will remain forever in the annals of the development of accounting thought.' Returning to Chambers' concern about appropriate use of words (see also chapter 6 endnote #36, this is captured in his U.S. Ohio State University Accounting Hall of Fame nomination: 'A voracious reader with a formidable vocabulary, he has even been known to study the dictionary. Possessed by a strong desire to see language used correctly, he studies the roots of words and that it is the right word in the context.'; accessed on 17 July 2017 at https://fisher.osu.edu/node/1947.

19. The poems by 'L.O.M. Bard' (1979a, 1979b, 1979c) and 'Ern Malley' (1979) appeared in *The Australian Accountant*.

20. The 1975–76 correspondence between the Chair of AARF, John Balmford and Chambers about Chambers' private ED on the proposed inflation accounting standard illustrates this—namely P202, #s9338a, 4938–4944, 10062.

21. Gaffikin (1988); Persson and Napier (2018).

22. For an account of Chambers' and others' views of what comprises a conceptual framework generally, and for accounting specifically, see Chambers (1976c, 1991c) and Dean and Clarke (2003a).
23. Chambers (1966, 4).
24. Chambers (1966, 367).
25. New insights into communication are discussed in Gleick (2011) and Clarke, Dean and Edwards (2013).
26. Comprehensive summaries of CoCoA appear in Chambers' ED, *Accounting for Inflation* (1975a; see para 44 for a succinct description of CoCoA), his August 1975 *Accounting for Inflation: Methods and Problems* (especially the symbolic representation of CoCoA presented on 33–4) and his *Auto-Bibliography* (1977a, especially 59–62). A contestable element in Chambers' definition of wealth is the measurement of liabilities at their face value at balance date when inflation and interest rates have changed. Ronald Ma raised this matter in the early 1970s but Chambers (1974b and 1976d) shows that he retained this view, suggesting that deducting the face value of the liabilities at balance date provided the best indication of an entity's wealth (general purchasing power), its capacity for adaptation. Staunton (2007) provides an extended analysis of Chambers' and others' views on how to account for the effects of purchasing power changes on liabilities.
27. Activities of the Accounting Researchers' International Association (ARIA) are touched upon in chapter 7 and described in detail in Edwards *et al.* (2013).
28. Chambers (1965a). Vance (1967) records the 1967 'Berkeley Symposium' papers.
29. Submissions are listed in Table 7.5.
30. Chambers (1976a, 1976b). See also chapter 2 extracts of detailed correspondence in 1972 with his student George Foster, based on P202, #s3829 and 3831. Analysis of this correspondence and Chambers' influence on Thomas' works awaits another occasion.
31. This was in line with the views of what was meant by experiencing a university education as discussed in the works of the likes of Cardinal Newman (1852), Whitehead (1929), Ortega (1946/63) and more recently Peliken (1992).
32. Brown (1986).
33. For the ramifications of inadequate accounting of mortgage-backed securities and the role of accounting generally in the GFC see the following: SEC (2008), Tett (2009), Valukas (2010), Laux and Leuz (2009, 2010), Magnan and Makarian (2011, especially 216).

Acknowledgments

This biography was finished around the time of the centenary of the birth of Raymond John Chambers, 16 November 1917. It is more than fifty years since his first classic, *Accounting, Evaluation and Economic Behavior*, was published, more than forty since *Securities and Obscurities: Reform of the Law of Company Accounts* (republished in 1980 as *Accounting in Disarray*) and over twenty since the unique *An Accounting Thesaurus: Five Hundred Years of Accounting*. Those works are drawn upon extensively in this biography of Chambers' intellectual contributions, as are other of his published works. Importantly, we also analyse archival correspondence previously examined only minimally.

While Chambers provided several bibliographical summaries of his work, without the benefits of reviewing and interspersing the text with evidentiary correspondence materials from the Chambers Archive, this study would lack much of the 'life' and nuances of the period covered. The 'semi-biographical narrative' draws on some correspondence material for the first time, but also codifies article and editorial length exercises by the authors drawing on parts of the archive related to theory development, measurement, and communication.

Analysing evidence from the Archive to better understand Chambers' intellectual contributions is a variant of what Cooperrider *et al.* describe in their 2008 handbook on action research as 'Appreciative Inquiry.' In this digital age the Chambers Archive is the model for what other universities and faculties should seek to establish to preserve significant contributions to the accounting discipline's intellectual heritage, and its origins, involving a leading thinker, like Chambers.

The Archive allows us to respond to those critics who claim Chambers' reforms were naive. They further reveal a man of theory and practice, whose theoretical ideas were solidly grounded on experiential observations from the practice of accounting. Many of his consultancy and other practical experiences have not been examined previously. This further differentiates our account from earlier analyses of Chambers' contribution to the accounting literature.

This exercise would be stillborn if not for the Herculean archiving work done by Angelika Dean and Cameron Esslemont, and the financial and other support provided by the University of Sydney, and specifically by, as it was called then, the Faculty of Economics and Business. Significant here was the role of Faculty Dean, Peter Wolnizer, as well as the financial support of the University of Sydney Accounting Foundation which Chambers had founded. We acknowledge also the assistance provided by the University of Sydney Archives Senior Archivist, Nyree Morrison, and by the University Archivist, Tim Robinson. All facilitated the professional archiving undertaken over nearly ten years. That work continues through completion of the digitization of the correspondence section of the Archive comprising over 40,000 pages, with the aim being its availability via the web.

Also, we appreciate greatly the support of the surviving Chambers' family members. They provide another differentiating feature of the present study, with reflections and photos that inject more personal insights into the account.

For an independent perspective we sought pre-publication reviews by non-Sydney School academics. Accordingly, we are extremely grateful to Philip Brown, Gary Previts, Sue Newberry, Geoff Whittington, and Steve Zeff who gave freely of their time to read the manuscript, identify errors and provide useful comments as we fine-tuned our draft ideas. Any remaining errors are of course our responsibility.

Again, our families have continued to endure and support unequivocally our work on this project, as they did with earlier ones. For that we are most appreciative. As always, the editorial advice of Carl Harrison-Ford is much appreciated.

Frank Clarke
Graeme Dean
Martin Persson

1 Growing Up:
Life on the Fringe—
rebutting Groupthink

A committee is unable, by its nature, freely to engage and disengage from its immediate attention [on] particular clusters of ideas in the search for a worthwhile conclusion.

—Chambers, 1972

The heady days of the sixties and early seventies don't seem to have left much trace. All the high talk of theories and principles seems to have been sidetracked by the institutionalization of think-work and publication by the many slow-moving and often confused boards, committees, and like bodies here, there and everywhere over the last decade.

—Chambers' letter to Norton Bedford, 1982[1]

This account draws largely on the material by Chambers published post-humously about growing up in Newcastle as a coalminer and newsagent's son whose stepmother provided him with what he described as a minimal 'bookish' experience. In 'Early Beginnings: An Introduction to *Wisdom of Accounting*' he observes:

High school opened up a new world. Our parents had had only an elementary education. Father, though an avid reader of newspapers, never bothered with books. Mother had a small shelf of novels of the time, but that was all. We had no "bookish" friends or relations. But, at school, English language and literature, French and Latin, Mathematics, Chemistry, Physics, everything was fascinating.

He humbly continues: 'For what had to be done, I achieved modest grades, but there was not time for browsing.'[2] That lament gives an insight into his subsequent desire to read across many areas. This is evidenced by the substantial library he bequeathed to the university, which is now part of the Chambers Archive. It contains his correspondence in the Archives of the University of Sydney and his collections of books, articles, newspaper extracts and other items in a branch of Fisher Library—the Burren Street Library, in nearby Macdonaldtown.

Early Education[3]

Newcastle and the Steelworks

Chambers was born in Newcastle, New South Wales, on 16 November 1917. Australia was a young nation, federated in 1901 and with a population under five million. Newcastle had been established as a penal settlement in 1801, but it grew quickly as Australian, English, Scottish, and Irish migrants arrived to work on the fertile hinterlands and in the coalmines. It became a city in 1885. Newcastle's industry would later diversify into iron, steel, and mineral sands mining.

Both Chambers' grandfathers were coalminers, one from Yorkshire, the other from Wales. His maternal grandfather emigrated to Australia in the 1860s to work in the coalfields of Ipswich, then Victoria, and finally in the Hunter Valley (New South Wales) where Ray Chambers' mother Louisa Moog grew up. His father, Joseph, came from an English family of underground coalminers from Barnsley, South Yorkshire (the family visited Joseph's sister in Barnsley during their trip in 1959). Joseph emigrated to Australia in 1912 to be joined by his parents and all bar one of his siblings in 1920. He settled in Newcastle around the age of twenty. Chambers' younger brother, Albert, and the family lived in a house Joseph had built overlooking the mouth of the Hunter River, several miles north from the harbour and the downtown business district. He had borrowed to build this house and another behind it.

Having no formal education or professional training, Joseph took employment as a labourer at the Newcastle Iron & Steel Works a mile upstream from the family's home. The Broken Hill Propriety Company Limited had established the steelworks in 1915. The operation was the first large-scale steelworks in the country and represented BHP's ambition to transition from its dependence on coal from the mines in Newcastle and silver, lead, and zinc lode deposits found in Broken Hill, the discovery of which had led to the company's incorporation in 1883. The large furnaces operated day and night and made Joseph's working environment both an uncomfortable and potentially hazardous one, with long hours working in rotating shifts, mornings, evenings, and on the weekends.

Islington, the Milk-Vending Business, and Newspaper Franchises

While the family was still living on the Hunter, Louisa developed a glandular disorder which proved fatal. Chambers recalls those events, observing that the goitre condition would have been curable just a few decades later and speculates on the immense stress that this must have caused his father. Two aunts, one from each side of the family, agreed to take care of the boys until Joseph had rearranged his affairs.[4] Chambers spent this time at a family farm in Quorrobolong, thirty miles away and close to another mining town, Cessnock.

Joseph remarried Esme Mabel May, who came from a family in the Northern Rivers district region of the state. The house on the Hunter River was sold and another one was built in Islington, a newly developed suburb close to the harbour and the business district. The family moved into this new house in 1927. Joseph also borrowed to buy several acres of land in nearby Mayfield.

Tired of working gruelling shifts in the steelworks, and longing for more independence, Joseph quit his labouring job in the mid-1920s and, again using borrowed funds, he bought a milk-vending business. This line of work, however, proved to be perhaps just as demanding. A central depot dispensed milk into a large tanker that then had to be driven to each customer's home. Deliveries were made seven days a week, and for the sake of freshness (there being no domestic refrigerators), milk was commonly delivered twice-daily, beginning after midnight and continuing during the day. Some of these sales would have been on credit, necessitating a weekly collection round as well. It is likely that the demands of these activities were the reason Joseph sold the business for a franchise to distribute a Sydney metropolitan newspaper in the Mayfield area, a venture that performed poorly as there was little demand for a Sydney paper at the onset of the Great Depression. The franchise was therefore sold for another franchise to sell a local evening paper. Concurrently the family re-entered the milk-vending business in 1930. These business activities were run in tandem, but income pressures meant that the family supplemented its income by growing vegetables at home and selling them locally.

Joseph's sales of the milk run and the Sydney newspaper franchise in the midst of the Depression resulted in a substantial loss of around 90 per cent of the initial purchase prices, which had included a large amount of goodwill.

Later in life, Joseph made another further poor financial decision by selling several acres of undeveloped land the family owned in York Crescent, Belmont, a suburb of Newcastle. The small amount received for the land forced Joseph to move to Sydney to take on odd jobs. Arguably those financial experiences influenced his son's thinking on the valuation of assets on the balance sheet, especially the nebulous 'goodwill' item. For the reporting of an asset Ray Chambers would require it to be severable and fungible. Chambers' son Kevin has spoken of one relevant asset sale, the York Crescent land sale:

> I don't think [Joseph] ever finished developing that [land] and I think he sold the lot of it for a very paltry amount of money but I believe there was enough space in the area that he owned to accommodate 40 houses. . . . I think Dad told me that he [Joseph] sold the whole lot and I think there were four houses half built in this area [at the time] . . . He sold the lot for £1,000 and thought he had made a lot of money but it wasn't enough for him to survive on. . . . I think his sons were both

furious that he had sold this property, particularly as they were both accountants and had some financial knowledge and he had none and he never consulted them. I think that was always something that stuck in both their necks.[5]

University Entrance Exam and the Scholarship

In 1930 Chambers enrolled at Newcastle Boys' High School, the main regional school, which had been established the year earlier when the former Hill High School had been split into two single-sex schools. The school was commonly referred to as 'the School on the Hill' and its campus remained on Newcastle Hill until Chambers' graduation in 1934, when it moved to Waratah, four miles from central Newcastle. His time at the institution coincided with that of several other boys who went on to achieve prominence in Australian life. One was Roger Levinge Dean, who later became a diplomat and served as the Administrator of the Northern Territory from 1964 to 1970.

Chambers describes school and homework as being sandwiched between work for the family's evening newspaper franchise and the morning and evening milk runs, each of two hours.[6] His home in Islington necessitated a daily two-mile walk and another five-mile ride by train for the next five years. The time demands of work and school led to a precarious but not uncommon situation for teenagers growing up in Newcastle in the 1930s, with little time left for team sports or other extra-curricular activities.

The family had no 'bookish friends or relations,' and there was little reading material at home. Nonetheless—or perhaps because of this—high school widened Chambers' horizons. Surrounded by teachers who were enthusiastic and passionate about their subject, he took great interest in subjects across the curriculum and achieved, in his words, modest grades.

In his third year of secondary study, Chambers' parents took him out of school to help the family with their businesses and to pursue a correspondence course in advertising and commercial art on the side. When he failed to show up for the 1933 academic year, however, Charles Herbert Christmas, the first headmaster of the Newcastle Boys' High School, wrote to the family urging them to contact him. Chambers and his stepmother called, and Christmas told them that someone with Ray's record should not forego the opportunity to enter one of the learned professions. He returned to school forthwith.

As Chambers was concluding his fifth and final year at school in 1934, the family again considered what he might do after graduation. He had expressed a desire to become a teacher, but there were no possibilities of pursuing this in Newcastle, as there were then no local institutions of higher education (Newcastle University College, later the University of Newcastle, was not established until 1965). The closest teachers' college was the one associated with the University of Sydney. But attending it seemed an unlikely prospect, given the family finances and the fact that their son's help was needed at home.

With university attendance looking unlikely, Chambers was once again enrolled in an accounting correspondence course in which Albert also was enrolled. This time it was one that led to a qualification in accounting and membership in the Commonwealth Institute of Accountants (later Australian Society of Accountants and currently CPA Australia). Perhaps Chambers was inspired by a maternal uncle, a practising accountant, who nonetheless was never consulted. Plans were changed again when the results of the Leaving Certificate examination for entrance into the university were published. Chambers' performance was not in his words 'satisfactory,' achieving only 'a second-class honours in mathematics and science, and an A-Grade in English—the seven-day working week had taken its toll.' But it was sufficient to give him the prospect of applying for two public service clerical positions in Sydney and the prospect of an exhibition scholarship covering tuition to attend evening classes at the University of Sydney.[7] Chambers' parents let Ray decide what option to take.

He moved to Sydney, worked during the day, and took evening classes at university.

Higher Education

A New Life and the University of Sydney

Chambers' move in 1935 had been made possible not just by the scholarship. His brother, Albert, had been appointed as a clerk in one of the steelworking industries in Newcastle and could continue to help with the family business in the morning and evening, for some years. A cousin and her husband were also already living in a house in Hurstville, five miles from the centre of Sydney, and were willing to let Chambers rent a spare room, where he stayed for the next five years. On the occasional weekends when he could afford the time and cost, he would visit home by taking the overnight steamer operated by the Newcastle and Hunter River Steamship Company. Incidentally, Albert would later move to Wollongong, south of Sydney, and work as an accountant for a private company.

Chambers enrolled part-time as an evening student in Sydney University's Faculty of Economics. He simultaneously took up a daytime appointment as a clerk in the accounting office at the New South Wales Department of the Attorney-General and Justice (now just the Department of Justice). Chambers recalled that 'the atmosphere of the metropolis, the content and milieu of clerical work and the substance and manner of university study, were all novel.'[8] He travelled between work and home by foot and by tram.

William Wentworth, a graduate of the University of Cambridge, and Charles Nicholson, a graduate from the University of Edinburgh, had helped establish the University of Sydney by Royal Charter in 1850, and its location on a hill overlooking the CBD had been granted in 1859. The Faculty of Economics had offered courses in accounting since 1907. When Chambers enrolled in a Bachelor of Economics degree, two of the ten course requirements were in accounting. This was later extended to three out of twelve courses in 1946, and in 1953 after Chambers' return to the university as an academic a full program of accounting was introduced.

At the time of Chambers' enrolment, however, he found that few people could articulate what economics was all about. This was so, he believed, because economics tended to not deal with matters that could be experienced directly but rather with abstract aggregates—and its sub-branch, accounting, appeared as a rather 'trivial pursuit.'[9] The material for the two accounting courses that he undertook was contained in two slim volumes of account-ing exercises, intended for memorization and rote-learning, written by the accountant on staff and a part-time instructor. The correspondence course that his family had enrolled him in but that had been put on hold offered much the same, with voluminous material written by contracted tutors and professional accountants. Nonetheless, Chambers pursued his university stud-ies with vigour and graduated in 1939. He became a professionally qualified accountant two years later.

Shortly after his graduation on 9 September 1939 (just six days after Britain declared war on Germany), Chambers married Margaret Scott Brown (of Scottish parents), who he had met in the Christadelphian ecclesia in Hurstville when he had first arrived in Sydney (Figure 2.1). The ecclesia was not far from where Chambers was boarding with his relations. His active engagement in the church, as a lay preacher and strong supporter, is remembered by the children. The Christadelphians were a small, fringe church group founded in the U.S. in the nineteenth century. The growth of the faith was limited, with ecclesia in only a few other countries, Britain, Australia, New Zealand and South Africa. In 2006 it was reported that there were about 50,000 members worldwide. A distinguishing feature is that its members do not join the military or the police force. The church did not have priests but relied on lay preachers drawn from the senior members of the ecclesia. The members believed, amongst other things, in a single being, God the Father (rather than the Trinitarian view of most Christian faiths) and that baptism should be something done only when a person reaches adulthood, when he or she can make an informed choice.

Interestingly, most university staff colleagues were unaware of Cham-bers' faith until they attended his funeral. This privacy feature is confirmed through conversations with the children and two of the authors (Clarke and Dean), which revealed also that his family were largely unaware of the extent of his academic achievements.

With Chambers maintaining a clear distinction between matters of work and family, his daughters recall that the family's social life was mainly with their mother's brother, sister, and their spouses, with the occasional card games every few weeks. The church also remained extremely important to the family, as son Kevin recounts:

> The Christadelphian Church was a very big part of my family's life. I remember being taken up to the Sunday school which used to be before the main meeting of the church and making my way up as years went by to different types of discussions with a Sunday school teacher who probably managed about eight children. After Sunday school then my parents would arrive for the main meeting of the church and then one of the members of the church would have prepared a sermon and this would be given and then bread and wine consumed by those who had joined the church. . . . I used to stay for the church service . . . after that we would go home and have lunch. . . . In the evening my father would come back to the church for a lecture again by one of the members of the church about some probably historical facts about early Christians or Israel.[10]

Inventory Work at the Shell Oil Company

Chambers could not see any possibilities for career advancement at the Department of the Attorney-General and Justice, so in 1938 he took up an appointment with the Australian subsidiary of the Royal Dutch Shell Group. Having first established bulk-handling facilities at Sydney Harbour, the company bought a large crude oil refinery in Clyde, an industrial suburb on the Parramatta River, thirteen miles west of the CBD. Throughout the Australian war effort, the refinery's normal operations were suspended, and it instead supplied petrol, oil, and lubricants to the armed forces.

Chambers first worked as an inventory control officer at Shell's bulk-handling facilities at Sydney Harbour and smaller regional depots spread throughout New South Wales. The job involved the detailed tracking of products and containers. In his second year, he was charged with keeping track of imported crude oil at the company's harbour facilities in Greenwich, on Sydney's lower North Shore. The work in Greenwich involved tracking the volume of inflow and outflow of crude oil as well as the measurement of its volume, weight, and temperature.[11] Once accounted for, the crude oil would then be shipped up the river to the Clyde refinery, where Chambers spent his third and final year working for the company in 1941. The shifting locations of employment led Chambers and Margaret to first move to Greenwich, and later Hurstville, a southern suburb of Sydney. They finally settled nearby in Blakehurst.

Electricity Meter and Allied Industries, and the Prices Commission

The decision to leave the Royal Dutch Shell Group came from Chambers' desire to put his knowledge in financial matters to the test. This led initially to employment with the Electricity Meter and Allied Industries. The company, which had been incorporated in New South Wales in 1934, was involved in the production of electric, gas, and water metres for houses and public utilities; it later became a producer of whitegoods. Interestingly, Chambers used his acquired knowledge in respect of utility companies in several later consultancies. He remained with the company for under three years, working in various capacities such as a statistical officer, supervisor, and inventory and production controller.

In 1943, and looking for a job that dealt more with financial matters, Chambers moved to the Prices Commission. According to responses from the children, it is possible that he also volunteered during this time in exercises for the defence of Sydney in case of an attack:

> Dad did not enlist as he was engaged in a government department at the time and it seems he was expected to stay on there. Margaret remembers a hard hat hanging in the hall and we think he may have been involved in the civil defence program as an air raid warden.[12]

The Australian government established the commission at the outbreak of war through the passage of the Price Control under the National Security Act. Sir Douglas Berry Copland—Sidney Myer Chair of Commerce at the University of Melbourne and the thirteenth child of a Scottish immigrant family in New Zealand—was appointed prices commissioner. Incidentally, Copland later became the first principal of the Australian Administrative Staff College and hired Chambers as a regular visiting lecturer (see chapter 5). The commission employed deputy commissioners, advisers, inspectors, and investigation officers nationwide, and its mandate over the war period was to regulate maximum prices of manufacturers' (as opposed to retail) goods during the war. These prices were regulated either formally, through a published price list in the *Commonwealth Gazette*, or informally through various meetings with manufacturers related to items such as lead, zinc, and copper.[13]

Working as an investigation officer for the Commission, Chambers was finally given the opportunity to apply his financial knowledge in the research process that led to the establishment of regulated prices for various goods. The formula for establishing prices was unique for each kind of goods. The formula also tended to be complex, taking into account several factors that had to be established before a decision could be made. In the case of tin ingots, for example, the Commission considered the maximum price of tin ingots in Australia before regulation, the export parity of those ingots after deducting transport charges and other costs, the ratio of exports to total production, and the fair margin of smelters of tin ore.

Another example was the regulation of prices of bicycle parts. Their regulation required the use of a basic price lists, a pre-approved annual percentage increase in costs, and an annual index number adjustment based on a pre-approved subset of parts held by a selected group of merchants. It is likely that this experience of working in the general measurement function of oil and public utilities and later the financial measurement function at the Prices Commission developed Chambers' initial and enduring interest in financial accounting measurements.[14] Chapter 7 reveals also that it was influential in several of his consultancies in these and related areas in the 1960s and '70s.

Accounting Flaws and a Scholarly Life

Lectureship at Sydney Technical College

In 1945 Chambers left the Prices Commission to take on his first full-time academic appointment, as a lecturer in the School of Management at Sydney Technical College. This move was presumably prompted by his experience working as a part-time correspondence teacher in auditing for the college while in his last two years with the Prices Commission. The college had begun in 1878, as a division of Sydney Mechanics' School of Arts— a community-based educational initiative to train men in mechanical craftsmanship—but had soon been taken over by the colonial government. In 1891 the college completed construction of its 3.5-acre headquarters in Ultimo, close to the central business district.

During the war, the college had operated as a teaching facility, factory, and camp under the Commonwealth Defence Training Scheme. After the war, it quickly grew to become the largest post-secondary school institution in the state, before various parts were rationalized as separate institutions, such as the University of New South Wales, the National Art School, and the University of Technology Sydney. The college itself was rebranded as the Sydney Institute of Technology in 1992, and its former headquarters was spun off as Ultimo College (one of seven separate campuses in the system).[15]

Bruce Brown, a University of Sydney graduate and full-time lecturer at the college, appointed Chambers. Another two full-time lecturers and a number of part-time teachers made up the faculty at a time when the School of Management was undergoing expansions to train returned servicemen in areas of foremanship and supervision in manufacturing. As part of its certificate program, the school offered courses in general, production, personnel, and sales management as well as a course in 'costing and control' as part of its certificate course program.

Chambers taught in all the courses, but the principal assignment was costing and control and his initial efforts were spent developing a new course in financial management. Due to the lack of material on matters of financial management, much of the material for this course had to be gathered from his wartime experiences, and from financial columns in local newspapers, financial reports of companies, and firms in the Sydney CBD. This foreshadowed much more extensive data collections that would underpin several books and academic articles in the 1950s and beyond. The new course was introduced in 1946, and the codification of this work led to his first book, *Financial Management*, published by the Law Book Co. in 1947 (subsequent editions appeared in 1953, 1967, and 1986).

The Sydney Technical College had a tradition of running five-year part-time trade-related diploma courses in areas such as mechanics, engineering, and architecture. These were popular programs, and by the time of Chambers' appointment, the college offered over twenty diploma courses. In 1947 the School of Management resolved to offer a diploma course of its own. Chambers' second major initiative was to design this course, which was aimed at individuals seeking to move into management roles and with some knowledge in the fields of accounting, economics, law, psychology, and statistics. The course was the first of its kind in Australia when it was introduced in 1949, and its designer remained at the school until the graduation of the first intake of candidates in 1953.

While Chambers was heavily involved in the operations of the School of Management, time was still found to engage with the accounting profession and to undertake research. He was a member of six professional associations and served on the Regional Research Committee of the Commonwealth Institute of Accountants and the Finance Management Panel of the Australian Institute of Management. In addition to publishing *Financial Management*, during this time Chambers also published fifteen articles in various journals (predominantly in *The Australian Accountant*, the journal of his professional body). One of his publications, 'How to Achieve Lower Costs in Australian Industry,' was awarded the Australasian Institute of Cost Accountants Fiftieth Anniversary Essay Prize in 1947, and his productivity quickly gained him considerable notoriety. It was perhaps this that led the Commonwealth Institute of Accountants to invite him to deliver a series of lectures on accounting for changing price levels, a pressing topic as inflation was rampant in post-war Australia and elsewhere. He gave these lectures, first to institute members in Sydney and later to attendees at the universities of Adelaide, Melbourne, and Queensland.

Return to the University of Sydney and Academic Expansion

In 1953 Chambers' rise in academic prominence led to a senior lecturer in Accounting appointment in the Faculty of Economics at the University of Sydney. At that time accounting as an academic discipline was still in its infancy in Australia. Largely due to two individuals, the University of Melbourne was perhaps the only institution with a distinction in the discipline. Alexander Fitzgerald had been appointed at Melbourne as a part-time lecturer in Accounting in 1925 and in 1954 promoted to the Gordon L. Wood Professor of Accounting. Fitzgerald was the most senior academic accountant in the country, and he had interacted with Chambers in his capacity as the President of the Commonwealth Institute of Accountants (1940–41) and editor of *The Australian Accountant* (1936–54). The other individual, Lou Goldberg, had been appointed as a lecturer in Accounting at Melbourne in 1946. This was the first full-time position in accounting in Australia. Goldberg assumed Fitzgerald's chair in 1958. Chambers had initially applied for this position but later withdrew his application.[16]

Back at Sydney, Chambers' appointment was followed in 1955 by that of Eugene Bryan Smyth to the first full-time chair in accounting at the New South Wales University of Technology. Incorporated by an Act of Parliament in 1949, it operated as a separate institution on the site of the Sydney Technical College until the early 1950s, when building began on its present Kensington site. It was renamed the University of New South Wales in 1958. Smyth previously held the position as the head of the School of Commerce at Sydney Technical College.[17]

Mathews recalls that the development of accounting departments in Australia was made possible by the support of the commerce and economics faculties, but that accounting as an academic discipline continued to be regarded with some suspicion.[18] Within the universities, professional accountants, working as part-time lecturers, wanted to hold on to their technical courses. On the other hand, full-time appointees such as Chambers, who sought to develop accounting courses with deeper theoretical grounding, had little material to draw on either domestically or from abroad. Chapter 5 indicates that business schools in the United States had accepted accounting as a legitimate academic discipline for some time but offered little material in this regard.

Outside universities, the profession was also divided on whether it was desirable for accounting to become an academic discipline based on more scientific rigour. Chambers was not oblivious to this rather precarious situation and the apprehension of some of his peers, stating in his 1953 appointment speech:

> Outside these walls and inside them perhaps, the accountant is a curious figure . . . they say ink runs in his veins . . . their hearts don't beat . . . they also have their rituals, doctrines and dogmas which is something they have in common with churchmen; they have their mumbo jumbo, their abracadabra, their folklore.[19]

Chambers regarded his position at the university as an opportunity to bring more discipline to the 'mumbo jumbo' and the 'abracadabra' that characterized accounting practice.

Although Mathews' observations regarding accounting academia were generally true, Sydney University provided as favourable a situation as one could expect. Syd Butlin, who had assumed the deanship of the Faculty of Economics in 1946, was overseeing a considerable expansion of the economics-related staff, and Chambers' appointment had been part of this process. Butlin was known for his frugality, resourcefulness, and open-mindedness. He too had grown up under trying circumstances, and his path had not been unlike that of Chambers. His father had been killed in a hit-and-run accident when Butlin was sixteen, leaving his mother and five siblings penniless. Butlin had helped his family survive by taking in washing, until he graduated from East Maitland Boys' High and like Chambers, won an exhibition scholarship covering tuition to attend the University of Sydney.[20] After graduating with a Bachelor of Economics degree, Butlin had been awarded additional scholarships to train as an economic historian at Trinity College, Cambridge, before returning to Australia to take up an appointment with the university.[21] Chambers recalls that Butlin's first-day instructions to him were simply to 'go, and do as you must.'[22] He set out to do so accordingly.

There were three part-time instructors in accounting working in the Faculty of Economics in 1953. Each instructor covered three courses of accounting in the Bachelor of Economics program, and this balance was retained after Chambers' appointment. The lesser teaching burden and Butlin's loose rein allowed Chambers to spend his time developing new teaching materials and establishing links between the university and the profession as well as other disciplines within the university. His efforts were fruitful. A credit course was established that focused on scrutinizing conventional accounting practices, principles, and doctrines. An Honours program in Accounting, focusing on the analytical, historical, social, and theoretical foundations of the discipline, was established in 1957. A separate department of Accounting was established in 1960 with Chambers as the professor, and daytime classes began to be offered the following year. To accommodate this expansion, there were several hires in the late 1950s and early '60s, including full-time appointees Alex Shaw and Ron Brooker as senior lecturers and Ron Brown as a lecturer; E.J. Walden, Hugh McCredie, and Peter Standish were taken on as part-time lecturers. Adding a legal dimension to accounting teaching and research, Pat Mills and Ron Bowra were appointed in 1962 and 1966 as reader and senior lecturer in Taxation Law. Chambers' importance rose in tandem with the prominence of the discipline, and he was promoted as associate professor in 1955 and foundation Chair of Accounting five years later. The full-time chair was the third of its kind in Australia.[23]

Sheltered from Groupthink

As this account demonstrates, Chambers' academic journey was embedded in practice. In an unfinished biographical manuscript, 'Life on the Fringe— an Accounting Odyssey,' which was found in his study after his death, Chambers writes about his early years:

> But I'd [have] liked to be an engineer, an architect, a medico. But they involved years of unpaid study, and my father, a small sole trader, had lost all he had in the Depression. But I could study economics and accounting at the university at night if I left home and earned my keep during the day. So I did.[24]

His upbringing and life in the Antipodes produced an outsider in the circles of accounting research in the 1950s.[25] It presaged his academic life on the fringe. But that isolation was not necessarily a bad thing—for it may have forged Chambers' thinking in a way that would likely not have been possible if a groupthink approach had been a factor. In his 1972 book Janis identifies three conditions that can lead to this: high group cohesiveness; structural faults, such as the lack of methodological procedures and the insulation and homogeneity of its membership; and the situational context, such as external threats, moral dilemmas, and recent failures. When it is present he suggests groupthink exhibits several symptoms: the overestimation of the stature and abilities of a group; closed-mindlessness to information that might challenge its assumptions; and the use of pressure to enforce uninformed beliefs and behaviour (e.g., through self-censorship).

When Chambers entered academia in the 1940s, the accounting profession in the U.S. and the U.K. displayed all those symptoms. Accountants were a highly cohesive group, with structural faults, such as no comprehensive system of thought, and the situational context was dire: there were problems of how to account for inflation, questions about the appropriate notion of depreciation, and concerns about how to put in place accounting that would lessen the opportunity for fraud. Faced with these conditions, the profession had responded with doubling down on their existing practices and the shunning of new ideas. But to combat groupthink, Janis suggests that one needs to do the opposite by seeking an outside expert and assigning someone to play the role of the devil's advocate. Being an outsider and a devil's advocate was something that Chambers knowingly took on, and in 'Life on the Fringe' he noted:

> What of the fringe? All professions and all professionals live on the fringe . . . accountants live on the fringe of business. . . . All academics live on the fringe . . . and if they give serious thought to the advancement of the art they serve, they will find themselves on the fringe both of the substantive professions and teaching profession. I have lived on the fringe in all three senses. [It] is always demanding, sometimes exhilarating, always adventurous. Top line persons in the arts, in sport, in science and business all live on the fringe. Some get their kicks out of doing what's not been done before, from outdoing rivals, some from public applause—some from simply pursuing goals of their choice which others have held to be unattainable. I've had my satisfactions and of all of these in modest measure.[26]

Chambers' path into academia, coupled with the aspirations of someone who sought methodological rigour found in other scholarly disciplines, meant that he was the ideal devil's advocate for his time. Faced with unsatisfactory accounting in Australia and groupthink among the learned circles of professionals and accounting academics in the U.S. and the U.K., he set out to rework accounting from the fringe. He describes this decision as follows:

> The flaws [of accounting] were universal—and if they could be excused or papered over in practice, that was not safe or serviceable ground for an extensively influential profession. I determined to try to set things right—by reworking the basic ideas, challenging conventional practices or habits, and teaching a set of ideas to the rising generation of practitioners. It would be uphill, against the tide of practice and practitioners. I addressed professionals, businessmen, lawyers—anyone who would listen. "Have gun, will travel—Have speech, will travel." But the bulk of Australian ideas and practices had been imported from the United Kingdom and the United States. I spent [1959] all over those countries trying to find whether anyone else was working on the same pattern—getting down to basics, as I was. I found no one.[27]

Chambers' correspondence indicates that the fact his ideas were not adopted (at least not directly) did at times cause him some discomfort later in his career. 'Life on the Fringe' also notes this and interview material indicates that he enjoyed reading biographies of individuals who had gone against the status quo, perhaps finding some comfort in the eventual success of many of their ideas (even if many of these were only accepted after their proponents' deaths). His extensive library (part of the Chambers Archive) includes hundreds of such business biographies.

By the time Chambers' wrote 'Life on the Fringe,' however, he appears to have come to terms with this fate. He concludes the manuscript stating that he is on firmer grounds than conventional practice:

> Why then should we persist in holding to ideas which fail to command general assent? In the first place, all people on the fringe . . . sooner or later dispose of the spur of external competition or criticism. One need then turn on his own cherished invention more intense scrutiny than at the point of creation or discovery. One looks for all kinds of evidence and argument beyond the level of common criticism. It's a game played against oneself, or against the best of tests one can discover in other domains of thought and inquiry. I'll mention only one class of tests—the test of history. If practice according to an accepted body of ideas is fundamentally sound, it should cease to be the target of criticism from within and from without. But the body of ideas underlying accounting has come up for robust criticism every five or ten years for most of this century.[28]

This would puzzle Chambers right up to his death. Significantly, as discussed in the concluding chapter, such criticism endured throughout the first two decades of the twenty-first century.

Notes

1. Chapter epigraphs:
   Chambers (1972, 156). See also endnotes #s38, 39, chapter 1 and Chambers' letter to Norton Bedford as Chambers approached retirement, P202, #6274, 27/10/1981. A few years later in a letter from Chambers to Briloff he lamented: 'Last year I spent a while as a member of the Australian Accounting Standards Board. I resigned after about 8 months. I found its exercises to be very much in the style of some of the remarks in the Christie article [possibly related to cross-sectional analysis procedures common to many market-based accounting research papers] you sent me. I'm not cut out for such boon-doggling.' (USA, P202, #7682, 17/02/1983)
2. Chambers (2000a).
3. The next three sections also draw on two of Chambers' (1991a, 2000a) accounts of his early childhood and career, Brown's (1982) earlier biographical work, and Clarke *et al.*'s (2012) account of the 'Sydney School of Accounting.' These are augmented by notes from the Chambers' children provided to the authors in responses to questions posed by the authors.
4. Chambers (2000a).
5. Extract from written response of Kevin Chambers to questions posed by the authors.
6. Chambers (2000a).
7. This and next section draws in part on Wolnizer and Dean (2000). The words attributed to Chambers are taken from an undated] two pages found in the Chambers Archive, titled 'Adventure in Accounting.' In another Archive entry (later published as 'Early Beginnings,' 2000a, 318), Chambers recalls that he had four options, and he resolved: 'If I could live away from home and meet the incidental costs of attending university out of a junior clerk's (thirty shillings a week to start) salary, I could combine the first and last of these options. Evening courses were available in Arts and Economics in the University, and as I had already begun to study accounting (an element in the Economics program) it seemed to make sense to enrol in [Sydney's] Faculty of Economics.'
8. Chambers (2000a, 318).
9. Chambers (1990a) contains more of his early thoughts on accounting as a profession and academic discipline.
10. Extract from written response of daughters, Rosemary and Margaret, to questions posed by the authors.
11. Discussion of Chambers' capital maintenance adjustment mechanism in chapter 6 shows how these exposures to practical measurement issues with oil influenced his approach to accommodating instability in the commercial currency unit due to changes in the general level of prices (inflation).
12. Extract from written response of Kevin Chambers to questions posed by the authors. It is possible that his Christadelphian faith may have precluded enlistment. In June 1942 Japanese submarines had shelled, unsuccessfully, part of Newcastle's heavy industry; and there was a midget submarine attack on Sydney Harbour resulting in some deaths.
13. For more on the work of the Australian Prices Commission, see Walker and Linford (1942).
14. For example, Persson and Napier (2014), Clarke and Dean (2010), Gaffikin (1988) and Brown (1982).
15. For more about this institution, see Neill's (1991) history of the Sydney Technical College.
16. Bill Stewart's response to Chambers' letter of withdrawal, P202, #229, 14/02/1958.

17. There has been considerable confusion in the literature about the nature and timing of the first accounting appointments in Australia (Carnegie and Williams, 2001 discusses this). Briefly, appointments included: Russell Mathews as Chair of Commerce, University of Adelaide in 1958; Reg Gynther at the University of Queensland in 1961; and Ken Wright, the University of Adelaide in 1962.
18. Mathews (1982).
19. Clarke, Dean and Wells (2010, 2012, 21).
20. The school was incidentally located close to Quorrobolong and the South Maitland coalfields, where Chambers spent some time as child with an aunt while his father was rearranging his affairs after the passing of Chambers' biological mother, Louisa.
21. For more about Syd Butlin's life and career, see his brother Noel Butlin's (1978) 'Fraternal Farewell' in the *Australian Economic History Review*. Noel, also a graduate from East Maitland Boys' High and the University of Sydney, had a distinguished career as an economic historian with appointments to the Australian High Commissioner in London, the Universities of Cambridge, Harvard, Sydney and Yale; and finally to the Australian National University.
22. Chambers (1991c, 144).
23. The formation, early appointments and growth of the Sydney School of Accounting is described in Clarke, Dean and Edwards (2010, 2012).
24. This was published in the Festschrift issue of *Abacus*, Chambers (2000b, 321).
25. For more about this, see Persson and Napier (2014).
26. Chambers (2000b, 322).
27. Chambers (2000b, 322–3).
28. Chambers (2000b, 325).

2   Chambers the Man

What impressed me most about Chambers was a quality in his character. . . .
Ray is his own man. His independence of mind makes him subservient to
no one. I have never met or heard of any practitioner (in a profession that is
supposed to place a premium on independence) who can match him.
—Edward Stamp, *Abacus*, December 1982

I know I'm a mixture of hard and soft, sociable and sole; not only have you
seen this but you captured it in masterly fashion, economically yet (may
I say) beautifully, in your seventh paragraph.
—Chambers' response to Stamp, December 1982[1]

Much has been written about Chambers' theoretical ideas, but little is
known about the man. This chapter explores several of his personas.

In the first epigraph, Stamp, a long-term friend and correspondent and
international accounting reformer in the 1970s and '80s, provides some
clues. These are elaborated in Stamp's 1982 *Abacus* Festschrift contribution
where he notes that Chambers:

> believes, rightly in my view, that the major advances in accounting
> thought are unlikely to emerge from committees, and in many ways
> he is a loner. . . . [with independence of mind] strength of his convic-
> tions . . . intensely disputatious and a doughty debater and polemicist
> [who] gives, and expects, no quarter in argument . . . [yet] as my wife
> and children and I have discovered [from his visits to our home], he has
> depths of kindness.[2]

In the epigraph reply to Stamp, Chambers observes that he can be both
'hard and soft' and 'sociable and sole.'

Chambers was a man on a mission, dedicated to searching for excel-
lence. Insights into this are gleaned from handwritten notes prepared for a
November 1982 farewell cocktails function held in the University of Sydney
Staff Club:

> Of all the things I have valued in University life, and also in my pro-
> fessional association, the greatest has been the opportunity for the

pursuit of excellence. The world is full of the dull, the humdrum, the pedestrian—that's what is fashionable (short-lived). . . . But, painstaking delivery, spirited lecturing, exact writing and venturous but rigorous thinking a case for which is enduring not short-lived—that is my idea of the spirit of the University and of the learned professions.[3]

In that pursuit Chambers was wont to express candidly his strong opinions on matters where firm knowledge had been obtained over years of research and analysis. Such features may have caused him problems in relationships with some in the business and academic communities. Again, his notes for that farewell function are appropriate:

The way we [Sydney School colleagues] have gone about our business— accounting and law—has not always attracted the esteem and approbation we have thought it deserved, inside and outside the University. We have experienced our share of what [Alan Sillitoe] described as the "loneliness of the long-distance runner."

Michael Gaffikin, who examined as part of his PhD Chambers' epistemological approach to his accounting reforms, came to a similar conclusion. He described Chambers as a loner, in the sense of a person possessing the spirit of a true individual.[4]

A voracious reader of all sorts of literature, he was also, as a later chapter indicates, an archivist who had filed and 'Dewey-classified' his notes and other materials and could retrieve just about anything he had read in an instant. And this was, generally, without the aid of the more recent computer-assisted retrieval. It is shown that this capacity to put forward supporting evidence irked many of his contemporaries as they debated contentious matters.

While becoming a little disillusioned after he retired, he proved resilient to the many hurdles faced and the failures that had occurred in his academic journey. That path entailed a daily routine of working long hours, beginning with travel to the university around 7–8 a.m. to beat the traffic, and returning home around 7 p.m. After dinner, talking with Meg, and having a Scotch with a dash of water, he would retire to his study at around 9.30 for several more hours of reading and writing. He slept for four or five hours, and then the cycle would be repeated.

We show Chambers was a devoted family man, with strong religious values, and he and Margaret shared an abiding interest in music and the arts. Excellence in performance fascinated Chambers, and he contrasted this with his perception of a lesser desire on the part of many of his associates to achieve similar excellence in accounting.

Some critics claimed Chambers was arrogant. The context often was that he did not accept that the world of accounting, finance, and management was changing, and that his ideas had not followed suit. However, he maintained that the financial fundamentals remained unchanged, and this is the opinion of the present authors nearly twenty years after his death.

Others have suggested also he was naive in pursuing regulatory reforms that were far too grandiose, too holistic, rather than seeking incremental reforms and being more political in his advocacy. This matter is explored in chapter 8.

Chambers' professional activities in public office as a councillor, New South Wales Division, National Councillor and National President of the Australian Society of Accountants, showed an ability to organize, administer meetings, and socialize with all and sundry. He was regarded by his professional colleagues as being as well prepared as he was well-attired, and an articulate spokesperson for his profession. An extract from a member of the Perth Stock Exchange and fellow ASA Councillor Bernard Wright, one of the many letters of appreciation from fellow councillors upon his retirement as National President, is instructive:

> I have heard it said that you are a controversial thinker and I think that was said in part from frustration but more particularly with envy. The range of depth of your thinking has been of undoubted value not only to . . . Councils of the Society . . . but also for the profession as a whole . . . history will prove that your areas of service . . . were always undertaken with the profession's welfare uppermost in your mind . . . I am sorry that I have had so few opportunities to work with you . . . [when I did] I learnt something of value and enjoyed your provoking me into thinking.[5]

Yet, as discussed in chapters 6 and 8, he was not always in favour with his councillor colleagues, especially on the big-ticket items from the 1960s through to the 1980s: for example, his contributions to CCA debates of the 1970s and especially his related chairmanship of the 1977–78 N.S.W. ASRC, his position on the twice-failed merger attempts of the two largest accounting professional bodies, and his views about what should be the ASA's conditions for its Meritorious Contribution to the Literature award.

Through his writings, his teaching, and his many conversations, Chambers constantly took a missionary stance—seeking relentlessly to reform the law of company accounts. Offence was frequently taken. His colleagues often saw in professional and university seminars, as Stamp acknowledges in the epigraph to this chapter, the feisty qualities of a skilful debater and strident writer. In such contests, however, no matter how vigorously things developed, our experiences accord with Stamp's and many others' view that he always 'played the ball and not the man.' Whittington and Zeff, however, recount the early 1970s debate between Chambers and Australian contemporary Reg Gynther over whether to report in the accounts specific asset and liability price changes (like changes in the replacement or current costs or exit prices) or to report general price level changes. They note Gynther's displeasure at what he perceived as playing the man when Chambers' called for 'an end to sterile argument and invention,' and 'the allegation of an "intellectual scandal."' They noted Gynther had publicly deplored Chambers' '"irritating" writing style and "unreasonable comments"' and described '"the allegation of an "intellectual scandal" as "offensive."'[6]

An extract from a letter to Stamp is apposite: 'Almost any attempt to fashion a consistent set of ideas will offend many people, for many different and indeed opposite reasons. Had I feared this, however, I wouldn't have lifted a pen.'[7] But when arguing for reforms he was adamant, as observed in another letter, this time to Geoff Vincent, then executive director of the Australian Society of Accountants, that ad hominem attacks should be avoided:

> [O]ne cannot expect (nor should one expect) editors to adjudicate, when sparring develops, on the validity of argument or the adequacy of evidence, between contributors. But surely editors can be expected to smell the searing flesh when one author comes out against another breathing fire and brimstone. The argumentum "ad hominem" is a bag of dirty tricks for bloodying a man's nose when you can't upset his argument.[8]

Similarly, in a letter to U.S. financial management academic of the era, Harold Bierman, he expressed a desire for courteous debates:

> I have a personal feeling . . . which forbids me regarding any person as an inferior, to be patronized or submitted to condescension on my part. I regard all as equal, and as my own work as open to criticism and objection as anyone else's. On this ground I myself would dislike a patronising or condescending attitude on the part of critics—I do, therefore, as I would be done by.[9]

However, while unwilling to change his 'in principle' ideas about what reforms were needed to rid accounting of its deficiencies and ensure an ordered commercial society, at the margin he did change his practical reform suggestions. This is attested in his 1970 and 1974 *Abacus* pieces—his 'Second' and 'Third Thoughts' (discussed in chapter 6). He was contemptuous of those academics who did not question the status quo. The academic's role was perceived by him, in conversation, to be an irritant, a facilitator of change. He notes this also in the Preface to his *Thesaurus*.

Chambers had strong views about how knowledge progresses. He was sceptical of what he viewed as the faddish fashion in much of accounting and finance to undertake large-scale market price-based research,[10] and as the Stamp and Chambers epigraphs suggest, of the drive by the profession and regulatory authorities to introduce more and more committees, producing their inevitable compromised, political solutions to practical problems.

Politicizing the process was anathema to Chambers. Consider this extract from his 1972 letter to U.S. certified public accountant Richard Knox, who had had expressed pleasure in a letter that Chambers had captured the practitioner's 'anguish' with the APB's myriad promulgations:

> [T]he present ineffectual mode of setting questions of principle will not be changed without something of a "palace revolution." Your reference to da Vinci employs almost the same turn of phrase I have used somewhere before. Freud, Einstein, Keynes, etc. had no committees. But that was before the unfortunate day when committees came to be considered as a proper way of discovery. What folly shall we have next?[11]

Several years later he reflected on the difficulty of getting academics and practitioners to appreciate the advantage of the division of labour between the two accounting arms. The context was academics being given either representation on professional committees or with the proliferation of the funding of 'named' professorships. This matter was discussed in several Chambers' letters including correspondence responding to Moonitz's note on the need for 'independence' which had appeared in the January 1979 issue of the AAA's *Accounting Education News*. Chambers observed: 'You know I support your view . . . without reservation.' Stressing the point made in the chapter epigraph by Stamp, Chambers observed that for professional fields generally: it is the function of academics to act as the "auditors," the monitors, of practice . . . as the "conscience" of the professions (all of them), and to pursue the logic of their fields without fear of the prevailing state of opinion.

He continues, confidently asserting that in accounting, however, 'the vast majority of academics seem to spend more time wanting to appear "on the side" of prevailing professional thinking and practice, than trying to advance the quality of both.'[12]

If Chambers was always confident of his views and positions, this was due in large part to meticulously kept and extensive, easily retrievable files on myriad accounting, finance, and management issues. As well, he was a keen reader. One of his contemporaries, Allan Barton, observed in conversation that, partly because Chambers had read so widely, he was 'a consummate wordsmith—he could have been a literary writer.'

A good example of confidence in his literary ability is an exchange from 1999 with the *Abacus* copy editor, Carl Harrison-Ford, when Chambers was proofreading his article, 'Simplicity in Accounting.' On the proofs Harrison-Ford noted:

> Proof reader assures me "corroborable" is not in the full Oxford English Dictionary and wonders if you'd prefer the use of "corroboratable." I leave this up to you as corroborable makes clear sense to me

and may be in use in accounting and other literature . . . and does not, in any case, seem an abuse of language. My computer's spell check recognizes neither word, but what would it know?

Chambers' response shows a determination to understand the correct use of language:

> I've used '[corroborable] for years, though I've never checked it with the OED. It seemed to me quite a handy word, but I've no idea where or when I first encountered it. "Corroboratable" sounds like a clumsy mouthful, sounds not even euphonious. I wondered whether there were other words of similar form to "corroborate," what the SOED (my 1936 ed) did to their derivatives. The first word I thought of was "ameliorate" of which "ameliorable" is given as a derivative. Perhaps there is some lexical rule that I know not of; and perhaps one precedent is not enough. But I'm reasonably content that the context (pp. 125–7) makes plain what was intended. And I'm content with "corroborable," and it seems you are too. Stet!

The word was retained. Further, the concluding sentence to Chambers' response to Harrison-Ford is an instance of his wit and a desire for research also to be fun: 'The meticulosity (!) of your proof reader provided some fun on the side!'[13]

'Adaptation' was another of Chambers' uncommon (to some) words. Consistent with the then-pervasive Austrian view of economics, for example that of von Mises, he felt the notion of a capacity for adaptation (rather than the more commonly used 'adaption') aptly captured his belief that knowledge of financial information about an entity's current financial position (its wealth) is a prius for managers and other interested parties making informed business decisions. The idea was critical for many of his theoretical forays. It was discussed in an exchange of letters with U.K. economist G.L.S. Shackle.[14] In one letter Shackle noted the similarities in their views, that they cover in the broad the same field, together with the lament that, in his formative education, he had not had the time to be properly exposed to Chambers' and other accountants' thoughts about the need to constrain accounting to the past and present. Interestingly, Shackle's later works would use the phrase 'time-to-come' and called for accounting to convey factual knowledge of financial position for decision making. Chambers replied:

> Your view of the relation between information about present status and imaginative constructions of future states tallies exactly with my own. I recall that in some of your work you mention the confusion which arises when economists write of "income" when often they mean expected income. Many people in my own field quote from

economists [he presumably was referring here, mainly, to Sir John Hicks] without noting that there is a difference between the attained and the imagined.

Chambers as Mentor

With his Sydney staff and junior academics from elsewhere submitting works to *Abacus* Chambers displayed strong mentoring and pastoral skills. Regarding his staff, this was achieved through meetings and paper reviews where generally he was critical, with lots of red pen scribbled on paper. He was quick and succinct in his reviews, reflecting his years of acquiring knowledge and willingness to pass it on. As well, Chambers frequently shared his musings in the form of mimeographed drafts of his papers with all staff, as those works were going through preliminary composition and then the often-lengthy journal review process.

The relationship he had with a master's student and University of Sydney tutor George Foster, who had just accepted a postgraduate offer to study at Stanford University in the early 1970s, illustrates well Chambers' caring and mentoring skills. In correspondence with the authors Foster observed:

> One aspect that I really admired was his advice to go to Stanford to do a PhD. His argument was that Stanford has "the best set of young academics in Beaver and Demski, where the discipline could be going. I don't agree what they are doing, but realistically it's in your best interests to get directly exposed to the leaders of this new wave and decide for yourself if you want to buy their approach." Very unselfish and for me the Stanford adventure has been great.

Foster continued:

> The one area the University of Sydney program in the 1960s vastly underplayed was quantitative/mathematical skills. I had a very rocky start at Stanford because I was very much out of my depth in these areas. Hard for Ray to appreciate the bridge that had to be built executing his sage and incredibly valuable advice to me and what was necessary to make the Sydney to Stanford transition work. Perhaps he thought "survival of the fittest" was a good test of my abilities.[15]

Confirming Foster's 'rocky start' at Stanford is the following from a 1972 letter (part of related correspondence during the year) written to Chambers from Foster's father. Foster had been enrolled in several courses at Stanford as part of a PhD program, and he apparently had found the settling-in process more difficult than expected. He was still finishing his MEc thesis at Sydney and asked his father to submit the latest version. He was comfortable enough to share his unease not only with his parents but his mentor. The father's letter notes:

> I am enclosing part of a letter received from George last Saturday. He passed all four subjects at the First Term Examination. . . . I believe and earnestly hope [the few week's break will] make him a more composed student from the one who, alone and somewhat confused, commenced the First Term. My wife and I wish to express to you our thanks for your help to our son while he was working under your direction at Sydney University.

This was followed not long after by the Foster family and George delivering Chambers a gift to acknowledge more formally that help.[16]

In June 1972 Chambers replied to a letter George had written to him noting that he had received formal notification of his master's degree being awarded. As well as congratulating George more generally, and on his recent marriage, Chambers noted:

> Third, congratulations on the Haskins and Sells Award. That is another feather in your cap (besides cash in the hand). Needless to say, it made me feel much better about the "straight talk" of my earlier letter. I would have been abashed if the work really crippled you—as you seemed to think it might. I guess you won't look forward with despair again. . . . Glad to hear you've been hearing and meeting some of the big names. Mixing it with those people can be helpful in ways you will only later realize. But those ways may have nothing to do with what you do with your head. I've criss-crossed the U.S. several times—from being known by others; but that doesn't mean I have given them anything to think about in a sustained way, or that they have given me anything of the same kind. What we have done and stand for here [at the Sydney School] seems to have had no impact on the drift of things there (or anywhere else).[17]

In chapter 9 we show that more than two decades later Chambers' frustration about his perceptions of minimal influence had not changed.

For his Sydney staff, while receiving Chambers' views on written work could be daunting, it was part of a constructive master—apprentice experience.[18]

Similarly, in respect of *Abacus* submissions, especially by junior academics, Chambers would spend hours reviewing and suggesting revisions to those papers that had the germ of an idea that he felt could improve practice. For senior academics he was less tolerant of preliminary works— he made the observation to Graeme Dean in the mid-1990s, when he was appointed editor of *Abacus*: 'Senior academics should know better than submit "half-baked" papers.' For their part, high ego senior academics sometimes viewed Chambers' editorial reports as abrasive.

Stamp's *Abacus* Festschrift contribution captures Chambers' support for novitiates:

> Indeed there are many younger writers on accounting who have experienced Ray's willingness, during his time as the Founding Editor of [*Abacus*], to devote hours of his time to patient correspondence with them in his desire to help them produce an article that would meet his exacting standards.[19]

During the first ten years at the journal, Chambers sought ways of promoting the new journal internationally. This entailed, amongst other things, a quick turnaround of manuscripts as he was often a sole reviewer. But he also sometimes painstakingly nursed submitted articles into acceptance.

An exemplar of this pastoral care is the editing suggestions with respect to a paper submitted to *Abacus* in early 1972 by a then relatively inexperienced U.S. author, Philip E. Meyer. The paper, 'The Accounting Entity,' was sole-reviewed by Chambers. Correspondence related to the article over several revisions is available in the Chambers Archive.[20]

The implications of the proprietary/entity notions underpinning the Meyer article were of great interest to Chambers at the time, and they resonate still.[21] The Sydney School held a strong position on what constituted the object of an accounting and how it should be accounted for. For the sake of generality, as noted in *Accounting, Evaluation and Economic Behavior*,[22] the term 'entity' is used to express that object. But that use should not obscure the fact that some specific person, household, business firm, corporation, association, or institution is in contemplation.

Prior to the paper's eventual publication in December 1973, Chambers cajoled Meyer to persist with what would prove to be a lengthy and challenging (approximately eighteen month) review process. Chambers' reviews were critical of certain parts of the paper—but in each review letter lengthy reasoning was provided as to how the paper might be improved. We draw on parts of that review process to indicate Chambers' mentoring skills.

The July 1972 Meyer brief response to Chambers' editorial review letter begins our review of several letters, extracts from which are reproduced below.

> I have received your letter of July 18 and thank you for your prompt response. Because the research effort underlying the paper encompassed the areas of extension that you cite, it is my hope to be able to make appropriate modifications and conclusions and send the revised version to you within the next few weeks (by mid-August).

Meyer responded on 30 August:

> The following changes are included in this revision:
>
> 1. The introductory remarks have been condensed to a level more applicable to an informed readership.
> 2. A review of the literature is set forth at the very outset so as to establish a common frame of reference between the author and potential researchers.
> 3. Immediately following the development of the eight pervasive theories comprising the entity concept framework, there is a discussion of comparative characteristics in an effort to discern truly distinctive features of each respective point of view.
> 4. Reference to specific financial reporting controversies are set forth—business combinations, inter-corporate investments, long-term leases, etc.
> 5. Special attention is devoted to the very crucial question of valuation in accounting—historical costs vs. contemporary bases.
>
> . . .

On 25 September Chambers replied:

> The final sentence of my letter of 18 July was a hint that your mode of expression is such that you come very slowly and in roundabout fashion to any point. I did not wish to be too critical; but the persistence of the same features in the revision prompts me to be more specific. The Introduction seems unnecessarily long—and it is made so by clauses or sentences which seem to be irrelevant. The expression is made ponderous by the use (or misuse) of terms which you could do without in the interest of clarity. Why use 'this question of well defined parameters'? What is the point of 'all such viewpoints are advocative in nature'? How can there be many interpretations of the entity concept? (Surely you mean that there are simply many different concepts). How can one 'co-opt common terminology'? (All these points on 1). There is similar prolixity and fuzziness throughout the paper.
>
> The 'Current State of Affairs' section is not well organized. You are leading up to an [8-class] analysis. [with] five paragraphs on different authors' views—. . . those paragraphs are curiously mixed up—both as to date and substance. Nowhere do you clearly identify authors with your 8 classes. . . .
>
> When you come to the detailed treatment of the classes of notion you identify, the treatment is descriptive more than analytical. As I said in my earlier letter, the object of such an analysis as yours is surely to reduce the confusion. This could be done by showing that some of the views are logically or practically identical (so that the apparent differences are verbal only) or that some of them are unrealistic (so that

they should be abandoned). You seem reluctant to make any attempt to judge between the different notions.

When you come to discuss the technical differences which might be supposed to arise from different notions of the entity, it is not made clear which notion leads to which rules. For example, the section on 'valuation bases' does not connect any specific notion of the entity with specific valuation rules. Then you decline to discuss certain valuation rules (foot of 25) without any indication of the possibility that they may have arisen from differences in view of what is being accounted for. . . . I hope you will not take all these remarks unkindly. I have gone to the considerable trouble of being specific about some things in the hope that you will appreciate my respect for your labor and in the hope that you may do something quite positive about reducing the messy state of the literature. The whole object of serious analysis where confusion exists is to reduce the source of confusion, to reach some conclusion which helps in this direction. To suppose that contradictory notions may be held about the same substantive things is contrary to the whole spirit of disciplined inquiry—it is anti-scientific, anti-intellectual. We must discriminate between what is good and what is less good if we are to advance our knowledge and competence.

Meyer was appreciative. Seeing a way forward, he was quick to reply to Chambers on 12 November accompanying the revised submission:

I appreciate your patient critique . . . the manuscript now contains a systematic categorization of entity views suggested by others, coverage of the 'theories' includes analysis of appropriateness and duplication, and much of the apparent overall verbose content has been eliminated. Two other aspects of your critique warrant comment.

My overall thesis does not suggest that one's perception of the accounting entity *ipso facto* offers insight into every ramification of financial reporting. Thus, my inquiry into the various theories has not resulted in my being able to document any *definitive* conclusions regarding the relative merits of replacement cost, discounted cash flow, current cash equivalent, etc. as measures of current value. However, the analysis was able to suggest that a current value basis is more meaningful than an historical cost basis, a conclusion that many, if not most, accountants have persisted in rejecting.

I also appreciate your comments regarding the importance of reducing the state of confusion and conflict surrounding issues in accounting. It was precisely in deference to this need that my efforts were undertaken. It is my opinion that because our professional and scholarly literature is so inundated with papers promoting particular theories of the accounting entity without systematically analyzing (or even acknowledging) *all* competing viewpoints, that creation of a neutral framework is warranted. The state of affairs is such that there often, if not typically, exists an unawareness as to what rival positions have been documented and what the similarities and differences are.

My contribution therefore is to set forth the parameters of the controversy so that intelligent and informed debate might ensue. Controversy cannot be resolved if the participants cannot even agree on what the subject matter is, much less not use common terminology or understand counterparts' positions. I too do not believe that 'contradictory notions may be held about the same substantive things [for it] is contrary to the whole spirit of disciplined inquiry—it is anti-scientific, anti-intellectual.' I too believe that 'we must discriminate between what is good and what is less good if we are to advance our knowledge and competence.'

There were more resubmissions and several proposed editorial changes for Meyer to consider before the paper was accepted. The process continued on 24 November with Chambers seeking to 'advise' Meyer on a possible way forward to achieve publication. Chambers notes, beginning with the positive remark, 'I hope my reactions are not wearing you down' and continues with:

I have pointed in the direction of what I consider clarification of the confusion. . . . You distinguish eight 'theories.' First, I think this should be eight conceptions; for each of them only represents the notion entertained about the 'entity' by the classes of person to whom you attribute them. An explicitly stated idea or set of ideas descriptive of the entity is not a theory, either of the entity or of the accounting for an entity class. But such a statement provides the elements which, together with other notions, may enable a conclusion (theorem or theory) to be deduced in respect of the accounting. I'll return to that shortly.

As I said in my last letter, it is quite possible that the distinctions you draw are distinctions based on the verbal forms used by writers. For example, look at the 'balance sheet equation' column of your summary appendix [which appears in the final published version]. Notwithstanding the different words, most of the entries are logically identical. Also look at the column 'Domain of the Assets.' (It seems to me this means who has dominion over the assets in some cases; but it means something else in other cases). The mere differences in the terms used do not, however, signify that their authors have distinctively different ideas about what things are assets of 'the entity.' Most of the authors entertain substantially similar views of what shall appear as assets, despite the differences in their verbal descriptions of the entity. And, while dealing with the appendix, the entries under 'concept of profits' do not represent a concept of profit in most cases; they represent who gets it whatever it is. I think this column should give a description of the concept—e.g., revenue gains; all residual gains; dividends plus interest; etc.

Now return to the deduction or inference mentioned at the end of my second paragraph above. If there are distinctive theories of accounting for the entity, each should be different in respect of what is considered to be assets, or what is considered to be liabilities or what is considered to be profit, or different in all three respects. What is 'considered to be,' assets, liabilities or profit must, of course, be derived in part by inference from the author's notion of the entity. But hardly ever, if ever, do authors derive their ideas in this way. That is why, in my view, they entertain very much the same ideas about accounting rules, methods and output, despite their verbal differences. . . .

I feel strongly (which I do as adviser, but not as editor) that most (but not all) of the differences in conception are really differences in emphasis, not in substance at all. But the emphasis does lead people to different ideas about asset and profit. That is why I think it is important to show that the many different conceptions have so many significant points in common.

The reason I write is that I still think your work on the matter is worthy of some firmer conclusion—and perhaps some tightening of treatment.

Meyer continues to show his appreciation of the review process with the response on 22 December: 'I have received your letter of November 28. . . . I recognize the goodwill implicit in your comments not to mention their inherent merit.' This was followed not long after by a letter from Meyer on 24 January 1973 accompanying his second resubmission. The letter acknowledges the author's appreciation of Chambers' advisory and editorial assistance:

I feel a true learning experience has occurred. The letter also summarizes the latest changes . . . [:]

1. The text has been 'tightened,' use of the word 'theory' has been curtailed, and more analysis appears earlier in the narrative.
2. The discussion of 'valuation' is placed in better perspective by virtue of introductory comments which point out the very ambiguity created by one-dimensional conceptions of the accounting entity.
3. The 'summary and conclusions' section has been rewritten in a manner which offers more depth. Important is the fact that a more forceful position is offered regarding the presence of many similarities among the various conceptions *and* the recognition that variations in terminology are not synonymous with substantive differences in conceptions.
4. The 'appendix' is restated in a manner which respects the homogeneity of entries contained in the various columns.

Chambers responded on 30 March, continuing to prompt Meyer to improve the piece, to revise it further. The concluding very positive sentence was indicative of Chambers' mentoring skills:

> I am sorry to have to continue in criticism of your paper. I am treating each version on its merits without reference to earlier drafts. My present difficulties are as follows:
>
> 1. You do not look critically at each of the conceptions you describe. Take the 'traditional proprietary' view, for example. You should point out that it is inconsistent with the nature of companies. Companies legally own or possess their assets; the stockholders do not own company assets. This makes the view you describe under this heading untenable as a description of the facts. Many of the other conceptions are subject to similar criticisms. As your object is presumably to do away with the confusion, you should put up the arguments against each and discuss those which are patently at odds with the facts.
> 2. Many of the conceptions you name are really different in name only. You may see this from your summary table. It is true that you mention some of the similarities, but you do not point out that the differences are really marginal, not substantial.
> 3. Your excursion into the valuation question leads you to say that seven of the eight conceptions entail the use of current values for assets. Yet the fact is that most of the proponents of those seven do not hold that assets should be valued at current values. You say nothing about this, nor about the grounds on which different views of asset valuation are held by different authors. It seems that your analysis should lead you to some synthesis which you could put forward as the ideal notion of the entity.
>
> I hope all this does not try your patience to breaking point.

No doubt this positive and considerate conclusion prompted Meyer to respond quickly. A revised manuscript and accompanying letter was received on 8 May:

> I welcome your critical comments for I suspect you perceive sufficient substance in my endeavor to justify continued attention. . . . Thus, we come to the specific matter of my reluctance to 'reject' particular conceptions of the accounting entity on the grounds that they are not substantially distinctive from other conceptions (see page 16) or because they do not reflect 'real-world' conditions. As a result of reviewing the paper, your critiques, and my own thoughts, I have rewritten the 'summary and conclusions' section of the manuscript in a manner which, I believe, points out quite definitively the susceptibility of the eight conceptions to such additional scrutiny. I specifically suggest that there are

but five 'pure' positions and that differences among these are invariably in degree only. The three 'non-pure' conceptions are specifically depicted as being neutralized versions of the 'pure' five. And with respect to the validity of views such as the 'traditional proprietary' view, there is specific reference to its authoritative, albeit tacit, support (e.g. earnings per share and the equity method). Whether the existing practices are valid is a matter specifically beyond the stated scope of my endeavor. I agree with you that discussion of valuation concepts is too vital and too complex to be afforded less than comprehensive coverage . . . the material has been withdrawn. Thus, the two substantive changes in the attached manuscript are the deletion of the (three page) valuation section and the completely revised 'summary and conclusions.'

While the process clearly was drawing to an end, still more advice and editing suggestions were proposed in Chambers' letter to Meyer of 10 October:

I had hoped that my several suggestions about redrafting your paper on the entity might have prompted you to tighten up and simplify its language; in particular to use consistently some of the terms (approach, concept and view) which occur in it repeatedly. But as you did not do so I have taken the liberty of thoroughly editing it. I have chopped out some sections which seem to get in the way of the main thread—particularly your pp 11–18 which in any case are too terse to match well with your treatment of the eight conceptions. And I have rewritten and added to the section which appeared under your heading 'Internal Consistency.' By separate airmail I am sending the retyped draft. Please let me know if there is anything to which you object. I have tried to follow your manuscript, its argument and sequence, even though I have added here and there an idea or an example which does not occur in the original. The appendix stands; it has not been retyped. Please read the copy with care and advise me immediately so that it can go to press.

The process ended after some minor suggested changes by both the author and editor. Meyer provides the final word: 'I appreciate your personal involvement in the development of the paper.'

Significantly, the Chambers Archive files reveal that this review process with a junior academic was, as Stamp also notes, not an isolated case.[23]

Recourse to observations from the family and some Sydney PhD students now allows us to say more about Chambers as a family man, as an effective doctoral supervisor, and a person showing resilience to setbacks.[24]

Chambers as a Family Man

Given long working hours and the enormous written legacy of those labours, it would not be unusual for the family to have to play second fiddle on occasions. To this end we sought from his daughters, Rosemary and Margaret, and son, Kevin, recollections of their parents during their childhood years. They reveal that their father was someone who cared deeply for his family, but who was also consumed by his work. Their mother was the head of social affairs and the home. We let the responses convey, at times, their differing recollections.

First, son Kevin noted that his father: 'always appeared to be somewhat austere to me and fairly standoffish. The house was really my mother's domain. She had control of this. She had control of this except when my father became furious about some infraction and then everyone dived for cover. My father had fallen I think into the habit of using the holidays to probably further his family's fortunes by doing things like painting the house rather than having a holiday and I remember one particular holiday when he spent two weeks just painting the house and I did complain to my mother. After that time it was interesting that I think my mother said this is unacceptable and insisted that two weeks a year be put aside for a family holiday and this subsequently came about and for about eight years in a row we used to go to Coolangatta as a family in my teenage years. On holiday my father seemed to be able to segment his days for certain things. I think he would allow two hours for the family and then lunch, then reading and then perhaps playing a game with his family and then some more reading.'

Kevin further recalls:

> I remember in particular still feeling cheated by my father particularly around Christmas time when my friends would go off camping with their families for at least two weeks. We never did such a thing and [later in the year] I did tackle my mother and father about this when I was about 16. I told them I was unhappy about this situation and my father immediately went up the street and bought a tent and the next weekend we went camping, unfortunately we went to Canberra in the middle of winter but he made an effort there. I think these turnabouts in spending time with the family were down to my mother rather than my father.

On the matter of the family and Saturday sport Kevin again had some positive and negative recollections of his father's and mother's actions:

> I do recall that I used to play sport every weekend, I would play tennis and my father would always be up and ready to take me wherever I had to go but then I had to spend about two hours and a few bus rides getting home from wherever I played and neither of my parents actually ever came to see me play which is somewhat different to

what happens today I think. I think if my father had turned up to such an event he would have found it a total waste of time and he was really not prepared to waste his time doing that. Contrary to my sisters' recollections I can't remember my father being very interested in my schooling at all. My father remained elusive particularly on Saturdays when he occupied himself doing things that he wanted to do around the house. I think these were times when he loved reflection on many issues and really didn't want to be disturbed and he would toil all day doing some tasks around the house either making fly screens, painting or in the garden which would take him all day but he didn't seem to have the need to talk to anyone during that time, I did try and insinuate myself in this from time to time but it was not successful.

Kevin then summarizes:

Having said all this about my father I can only say that he was very strong on family and wished to involve himself with his family and have his family around him, I think that the young children did worry him enormously as they did mess up the house and his things and he found this particularly irritating. It was interesting then to see him actually have an epiphany one day and I think he decided that it really wasn't worth getting upset about and he allowed the children from that time on pretty free rein with whatever they wanted to do around his house. He certainly seemed much more relaxed in his later years.

The daughters' joint recollection focuses mostly on the positive reflections of Kevin.

Our parents were very interested in our grades at school and willing to help with homework and projects etc. while we were young. We were fortunate to enjoy holidays at the Blue Mountains or at the beach very regularly. This was when Dad really engaged in family life, uninterrupted by the demands of work. We all played games together of an evening after days outdoors enjoying the natural environment— bushwalking, swimming etc. As we grew up, we were expected to take care of our own studies and dad would retire to his office after dinner, and we would go to our own rooms to work. I think Mum often felt pretty alone of an evening.

This last point is confirmed by Chambers' comments to one of the authors (Dean) that after dinner he would return to his study for several more hours of work.

Overseas Travels and Rejecting Invitations for Chair Positions

As his ideas became more widely known in the late 1950s and through the 1960s, Chambers received many offers to move overseas. His strong family ties are shown to have been a, if not the, major reason for rejecting such offers.

Considerable evidence of Chambers' attempt to promote his ideas in North America appears in the Chambers Archive. He undertook several sabbaticals in the U.S. and Europe/U.K. The first, and longest, covered all of 1959. Subsequent trips occurred until his formal retirement.

Chambers' family provide some reflections about the 1959 sabbatical and have also provided photos—some are reproduced as Figure 2.2. His post-humously published Probus lecture 'Life on the Fringe' hints at those travels adding some pressure to his already hectic early academic life in the 1950s and '60s.

It also notes his frustration at his reform ideas being rejected. Summary notes prepared for the Probus lecture are insightful about those frustrations:

> About 10 years through the 1950s, I constructed a style of account-
> ing that many professionals and others said we should have but which
> could not be devised. All over Europe, Britain and the U.S. [throughout]
> 1959 I tried to find a hint that others were on a similar track. Found
> none.[25]

Chambers experienced other frustrations related to financing his fam-
ily to accompany him on that trip. The winter of 1958 was an especially anxious period. In March he had applied to the vice-chancellor for study leave to explore developments in regulatory reform, and in particular to participate on breakthrough, scientifically grounded accounting research with overseas (mainly British and North American) scholars. He received formal approval from the Senate in May but the final letter from regis-trar, Margaret Telfer took another four months to arrive. It notes: 'study leave . . . has been granted by the University for the purpose of examining work being done towards the integration of studies in accounting, eco-nomics and administration, towards rigorous theoretical study of account-ing methods and concepts, and the relationship of this to the business and professional environment. It is intended to discuss these matters with a number of persons in the Universities—in particular California, Chicago, Columbia, Harvard, Michigan, New York, Ohio, Virginia and Yale; with persons engaged in the professional practice of accounting; with officers of professional and regulating bodies; and with some financial executives in industry. These studies may require up to eight months in the United States and Canada.'[26]

Other correspondence reveals that, in addition to the half salary and half travelling allowance paid in advance, the 1959 trip was funded from a £250

Sydney University travel grant and a £100 Institute of Chartered Accountants in Australia travel grant. There was a major concern still that the family might have to return to Australia after the first stage of the trip—the European leg—unless additional funding was forthcoming. Further funding requests were rejected by the Carnegie Corporation's British Dominions and Colonies Program and local bodies such as the Public Accountants' Registration Board (PARB). The proposed first stage of approximately five months involved pre-arranged visits to institutions such as the universities of Bristol, Manchester, and Oxford as well as the London School of Economics. Visits were also scheduled with academics, practitioners, and regulators at institutions in Austria, Belgium, France, Germany, Switzerland, and the Netherlands.

With the departure for England fast approaching, in August 1958 and on the advice primarily of U.S. academics William Paton and Robert Dixon, Chambers applied for a Relm Foundation Fellowship Grant. The foundation was attached to the University of Michigan. Three months passed. Finally, early November and just a month prior to departure, news arrived that a U.S.$5,000 Relm grant had been awarded. Relief must have been palpable. Chambers recounted to his relatively unknown (in accounting circles) U.S. colleague Ernest Weinwurm that: 'This removes a great deal of the immediate anxiety, and permits me to plan with some assurance.'[27]

Departing Sydney on the SS *Arcadia* on 28 November (Figure 2.3), the family arrived in London on 29 December. With the European leg completed as planned, the family left England on the *Empress Britain* in the middle of May for Montreal, spending two weeks in Canada before moving to the U.S.A. A three-month teaching stint at the University of Michigan started the U.S. leg. This was followed by seminar visits to over a dozen other institutions, including Carnegie Mellon, Chicago and University of Illinois at Urbana—Champaign before Stanford, University of California Berkeley, and University of California Los Angeles.[28]

All three children have fond memories of their grand tour. In a joint response to a question about it daughters Rosemary and Margaret observed:

> We travelled for a whole year together as a family unit, dependent on each other's company for long periods. In between Dad's work commitments, we drove through many different countries appreciating their cities and their natural wonders . . . exotic places like Sri Lanka and Port Said. . . . We lived in Richmond for about 3 months, . . . before the long car trip through the United Kingdom as well as France, Belgium, Netherlands, Germany, Austria, Switzerland and Italy. . . . "The Trip" . . . opened our eyes to so much about the world and our privileged place in it. We think Dad wanted to know about the world himself and to share that knowledge with us . . . it involved a tremendous amount of planning and costing but the experience was enormously enriching for us as

individuals. It was also a shared and priceless treasure for our family and has given us a sense of belonging to each other in a remarkable way. His achievement in accomplishing it was a matter of determination over a long time and in challenging circumstances. This determination was a signature aspect of his character.

Son Kevin was equally effusive:

The trip—I must say that from my point of view this is the most memorable trip I have ever been on, I am so grateful to my parents for taking all of us away on that trip. . . . I think my father planned that to the last penny and to the last day. . . . He used to keep a diary about what we spent the money on and he worked out every day what he had done . . . it was the greatest gift I think that I have been given by my parents.

It was unusual for an Antipodean accounting academic and his family at that time to travel extensively overseas. Chambers' sabbaticals and other special leaves, however, reveal an accounting internationalist, with five trips round the world between 1959 and 1982 visiting numerous countries, especially the United States. He criss-crossed the U.S. in 1959, 1962, and 1966 and was the AAA Visiting Overseas Scholar in 1976. His last pre-retirement visit to the U.S. was in 1980.

In 'Life on the Fringe' his travels were described as being like a:

Have gun will travel—Have speech will travel. . . . I became well known. I was invited to speak all over the place. In 1966 I went by invitation on three or four day visits to the University of California at Berkeley. Out of there I made sorties to Alabama, New York, Los Angeles, to Sydney and back, to Michigan, Stanford University, Washington University (Seattle), Edmonton, Saskatchewan, Oregon. The family were in tow on many occasions.

On such visits Chambers felt like; 'an academic gadfly—on the fringe—for one can only generate impressions, not convictions in such short spells.'[29]

In his many U.S. travels Chambers accepted semester-length endowed chair appointments, such as the Edmund P. Learned Professorship at the University of Kansas, the George A. Miller Distinguished Professorship at the University of Illinois at Urbana—Champaign, and the Walker Ames Professorship at the University of Washington (Seattle). In what was an unusual situation from late 1950s to the end of the 1970s Chambers was overseas on eight separate trips for approximately four and a half years on relatively short-term (less than a year) visiting appointments.

As well, Chambers received numerous invitations to accept longer professorial appointments (one year or more) or longer term teaching invitations in several major U.S. universities, such as University of California Berkeley, Columbia University, University of Kansas, Harpur College, N.Y., DePaul

University, University of Illinois at Urbana—Champaign, University of Michigan, New York University, Ohio State University, University of Utah, and University of Virginia. More than once it was suggested he would be better able to pursue his reform program, and with a more lucrative stipend and research allowance.[30]

The tone of just one invitation is illustrative. On 2 January 1962 Ernest Weinwurm wrote:

> Of course it is wonderful that you come again [to the U.S.A. this year]; as you know I have been in favor of your staying here permanently to help to promote a new scientific approach to accounting. Your assistance is needed in view of the small group of those interested in that all-important project.[31]

Chambers' responses to those invitations confirm that, while adamant his work goals would be more easily achievable from a U.S. university base, several factors militated against such a move. These included a desire to stay in Australia to change things locally through his professional association networks—he was at various times a state councillor, then state and national president of the ASA. He wanted to be the first academic to achieve national presidency and in this he enjoyed success. But critically, he was loath to spend any more time away from his family. This, along with further information from his children, reveals a family man who was devoted to his children, grandchildren, and wife—and someone who did not want to dislocate them. The following extract responding to one of many chair invitations, from Robert Sterling, this time in August 1969, shows he was very comfortable in his own city and in his own skin:

> I'm sure I would be financially better off in the U.S. But I have long been accustomed to thinking that so long as I have sufficient to keep me in reasonable comfort, the chance of carrying on what I have been trying to do is more important. For that purpose location is immaterial—I am what I am wherever I am. And while I walk a tight-rope intellectually, it is a little comforting to be able to get back among my own family and familiars. Were I younger it might be different—but children and grandchildren are special kinds of ties.[32]

Appreciation for Music and the Arts

Chambers' daughter, Rosemary Pearce, had spoken of her parents' enjoyment of the arts. This is confirmed in the joint response of the daughters to a question on this:

> [Mum and Dad] were interested in art as an opportunity to "broaden their mind." Classical music, popular musicals, opera, ballet & cinema were all valued. We don't recall a "passion" for any of them in

particular, rather an enjoyment and appreciation of creativity and talent in all forms. We were taken as children to orchestral concerts at the Sydney Town Hall. We would go to the Art Gallery sometimes and we remember quite a number of books about Australian artists in our library at home. Dad had a lovely singing voice, which we heard and loved as young kids. Then later, he stopped singing. He'd also taught himself to play the piano and would rattle off some popular ditties until he stopped that too. Life probably became busier.

Kevin, however, has a somewhat different view, noting: 'that my [older] sisters have suggested that my father had a good voice. I cannot recall this, he did sing in church but that's the only time I ever heard him sing. [Mum and Dad] did try to involve themselves in things that were outside their comfort zone I think, in terms of music, drama and dance and I think this was a genuine attempt by my father in particular to broaden his own horizons.'

Several letters in the Chambers Archive indicate Chambers' fascination with the arts. Consider this extract from a letter to Moonitz in March 1991:

It was interesting to hear of the similarities of the backgrounds and musical accomplishments of you both [Bill Vatter and Moonitz]. I fear I'm just an onlooker (or is it, onlistener?). But all the musical, dance and theatre arts entrance me. I admire the apparent ease and grace of performers and the inventive skill of composers, knowing all the while that it is not produced without great labour. Then I ask myself, especially when I see other accountants in the audience, why is it that accounting is so clumsy, graceless, discordant, undisciplined? I tell myself it is because we do not work as hard at our trade as musicians do at theirs; that we haven't learned the virtue of simplicity and the value of concord in what we do. But who's about to agree with that?[33]

Academic Supervisor

When Chambers joined the ranks of those already appointed to chairs in accounting in Australia—Fitzgerald, Goldberg, and Mathews—there had not been any accounting PhDs awarded in Australia.[34] This situation persisted until the early 1970s. The University of Melbourne awarded the first two accounting PhDs in 1973, to Peter Hain and Bob Clift, while Peter Standish (an early 1960s staff member at Sydney) was awarded an Australian National University PhD in 1975. While a few of his students worked independently, most met regularly as part of Chambers' uncompromising and demanding supervision. The first PhD awarded at Sydney was to

Murray Wells in 1974. Others quickly followed, with the last of Chambers' Sydney PhD students being Peter Wolnizer, who graduated in 1986. Later Chambers co-supervised with Wolnizer Brian West's PhD at Deakin University. This was Chambers' last supervision. It examined 'Professionalism in Accounting' and was awarded the American Accounting Association's Best PhD Manuscript Award in 2003.

The fact that eighteen candidates who studied and worked within the Sydney School during the Chambers years were subsequently appointed to chairs is evidence of both the rigorous training they received and the work ethic to which they were exposed (Figure 2.4). This enduring legacy is well described in the Sydney School monograph.

Chambers took many of the Department of Accounting staff during the period on his academic odyssey, not as acolytes but as confreres in a common endeavour to, improve corporate reporting. Examples of this may be seen in Wells' PhD and related articles on the development of 'costing for activities' and his 1976 'Revolution in Accounting Theory' article in *The Accounting Review*; in Walker's 'consolidated financial statements' PhD and analyses related to creative accounting, true and fair view, public sector infrastructure valuation, the assessment of the effectiveness of the Accounting Standards Review Board and on regulation more generally; in the adoption of a 'balance sheet approach to teaching' by Birkett, his articles on accounting education and competencies for the professional accounting bodies and subsequent work on management accounting at the UNSW; in Gray's PhD and seminal examinations of 'international accounting and culture'; in Clarke's PhD and articles on the 'accidents of history' and 'price and price variation accounting'; in Clarke and Dean's articles and monographs on 'audited accounting and corporate failures'; in Wolnizer's doctorate and articles on 'audit independence' (an area that Chambers had only touched upon relative to his explorations into managerial and financial accounting); in Chambers and Wolnizer's two major 1990s articles on 'history and meaning of true and fair view'; in Gaffikin's PhD and related works on 'philosophy and critical accounting'; in Craswell's PhD on 'audit qualifications in Australia and his work on audit fees'; in Poullaos' PhD and related examinations of the 'sociology of the accounting profession'; in Johnstone's PhD and related articles 'critiquing the use of tests of significance in empirical accounting research'; in Pererea's PhD on 'asset valuation'; in Rahman and Islam's PhD analyses of 'international accounting standards setting'; and in myriad other works.[35]

Resilience to Setbacks

Finally, and briefly, Chambers showed himself to be a man of resilience when faced with setbacks. Evidence of this appears in 'Life on the Fringe.' Some instances are discussed below, others later.

Figure 2.1 Ray and Margaret's Wedding

Ray and Margaret Chambers on their wedding day (9 September, 1939) at the entrance to the Christadelphian ecclesia, Hurstville, a suburb of Sydney.

Figure 2.2 Ray and Family

Above: Ray and Margaret with their children.

Top row—Rosemary Pearce and Margaret Kaye;

Bottom row—Kevin, Margaret and Ray.

Below: Margaret and Ray with some of their grandchildren

Figure 2.3 Ray and Family Travelling

Family and two unknown travellers departing Sydney on the SS *Arcadia* on their '1959 Trip'—left to right at the railing: Ray, Margaret, unknown, son Kevin and daughters, Margaret and Rosemary, unknown.

Ray and Margaret with their daughters enjoying holiday time in the early 1950s in Australia's snow fields.

Figure 2.4 Ray and Colleagues

Above: Thirteen of the Sydney School professors who attended the October 2010 Golden Jubilee of the founding of the Sydney School of Accounting.

Top Row: David Johnstone, Hector Perera, Michael Gaffikin, Allen Craswell, Murray Wells

Middle Row: Ian Eddie, Sid Gray

Bottom Row: John Staunton, Frank Clarke, Graeme Dean, Atiqe Islam, Peter Wolnizer. The 'professors' were joined in the photo by the Keynote Speaker, APRA Chairman and Sydney graduate, Jim Laker, third from the left, between Frank Clarke and Graeme Dean.

Below: Ray Chambers, Murray Wells, Cliff Dodds (immediately behind Chambers), and ASA colleagues enjoying themselves at the April 1982 ASA Congress—'A Roman night.'

Archive files show that in 1949 he unsuccessfully applied for the position of secretary of the Snowy Mountains Hydro-Electric Authority, and prior to joining the University of Sydney as a lecturer he unsuccessfully applied for a readership in Commercial Studies at the University of Adelaide.[36]

Employment setbacks continued after his appointment at Sydney. These included applying for, then withdrawing from, the chair position at the University of Melbourne, which was awarded to Louis Goldberg in 1958; failure to obtain approval for the running of a management education program at Sydney University in the late 1950s; several unsuccessful funding requests for his first sabbatical; failure to have *Abacus* initially operating as an international journal; repeated failure in the 1960s and '70s to achieve the formation of an international group of elite accounting academics; and in 1974, failure to be appointed as the first Professor of Management at the new Australian Graduate School of Management at the University of New South Wales. This position was awarded to Professor Philip Brown, also an inaugural AAHoF inductee, who became internationally regarded for his empirical-based research. In 1979 Chambers unsuccessfully applied to be a foundation member of the newly created National Companies and Securities Commission.

All of these were likely viewed as setbacks by Chambers, but from the outside it was difficult to see that they affected him visibly, especially in relation to his professional activities and academic output. Letters in the Archive further confirm this. They reveal a person keen to get on with things, someone who always congratulated graciously those who got the job ahead of him (e.g., letters to Lou Goldberg in the 1950s and Phil Brown in the 1970s).

While resilient to those setbacks and generally confident, in the late 1980s and early 1990s Chambers expressed doubts about the effectiveness of his career. He mentioned in conversation that more than once he was surprised, disappointed, and even irritated that staff at Sydney had not made better use of his talents in retirement, especially in respect of teaching—especially in the honours and advanced undergraduate classes. The introduction to chapter 9 elaborates on some of those frustrations. It reveals that he was more than happy to accept post-retirement offers of several short-term teaching and research supervision appointments at Deakin University in the 1990s. His former PhD student Peter Wolnizer, who by then had been appointed Dean of the Business Faculty at Deakin, organized this.

Notes

1. Chapter epigraphs:
   Prominent U.K. accounting reformer, Edward Stamp, 'R.J. Chambers: Lauditio viri veritati studentis,' *Abacus* December 1982 Festschrift 'Special Issue,' page182.
   Chambers letter to Eddie Stamp following Stamp's article in the *Abacus* December 1982 Festschrift 'Special Issue'; P202, #6545, 8/12/1982.

2. Edward Stamp, 'R.J. Chambers: Lauditio viri veritati studentis,' page 183
3. Chambers' handwritten notes, P202, #10838, 11/11/1982.
4. Gaffikin (1988, 1994).
5. ASA Councillor, Bernard Wright to Chambers, P202, #5681, 06/06/1979.
6. Whittington and Zeff (2001, 228). Chambers would reject Gynther's claim. But as suggested by Whittington and Zeff, in the heat of written or verbal debates with the likes of Mathews, Gynther, Littleton, and even Stamp, Chambers was relentless in developing arguments to defend his position. His opponents often took offence at his apparent inability to compromise. Compromise is something we note in several places in the biography that Chambers viewed as unscientific; this adherence to logic was often interpreted as 'playing the man.'
7. Chambers to Stamp, P202, #8243, 16/09/1965.
8. Chambers to ASA Executive Director, Geoff Vincent, P202, #6171, 16/02/1981.
9. Chambers to Bierman, P202, #8579, 30/06/1974.
10. Chambers (1974b). See also endnotes #s32, chapter 3, 51, chapter 3, 43, chapter 5, 18, chapter 9.
11. Chambers to Richard Knox, P202, #9026, 09/05/1972. Knox had expressed pleasure in his letter, P202, #9025, 30/08/1972. There are similar comments in many other letters in the Archive.
12. Chambers to Moonitz, P202, #5800, 08/05/1979.
13. The Chambers and Carl Harrison-Ford correspondence is available at P202, #9893, 22/02/1999 and #9894, 24/02/1999.
14. November 1975 exchange between leading 1960s and 1970s U.K. economist, G.L.S. Shackle, P202, #s4856, 07/11/ 1975 and #4858, 06/02/1976 and Shackle's lengthy handwritten response to Chambers, P202 #4857, 15/11/1975.
15. Email from Foster on 30 August 2016 in response to authors' request to use the correspondence between himself and Chambers.
16. Correspondence between Foster and Chambers, P202, #3829, 17/01/1972; also throughout 1972, including P202, #3831, 29/06/ 1972.
17. Chambers to Foster, P202, #3831, 29/06/1972. Foster was quick to hit his straps in the U.S., as he was awarded in 1977 and 1978 the American Accounting Association's *The Accounting Review* Manuscript Award. This had not been achieved before or since.
18. This aspect is addressed in Clarke *et al.* (2012, 90–4).
19. Stamp (1982, 183).
20. Refer especially to P202, #s4157–4170.
21. Dean *et al.* (2016).
22. Chambers (1966, 50–1).
23. Some manual copies of Chambers' other *Abacus* reviews in early *Abacus* volumes are available in the Archive; however, most were destroyed after about twenty years due to storage space limitations. Reviewing computer files and the residual hard-copy files of the first ten years of *Abacus*, show that Chambers was often a sole reviewer, with several reviews being in respect of junior academics' submissions.
24. In the section below and in later chapters we provide extracts from responses to questions sent to Chambers' children.
25. Chambers (2000b, 326).
26. Sydney University Registrar, Margaret Telfer to Chambers, P202, #377, 29/09/1958.
27. Relm Grant details, P202, #350, 24/10/1958 and P202, #387, 13/11/1958. The role played by Weinwurm in developing Chambers' ideas on measurement and theory is outlined in Dean and Clarke (2010a).
28. Persson (2013, chapter 5) and the paras immediately below.

29. Chambers (2000a, 326). The many people and places Chambers visited on his 1966 leave are noted in the 'Life on the Fringe' article. Interestingly, during the 1950s and 1960s all overseas leaves were approved personally by the Vice-Chancellor.

30. Those, often year-long, invitations included: Maurice Moonitz, UCLA Berkeley 1961–62,P202, #7705, 27/09/1961 and Chambers' response #7706, 11/10/1961, Dean Courtney Brown, Columbia University, Graduate School of Business, P202, #731, 06/11/1961 and Chambers' response, #732, 17/11/1961, Ernest Weinwurm at De Paul University, P202, # 8128, 02/01/1962 and Chambers' response #8129, 15/02/1962, Robert Sterling at Harpur College, New York, USA #1972, 16/11/1965 and Chambers' response, #1973, 22/11/1965, Robert Dixon, University of Michigan, P202, #2809, 24/02/1969 and Chambers' response #2810, Frank Kaulback, University of Virginia, P202, #3388, 24/09/1971 and Chambers' response #3389, 05/10/1971, Abe Briloff, New York University (not on file) and Chambers' response, P202, #4501, 17/04/1973, Felix Kollaritsch, Ohio State University, P202, #4843, 06/01/1976 and Chambers' response #4844, 14/01/1976, Norton Bedford, George A. Miller Distinguished Professorship at the University of Illinois at Urbana—Champaign, P202, #5994, 29/01/1980 and Chambers' response P202, #5995, 12/02/1980, Daniel MacDonald, Simon Fraser University, Canada, P202, #6905, 27/04/1983 and Chambers' response, #6906, 06/07/1983; and several times from Robert Sterling at the University of Kansas—the Arthur Young Chair (P202, #2887, 23/07/1969 and Chambers' response #2889); and later, the Eccles Endowed Chair of Business, University of Utah, P202, #7628, 19/06/1984 and Chambers' response #7629, 01/08/1984.

31. Weinwurm to Chambers, P202, #8128, 02/01/1962.

32. Chambers to Sterling, P202, #2889, 20/08/1969.

33. Chambers to Moonitz, P202, #7345, 21/03/1991.

34. Whittington and Zeff (2001, 206, footnote, 16) state that several Australasian accounting academics had been awarded PhDs at overseas institutions, the first being Allan Barton in 1961.

35. Thirteen of the eighteen professors are in the photo on 43, attending the October 2010 Golden Jubilee of the founding of the Sydney School of Accounting.

36. Respectively: P202, #10747, 04/09/1949 and P202, #10769, 04/06/1952.

3 Historian:

Past, Present, Future

Whether he believes it or not, Ray has made the future of CoCoA secure. Let us hope that in his retirement he will further enrich the literature of accounting by giving us his thoughts on the history of accounting ideas.
—Stamp, *Abacus* December 1982[1]

As Chambers was a practising archivist (chapter 4), he drew heavily on historical sources in developing ideas, advancing arguments when debating fellow academics, or drawing attention to his practitioner colleagues of misleading accounting practices. The extract from the Introduction to his *Accounting Thesaurus* is instructive:

> But today's [accounting] practices have emerged from a wide and conflicting array of demands and circumstance. The rising need in commerce for systematic bookkeeping from the 15th century onwards; the foreign engagements of European venturers from the 16th century; the growth in the size and diversity of firms, and the growing investment in durable and costly equipment, in the 18th and 19th centuries, arising out of the industrial revolution; the emergence of large partnerships and corporations as the dominant form of business in the 19th and 20th centuries; the growth of personal investment in corporate securities, and of public regulation of their issue, over the same period; the drive for recognition of accounting as a profession from the mid-19th century; the introduction of the study and teaching of accounting to the institutions of higher learning, and the rise of a largely descriptive literature in the 20th century—these have all left their marks on the 20th century doctrine and practice.[2]

This passage suggests that any reformer of accounting 'doctrine and practice' needs to have a good grasp of the history of accounting thought if reforms to the current 'faulty instrumentation' are likely to prove relevant, reliable, and enduring. On the next page, however, Chambers notes that reformers have paid scant attention to accounting's history:

> [S]eldom is more than passing attention given in manuals, textbooks and instruction in accounting to the dicta and practices of the past, their origins and their consequences; or to seminal ideas from other fields of scholarship that could aid in the resolution of past debates and present dilemmas. Yet without knowledge of the origins and associations of what are now traditional or conventional practices, we can neither understand them, nor wisely shape the future of accounting. Hence this thesaurus—a view of the past with an eye to the future.[3]

Given this interest in the history of accounting, it is worthwhile to compare how Chambers' motives for drawing on historical sources compare with the most common ones found among accounting researchers and historians.[4] Several accounting historians identify a number of goals amongst researchers drawing on historical sources.[5] The earliest was to enhance the status of their discipline among practitioners and academics from other disciplines by appealing to the historical origins of accounting. The purpose was to reinforce the notion that accounting is not merely a technical endeavour but one with a rich and important past. A more recent goal has been to use historical sources to reinterpret the past in order to offer new perspectives on contemporary issues, an approach that has been made more popular with the emergence of what Miller, Hopper, and Laughlin termed 'new accounting history.'[6] And a third goal has been to solve present problems, by using historical accounting sources as repositories of knowledge that can inform the present. Previts, Parker, and Coffman argue that this can aid in the teaching of accounting, in selecting among regulatory alternatives, and in selecting from alternative accounting methods which to use within a company.[7] While Chambers was instrumental in bringing about accounting as a respected university discipline in Australia,[8] his historical approach did not stem solely from a desire to increase the prestige of his discipline (i.e., the earliest motivation). The passage quoted from the Introduction to *An Accounting Thesaurus* shows his desire was also to use historical accounting sources as a means by which to improve and solve contemporary accounting problems in all three senses suggested by Previts *et al.*

Drawing on historical methods and sources, accounting academics have pursued a number of different historically informed subjects. Previts *et al.* list a number of these: general, bibliographical, biographical, critical, historiographical, and institutional research as well as studies about the development of accounting thought.[9] Chambers' pursuit of 'knowledge of the origins and associations of what are now traditional or conventional practices'[10] lies squarely in the category of studies about the development of accounting thought. Yet Chambers shared little with his contemporaries who were pursuing similar ideas. During the time that he was writing, there was a tendency among accounting academics to view the development of accounting knowledge as inherently progressive. This is evident in the title of Ananias Charles (A.C.) Littleton's book, *Accounting Evolution to 1900*, on the historical development of accounting knowledge and his *Thesaurus* introduction:

> Accounting is relative and progressive. The phenomena which form its subject matter are constantly changing. Older methods become less effective under altered conditions; earlier ideas become irrelevant in the face of new problems. Thus surrounding conditions generate fresh ideas and stimulate the ingenious to devise new methods. And as such ideas and methods prove successful they in turn begin to modify the surrounding conditions. The result we call progress.[11]

Carnegie and Napier refer to Littleton's and similar accounts of the evolution of accounting knowledge as 'Whig histories,' characterized by a constant sense of progression from the primitive practices of the past to the sophisticated ones of the present.[12] Chambers was more careful in his assumptions about the past. Although he had no interest in using various social theories as is common today, he was before his time in that his historical enquiries exhibit scepticism about our past in much the same way as do narratives now emerging from the 'new accounting historians.' The introduction to *An Accounting Thesaurus* indicates Chambers was acutely aware that accounting practices do change over time, but he was careful not to use notions such as progress where there is no evidence that such a notion is warranted. In much the same way, one of his Sydney colleagues, Clarke, described the CCA debates in the 1970s using the subtitle: 'Progress or Regress?'[13] Chambers had little interest in justifying contemporary accounting practices, most of which he believed to be faulty. His interest was in identifying how these practices came about, convinced that the answer was hidden somewhere in the sequence of events that had led to the present.

Some of the ways in which Chambers used historical methods and sources in his work meshed with his work as an archivist (chapter 4).

History as a Method of Inquiry

Chambers' use of historical sources as a method of inquiry is persuasive throughout his work, whether he is dealing with the development of accounting theory, the function of financial statements, accounting for price and price-level accounting, or the legal override, 'true and fair view.' He was conscious that these sources and methods tended to make up most of the body of his work. In 1964 he wrote to the U.K. reformer, Edward Stamp, then a senior lecturer of accounting at the Victoria University of Wellington, detailing his progress on what would be published as *Accounting, Evaluation and Economic Behavior*:

> I have been working for several years to bring together in an extended treatment a theory of accounting, but it will be some time yet before it is

completed. *I think I know the beginning and the end; it's putting some body in the middle that is difficult.* (emphasis added)[14]

As he alludes to in this passage, Chambers approached his subject with a carefully planned starting point and a deep sense of direction. This starting point was located either in the past, such as the historical origins of an accounting practice, or in the present, such as a contemporary accounting practice. The ending point would usually be the present-day iteration of the original practice coupled with the ideal treatment of this practice. Chambers is referring to the ending point in his letter to Stamp, but in either case it was the part in the middle that required historical resources, methods, and careful attention. A mistake in this middle part would lead to failure in connecting the starting and ending points.

To appreciate fully the care with which Chambers pursued this task, it is helpful to understand his views on what constitutes 'research' in accounting. He was in the earliest stages of his academic career in 1955 when Sir Alexander Fitzgerald, then a professor at the University of Melbourne and the most senior accounting academic in Australia, inquired about his thoughts on the matter. Chambers responded:

> Research means broadly an examination of the scope and content of knowledge. . . . At some stage this will involve grubbing for the facts; at other stages, before and after searching for the facts, it will involve cerebration . . . as much a part of the process as accumulating facts . . . [and] this requires that no relevant facts shall be overlooked . . . [in] the ordering of the facts and the making of inferences that great care is needed to avoid erroneous conclusions.[15]

As is made clear in his letter to Fitzgerald, Chambers did not intend to imply to Stamp that facts were just the 'stuff' one puts in the 'middle' to get from the starting to the ending point. It was quite the opposite; it involved both 'grubbing' and 'cerebration.' Only the successful accumulation, examination, and ordering of facts could lead to a valid conclusion. This accumulation of facts and the convergence of overwhelming evidence to support an ending point is a recurring theme in his work. It is indicative of what he considered to be 'empirical research' (i.e., research based on observation) in accounting. This is also a view that would have been widely shared by his contemporaries before the use by researchers of statistical research methods and examinations of large datasets of numerical values (of accounting numbers reported in companies' financial statements and their share prices) in the 1980s.[16]

Three early 1990s examples of Chambers' use of history as a method of inquiry are considered: *Foundations of Accounting*, 'A True and Fair View of Position and Results: The Historical Background' (with Wolnizer), and 'Historical Cost—Tale of a False Creed.' Chapter 9 refers briefly to several other historical papers that he wrote toward the end of his life.

Foundations of Accounting

Chambers' major works exhibit use of a historical method of inquiry addressing a particular area of interest. His *Accounting Thesaurus* traces the historical origins of hundreds of accounting terms, whereas *Securities and Obscurities* revisits and reinterprets British Joint Stock Companies Acts from 1844 and 1856, and in *Accounting, Evaluation and Economic Behavior* he sets out an accounting theory based on the historical and social context of human action and the role of accounting. As these works are covered in other chapters, let us here review the *Foundations of Accounting* to illustrate his method of using historical inquiry to connect starting and ending points. Deakin University Press published *Foundations* in 1991, and Chambers used it for teaching accounting theory in the graduate degree program at Deakin University during a visiting professorship there in the early 1990s.

Chambers sets out his ending point on the first page: '[to] yield an accounting that is realistic, theoretically supportable, and practically serviceable.' To arrive at this ending point, his starting point explores observations and conclusions in other domains of knowledge that have a bearing on that of accounting. The first two chapters define the notion of what constitutes a 'foundation' and demarcate the field of accounting from other fields of practice and study. The remaining chapters constitute Chambers' middle, that is, the tracing of the commercial, legal, economic, financial, metrical, psychological, axiological, organizational, linguistic, social, and data processing foundations of accounting (in that order). Throughout these chapters, the book also presents the reader with questions designed to spur creative thinking and, in so doing, aid in escaping current dogma in accounting thought and practice. The emphasis is on being constructively critical and the convergence of overwhelming evidence towards a single point.

An example of this approach is the section discussing the legal foundations of accounting. Chambers traces how the notion of an 'asset' has drifted from something specific in the field of law to something much looser in the field of accounting. His starting point is the legal definition of an asset from *The Law Dictionary* published in the early nineteenth century: 'Assets . . . [are] goods [that are worth] enough to discharge the burden which is cast upon the executor or heir, in satisfying the debts and legacies of the testator or ancestor.'[17]

He notes that the term did not appear in accounting documents, manuals or textbooks until the end of the nineteenth century. When it eventually appeared, its initial definition was the same as it had been in the legal domain: something that the owner could turn into money or use to settle debts. Chambers then shows how the original meaning of the term has been progressively eroded. Early indications of this appear in an introductory accounting textbook by Hatfield published in 1909, which speculated that one could include among 'assets' items without traditional property rights, such as an advanced payment in exchange for a future service.[18]

This shift probably came about because Hatfield was a trained economist and the idea of 'the service potential of assets' underpinned contemporary views of the U.S. economist Irving Fisher and, among others, the economist trained-cum accountant, John Bennet Canning, who in 1929 noted that '[a]n asset is any future service in money.'[19] This notion became increasingly accepted, so much so that less than ten years later, Sanders, Hatfield and Moore suggested in their monograph on accounting principles that all deferred charges and prepaid expenses are 'assets' while their 'expenses' are held in suspense until an exercise date in a future period.[20] Fast forward to 1957 and the definition of an asset was widened further in the U.S. as the AICPA suggested that all unexpired costs should be viewed as 'assets' with the expectation that a corresponding revenue is to be received in a future period.[21]

Through his careful ordering of the intellectual transformation of the term, Chambers demonstrates how a precise definition of an asset as something with spending or debt-paying power was borrowed from the legal domain and subsequently turned, via recourse to the domain of economics, into something loose and ambiguous that incorporated ideas around future prospects and unexpired costs. This transformation may be unique to the field of accounting; it certainly did not happen in the hands of legal scholars. Chambers concludes with this fact, citing a more contemporary legal definition of an asset in *Jowitt's Dictionary of English Law*: 'assets [are] . . . property available for the payment of the debt of a person or corporation.'[22] A similar approach of tracing ideas is used throughout the *Foundations'* other domains of knowledge and covers various terms such as liabilities, equity, and net income.

A True and Fair View of Position and Results: The Historical Background

In addition to *Foundations*, the use of history as a method of inquiry permeates Chambers' early 1990s articles, such as 'A True and Fair View of Position and Results: The Historical Background' and 'Historical Cost—Tale of a False Creed.' He wrote the former with Wolnizer and presented it at the Congress of the European Accounting Association in April 1990. In 1991 it was published in *Accounting, Business and Financial History*.

In 'A True and Fair View' the authors sought to provide a historical background to the true and fair view clause from the British Joint Stock Companies Acts of 1844 and 1856. Their starting point is one of speculation: that the meaning of a 'true and fair view' has drifted through the decades because those who had introduced the term had failed to define it clearly. In order to establish whether this is the case, they began by examining usages of the term leading up to 1844. The analysis suggests that the Corporation of the Governor and Company of the Mine Adventurers of England in 1710 provided the first known reference to a true and fair view. They then consider a number of contractual references by lawyers and writers in the period 1628–1883; twenty-four partnership agreements from 1714 to 1829; and seventy deeds of settlement from 1827 to 1843. Also examined is the usage in the academic accounting and economics literature, drawing on more than twenty authors. The starting point in the former is Pacioli's 1494 treatise on double-entry bookkeeping, and in the latter, it is Adam Smith's 1776 *The Wealth of Nations*.[23]

After considering the empirical evidence and presenting it in the middle of the article, the common usage of a 'true and fair view' (importantly of financial position and financial performance) among accountants, economists, and lawyers, and in the writings of contracts, partnership agreements, and deeds of settlement, is found to be dependent upon knowledge of current market prices of assets and liabilities.[24] The article concludes that, although not clearly defined in the legislation, the drafters of the two Companies Acts had not anticipated for a 'true and fair view' to be interpreted to mean the use of historical costs on the balance sheet. A number of court verdicts in favour of the use of up-to-date prices that were handed down subsequent to the passage of the two acts reinforced this position.[25]

The ending point is of a familiar kind, with its emphasis on the convergence of evidence:

> The evidence seems to converge on the conclusion that a full and fair balance sheet and a true and correct view of the state of affairs would not be given unless asset valuations were such that the money and money's worth available to meet debts and otherwise to carry on business were fully and fairly depicted.[26]

Historical Cost—Tale of a False Creed

Chambers was the sole author of 'Historical Cost—Tale of a False Creed,' which was presented by Michael Gaffikin (Chambers was recovering from a fall) at the Congress of the European Accounting Association held in Turku, Finland, in 1993 and published in *Accounting Horizons* the following year. In some respects, this article is a continuation of the previous one, but with a broader field of investigation. Instead of examining the slippage of equating a 'true and fair view' with the use of historical cost, it investigates the prevalence of the historical cost accounting doctrine more widely. Chambers situates his inquiry as follows:

> [Entering academia] I had now two puzzles: how to devise a form of accounting that would yield the necessary information on the component and aggregate amounts of property and debt from time to time, and how to explain the emergence and survival of a body of universally endorsed accounting rules that did not yield information of that kind. The solution of the second puzzle, it seemed, must lie in some unnoticed historical circumstance which interfered with the exercise of ordinary common sense. . . . Only now, after a further quarter century, has a plausible solution of the second emerged from the cluster of circumstances now to be explained.[27]

His investigation into the origins and the prevalence of the cost doctrine begins with the exposition of double-entry bookkeeping found in Pacioli's treatise from 1494 and the use of current market prices in private ledgers, such as the accounts of the Venetian merchant Jachomo Badoer (1436–40), which would not have been accessible to writers of accounting manuals at the time. Chambers then traces this doctrine through the emergence of the corporate era and an organized accounting profession. Finally, he contrasts this doctrine with the common practice of asset revaluation of properties in the U.K. and in the U.S. up until the formation of the SEC in 1934. His ending point returns to the convergence of evidence:

> The bookkeeping manuals and textbooks, legislative and judicial utterances, and individual and collective professional contentions and dicta of the past 500 years, provide some evidence pertinent to these matters. The material is scattered and diverse, but it appears to converge on the conclusion that cost-based doctrine and practice were founded, and have been sustained, by assiduously taught but commercially false beliefs.[28]

The three items examined are not exhaustive, but they do demonstrate Chambers' general approach to history as a method of inquiry. He draws on a large number of empirical observations from a diverse set of sources that are often spread over several centuries. In *Foundations*, Chambers' knowledge of the breadth of the subject matter is on display as he canvasses eleven other fields of knowledge for clues as to how one might develop a more serviceable accounting system. In both articles considered here, his depth of knowledge of the subject matter becomes apparent in the tracing of the true and fair view and the cost-based doctrine over five centuries. The result— what Chambers describes as his 'middle part'—is unlike much of the work in accounting history today, which tends to draw heavily on social theory but seldom offers the empirical richness that is on display in these two works.

History as a Subject of Interest

Chambers' primary interest resided in studies of the development of accounting thought, and in doing so he harboured a healthy scepticism of the often taken-for-granted notion of accounting as inherently evolutionary and progressive. The process of revisiting events in accounting's past therefore required the careful retracing and bringing together of often forgotten or lost ideas, the result of which necessarily took the form of a carefully constructed account.

His mode of representation touches upon an ongoing debate between traditional and new accounting historians about the role of story-telling in accounting research that draws on historical methods and sources.[29] Traditional accounting historians argue for narratives solely based on historical evidence, such as a carefully examined archive, and that detours from this evidence place at risk the historical accuracy of the account.[30] New accounting historians, however, argue that histories are best understood when displaced from their archive and put in the wider social context, often through a theoretical lens of some kind.[31] This has led to a common conception that traditional accounting historians are narrow both in focus and in use of empirical evidence, whereas new accounting historians are more liberal and able to draw on a wider range of historical sources.

Most of Chambers' work predates the debate between these groups, and his historical approach is not easily categorized in the manner described above. On the one hand, Chambers had little interest in drawing on 'theoretical lenses' that happened to be in fashion when considering his historical sources. A 1990s letter to Gaffikin posing nineteen questions about the purpose of 'critical accounting research' indicates that he harboured some serious doubts whether such an approach could ever be useful.[32] On the other hand, chapter 6 shows that, when warranted, he drew on various theories on human behaviour, communication, measurement, and decision making in his work in accounting theory (e.g. the use of the homeostasis model of human behaviour in *Accounting, Evaluation and Economic Behavior*).

Chambers' selection of entries in his *Thesaurus* was also wider than the caricature of the concerns of the traditional accounting historians. When constructing his accounts of the development of accounting ideas, Chambers was eclectic, considering all sources he deemed appropriate for the task. In the case of tracing the drift in the definition of a 'true and fair view,' for example, this meant over a hundred references to contracts, partnership agreements, deeds of settlement, and academic literature spanning over four centuries.[33] Thus, his historical approach breaks down the traditional and new accounting history dichotomy. The debate is also sidestepped by his focus on the narrative mode; that is, the careful ordering of facts forming a sequence of events that are tied together in a 'story.'[34] Whereas he might not have put his historical approach in these terms, his approach is nonetheless methodologically valid, and narratives have traditionally been seen as the most effective method of uncovering our past and how this past informs our present.[35]

Irving Fisher and John Bennet Canning

The contributions of the economist Irving Fisher and John Bennet Canning to accounting were considered by Chambers in major review articles.

They are interesting in so far as they are different from the topics Chambers tended to pursue, often focused on commonly known ideas, methods, and terms within the practice of accounting or on contemporary work by other accounting theorists that had the potential to be adopted in practice.[36] In this instance, however, he examined two publications that had been influential within some academic accounting circles but otherwise enjoyed little success in swaying accounting practice. Therefore, the exercise became one of interest in understanding both Fisher's and Canning's historical influence as opposed to one of dismantling false doctrines and opposing ideas (although Chambers certainly disagreed with both authors).

Fisher's Intellectual Contribution to Accounting

Chambers' 'Income and Capital: Fisher's Legacy,' a study of Fisher's 1906 *The Nature of Capital and Income* was published in 1971 in the *Journal of Accounting Research*. His examination of the intellectual contribution of 'Canning's *The Economics of Accountancy*—After 50 Years,' was published in 1979 in *The Accounting Review*. Several matters are worth noting about these subjects. Both Fisher and Canning were trained economists and worked mostly outside the field of accounting; although Canning taught accounting for many years at Stanford University, directing and managing its accounting program. The articles appeared several decades after the books' publications, which might seem odd or untimely, but Chambers often used ideas from other disciplines, so long as they had a bearing on accounting, and he was well read on the history of ideas and knew that it could take ideas often several decades before reaching widespread acceptance. He was presumably not bothered that some time had passed since their initial publication and still saw an examination of them as an important exercise in evaluation.[37] In addition, each article focuses on an individual and his contribution, as opposed to the works of a collective or group.

Chambers' experience with, and disdain of, groupthink among various accounting standard setters and committees (also discussed in chapters 1, 3 and 6) may have influenced the decision to choose Fisher:

> A committee is unable, by its nature, freely to engage and disengage from its immediate attention [on] particular clusters of ideas in the search for a worthwhile conclusion . . . [This] requires the concentration of one mind. But a committee has not one mind. It has many minds. At any stage in the deliberations of a committee, each member will have different sets of ideas in the back of his mind, waiting to be drawn upon, and each will tend to value those ideas differently from other members. Debate follows. Sharp lines are drawn, lines which prevent the free association of ideas and lead to premature commitment. Committees are impatient with involved argument. They tend to brush aside evidence. . . . They tend to seek verbal consensus rather than understanding and to value convergence of opinion rather than the convergence of evidence.[38]

The above passage makes it clear Chambers felt that groups tended to produce sweeping political agreements as opposed to deep systematic thought and that this was antithetical to the convergence of empirical evidence that he sought in his own research. This is also well captured in the chapter 1 epigraphs and in this extract from a 1979 letter to a U.S. contemporary Abe Briloff:

> It is this plethora of "non-argument" [in committee-based decisions of standard-setting boards] that forces me to the conclusion that standards must be specific, and specified. Financial dealings may be different as between firms; but their elements are all the same. There will be no disciplined accounting, and no effective disciplining of accountants (by their own professional bodies or otherwise) until that is recognized. Basically, financial statements are linguistic. If by the same basic words and numbers they do not mean the same thing, they are farcical . . . when words and numbers can mean virtually anything, they convey no useful message. Last year I chaired a committee appointed to review Australian standards [the ASRC Report discussed in chapter 8]. Its report . . . concluded that there is no certain way of getting order out of present chaos other than by legislation (which is "anathema" to the profession in many places).[39]

That the choice had fallen, in particular, on Fisher's *The Nature of Capital and Income* was probably because it had become an authoritative source in the field of economics, rather than had affected substantially accounting practice.

The review of Canning's work, it seems, resulted from an invitation by the book review editor of *The Accounting Review*.[40] It was an extension of his Fisher investigation, as Canning had drawn on Fisher's work, which had been widely cited and was considered a seminal contribution at least among accounting researchers. In essence, Fisher and Canning represented an emerging stream of thought among some accounting researchers who considered assets in terms of their service potential and welcomed the use of valuation methods to estimate their value. Hatfield, mentioned earlier, would have been part of this stream as well.

Chambers begins his examination of Fisher's work with what he finds positive, such as the description of interdependence between wealth, property rights, and double-entry bookkeeping. Fisher's argument is that there cannot be wealth without property rights. At the same time, there cannot be property rights without wealth. He goes on to venture that this is the basis for the double-entry bookkeeping relationship between equities and assets.

In essence Fisher emphasized income rather than, as Chambers did, financial position and he saw income as forward looking. Income was consumption, antithetical to Chambers' view of income as an entity's change in financial position from period to the next, viz its increase in wealth. Not surprisingly, Chambers regarded Fisher's work as quite ambiguous. Some ideas appear to be based more on his hypothetical scenarios than on empirical observation and the convergence of evidence suggesting a particular conclusion. This lack of clarity, Chambers notes, has led to a situation where the book has been used, perhaps mistakenly, to support the use of future prices in financial reporting (e.g., the use of various discount methods; and recourse to the future service potential idea in asset definitions). Chambers speculated as to the ramifications of this slippage for the accounting literature near the end of his review article:

> In the most general terms, Fisher provides grounds for both measures and valuations (i.e. anticipatory calculations). The distinction between them and the necessity for both have been the burden of much of my own work. It is a matter for speculation how different the literature and practice of accounting might now be if this distinction and this necessity had been clearly pointed out by Fisher and those who have found support in parts of his work.[41]

Such a slippage has persisted. It underpinned Chambers' debates with Ricco Mattessich in the 1970s and beyond which are discussed in chapter 6, and his correspondence with G.L.S. Shackle noted in chapter 2.

Canning Spreads Fisher's Ideas in the Field of Accounting

Chambers' suspicion about how ambiguities regarding accounting measurements and anticipatory calculations in *The Nature of Capital and Income* had drifted into the field of accounting led him, through invitation, to review Canning's book eight years later on its fiftieth anniversary. He begins by asking a rhetorical question: how could one do justice to a book written half a century ago when the state of the art of accounting was so different then? He admits that the process is challenging but possible as long as one is careful to consider the wider social context in which the ideas were conceived as well as the antecedents in the literature and practice. If one can accomplish this, there is the benefit of the historical perspective that is only possible several years after the events as one can be 'more objective and dispassionate about matters in which one was not personally and actively engaged.'[42]

One of Canning's main aims was to help rid the accounting literature of its laxity in methods and terms. Given Chambers' similar goal, he found this part of the work to be the most worthwhile. In particular, he credits Canning with being one of the first Anglo-American academics to set down the rules for aggregative measurements in the field of accounting. For the aggregate of two measurements to have a meaning, the things measured must belong to a common population (that is, the same attribute or property being measured) and the measurement method and circumstances must be similar. The unit of measure must also have a common significance, a uniform magnitude (or be convertible into such a magnitude), and the degree of error cannot vary significantly between different measurements. Although convinced that it should have represented a breakthrough for standard setters and the literature on accounting measurements, Chambers notes that this contribution has gone mostly unnoticed:

> [It] has amazed me for years that . . . [i]f individual measures are to be merged, it is useless from the outset to define or make individual measures which are "sensibly unlike." Understanding and acceptance of the rules would impose an unavoidable limitation on the invention or adoption of "individual measures" of unlike properties where the individual measures are to be aggregated or related. But, as we shall see, Canning himself at a number of points overlooked this limitation.[43]

Whereas Canning's major contribution in establishing the need for uniform measurements had gone largely unnoticed by the author himself and by accounting scholars, Chambers found that the use of anticipatory calculations, handed down from Fisher, to be the most commonly quoted section in the accounting literature. This unfortunate circumstance had led to several accounting theorists picking up ideas around anticipatory calculations instead of focusing on the need for uniform measurements.

Reaching his ending point, however, Chambers observes that none of the fundamental measurement ideas presented by Canning appear to have had a discernible impact on standard setting and financial reporting practices:

> These critical observations [i.e., the use of different measurement rules] were enough to indicate the potential fruitfulness of a comprehensive study of theory and practice . . . Yet, 50 years later, many [similar] observations may still be made of accounting theory and practice. Indeed, in that interval, there has been such a proliferation of alternative rules, definitions and practices, that the diversity of which Canning complained has become greater rather than less; and much of the debate that rages consists of argument which to one party or the other, is still "amazingly inconsequential."[44]

This highlights once again the point made in the Prologue that accounting and related discipline fundamentals (in this case the principles of measurement) have remained the same, while at the margin some other aspects of accounting, finance, and management have changed.

Chambers' two review articles exemplify his interest in the development of accounting thought as a historical subject itself. He wrote them with the aim of understanding each subject's contribution to thinking in certain academic accounting circles around assets as unexpired costs. The origins of these inquiries stemmed primarily from academic curiosity and interest (i.e., history as a subject of interest), as opposed to the need for the reform of accounting practice, which had been the case with the material on the cost doctrine described in the previous section. The historical method, however, remained the same regardless of the subject matter. In these works, we again see the tracing of ideas through time. Chambers places the authors' work in their wider social context, with the aim of understanding them in the period in which they were written and to trace their contemporary significance. This is a hallmark of his historical method, as he stated in *An Accounting Thesaurus*, to provide 'a view of the past with an eye to the future.'[45]

History as a Component of Accounting Theory

History has played a prominent role in much of Chambers' work, both as a method of inquiry and a subject of interest. It has also influenced his thoughts on issues of accounting theory. In an article in the March 1989 issue of *Abacus*, 'Time in Accounting' (he had presented this at the 1988 Accounting Historian's World Congress), Chambers examines the role of the passage of time and the trick that it has played on accounting users and researchers alike. He notes: 'the cavalier fashion in which dates and times are treated in expositions of accounting ideas and in accounting practice. I am of the opinion that a great deal of what passes for explanation and justification in accounting is deficient and misleading through disregard of the disciplinary nature of experienced time.'[46]

He then explains that accounting researchers, practitioners, and users speak of the passing of time as well as present and future time, often imagining time as a form of continuum from the past to the future. Although this is common when discussing time, the notion does not hold up when one is considering human action and decision making. Chambers instead describes time as a datum, a reference point against which measurements and comparisons can be made to inform present and future decisions. This reference point, however, is often obscured as limitations in human memory force us to rely on written records of our past. Digressing, 'Time in Accounting' illustrates this point with several coloured figures, the different colours representing the past, present, future. The use of a picture or an illustration was something Chambers used deftly in articles and his presentations (two are reproduced in Illustrations 3.1 and 3.2).[47]

The illustrations show that the quality of those records—the quality of the financial statements in the case of financial decisions—as well as faulty recollection of past events often hinder our ability to make 'good' decisions:

> We commonly claim to be guided by experience; we often are very confident of what we claim to know by experience. But, on reflection, experience turns out to be a compound of quite dubious

character. It includes events in which we have been participants as principals, as agents and as observers; different roles, different experiences. It includes the judgments we have made of the relationships of antecedents to events, and of antecedents and events to their consequences.[48]

Whereas past events can be obscured, future events are inherently even more uncertain. But how obscured could our views of accounting's past be? Chambers thought that it was potentially extremely so. As an example of this, we present his analogy in correspondence with Robert Anthony, accounting professor at Harvard University in the 1960s,

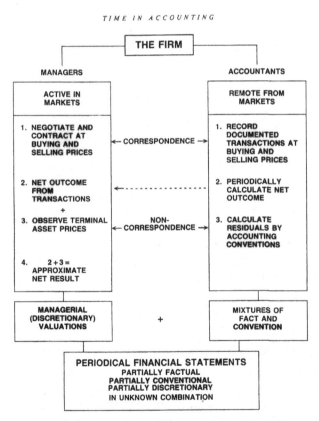

TIME IN ACCOUNTING

Illustration 3.1 Fact, Convention, and Judgement in Accounting

Reproduced from Chambers' (1989) 'Time in Accounting,' this diagram seeks to differentiate fact from convention and the related judgement in accounting.

Illustration 3.2 Integration of Financial Calculations

Chambers prepared this illustration to demonstrate visually how financial calculations are integrated with the data in reported financial statements when capital budgeting decisions are being considered. This was first discussed by Chambers (1977b), an October 1977 Shaoib Memorial Lecture for the Institute of Cost and Management Accountants of Pakistan, Karachi. He coined the term in the capital budgeting literature, 'DCEF,' to represent 'discounted cash equivalent flows.' It was the focus of his 1978 ARIA 'Taxi-Symposium' paper and several *Abacus* articles (including: Peasnell, 1979, Chambers, 1981 and Madan, 1982).

questioning the historical justification for the use of dated entry prices in contemporary practice:

> I make as a start the bald proposition that the existence of practices proves nothing except that they are the practices of a people at a time and place. The obstetricians of Semmelweiss's age had their practices and they were not to be scorned. Everybody (except Semmelweiss) held to their views and their practices. Could not all the widowers and expected mothers and motherless families have

demanded the adoption of Semmelweiss's views, as the lives of numberless women depended on it? No, they could not; because they were in the hands of an established body of experts. We today would regard the then generally accepted practices as unhygienic and barbarous in the extreme, though the practitioners of the time found them quite 'useful.'

Sea-faring merchants before the fifteenth century had their practices—quite useful ones—including the practice of never sailing beyond the sight of land. Was it the stay-at-home venturers who were strong enough to demand that their captains forsake this principle? Certainly not. If they ever thought of the possibility of greater gains from abandoning this principle they could not have made it effective, because they too were in the hands of experts—the navigators.

There was a time before the number zero was invented; was its adoption a mistake? Clearly for centuries, if not millennia, people got along without it; their practices were quite 'useful' to them. I could multiply this type of illustration manyfold. But it would only serve to point out two things (a) that the existence of any practice is only a function of knowledge and belief and (b) that the people for whose 'benefit' practices exist are seldom able to decide what is best for their purposes either because they act in ignorance of alternatives or because they are in the hands of 'experts.' I am not in the least on shaky ground; the whole of human history is studded with examples of well-established practices which have been demonstrated to be useless at best and positively inhuman at worst.[49]

To Chambers, the combination of not understanding our past and not distinguishing it from our future has led to an untenable situation for accounting theory. In 'Time in Accounting' he expressed it:

An accounting, historical and factual, locked by explicit reasoning to the processes of judgment and choice, is a widely entertained ideal. But, if the reasoning disregards the uniqueness of moments of choice and the irreversibility of time, the ideal is set aside—if not deliberately, then carelessly or indifferently. The false, mistaken, idea that supplants it may long command allegiance; that allegiance, crystallized into a "tradition," may long subvert attempts to attain the ideal. The failure of decades of costly effort to eradicate the known flaws in accounting doctrine and practice should be clear evidence of their intractability. . . . The present products of accounting, . . . [are] anachronistic to the core. Whether the prevalent mode of accounting should survive or should be replaced by a temporally well disciplined alternative is a matter of choice by those who assume the task of advancing the functional fitness of accounting.[50]

It is worth noting that concerns about the quality of our records and of our recollections resonate with his historical method, based on the careful chronological ordering of events and facts. They also resonate with the depth and breadth in which he pursued his chosen inquiries, often drawing on material spanning several disciplines and centuries. He was convinced that it was necessary to present this material in the middle.

Looking Forward

Chambers expressed serious concerns about positive accounting research when it emerged in North America in the 1970s.[51] Later, he became increasingly concerned about critical accounting research that emerged in Europe in the 1990s, as evidenced in the undated letter to Gaffikin quoted above.[52] With these developments and the declining interest in the substance of the accounting function (i.e., the measurement of transactions and production of financial statements that tell it as it is), he would have found himself increasingly isolated among peers who no longer pursued accounting topics with the same empirical breadth and depth that he had advocated.

As he had pointed out in that letter to Anthony in October 1962[53] and in several of his articles, such as 'Time in Accounting,' he saw these developments as both unfortunate and risky. Without a proper understanding of the historical developments of accounting thought and practice, it becomes increasingly likely that the current generation of accountants lack the necessary insight to improve their own discipline. This observation applies equally in the early decades of the 2000s.

Yet, Chambers remained confident that evidence-based and thoughtful research would eventually prevail, as even the best developments sometimes took a considerable time to find acceptance. In his own words:

> From the time of Plato (5th century BC) to the time of Kepler (17th century AD) the paths of the planets were believed to be circular—22 centuries to demolish a mistaken belief. Though some Greek philosophers of the 4th century BC believed in a heliocentric universe, the geocentric doctrine prevailed for over 20 centuries. Though some Greek philosophers had believed in an earth in motion, for 20 centuries the doctrine of stationary earth persisted. . . . More recently, such eminent scientists as Kelvin, Mach and Rutherford held firmly to beliefs that were discarded, because disproved, within a generation of their utterance. As for technology, the following periods elapsed between the conception of the basic idea and its fruition—photography, 56 years; television, 63 years; antibiotics, 30 years; zip fasteners, 30 years; instant coffee, 22 years. In the light of this it is perhaps understandable that the emergence of an agreed, serviceable form of accounting from a trial and error stage, through speculation, experimentation and confirmation to execution, cannot be expected to occur speedily.[54]

Notes

1. Chapter epigraph:
   Extract from an article in the *Abacus* December 1982 Festschrift 'Special Issue' by outspoken 1970s and 1980s U.K. academic, Eddie Stamp. Endnote 18, Prologue provides details of the relevant letter by Barton to Chambers, #6549.
2. Chambers (1995a, xi).
3. Chambers (1995a, xi).
4. Carnegie and Napier (1996).
5. For example, Carnegie and Napier (1996).
6. Miller, Hopper and Laughlin (1991).
7. Previts, Parker and Coffman (1990b).
8. For example, Clarke, Dean and Wells (2010, 2012).
9. Previts, Parker and Coffman (1990a).
10. Chambers (1995a, p. xii).
11. Littleton (1933, 361); cited in Carnegie and Napier (1996).
12. Carnegie and Napier (1996)
13. Clarke (1977).
14. Chambers to Stamp, P202, #7987, 19/03/1964.
15. Chambers to Sir Alex Fitzgerald, P202, #84, 13/05/1955.
16. Whitley (1986); Edwards *et al.* (2013).
17. Tomlins (1820).
18. Hatfield (1909).
19. Canning (1929, 22).
20. Sanders, Hatfield and Moore (1938).
21. AICPA (1957).
22. Jowitt, Jowitt and Walsh (1977, 144).
23. Pacioli (1494) and Smith (1776).
24. The qualifiers 'financial position' and 'financial performance' are often overlooked when the true and fair phrase is examined. This is discussed in Chambers and Wolnizer (1990).
25. *Ex parte Holme* (1852) 22 L.J. Ch. 226; *Binney v. The Ince Hall Coal and Cannel Company* (1866) 35 L.J. Ch. 363; *City of Glasgow Bank v Mackinnon* (1882) Court Sessions Cases 4th series 535; and *Re Spanish Prospecting Co. Ltd* [1911] 1 Ch. 92.
26. Chambers and Wolnizer (1990, 211–12).
27. Chambers (1994, 77). We reconsider the two puzzles and the related riddle of the money illusion, especially in chapter 9.
28. Chambers (1994, 76). Using path dependence Edwards (2016) suggests a different reason for historical cost valuation dominance prior to and since the Renaissance.
29. Carnegie and Napier (1996).
30. Keenan (1998).
31. Napier (1998).
32. P202, #7442, 01/02/1995; as noted in Dean and Clarke (2010c). As endnotes #s10, chapter 2, 51, chapter 3, 43, chapter 5; 18, chapter 9 as well as their related text indicate, Chambers was also sceptical about the utility of share price-based empirical accounting research in improving accounting practice.
33. More on this appears in Chapter 8.
34. As adopted in Herman, Jahn and Ryan (2013).
35. Funnell (1998) discusses narratives in accounting history).
36. Consider Chambers (1961, 1964a, 1967b). Others would review the works of Canning, like Whittington (1980) who included a lengthy commentary about

Canning as one of the early pioneers of income measurement and price-level accounting and Zeff's (2000) article-length review of Canning's academic career.

37. Chambers (1980a) discusses this.
38. Chambers (1972, 156). For similar observations about committees see endnote #1, chapter1, immediately below endnote #39, chapter 3 and in later chapters.
39. Chambers to Briloff, P202, #5770, 21/02/1979.
40. Steve Zeff in an a 14 November 2017 email to the authors noted that when Editor of *TAR*: 'I had asked Tom Burns, my Book Review Editor, to invite Ray to do the Canning review, it was natural for him to do it, because he had already reviewed Irving Fisher's book.' Zeff indicated it was one of several reviews: 'I instructed Tom . . . to secure review articles on Paton and Littleton's monograph after 40 years (written by Yuji Ijiri), on Canning's "Economics of Accountancy" after 50 years, and on Edwards and Bell's book after 20 years (done by Larry Revsine). I am sure that I told Tom to invite Ray to do the Canning review.'
41. Chambers (1971a, 149).
42. Chambers (1979a, 764).
43. Chambers (1979a, 766).
44. Chambers (1979a, 764).
45. Chambers (1995a, xii).
46. Chambers (1989a, 7).
47. Chambers' hand-drawn illustrations are available at P202, #12818.
48. Chambers (1989a, 8). The attention to detail in the preparation of illustrations was one of Chambers' teaching strengths. An aside in a letter from a Hong Kong ASA representative, Baldwin Wong, P202, #5853, 26 /05/1979, is indicative of Chambers' strong teaching abilities: 'You may be very interested to know that the participants of your recent course rated you as the best lecturer in all the courses ever offered by the Hong Kong Society of Accountants.' In another, Jay Smith, Chairman of the Department of Accounting, University of Kansas, commented on Chambers' enthusiastic approach to teaching: 'Graduate students were high in praise. . . . You really "turned them on." ' see (P 202, #3064, 25/05/70). Well-known 1990s Australian businessman and former student Tony Berg was effusive about Chambers' educator skills—see P202, #7318, 15/07/1991: 'Ray Chambers has done more than anyone I can think of to make accounting information relevant to its users, and even though the profession itself has moved slowly and reluctantly in response to Ray Chambers' wisdom, his students have benefited enormously from the insights gained from him.' The Archive reveals many other positive reflections. On his teaching abilities generally see the observations in Wolnizer and Dean (2000).
49. Chambers to Anthony, P202, #8481, 22/10/1962.
50. Chambers (1989a, 20). This aspect is discussed in his 1961 *General Theory* monograph (especially paras 55 and 119) and he would return to the issue in his *Accounting Horizons* article (endnote #11, chapter 9.
51. Chambers (1993), 'Positive Accounting Theory and the PA Cult.' See also endnote #43, chapter 5 and related text discussion about testing accounting quality.
52. P202, #7442, 01/02/1995.
53. Chambers to Anthony, P202, #8481, 22/10/1962.
54. Chambers (1980a, 167). In his *Thesaurus* Chambers adds to this quote in square brackets that some evidence for this view is provided in Stephen Rosen (1976).

4 Archivist: Classifying, Searching for Order

We think we think. But what we think is often vague, ambiguous and disconnected. Only the discipline of writing forges thoughts into serviceable shapes and systematic patterns. Writing maketh an exact man, said Bacon; but seldom, I suspect, at the first attempt. I know that 'Chambers later' has frequently thought differently from 'Chambers earlier'; and that 'Chambers now' has often wanted to know what 'Chambers then' thought, for the purpose of completing some uncompleted business. But I kept no index. I have preferred usually to think afresh about a matter in hand, rather than run the risk of repeating my own mistakes; and that very process has revealed mistakes. But, at last I found I needed an index of some kind.

—Introduction to *R.J. Chambers: An Auto-Bibliography*, May 1977a[1]

In *The Measure of Reality* Alfred W. Crosby explains how 'Western Europeans were among the first, if not the first, to invent mechanical clocks, geometrically precise maps, double-entry bookkeeping, exact algebraic and musical notations, and perspective painting.'[2] And, although he declares that 'By the sixteenth century more people were thinking quantitatively in Western Europe than in any other part of the world'[3] and later, 'that double-entry bookkeeping brought an order to commerce,' he fails to explain how the archivists generally made possible the explanation of such innovation. For it was only because of meticulous archives that the telling of this history was possible. For example, towards the end of the sixteenth century Francis Bacon, the 'father of empiricism' and of the inductive method of science, had noted the need for classification to better understand natural history.

Chambers clearly saw value in systematically storing a large collection of accounting and cognate discipline materials. Several entries in section 212 of his *Thesaurus* give a clue to his thinking. Pareto is included, with the quote that 'classification is a first step that is almost indispensable if one would have an adequate grasp of any great number of differing objects.'[4] While Larrabee observes that:

The limited spans of human attention and memory [mean] . . . the only way in which a human mind can cope [with numerous and diverse things] in thinking is by grouping individual items into classes to which names or symbols are usually attached.[5]

An orderly commerce was Chambers' avowed pursuit and that of the Sydney School of Accounting from its origins in the early 1950s.[6] *Orderly*, in the sense that accounting statements of the financial position of commercial entities needed to *tell it as it is*. The work of the school's members is instructive; most recently Clarke *et al.* (2014, 2016) suggest that it is doubtful that accounting statements have ever done so for the majority of companies, except by accident. Bookkeeping without imputation is not a mechanism for determining financial position.

Accordingly, many of Chambers' forays into accounting-related policy matters were driven more by seeking to unearth the wisdom of accounting than the intricacies of its techniques. Informing the necessary legal (chapter 8) and management education reforms (chapters 5 and 9) were his encyclopaedic records of the relevant material begun in the late 1940s. From that early stage in his academic career he maintained an ordered set of correspondence that forms the basis of what became the R.J. Chambers Archive. Those forays were underpinned by a view of commercial (financial) matters not as isolates, but as interconnections—especially the interconnectedness of accounting, finance and management, and accounting, evaluation, and economic action. The Prologue notes his view that the fundamentals of those relationships endure.

The previous chapter reveals Chambers' penchant for an understanding of historical antecedents of whatever was the current focus. He noted in the new introduction to the 1974 Scholars Book Co. reprint of *Accounting, Evaluation and Economic Behavior* that he loved mathematics, especially Euclidian geometry and related arts like classificatory schema. Hence there should be no surprise in his enduring belief that for there to be order in business, a classificatory schema of business matters was essential.

The following section, which describes the Archive's features, affords us a unique view of the environment in which Chambers worked and how his reforms were forged.

To put this into perspective, first we examine Chambers' activities as a member of the N.S.W. Division of the Business Archives Council of Australia (BACA). By the 1950s there was a national Business Archive Council with divisions operating in Australia's major states. A similar body existed in the U.K. In N.S.W. it was a Sydney University-based organization that began operations in the mid-1950s, so Chambers was well aware of its existence and functions. In the early 1960s the BACA administered a journal, *Archives and History*, which was the antecedent of *Australian Economic History Review*. Later developments indicate why Chambers was interested in the Council's archival preservation work from the time he joined the University. Around 1960 he became a committee member and then secretary of the Council, continuing in one or more of those positions until the organization merged with the Records Management Association in 1969.

That interest is implied in a letter written to Chambers by the BACA secretary: 'We thank you for your past support of the Council [as a member and officer], and look forward to your continued co-operation in the work of encouraging preservation of business records and interest in business history in Australia.'[7]

Chambers clearly had a keen interest in history and used historical methods from his early days in academe. He would not only seek to obtain, preserve, and classify business records, but he added substantially to them through his own works. It was only natural that he would apply such archival-type ordering to his correspondence files and related materials.

The Chambers Archive and His *Accounting Thesaurus*

Both the Archive and the *Thesaurus* provided ideal foci for many of Chambers' criticisms of conventional accounting. His ideas evolved by looking outside the conventional wisdom for innovative solutions to ongoing accounting problems. Instances described in detail in this chapter are the 'case against conventional consolidation with the proposal for an alternative group accounting,' and recourse to the use of the 'double account mechanism to resolve problems related to large sunk cost items,' such as the accounting for long-life assets, accounting for mining expenditures and accounting for the cost associated with purchased goodwill. Regarding the use of the double account mechanism Chambers was well aware that it had been in use for over 150 years in capital-intensive transportation industries, like the railways and canals, as well as in Anglo-American local councils. But he sought to apply it to a different commercial setting. Other problems and Chambers' innovative attempts to resolve them are discussed in subsequent chapters.

The Chambers Archive

Having maintained for many years an extensive amount of professional and academic material in folders and filing cabinets, Chambers used an abridged Dewey classificatory system to store and retrieve items. His articles, submissions to government and professional enquiries (listed in Tables 7.3–7.5) were informed by particulars of practice that he was wont to draw upon. Indeed, one of the current author's (Dean) first jobs in 1974 as a research assistant was to file and catalogue (under direction) Chambers' cards and his substantial collections of newspaper cuttings, articles, and related materials on accounting and related disciplines.

Following Chambers' death, ongoing professional archival work has meant that a summary paragraph form of the hard-copy correspondence collection and the materials collection is now nearly fully searchable, even by international researchers using the internet. A description of each item held in the archive is available at http://sydney.edu.au/arms/archives/chambers_items871.shtml. Fisher Library is reviewing the extent of the materials available on this site as the book goes to print.

The full collection comprises the hard-copy correspondence held in the University of Sydney Archives of more than 15,000 correspondence and related items. It also contains book and article hard-copy libraries stored elsewhere in the University. Augmenting this hard-copy collection are digitized copies of most items. It is proposed that the correspondence and digitized summaries of the four libraries will be searchable across multiple classificatory types which have been manually inserted into an itemized information set.

Those libraries cover:

- Personal Papers with over 12,000 correspondence items;
- Personal Library with over 2,500 books;
- Personal Reading Material with over 2,000 items; and
- Published Works Abstracts with over 300 items.

An earlier digitized version was accessible for several years from the Faculty of Economics and Business website.

It is worth recalling that upon hearing of Chambers' death U.K. economist-cum-accounting theorist Geoffrey Whittington emailed one of the present authors with the following: 'Visiting the Sydney Accounting Department will be a bit like visiting the City [of Sydney] and finding the [Harbour] Bridge missing.' He continued with this prescient plea: 'I don't think there can be any doubt that he has earned a significant place in the history of our subject, and that many PhD theses will be written about his work, so I trust the Archives will be preserved.'[8]

That plea was heard, but only just in time. Below we mention briefly the dramas facing the Archive. In the mid-1990s as a consequence of the decision by the university to develop the Darlington Centre on the eastern edge of the Sydney campus, Chambers and part of his archive were moved to an annex in the grounds of the Newtown North Public School. Curiously, some of the Archive materials remained in an academic's room in the Economics Faculty's Merewether Building. What bizarrely occurred a few years later following Chambers' death as described in 2006 by Clarke, Dean and Wolnizer:

> The collection had a lucky escape from destruction following several moves after Chambers officially retired in 1982. Physical moves continued . . . after Chambers' death . . . papers were boxed . . . in rather insecure storage in a University-owned building that was scheduled to be demolished. . . . Peter Wolnizer as dean of the Faculty of Economics saw urgent manoeuvres to ensure the Collection was recovered

from its several locations and re-assembled in a similar form (layout of room, etc.) to when Chambers was researching. The Collection was saved from imminent destruction, which would have been a tragic loss not only for accounting historians, but also for the history of accounting . . . Graeme Dean assumed principal responsibility for managing the archiving and digitizing processes.[9]

The salvage allowed the development of one of the most comprehensive and fascinating accounting collections, comparable with those of international researchers such as the U.S.A.'s Abe Briloff, John Bennet Canning, and Kenneth MacNeal, the U.K.'s Harold Edey, and Australia's Lou Goldberg.[10]

With the Chambers' correspondence files preserved, Whittington's prescience about prospective theses would soon be borne out. The maintained databases, in hard copy and digitized forms, have underpinned several PhDs at Sydney and elsewhere including those by Sydney's Martin Bloom (2008), John Staunton (2007) and Lachlan Tuite (2013), and Royal Holloway's Martin Persson (2013). Prior to these doctorates, recourse to historical method is evident in all the 1970s and 1980s PhDs emerging from the Sydney School of Accounting—namely those by Clarke, Craswell, Islam, Johnstone, Perera, Rahman, Walker, Wells, and Wolnizer.[11]

The historical lens adopted in those theses differentiated them from many doctorates undertaken at other Australian and overseas universities. Policy reforms were sought via unravelling the nuances in the antecedents of accounting's current disorderly state. They covered a broad spectrum— from goodwill accounting, consolidation accounting, accounting for liabilities, accounting standards setting, auditing and auditing independence, as well as cost accounting and accounting for price and price level changes.

An Accounting Thesaurus

After retirement Chambers' academic enquiries continued as he revisited an old project. It was a daunting exercise but led to the publication of *An Accounting Thesaurus: 500 Years of Accounting*, which was launched at the university in June 1996. It remains the only thesaurus of accounting.

Several years after its publication, George Staubus referred to it as Chambers' magnum opus.[12] This was significant, albeit contestable, as Chambers had published in 1966 what many regarded as his most significant work, *Accounting, Evaluation and Economic Behavior*. The raw materials for the thesaurus were close at hand. Ever since he had started serious study, Chambers had maintained the practice of keeping notes—'quotable quotes' from the things he read.[13] Like some before him, exemplified by Sir Francis Bacon, Chambers loved to record and catalogue things. It was thought essential to the discovery of accounting knowledge.

Being close to seventy, Chambers resurrected this chartulary of accounting and related ideas. While he had an abundance of materials, there was

Figure 4.1 Ray and the Thesaurus

Photo: Chambers at the launch of the *Thesaurus* in the University of Sydney's McLaurin Hall

no roadmap for a thesaurus such as this. Additionally, his computing skills were limited. One of the authors (Dean) recalls several occasions when a frustrated Chambers would call from his home after dinner with a computing problem. A late-night drive to lend assistance was usually the best way to solve the problem quickly.

Chambers was never deterred, and he pursued the mammoth task with great passion and determination. Regarding its ambitious scope Chambers observes in a note on the book's inside cover:

> Using an ingenious and unique decimal classificatory system of the whole of accounting knowledge, the book aims to give a historical perspective as well as an up to date overview of what accountants, were, are and do, and is intended as a reference book and a research aid.

The *Thesaurus* Preface provides a further justification for the project:

> Much of the wisdom and the folly of the past are now little known, for the sources are scattered or remote. Reliable knowledge pertinent to accounting—economics, law, psychology, mathematics, administration and so on [his foundations of accounting]—is often disregarded, for its sources, too, are diverse and have seldom attracted the close attention

of those who have shaped the present common style of accounting, and may shape its future.

In response to the University of Sydney's Chancellor, Dame Leonie Kramer's book launch, Chambers noted further aspects of the scope and limitations of his work:

> The project stemmed from a dissatisfaction with accounting practice and teaching about the mid-twentieth century. [I viewed] Accounting— as memory; as instrumentation of regulation of economic behaviour; as a means of coordination. Teaching and learning were by rote with only a vague association with economics in which Faculty it was taught. Manuals and textbooks were regurgitations of what had appeared in their precursors for decades. They lacked any clear association with commerce and government. . . . Hence the thesaurus—an exercise in setting side by side what seemed to be wise and foolish, what seemed consistent with what was inconsistent—what seemed to be realistic with what was admittedly false or synthetic. I could not pretend to canvass the whole of the wisdom of economists, mathematicians, psychologists, political and social scientists, logicians, philosophers.[14]

Early Versions of the Thesaurus

The Chambers Archive preserves multiple versions of his *Thesaurus* dating from the middle of the 1980s and with many handwritten changes. Those versions resulted from the actions of someone who refused offers of research assistance in the tedious process of verifying back from the original sources his handwritten card index entries. The final version was completed in late 1995. The characteristics of those earlier versions are that they are less condensed and have more quotes from the one author in the same section. The final version evolved as Chambers realized the need to fine-tune the many entries into a workable number, not to have too many of his own entries, and to have competing ideas in each section.[15]

In the Preface Chambers tells of his return to a long-held missionary-like goal:

> The justification of this selection, from diverse ages and fields of inquiry, lies in a belief in its potential, as an irritant or stimulus, in advancing the development of a demonstrably rigorous and serviceable accounting in a world that cannot do without it.

Not everyone could see the value in such a massive exercise. It is worth mentioning, for example, the observations of another U.S. contemporary of Chambers, who observed in 1996 to two of the authors that he was unclear as to how the material in the *Thesaurus* could be used. They responded that several articles would have their catalysts from debates in that *Thesaurus*. Chambers had made a similar claim in a 1993 letter to Sterling that the *Thesaurus'* contents:

> have suggested to me scores of articles (even dissertations) that could be written on the worthwhile, the transient, fashionable, the zany, ideas and arguments that have made accounting what it is. (One of the by-products is the paper I enclose, which has been accepted for *Accounting Horizons* early 1994.)[16]

Still, it is likely that few would dispute that the *Thesaurus* is a major work, and time will be the arbiter of Staubus' and others' observations.

But none of this says anything about the drama in getting the *Thesaurus* published. Fortunately, we have the correspondence regarding this in the Chambers Archive.[17] Chambers received the disappointing news that Pergamon Press, part of the Elsevier Science group, had rejected his proposal to publish the *Thesaurus*, now close to finalization after nearly a decade of assiduous effort.[18] One can only imagine how this hit him. But, never one to give up, he set about seeking a subvention from the University of Sydney Accounting Foundation which he had helped found, especially through his own initial funding sources.[19] To Chambers' relief, a $25,000 subvention was provided and Pergamon Press agreed to publish this work. When he received the first printed copy in the post[20] the lengthy project was near its end, at least for Chambers. The hard-copy book proved a success, achieving several print runs. Others, especially Bob Walker, have pursued this exercise, with it now being available online at http://setis.library.usyd.edu.au/chambers/*body.html*.

But how useful are the Chambers Archive and *Thesaurus* for teaching and research?

Before answering we digress, noting that the commercial and academic environments that Chambers faced were difficult. It was rare for accounting academics to engage in what could, at times, be hostile public debate. But Chambers did, over several decades.[21] To be effective over a sustained period this demanded a vast reservoir of knowledge and authoritative references. One had to be sure of the territory, if one's integrity were to be maintained. The material in the Archive proved invaluable as the evidence it provided often gave Chambers' argument an evidential authority.

Without the Internet and advances in IT, it was not an easy task. If something seemed interesting, then it had to be preserved. Such underlay the retention of the trays of cards, newspaper cuttings, and hard copy of articles; with their referenced quotes and other details to be drawn upon as the occasion warranted. Those sources meant Chambers was able to refer to an eclectic range of sources to support what were perceived by many as radical solutions to many 'recycled' accounting problems.[22]

Returning to the question about teaching and research we now consider a few examples briefly. Other chapters also reveal clearly how Chambers explored the history of current practices to identify the prevailing circumstances and to ensure that proposed reforms addressed the problems with workable solutions.

What was also novel in his works was an overarching desire to treat these matters as part of a resolution within his broader accounting theory reforms—not to view the latest problem as an isolated issue. Resolution of problems related to asset valuation, takeover sagas, price and price level changes, and addressing legal anomalies in respect of corporate financial reporting—all of which, as chapter 6 notes, were to be considered part of his holistic, theoretically grounded reforms.

Innovative Reporting Proposals

Chambers' innovatory solutions to two enduring and major reporting problems are considered—how to account properly for corporate groups, given that a large proportion of business is conducted through them, and his advocacy of the double account reporting system to address a class of unresolved financial accounting problems related to accounting for sunk cost items, namely, how to account for purchased goodwill, mine development costs, the purchase price of highly specialized plants, and other 'costly' items.

Chambers on Group Accounting

Throughout the twentieth century, recurring booms, economic vicissitudes, and financial imbroglios have produced anomalies with respect to the serviceability of conventional consolidated accounting for corporate groups. Most recently in the Global Financial Crisis this resurfaced with the undisclosed roles (notwithstanding bank groups following consolidation accounting rules) of the 'off-balance sheet' shadow banks.[23]

Such problems had a long history prior to the GFC and Chambers had addressed the issues in the late 1960s when he proposed an alternative group accounting mechanism. In a 1968 publication of a national practitioner group, the ASA he had written that 'consolidated accounts are not really necessary.' The *Thesaurus* (*AAT*: s. 488, 477–78) records that another 'Sydney Schooler' Bob Walker (1978) wrote 'By 1940 consolidated reports had become an accepted vehicle for corporate reporting . . . but uncertainty about what those statements were supposed to show was reflected in an inconsistent and confused array of practices and rules.' Australian examples of confusion and uncertainty included the early 1960s unexpected receivership of electrical retailer H.G. Palmer Ltd (and its related Group companies), which was left high and dry when its owner, the MLC Limited, a listed life insurance company, quite properly (from a legal perspective) declared its wholly owned subsidiary, the H.G. Palmer Ltd and its Group of companies, as being separate entities. The H.G. Palmer parent company had, prior to it being placed in receivership, reported a consolidated group profit in each of the fifteen years since its incorporation.

Earlier *Thesaurus* references had criticized the notion that corporate groups were more than a convenient accounting way of describing the relationship of legal entities and groups—for example, in 1919 Webster at *AAT* (s. 481, 462) noted 'many lawyers were opposed to the presentation of consolidated accounts by companies to their stockholders,' and, within the same subsection at *AAT* (p. 463), in 1970 Jones observes that: 'no group of companies is recognized by the [U.K. Companies Act], the attribute of legal entity is not conferred upon the group as such . . . creditors can look for satisfaction of their debts only to the assets of the one company to which they have extended credit.'

Still in that subsection (*AAT*, s. 481, 463), it was not a surprise to see the 1978 entry of the N.S.W. Government ASRC (more on which appears in chapter 8) that: 'a group is not a legal entity capable of issuing shares, owning assets and owing liabilities. It cannot have a state of affairs, nor earn profits . . . sue or be sued . . . no set of consolidated statements can give a true and fair view of anything.'

Notwithstanding the argument in Chambers' 1968 article, in 1973 in *Securities and Obscurities*, and reiterated in the 1978 ASRC Report, the ICAA and the ASA (*AAT*: s. 481, 463) relied on the broader 'economic' control criterion to expand the definition of 'economic entity' to include 'the group comprising the investor [company], its subsidiaries and the investor's ownership interest in its associated companies.'

The notion of an economic group, rather than a group based on the criterion of a subsidiary requiring more than a 50 per cent share ownership, had triumphed as the basis of promulgated professional standards on accounting for a group. It remains the case towards the end of the second decade of the twenty-first century.

Group accounting in the form of conventional consolidated financial statements rests upon a number of dubious assumptions: that the group is an *economic* entity possessing the legally determined features of ordinary companies; that the profits and losses of the subsidiaries would flow from each subsidiary to its owner (more or less) automatically and should be accounted for on that basis; that all transactions between the related companies are *sham* and their financial impact should be eliminated when assessing their overall financial effect on the group's combined wealth; and most importantly, that consolidated financials could provide information not available from the accounts of the individual companies. According to Webster in 1919 (*AAT*: s. 486, 470) for example, the object of a consolidated balance sheet is to 'show the true financial position of accompany and its subsidiary,' while in 1949 Childs (*AAT*: s. 486, 471) held the view that the transactions should be accounted for 'as though they were in fact those of one company.' In 1959 the AICPA published the Committee on Accounting

Procedure's ARB 51. It opined that the consolidated financial statements were to be prepared to show the 'results of operations and financial position' from 'shareholders and creditors of the parent company's viewpoint.' And in 1962 Wixon (*AAT*: s. 486, 471) suggested that the statements were to report on companies operated under 'common control' rather than 'a legal unit.'

Taken together the ideas conveyed in the Peloubet, Garnsey and Robson quotes in the *Thesaurus* appear as a most likely influence on what some commentators had viewed as Chambers' 'revolutionary' ideas. Peloubet noted that the group accounts format of consolidated statements 'when correctly drawn up . . . are frankly and plainly statistical statements.' Garnsey also in his 1923 listing of the four ways of presenting group data appears influential. For his '(iii)' suggests 'as a separate statement a summary of the assets and liabilities of all the subsidiary undertakings taken together.' Robson in 1936 revived Peloubet's statistical summary notion, aggregating the assets and liabilities of the subsidiaries.

Chambers' alternative to consolidated statements in 1968 entailed a form of equity accounting with aggregative annexures providing explanatory information. He provided more detail in the 1973a and 1978 ASRC works, albeit still 'in principle' with no numerical workings. The 1977 *Auto-Bibliography* summarized this style of group accounting as an integral part of his CoCoA system: 'In place of consolidated statements there will be (in addition to and in similar style to the legal accounts of any holding company) an aggregate statement of assets, equities and results of subsidiary and associated companies, in columnar or other form, under whatever class-headings are deemed appropriate.

a) There will be no off-sets or "eliminations," since the companies are legally independent.
b) There will be a reconciliation of the holding company's legal balance sheet figures with the figures shown in the aggregate statements.
c) Since all companies will use the same accounting, there will be no "goodwill on consolidation" and all [asset and equity] items or groups of items as at a given date will be properly aggregable and relatable.'[24]

However, it was left to others to work out and gradually refine the details of what a colleague, Clarke, had commenced in the Sydney MBA curriculum during the early-to-mid 1970s.[25]

During the three decades prior to 1975 a number of Australian corporate groups had proven themselves to be more than a handful for the regulators. Clarke, Dean and Oliver (1997) and Clarke and Dean (2007) analyse those failures, revealing how Australian creditor sagas, especially related to employees in the 1980s and '90s, also proved embarrassing. These included: the treatment of employees' entitlements for long-service, leave and redundancy payments upon the cessation of a group's subsidiary businesses because of the bankruptcy of the relevant group parent company; and disputes at the major mines of the N.S.W. country towns of Cobar and Woodlawn. In those cases it was claimed that the parent companies were not legally obliged to meet the liability for the amounts due to the employees of each of the separate wholly owned subsidiary operating companies which, by then, had minimal funds.

These actions reinforced the more than a century-old U.K. *Salomon v. Salomon* principle that each company was a separate legal entity liable in the first instance for its debts. The same happened a few years later at the N.S.W. city of Newcastle with the actions of another parent company, STP, and Bond Corporation's milking of its subsidiary, Bell's 'cash box,' as if the assets of Bell (a listed company) were available for use by its majority shareholder. Alan Bond, the Chairman of Bond Corporation was sentenced to gaol after pleading guilty for fraud. Perhaps the highlight event, because also of the industrial relations implications nationally, was the late-1990s 'Waterfront' affair in which the employees within the Patrick Corporation's stevedoring group had been contracted by a separate, now insolvent subsidiary company of the 'Patrick group.' The interface between group accounting and social (industrial relations) ramifications was clear. Importantly, it also confirmed the idea that assets of the group companies were not (in the absence of cross guarantees) automatically available to meet the debts of any company within the group.

Based on a numerical illustration first presented publicly in 2002, the 2014 Clarke *et al.* iteration of the Chambers' alternative market price group accounting[26] is drawn upon here to show, in principle, how the consolidation financial reporting problem can be mitigated.[27] The method shows that the general mode of Chambers' CoCoA form of mark-to-market accounting is workable; it can accommodate an effective accounting for related companies. While not presently achieved, a commonly declared overall objective of consolidation accounting is to give greater insight into the wealth and progress of related entities than can be provided, as occurs under conventional accounting, by simply reporting their investment cost at acquisition date. Consolidation accounting sidesteps the *Salomon v. Salomon* principle. It does this within a corporate group setting through the aggregation of the physical and financial aspects of the separate entities' assets, liabilities, revenues, and expenses, injecting consolidation-specific data and adjusting legitimate transaction data through the elimination rule, under the umbrella of a supposed group entity approach.

Proposing in 1968 that 'consolidated statements are not really necessary,' Chambers could not have foreseen the extent to which corporate groups in Australia and elsewhere would dominate the business landscape over the next half century.[28] In that article he railed against the way in which his understanding of the function of accounting to report the wealth and progress of business entities within a legal, social, and economic framework was being frustrated by attributing a legal status to a group of related companies. No such status pertained. The group, he explained, was an *accounting fiction*. This point was later discussed in detail in a legal article, 'Law and Accounting: Separate Legal Entity and Consolidation Accounting.'[29] One Australian radio commentator, referring to the group fiction idea, aptly described it as akin to the Australian Aboriginal mythological creature, the 'bunyip.'

When Chambers first proposed his group accounting reform, a corporate group was deemed for reporting purposes when a company held more than 50 per cent of the issued shares in another, thereby making the latter a subsidiary of it. A corporate group, however, could not own assets or incur liabilities, earn revenues or incur expenses. Then as now, this was the domain only of legal entities. They were and remain the assets and liabilities *of* the separate companies comprising the deemed mythical group. This arises because of proprietary rights, which a group of companies does not have. Chambers outlined a general proposition for an alternative form of group accounting that would not only accord with the law and his CoCoA system, but would better provide the aggregative group financial information that consolidation was intended to give when first proposed in the early years of the twentieth century.[30] Most importantly, his general proposal would achieve this without improperly attributing to the fictional group any proprietary rights regarding the aggregates of the so-called group assets, liabilities, revenues, or expenses that were not its legal due.[31]

Chambers suggested that, were there to be a professional and legislative rethink of how to affect the capital boundary in relation to what are currently defined as 'related companies,' his alternative presentation of the aggregative data would provide a workable outcome.[32] The overall effect of CoCoA is to remove most of the causes for the creative consolidation accounting that have been identified elsewhere.

As a consequence of applying the accounting standards in the preparation of the consolidated statements creative accounting abounds. Consolidated amounts for assets, liabilities, revenues, and expenses and the separate items of each classification may differ from the aggregations of those in the separate accounts of the parent and its subsidiaries. Further, the consolidated amounts arising from the use of tax effect accounting may differ, insofar as the net effect may well be a debit in the consolidated statements in contrast with a net credit on an aggregated basis in accord with accounts of the separate companies. That and other consolidation adjustments (eliminations and the like) could have the effect of changing an aggregated net profit in accord with the separate subsidiary accounts to a 'consolidated loss.' Further, the consolidated statements ordinarily have items for which there is no comparable item in the accounts of the parent or any of its subsidiaries—they are purely artefacts of the consolidation system. Examples include 'Goodwill on consolidation' and 'Gain on bargain purchase' (previously described as 'Negative goodwill on consolidation' or a 'Discount or premium on consolidation').

In brief, whatever group detail is thought necessary by the financial pundits could be provided in Chambers' alternative group accounting format, as each of the related companies would be required to comply with the disclosure requirements for separate companies under the relevant companies' legislation. Drawing on the ideas of Peloubet, Garnsey and Robson, Chambers' accompanying statistical summary (schedule/annexure) feature gives only the types of aggregate data usually required to prepare the conventional analytical metrics. But there is a major difference. Because under CoCoA the current market price data are adjusted by the capital maintenance adjustment, the reported amounts for the assets, liabilities, and profits are all stated in terms of the general purchasing power of money as at the date of the statement of financial position. Being homogeneous in that way, they are capable of having mathematical processes legitimately applied to them.

In Chambers' statistical schedule each total for paid-in capital, capital maintenance, profits, liabilities, and assets is the unadjusted aggregate of the amounts in the subsidiaries' accounts. The amount for the residual equity owned by the parent company is the aggregate of the amounts shown in the parent's statement of financial position as its investment in its subsidiaries. The ('held by') others amount is the residual equity other investors have in the subsidiaries, including any indirect investment in a subsidiary. Subsequently, Clarke, Dean and Houghton suggested that a spreadsheet listing of all cross claims within the group, as well as the external claims of each group company, should also be disclosed (see endnote #31, chapter 4). Similar schedules could be prepared for within the group revenues and expenses as well as those with external parties.

Chambers' Double Account System Resolves 'Recycled' Sunk Cost Problems

While new ideas are usually the means of economic advancement, sometimes the revival of old ones in a different setting is equally effective. When he was invited by Sir Allan Knight, then Chairman of Section No. 3 of the Hydro-Electric Commission of Tasmania, to contribute a paper at the May 1975 second biannual conference of the Electricity Supply Association of Australia it was seen by Chambers as an opportunity to resurrect for general use the centuries old double account system. The system was somewhat discredited, now untaught, but still used in limited settings. As Brief contended, it is 'based on what are essentially cash accounting methods.'[33] The conference was particularly relevant for it occurred during the highest inflation period in the latter half of the twentieth century in Anglo-Saxon countries.

Chambers readily accepted the invitation. In his view, the energy industry with its history of pressing for replacement price asset valuations during periods of increasing energy generation price changes, its government pricing regimes, and the massive (up front) costs for infrastructure assets needed for electricity generation, begged for the revival of the double account system 'with a market price twist.'

Large expenditures necessary before an industry could commence its operations were common during the Industrial Revolution and especially in respect of the building of canals in Britain, turnpike roads, and later the permanent way afforded by railway tracks. The large sums necessary were raised from the public and/or government, contracts were let, the infrastructure was built, and the cost recorded in a capital account. Those capital costs were for all intents and purposes one-off large expenditures to be accounted for in an innovatory (in this setting) two-tiered balance sheet. Under the double account (two-tiered) method of reporting *capital* assets—the initial reported purchase cost of the assets which, although requiring further periodic maintenance costs—remained constant. Importantly, there was no need for reporting annual amortization charges. The top tier contained purchase cost of the long-life asset (e.g., the canal or railway line contracted cost of its construction, augmented by other formation costs including initial loan interest costs) and the capital outlay required to finance it. The bottom tier or revenue account contained the normal cash-based operational outcomes of trading, incorporating periodic profit and losses that included the annual maintenance costs. The method also included in the bottom tier, as part of what some labelled the General Balance Sheet, items such as short-term fixed assets, land, investments in securities, amounts for working capital, etc., and their associated loan funds. The two-tiered structure is illustrated in Chambers' conference paper with its hypothetical electricity company balance sheet; it is reproduced in Table 4.1.

It was argued that many recurring accounting manipulations related to the amortization charges of major capital items would be mitigated by this method. The link with cash movements no doubt also appealed to Chambers. Entries in the *Thesaurus* are again useful in understanding the method. Consider, for example Manson (*AAT*, s. 387, 395), who in the early 1900s observes that:

> Under the double account system, a more marked line is drawn between capital and revenue. In a sense, every increase in the value of a company's assets is a profit, or more properly a gain—that is—the company is so much the richer, but it is not a "profit arising from the business of the company," so as to be available—in the view of the advocates of this system—for the purposes of dividend. . . . Profits in this sense

[consistent with the UK judicial law of the time] are the excess of revenue receipts over expenses properly chargeable to revenue account.

The history and examples of the method are described in an article, 'The Origins and Evolution of the Double Account System: An Example of Accounting Innovation.'[34] There, U.K. academic Dick Edwards describes the method as an exemplar of accounting innovation where long-lived assets played a major role in the business involved. He shows how it was developed by railway companies early in the nineteenth century in Britain, and that it was still being used by British local municipalities up until the early 1990s. Nearly twenty-five years later, Australian accounting practitioner Martin Bloom observes that the method was still practised in India in the early 2000s.[35]

Its significance is noted in Chambers' 1976 observation:

> In the double account system . . .: sunk costs were represented separately from financial operations on current account. There are good reasons for recourse to the same device in respect of purchased goodwill, mine development costs, highly specialized plant and other "costly" items.[36]

Chambers' use of the method in the May 1975 conference paper was 'CoCoA with a double-account twist.' Appearing a decade after publication of *Accounting, Evaluation and Economic Behavior* it was an illustration of 'Chambers later' differing from 'Chambers earlier.'[37]

Accounting, Evaluation and Economic Behavior was specifically directed toward outlining an accounting under *all* the price and price level changes that occur normally under *all* economic conditions. So it was aptly suited to the inflationary circumstances of 1974 and 1975 of near to 25 per cent in Australia and 20 per cent in the U.K.; and the reporting of CoCoA data within a double account system was a better way to account for the massive (up front) costs of the non-adaptive, risky infrastructure assets needed for electricity generation.

In the U.K. the Inflation Accounting Committee (under the chairmanship of Sir Francis Sandilands) had reported in September 1975 recommending a system of Current Cost Accounting (a 'value to the business' form of replacement price accounting). It had expropriated Chambers' CCA label, causing Chambers to adopt the label CoCoA.[38]

Replacement price valuation for assets was the flavour of the month in the U.K. and elsewhere in 1974–75. Interestingly, a subsequent U.K. government inquiry into nationalized industries produced the Bryant Report of 1992. It recommended asset (especially infrastructure) valuation based on current cost accounting and, where prices for services (such as energy) were being set by government-led commissions, using rate of return calculations drawing on reported CCA-based asset information. So, it was not surprising that, at the Tasmanian conference held during the mid-1970s, there was a push for a form of replacement price valuation.

As usual, Chambers' Tasmanian paper did not overly deal with matters of detail; he concentrated on the broad ideas underpinning his variant of the double account system as a novel way to resolve the problem at hand. This was his way of setting out the broad principles, leaving it for others to pick up the details later, such as Wells (1984) did in respect of accounting for nationalized industries, and as Clarke and Dean (2002, 2007) did regarding group accounting. Writing to John Sutcliffe, a practitioner who attended the Tasmanian conference and who corresponded with Chambers proposing another form of market price accounting to assist in the setting of electricity tariffs, Chambers noted:

> My paper did not attempt to tangle with specific laws or regulations governing utility accounts. Nor am I confident that I could do justice to all the rules relating to sinking funds, and so on. But it does seem to me on reading your letter that the whole subject of utility accounts could do with a new look.[39]

A few years after the Tasmanian paper Hector Perera's PhD thesis (supervised by Chambers) used an electricity utility case study to explore the intricacies of inflation accounting. Perera provided an accounting reform proposal using the double account mechanics.[40] And about thirty years later Bloom (also in a Sydney-supervised PhD, but this time by another Sydney Schooler, Dean) provided detailed illustrations of how a form of the double account system could be used to account for purchased goodwill in respect of Dot.com companies whose major asset was goodwill.[41]

Chambers had, either directly or indirectly, influenced these novel works which sought solutions to the types of problems that had for years befuddled accounting standards setters (and still do). Their thoughts had been stuck in a conventional groove from which he had sought to extricate them.

Chambers' Tasmanian paper used an electricity utility accounting example (see Table 4.1) to capture the appropriate risk attendant upon an entity's now appropriately disclosed disposable asset backing. In such long-life-asset cases the most likely higher rates of return achieved were shown to be due to the risks associated with investing in non-adaptive, and hence risky, assets. His hypothetical electricity company balance sheet reveals clearly some of the standard double account features, accompanied by Chambers' twist, namely, in determining the utility's current financial position, fungible assets were reported at their cash equivalents. The investment in Long-Term Plant was not fungible, and hence not part of the entity's current financial position. It was reported in the 'top tier' of the Balance Sheet 'at cost,' and accompanying it was how it had been financed.

Table 4.1 Balance Sheet of a Utility as at 31 December 19x5[i]

<u>*Investment in Long-Term Plant, at cost*</u>	$1,400
Less amortization to date (invested in other assets)	<u>500</u>
Provided by Loan and other Funds	<u>900</u>
Current Financial Position	
<u>*Assets*</u>	
Office and other Buildings and Land	300
Short-Term Plant, Vehicles, etc	200
Inventories	200
Investments in Securities	50
Receivables (this item and all the above are at approximate market value)	300
Cash	<u>50</u>
	<u>1,100</u>

<u>*Financed out of—*</u>		
Loan Funds	1,500	
Less invested in Long-Term Plant (see above)	<u>900</u>	600
Capital Grant (original sum)	300	
Capital Maintenance Reserve	<u>80</u>	380
General Reserve		50
Accounts Payable		<u>70</u>
		<u>1,100</u>

i The hypothetical utility example is reproduced from Vol. 4 of *Chambers on Accounting* (1985, 145).

This illustration is more detailed than the one proposed in his 1976 *Abacus* article 'Continuously Contemporary Accounting: Misunderstandings and Misrepresentations.'[42]

Fifteen years later Chambers would recommend in principle this form of accounting for large up-front mining expenses to Australia's National Audit Office, then considering proposed changes to Section 301 of the Corporations Law Act. The NAO had asked Chambers to consider a market price system rather than the Current Cost Accounting proposal it had put forward for consultation.[43]

Those two lengthy practical illustrations reveal Chambers' desire to look outside the square, to be innovative in seeking ways to resolve recurring, and what many perceived to be insoluble, practical problems. Similar reasoning underpins solicited 'expert opinions' aimed at resolving practical problems that are revisited in a later chapter. Those opinions reveal a person immersed in practice. They also show how important it was for him to support his ideas by being able to draw on the multitude of archived source materials he had so orderly classified over the decades. His archivist tendencies certainly had served him well here, as they did elsewhere.

Notes

1. Chapter epigraph:
   Introduction to *R.J. Chambers: An Auto-Bibliography*, ICRA Occasional Paper #15, May 1977a.
2. Two of the present authors (Clarke and Dean) have explored this speculation in Dean, Clarke and Capalbo (2016).
3. Crosby (1997, page before Preface).
4. Pareto (1916, 7).
5. Larrabee (1945, 29).
6. Clarke *et al.* (2012).
7. Letter from Business Archives Council of Australia Honorary Treasurer H. McCredie to Chambers, P202, #11292, 05/06/1967; see also letter from Business Archives Council of Australia Secretary John Linton to Chambers, P202, #3862, 18/10/1972 with a similar comment about Chambers continuing to support the Council.
8. Geoffrey Whittington email to Graeme Dean, 13 September 1999.
9. Dean, Clarke and Wolnizer (2006, 150). Digitization of correspondence has been completed but is not yet available on the internet. As this book goes to press the hard-copy book library and related articles and other materials are available in Burren Street Library, a branch of University of Sydney's Fisher Library; whether such hard-copy collections will be retained is problematic.
10. Endnote #3, Prologue.
11. For details see Clarke *et al.* (2012, especially 32–5) and chapter 2 above.
12. Staubus (2003). Clarke (1996) and Previts (1996) were equally effusive about this novel work.
13. Examples of Chambers' early handwritten quotes are listed in the Archive #s500a and 9894.
14. Handwritten notes of a response by Chambers to the official launch of his *Thesaurus*, P202, #7465, 05/07/1996.
15. Draft versions of the *Thesaurus* are held in the Archive, P202, #9869.
16. The article was 'Historical Cost—Tale of a False Creed'—see Chambers to Sterling, P202, #7421, 23/11/1993. In more recent times several articles have been written including Edwards *et al.* (2009, 2013) and Edwards (2016) and dissertations (see endnote #35, chapter 2 and its related text).
17. These include catalogue entries: #7462, 7463 and 9867. Such delays are not uncommon in getting manuscripts reviewed and published.
18. Interestingly, in a 1993 letter to Sterling (P202, #7421, 23/11/1993) Chambers reflects on how difficult it has been to get unorthodox views published, as evidenced by what happened with his two books, *Accounting, Evaluation and Economic Behavior* and *Securities and Obscurities*, and Sterling's (1970) classic.
19. Clarke *et al.* (2012, especially 109–13) for details.
20. Letter from Elsevier Editor David Sharp to Chambers, P202, #7462, 19/12/1995.
21. Table 7.3 below; and Clarke, Dean and Wells (2012, 96–7; and Appendix III for details). Another contemporary to engage in such press releases was U.K. academic, Eddie Stamp.
22. The notion of recycling problems, not resolving them, was noted by Chambers' colleague and friend Bob Sterling (1979).
23. Clarke *et al.* (2014, esp. 122–29), FSB (2012), Pozsar *et al.* (2010), Tucker (2010, 2012).
24. Chambers (1977a, 62).
25. In particular, see Clarke and Dean (1993), Clarke, Dean and Oliver, 1997, 2003, Clarke, Dean and Houghton, 2002, and Clarke, Dean and Egan, 2014)

and endnote #31, chapter 4. For a summary of the MBA curriculum refer to Clarke *et al.* (2012, 138–9).

26. Clarke, Dean and Houghton (2002) and Clarke *et al.* (2014, 141–9).

27. Accounting aficionados wishing to follow in more detail through a series of transactions how the CoCoA group accounting mechanism works should refer to Clarke, Dean and Houghton (2002).

28. The Chambers Archive reveals in private correspondence that Chambers (1968a) changed his mind regarding support for conventional consolidation statements he had supported in *Accounting, Evaluation and Economic Behavior* (1966, 288). Consider P202, #s8727, 8731, 8733. Another Sydney School of Accounting member, Bob Walker (1976, 1978), provided criticisms of conventional consolidated statements. Around the time of the publication of Chambers' 1968 article Walker had just completed a MEc which involved honours lectures with Chambers and the writing of a thesis. It would be followed by his PhD examining consolidated financial statements which was submitted in 1976.

29. Clarke and Dean (1993).

30. *AAT* (pages 75–6 above) noted this feature.

31. With his proposal disputed and derided, few critics, however, acknowledged that Chambers did not claim that aggregative group financial data might not be useful, even necessary, for the effective management of the group affairs. As noted earlier, several academics and practitioners had promoted a similar idea. Chambers returned to this idea in 1973 in *Securities and Obscurities* and again in the 1978 N.S.W. government-initiated ASRC's Report, *Company Accounting Standards*. Chambers chaired that committee (see Clarke *et al.*, 2012 and chapter 8 of the biography). In November 1979 Chambers and a co-author of the 1978 N.S.W. ASRC Report Sri Ramanathan were invited to comment on Schedule Fourteen of the draft Sri Lankan Companies Act. They submitted thirty four A-4 typed pages of suggested amendments to the Sri Lankan Registrar of Companies and the Minister of Trade and Shipping. A major element related to Group Accounts presentations (see P202, #9540, 27/11/1979).

    In 1997 Chambers' alternate group accounting proposal was revisited in Clarke and Dean's (with Oliver) *Corporate Collapse*. A decade later their *Indecent Disclosure* fleshed out a workable mechanism using a numerical example. That example had first appeared in the *Australian Accounting Review* (Clarke, Dean and Houghton's 2002). It contained for the first time, as part of the related parties' statistical schedule, a spreadsheet listing of cross claims arising from inter-group transactions. As no refutations of this idea have been forthcoming the biography text provides a reduced non-numerical example with a few updates from the 2007 explanation. It is in principle similar to what also appeared in Clarke *et al.*'s (2014) *The Unaccountable and Ungovernable Corporation*.

32. Endnotes #23–29 and 31, chapter 4.

33. Brief (1966, 3). This emphasis on cash reporting appealed to Chambers, perhaps because CoCoA is primarily a cash-based system augmented by price variation and capital maintenance adjustments (see Chambers, 1975a for a description of this cash and cash equivalents system). Co-incidentally, in correspondence in 1972 with Homer Kripke (see Page 190 of the biography and endnote #38, chapter 8), the valuation of railway infrastructure was addressed. It had been considered earlier, in principle, in Chambers (1970a); and then later through a lengthy infrastructure example in the Chambers (1973c) paper presented at the Mt Isa ASA conference, 'Mining, Taxing and Accounting' (see also endnotes #36–37).

34. Edwards (1985). For those wishing to better understand the double account mechanism Edwards (1985, 32–3) illustrates the method with several pro-forma examples, as well as including an extract from the 1838 published accounts of the London and Birmingham Railway. Also, we refer to an extract from a hypothetical utility company example by Chambers in Table 4.1 of the biography.

35. Bloom (2008, 138).
36. Chambers (1976d, 145). He had alluded to this idea in an ASA State Convention paper, 'Mining, Taxing and Accounting' (1973c), and he would provide an even more detailed illustration in his seminar paper 'Inflation accounting and the electricity supply industry' (1975c).
37. Chambers, P202, #5175, 15/07/1977, retraces the history of his thinking about how to account for 'sunk costs,' a conundrum that has bedevilled accounting standards setters for decades.
38. This is discussed further in chapter 6.
39. John Sutcliffe to Chambers, P202, #10102, 24/09/1975 and Chambers' response to Sutcliffe, P202, #10103, 23/10/1975. Prior to the Tasmanian conference Chambers wrote to a fellow General Management Group luncheon colleague, Sir Frederick Wheeler, Q.B.E., then Secretary to the Federal Treasury, noting: 'I was interested to hear over lunch yesterday of the discussions you recently had on the so-called "Accounting for inflation" problem [in the public sector]. A great deal of publicity has been given to some of the proposals [like CPP and CCA] made in respect of private sector accounting. But much of the reporting is descriptive only and most of the proposals discussed can be shown to be logically fallacious and practically misleading.' (P202, #4425, 24/04/1975). Also, he sent Wheeler his Tasmanian conference paper and several other articles. Wheeler responded somewhat belatedly, noting that Chambers' ideas indeed differed greatly from those in the recent Mathews and Sandilands Reports. (P202, #4454, 19/09/1975)
40. The Archive has several letters from Chambers and Perera, P202, #s5407, 5408, 5409, 5410, 5411 sent to possible publishers outlining Perera's innovative thesis. They highlight the difficulties at that time of getting theses published using Anglo-American data.
41. The 'double account' idea appeared elsewhere. Chambers supervised a staff member of the time, Trevor Wise, until he moved to the University of Melbourne in the mid-to-late 1980s where he completed his PhD in the early1990s. His examined how to account properly for oil companies' operations; focussing on how to account for the underground reserves and sunk costs in bringing those reserves to the surface.
42. Chambers (1976d, 145–6).
43. Chambers' letter to a representative of the National Audit Office, P202, #9684, 09/12/1991.

5 Management Educator

My own conclusion, long ago, was that reform is slow; it proceeds through the educational processes in civilizations organized like ours; and one way of stimulating the rejection of what is parasitic is therefore to force educators themselves to recognize it.

—Chambers' letter to Abe Briloff, 1983

Perhaps the most striking feature of the human condition, . . . across all fields of knowledge and inquiry, is the reluctance of the masses to tolerate things different from what they have become accustomed to. The tiny proportion of the world's population that is inveteratively inquisitive has always had the greatest difficulty in having novelty accepted. Accounting is . . . the business of 'the masses'—the vast number of practitioners and teachers who are not even mildly inquisitive. Their penchant for crooked thinking and closing their eyes to the commonplaces of everyday life is a universal. Much more comfortable is it to mouth the creed of the last generation than to take issue with its oversights, tergiversations and humbug.

—Chambers' letter to Tom Lee, 1990[1]

While Chambers' technical college teaching posts were across the accounting sector, by the mid-to-late 1940s management was his clear focus. His many early works reveal an understanding (not shared by many) that accounting, finance and management disciplines were not isolates but integrals. That they were applied disciplines would influence substantially his reasoning. The first edition of *Financial Management* was published in 1947, followed closely by articles during 1948–50 which included 'Business Finance and the Analysis of Financial Statements,' 'The Training of Accountants,' 'Accounting and Management,' 'Incentives for Industry,' 'Accounting and Shifting Price Levels,' 'Budgetary Control' and 'Depreciation and Replacement Cost.' This view of the commercial world and accounting's function would also underpin his early University of Sydney Extension and Appointments Board lectures, as well as his involvement with the Australian Institute of Management (AIM) and invited Mount Eliza (Victoria) Australian Administrative Staff College (AASC) lectures which began in 1958 and continued for over a decade.[2]

The following from 'An Academic Apprenticeship' illustrates Chambers' observations of early management, especially *financial management* and its connection (or lack of it) with accounting:

> My experience [in the late 1930s and 1940s war years] of manufacturing and distributions was of firms that depended for action on prompt factual information on physical flows and stocks, and on physical specifications of inputs and outputs and indicators of performance. By contrast, the kind of accounting I had learned, and on which all firms presumably depended, was of the conventional, historical kind—long out of date in many respects and having little relation to immediate exigencies, except for cash, receivables and payables.[3]

Early Thoughts

Sydney Technical College

Chambers' first full-time academic position was as a lecturer at the School of Management at Sydney Technical College in 1945, which grew to become the largest post-secondary educational institution in the state before various parts were spun off as separate institutions. In the School of Management, Chambers worked alongside Bruce Brown, another two full-time lecturers, including Bryan Smyth who later became the foundation Professor of Accountancy at the University of New South Wales and several part-time teachers. At this time of tremendous growth, it was commonplace for a small group of individuals to cover all the courses offered at its three locations in Sydney, Newcastle, and Wollongong. Chambers, however, still found time to introduce a course in financial management in 1946 and a graduate diploma course in management in 1949. Moreover, because there were no courses in financial management in Australia at this time, he had to hand-collect much of the material from local sources such as newspapers and firms in the Sydney central business district in between his various teaching assignments.

While teaching and developing coursework, Chambers actively sought opportunities to put his new educational material on accounting and financial management to wider use. One part of this effort was publishing articles in *The Australian Accountant*, a practitioner journal and the only professional outlet for accounting in Australia at the time. These articles covered the relationship between accounting information and various internal and external decision uses as well as more topic-specific areas such as accounting measurements.[4]

The other part was the teaching of the material outside the college. This began with Extension and Appointments Board lectures on behalf of the Centre for Continuing Education in 1946. This centre had been established at the University of Sydney in 1886—the first lecture series delivered by the

English classical scholar Walter Scott (1855–1925) and author of *The Principles of Cost Accounting* which was published posthumously in 1944. It remains the longest running adult education program in the country. Chambers' first lectures were on the subject of financial management,[5] but over the next two decades he gave more than thirty lectures on a diverse set of topics, such as corporate governance, incentive problems, and investor relations. Some of these were day-long engagements and, at least for the later ones, he enlisted his colleagues to assist in teaching the often-voluminous material they covered.[6]

His second appointment was as a member of the Australian Institute of Management in 1951. The institute had been founded as a non-profit organization in 1941, with the sole purpose of advancing managerial education in Australia (it is the largest such organization in the country today). Its initial name had been the Institute of Industrial Management, but the new title was adopted in 1949. Omitting 'industrial' from its name recognized management education had to be broader and more inclusive of its neighbouring disciplines, such as accounting. This had been the same line of thought that underpinned the development of Chambers' teaching material and had been adopted in his published works.

At the AIM, Chambers served on the Financial Management Panel, which ran a series of conferences, lectures, and forums on financial management for executives.[7] The institute was organized in a number of divisions and Chambers worked out of the Sydney office of the New South Wales and Australian Capital Territory division. There were also offices in Adelaide, as part of the South Australian division, and Melbourne, as part of the Victorian and Tasmanian divisions. Offices were set up in Canberra in the late 1950s, and Darwin in the mid-1970s. As part of the panel, Chambers would have had influence over the design of lecture series and occasionally he delivered lectures.[8] On these occasions, he often drew on newly developed material, such as that in *Accounting and Action*, which he presented for the first time during a lecture in Newcastle in 1958.

The Training of Accountants

Chambers' initiative to participate but also shape the activities of the Sydney Technical College, the Centre for Continuing Education and the AIM came from an early conviction that accounting- and management-related curricula were in desperate need of reform. Being extremely dissatisfied with the state of the accounting profession, he was an agent of change in the education of its current and prospective members. Some thoughts on this matter are set out in 'The Training of Accountants,' which was published in *The Australian Accountant* in 1948. There he began by distinguishing between the *training* of specific methods and procedures, which tended to restrict critical reasoning, and the broader notion of education for which the profession should strive:

> Education may be considered as a process by which the innate qualities of the student are drawn out and developed, and by which the student's mind is enriched both because of the experience suffered and because of the knowledge gained. Teaching to be really educational should, therefore, aim to provide such stimuli for the student that he goes forward seeking an understanding of the principles of his subject rather than sitting back smug in the knowledge that he "swatted" the correct material for the examination.[9]

Accounting, Chambers continued, has been a subject of 'much training but little education.' He based this impression on two pieces of evidence. The first was his accounting teaching experience; the second, the borrowing records of the Commonwealth Institute of Accountants' library. According to these records, the members of the institute seldom borrowed items outside the standard accounting textbooks and very rarely consulted literature from neighbouring disciplines of economics, finance, management, and statistics. This limited reading had turned what should be a broad educational experience into the training of accounting procedures and techniques, often through methods of rote-learning and memorization. Such an environment did not allow teachers or students to be sufficiently critical of their subject, which was evident in the lack of a comprehensive body of Australian accounting literature and his need to develop his own teaching material.

To transition from accounting 'training' to 'education' and thus elevate the professional status of the discipline, Chambers proposed three steps. First, the accounting 'course of study must resemble in admission qualifications, in structure and in scope, other University courses.'[10] Second, the curriculum must include training in scientific methods and, third, courses should include both practical and theoretical material. He believed that this new theoretical material should be integrated into the existing curriculum and had to cover areas such as the historical development of accounting theory; the relationship between economic and accounting theory; and the relationship between accounting and general management, which would have come from his managerial teaching experience. 'A sound accounting syllabus,' he wrote: 'should recognize that many professional accountants become directors of companies; that quite a number of commercial accountants become directors or managers of the enterprises they serve; and that all who progress no further than the middle executive level are constantly in contact with other specialists in a service capacity which they are only qualified to fill if they acknowledge explicitly the limitations of their techniques and the importance of the *facts* which they endeavour to record. Recognition of these things should take the form of some managerial studies in formal training for accountants, firstly, so that a narrow technological bias may be corrected, and secondly, so that accounting may be set in its true perspective in the field of business.'[11]

That experience demonstrates an emphasis on situating accounting in the context of other managerial disciplines. In terms of concrete proposals, he presented a sequence of coursework divided into the fields of accounting and auditing, law, and economics and business. This started with intermediate accounting and auditing and then transitioned into business statistics, advanced accounting, auditing and investigations, and the history of accounting theory and practice. The inclusion of 'investigation' is again demonstrative of his emphasis on making connections between accounting and other disciplines, in this case between the narrow field of auditing and the broader, investigation field. The second field would include commercial, company, and taxation law, and the third started with scientific methods and transitioned into general economics, financial economics, and business management.

In 1948 Chambers still had to decide on the relative weighting of the different courses in his proposed curriculum. He also admitted that his proposal should be seen as a long-term goal that might only be reached gradually. Nonetheless, he felt comfortable that the curriculum would, when implemented, accomplish the goal of 'a wider training and a more selective training for accountants, as a basis for a broader outlook on business and community life than narrow specialization bestows.'[12] And as his educationalist experience deepened over the next two decades, further details of Chambers' vision for managerial education reform would emerge.

Second Thoughts

The University of Sydney

Chambers' appointment at Sydney University was part of a series made by Syd Butlin aimed at expanding the Faculty of Economics. Butlin was known to be a resourceful and frugal dean with little interest in micromanaging his staff. Chambers was therefore given considerable freedom to 'do as you must,' a directive he took to heart as he set out to continue his reform of accounting education.[13] And, operating with considerable autonomy, Chambers would remain with the university for the rest of his career.

In the Faculty of Economics he joined three part-time instructors in accounting covering the coursework in accounting in the Bachelor of Economics program. Throughout this period of rapid expansion and transformation, however, Chambers remained closely engaged in all matters of the department (even down to the reviewing and editing of the staff's drafts of student exam questions). This meant that Chambers was demanding of both his faculty and students, but he was never perceived as unfair or heavy-handed. Instead, the result of his efforts was the fostering of collegiality and a tight-knit community that rallied around his goal of reforming accounting education and financial reporting.[14]

With the support of Butlin and the Faculty, and based on his experiences, Chambers began reshaping managerial education at university soon after his initial appointment. His first change to the curriculum was the introduction of coursework on accounting theory construction, analysis, and historical development.

The introduction of an honours program in accounting in 1957 followed. It comprised the fourth year of a student's regular degree program and covered business finance, history of accounting, and the development of accounting thought. The literature for this program was drawn from a wide range of sources and comprised original documents or material focused on the historical developments of certain aspects of accounting. The selection was consistent with Chambers' vision to equip students with the necessary foundation to think critically about contemporary accounting practices and link their subject to other managerial disciplines.

Initially students would read such items as the original British Joint Stock Companies Act of 1844, official U.S. SEC regulations, and Chambers' 1947 *Financial Management*. Then serious scholarly material was introduced— from some of the most prominent accounting thinkers of the time—such as James Don Edwards' *History of Public Accounting in the United States*, Paul Garner's *Evolution of Cost Accounting to 1925*, and Littleton's *Accounting Evolution to 1900*. Finally students were introduced to alternative ways to think about accounting, such as those proposed in the early twentieth century U.S. writings of Sprague, Hatfield, Paton, Canning, Gilman, and Sweeney.[15]

In developing further coursework, he drew on his international experiences of having canvassed the curriculum of various universities abroad. Upon his return to Australia at the end of 1959, Chambers was one of few local academics who would have had such a broad knowledge of foreign institutions and their managerial education curricula. However, as none of the institutions he had visited offered the kind of material that he had sought to develop in Sydney, Chambers found himself designing coursework from scratch yet again. He introduced a Master of Economics in Accounting in 1966. This was followed in 1967 by the introduction of courses, Development of Accounting Thought, Foundations of Continuously Contemporary Accounting, and revisions to the undergraduate Auditing program. He then introduced the MBA program (Accounting and Finance specialization). It spanned six nine-week term units (i.e., two years) with classes delivered twice a week in the evening. Each unit was given a theme that built upon the content of the previous one, starting with 'The Structure, Management and Regulation of the Modern Corporation' and ending with 'Corporate

Dilemmas, Difficulties and Disasters' in the fifth. In the capstone unit Chambers delivered 'Reconstruction of Accounting' to highlight the underpinnings of his accounting system, Continuously Contemporary Accounting. In the 1980s Murray Wells later redesigned this program into a general Master of Business Administration offering.[16]

Chambers' final major change to the university curriculum was the introduction of a PhD by thesis program in 1972. Modelled on the traditional British doctoral program, it consisted primarily of closely supervised independent study. This contrasted with the contemporary American program, which had a significant portion of required coursework. He worked closely with nearly all the students accepted into this program under his supervision, with the first doctoral degree awarded to Wells in 1974. Chapter 2 showed that many doctoral degrees were awarded over the next decade. Upon graduation, several of these individuals came to share his convictions regarding the future direction of accounting education and curricula.

Australian Administrative Staff College

While working at the university, Chambers continued to seek external opportunities to teach his new educational material on accounting and financial management. Such an opportunity arose when Harry Slater, Fitzgerald's successor as the editor of *The Australian Accountant*, accepted an administrative position at the newly established Australian Administrative Staff College in December 1956. Slater was promoted to dean in 1963.[17]

The inspiration to establish a college for education in advanced administration in Australia had its origins in March 1955 in a speech given by Noel Hall to the New South Wales Regional Group of the Institute of Public Administration. Hall had been a professor of Political Economy at University College London and later spent some time at Princeton University's Institute for Advanced Study. He had then returned to Britain to establish the Administrative Staff College at Henley-on-Thames in 1945 (today known as Henley Business School at the University of Reading). He later served as the principal of Brasenose College, a constituent college at Oxford University, from 1960 to 1973.

Hall was known for his work on business theory and education, and as the first principal of the college he had designed its curriculum. This curriculum drew its material from prominent guest lecturers and the writings of Lyndall Urwick, a well-known British management consultant and later one of the founders of *Administrative Science Quarterly*. Its emphasis was on discerning the qualities of good administrators, and it drew inspiration from influential public servants including Donald Banks, Geoffrey Heyworth, and Hector Hetherington.

The University College had been established to offer instruction in advanced administration to senior executives from Her Majesty's Civil Service, nationalized industries and private enterprise. The Australian counterpart was established to fulfil a similar function, drawing senior executives from private enterprise, trade unions, and federal, local, and municipal government departments. The executives were admitted based on their experience, not necessarily their formal education, and the college sought a balanced admission with individuals drawn from a variety of fields. The average age of the British executives attending the college had been thirty-eight years, and it was envisioned that the executives attending the Australian college would be of similar age. In this regard the college did not seek to compete with university undergraduate programs or the Australian Institute of Management, where Chambers had been delivering lectures to younger professionals.

Douglas Copland, the former dean of the Faculty of Economics and Commerce at the University of Melbourne, had been appointed as the inaugural principal of the Australian Administrative Staff College. Harry Slater was then recruited with other administrative staff to prepare for the first cohort of executives starting classes in September 1957.[18] The structure and content of the curriculum were similar to those offered at Henley, with an additional focus on Australia and its relationship with the world economy. Each session was three months and in residence at the college, which was located in Mount Eliza, Victoria. Each cohort consisted of forty executives, divided into four groups with their own group leader. The principal delivered lectures together with other visiting authorities in various managerial fields.

The coursework topics entailed an introduction to administration, internal organization, accounting and financial control, external relations, and the establishment, growth, and adaption to change. As in its British counterpart, each student also had to read two biographies and write an essay on the qualities of a good administrator.[19] Slater reached out in June 1960 to see whether Chambers would be willing on an adjunct teaching basis to deliver one of the sections, titled 'Delegation, Control, and Accountability,' as part of the accounting and financial control curriculum. Chambers agreed to this, and the lecture was such a success that he continued to deliver the accountability section to another ten cohorts.[20] His last lecture there was delivered in 1976. The college merged with Melbourne Business School, the graduate business school of the University of Melbourne, in 2004.

Educational Policy: A Suggestion

Chambers' thoughts on managerial and accounting education continued to evolve in the 1950s, informed by his commercial education and Prices Commission experiences. The products of this are to be found in 'Educational Policy: A Suggestion,' which was published in *The Australian Accountant* in 1956.

Having made the case for the desirability of education over training in 'The Training of Accountants,' Chambers began with what he saw as the three major sources that dictate the content of this education. The first, customs or conventional practices, was the least justifiable. The second was current practical needs, and although occasionally necessary ran the risk of not giving the student a general sense of the subject and the relationship between its constituent parts and other disciplines. The third was the striving for more encompassing 'concepts of professional education and competence.'[21] If the concepts are well defined and desirable, however, the third source could guide curriculum design to encompass both particular expertise and a broader understanding. He argued that the relative weight of the sources was due for a realignment:

> The absence of theoretical and analytical material, and the belief that accounting is essentially a set of definite and questionable procedures, would have obliged them [i.e., educators] to fill out the course with specific types of accounting. . . . The consequence has been that students find little more in the whole subject than rules and technicalities. . . . To depend on variety when there was little depth was good enough in its time. But now variety may well be replaced. There is a large and growing literature devoted to the discussion of accounting ideas, and techniques may well bow to it.[22]

Drawing on the third source as a guide to curriculum design, Chambers proposed several competences that all accounting students should seek to develop. The simplest was the skill to prepare accounts. Another was the fostering of an understanding of the underlying forces of these accounts. The third, and the most difficult to attain, was the ability to think clearly and to reason cogently. The last had not been sufficiently developed in current accounting curricula. The emphasis on detailed rules for accounting procedures, derived from customs and conventional practices, did not do enough to aid students in critical thinking of the kind that is desirable in a professional. As an alternative to current educational practices, Chambers sought a curriculum that: 'should develop breadth of vision and understanding. This it will be able to do if it incorporates some studies which serve to portray accounting in its *historical setting* and in its *contemporary business environment* [emphasis added], and if it includes some studies at greater depth, even if this means fewer superficial studies of particular sorts of accounts. Rather than a lot of slim sandwiches, a few "dagwoods" would seem to be the appropriate diet.'[23]

Unlike the curriculum proposed in 1948, which was divided into accounting, law, and economics, Chambers now sought to develop the coursework along three stages. Each stage contained three streams of courses: technical, legal, and theoretical. The technical and legal streams covered current accounting practices and this knowledge was necessary, but it was the theoretical stream that enabled students to think more critically about their subject matter, through the introduction of its historical development, its relationship to other managerial practices, and to alternative accounting methods to those currently used in practice.

Chambers conceded that some of the necessary literature for his ideal curriculum had yet to emerge. These difficulties, however, were not insurmountable. At the University of Sydney he had proved as much through the development of accounting coursework, drawn from the literature and source documents (e.g., U.S. SEC pronouncements and the U.K. City Takeover Code). As such, he concluded the article:

> Whatever merits or faults the main proposal of this note may have, a point mentioned at the beginning stands clear. Educational policy and standards need to be developed deliberately, with an explicit and widely known purpose. . . . Progress on a broad front will not be achieved without common knowledge of what is considered to be an ideal professional education.[24]

Third Thoughts

The Institute of Management Sciences

From the 1960s Chambers became increasingly engaged with the development of accounting and managerial education internationally. This primarily took the form of extensive visits to the United States, which was at the forefront in the establishment of dedicated schools of business.[25] After his first sabbatical, we noted he returned to the U.S. on five occasions (1962–80) to spend significant time at various institutions. He also visited prominent universities in other countries, including Lancaster and the London Business School in England, Glasgow and Edinburgh in Scotland, Simon Fraser, British Columbia, Saskatchewan, and Alberta in Canada, the University of Singapore, the Universities of Canterbury, Wellington, Massey and Otago in New Zealand, Waseda, Kobe, Soka, Hitotsubashi in Japan, and the University of Cape Town in South Africa.[26]

The university visits were of two kinds. The more traditional involved the delivery of an occasional lecture, seminar or speech. The most prominent of these was Chambers' appointment as the inaugural American Accounting Association's Distinguished Visiting Lecturer, which involved his touring ten universities in 1976. Less traditional visits were Chambers' semester-long teaching appointments. Several of these were in the form of endowed chairs, such as the Edmund P. Learned Professorship at the University of Kansas, the George A. Miller Professorship at the University of Illinois at Urbana—Champaign, and the Walker Ames Professorship at the University of Washington (Seattle). Because of the nature of these latter arrangements, Chambers engaged in the development of curricula (available in the

Chambers Archive) and in coursework at these institutions in ways not possible during a more traditional academic visit.

In addition to this influence, Chambers' interest in the development of accounting and managerial education was shaped by the activities of the College of Measurements at The Institute of Management Sciences (TIMS). The institute had been established in December 1953, during a gathering of management academics at Columbia University in the City of New York (today Columbia University). Its purpose was to promote 'scientific management,' an approach to managerial research which had emerged after World War II and was based on the same scientific methods of experimentation, inquiry, and research found in the natural sciences.[27] This institute merged in 1995 with the Operations Research Society of America to form the Institute for Operations Research and the Management Sciences (INFORMS).

The founders of TIMS believed strongly that knowledge is best advanced when different disciplines come together. The institute was therefore set up to allow for dedicated colleges, the purpose of which was to draw on the expertise of specialized disciplines and apply that to specific areas of scientific management. One such section was the College of Measurements, which had been established in 1958[28] through the initiative of Ernst Weinwurm—former TIMS President in 1954 and Associate Professor of Accounting at DePaul University—after he had failed to find support for the arrangement of a similar group under the auspices of the American Accounting Association.[29] This new college had the full backing of the 1958 institute president and college founder, George Kozmetsky, as well as 1959 president-elect Melvin Salveson.[30]

Chambers joined the College of Measurements in 1960 and TIMS the following year. He remained a member in the latter until 1971. His decision to join came through his association with Weinwurm, who had corresponded with Chambers after reading his 1955 'Blueprint for a Theory of Accounting.'[31] As Dean and Clarke show in their work in *The Accounting Historians Journal*, from the beginning of their correspondence it became clear that both scholars were deeply concerned with the promotion of a more scientific approach to accounting research and education.[32] These shared concerns would lead to a friendship spanning almost thirty years, and Chambers often arranged to see Weinwurm during his visits to the United States.

The correspondence with Weinwurm, and participation in the activities of the College of Measurements, led Chambers to become increasingly concerned with the measurement function of accounting. On the urging of his new colleague, Chambers turned to 1950s and '60s general literature on measurement and read such items as Churchman's (also a TIMS member) *Prediction and Optimal Decision*, Hempel's *Fundamentals of Concept Formation in Empirical Sciences* and Margenau's *The Nature of Physical Reality*.

Early evidence of the influence of this literature on Chambers came during a presentation on measurement at a TIMS meeting in Chicago in 1959.[33]

This same literature eventually led to a permanent shift in Chambers' views on accounting measurements and the establishment of current exit prices as the uniform measurement basis for his accounting system, Continuously Contemporary Accounting. In fact, according to his recollection of these events, the notion of scientifically proper measurements was so important that from the mid-1960s it became a cornerstone of much of his views on accounting—including the education and training of accountants.[34]

Professional Education

Chambers' increased concerns about 'scientific methods' and that accounting should be based on a measurement system that conforms to the type of valid measurements applying in the natural sciences are evident in his 1960s writings. This was also the case in his works on accounting and managerial education, the manuscript 'Professional Education' being an example. Chambers had written this in response to a 1964 report on the subject by Vatter, which had been commissioned by the Australian Society of Accountants, the ICAA, and the Australasian Institute of Cost Accountants.

In 1965 Chambers presented the manuscript during the Australasian Association of University Teachers of Accounting Conference, Melbourne. His critique of the report was that it lacked precision in definition of the subject matter (both accounting and education) and that it was too narrowly focused on technical details. As he had argued in 'The Training of Accountants' and 'Educational Policy: A Suggestion,' Chambers had no interest in solely technical programs of this kind. Instead, he opted for an educational program that both probed deeper and stretched wider:

> We seek broadly a good professional man. The first requirement shall be that he is technically expert in a limited field. . . . The second requirement shall be that his conception of his professional task is tempered by an understanding of and a sympathy with the environment of that task. At its simplest, this means an understanding of the place of the expert and the function of his task in the immediate environment.[35]

With the aim of producing a 'good professional man,' Chambers proceeded to list eight attributes he believed to be necessary as a foundation for the specialized practice of accounting. Some of these would have been familiar to Chambers' earlier readers, such as knowledge of business systems and communication; legal and social processes; as well as markets and prices.[36]

The other components were new. Three of these appear to have been influenced by his experiences at TIMS and its goal of scientific management. In addition to the earlier requirement for an understanding of the historical development of accounting, he was now convinced that an ideal curriculum should include knowledge of the historical development of science and the scientific method. Coupled with this, he also felt that the accountant should be trained in the current state of the art of empirical inquiry and possess an understanding of the relationship between experience and expectations (i.e., the distinction between empirical observations and predictions). This, of course, resonated with the earlier emphasis on fostering a critical spirit that enabled students to question current accounting practices.

The remaining components once again appear to have been influenced by Chambers' correspondence with Weinwurm and his experience participating in the College of Measurements. The first was knowledge of the cognitive limitations of individuals and the second, 'knowledge of the theory and methods of classification, measurement and calculation.'[37] Chambers emphasized that it was particularly important to teach students to distinguish what can be measured, to understand the conditions under which this is the case, and when calculation is therefore necessary. Consistent with his long-term goal of tying accounting education to the wider context of managerial education and the business environment, Chambers observed:

> It will be apparent that this list has two features. Every item has a specific relation to the actual practice of accounting as a general expertise. And every item has also a wider aspect which contributes to awareness of or sensitivity to the general characteristics of living, in large or small groups as occasion demands.[38]

In terms of the required material and the teaching of a curriculum of this kind, Chambers argued that the nascent accounting literature no longer posed a problem for implementation. Instead, he suggested the compilation of literature from relevant disciplines, much in the same way that TIMS had done through its system of specialized colleges. And since this process did not necessarily depend on the development of new literature, he maintained that the accounting profession no longer faced a major problem. The task essentially fell on the teachers of accounting to compile the necessary literature. He wrote:

> Being integrated with what we believe to be necessary professional education, the treatment does not depend on the availability of general texts in the related fields or on the "servicing" of studies by experts in those fields. It depends rather on the actual interweaving of the appropriate propositions or findings of experts in other fields with the technical features of accounting as and when they become necessary. The task is entirely in the hands of teachers of accounting as such. They alone have the particular orientation necessary to select from the findings of logicians, scientists, psychologists, economists, and others, those which are pertinent to accounting.[39]

Whereas the previous articles on reforming accounting education had offered various fields of study and several stages, Chambers did not want to impose such a restriction on the current proposal. This was so because the weighting of his components was not essential to the general goal of integrating accounting with its educational and professional environment. Instead, what mattered was the unshackling of accounting from 'long-standing habits' and towards demonstrable empirical inquiry. He noted that this had caused accounting education and practice so much harm:

> The myths, the fictions, the unsystematic nature of present doctrines, we have gone on accepting, largely we believe because of the long divorcement of accounting from other fields. Ill-considered accretions will only compound the present confusion; a major reconstruction, one could hope, would do much to eliminate the illogical, the patently irrelevant, and the obfuscating features of doctrine and practice.[40]

His views on the latest suggestions in Australia to replicate overseas management education programs are well summarized in a March 1966 letter to the editor published in the *Australian Financial Review*. As was common in his writings he uses analogy, hyperbole and careful observations to capture his concerns:

> The soft habit of taking our ideas from others is far too prevalent . . . [as is accepting the view that] teaching institutions should be staffed by people who have "practical" experience and who are actually consultants or advisers to business. . . . I have not heard it said that people who need psychiatric advice should consult neurotics or psychotics; or that to be a psychiatrist one must be round the bend. More human knowledge originates in a patient and careful observation (without involvement) than ever emerges from participation. And most of the advances in human knowledge arise from being sceptical about the "conventional wisdom" of the practitioner.[41]

An Educational Legacy

Chambers was instrumental in pioneering a type of managerial and accounting education in Australia. Through his appointments at the Sydney Technical College and the University of Sydney, as well as his guest lectures at the Australian Institute of Management and Australian Administrative Staff College, he remained an innovator. Each engagement ran parallel with the introduction of new degree programs, coursework, and educational material that linked accounting with other managerial subjects in ways that had not been done before in Australia. In hindsight, it has also become clear that those who were exposed to this innovative material benefited greatly from it, such as the graduates from Sydney's Master of Economics in Accounting and PhD by thesis programs.[42]

In another sense, much of Chambers' educational vision remains unfulfilled, as indicated in his 'unfinished business' discussed in chapter 9. Whereas the details of 'The Training of Accountants,' 'Educational Policy: A Suggestion,' and 'Professional Education' vary, there is a unifying theme of exposing accounting students to a wider array of neighbouring disciplines and their relationship with the subject of accounting. There is also a unifying theme of forcing students to probe deeper into the historical roots of accounting and to question contemporary practices. What has transpired since those articles were written, however, is the proliferation of accounting curricula that are increasingly dogmatic and aimed at passing professional examinations rather than encouraging critical, constructive thinking. Chambers viewed this as a regression. Contemporary accounting students are rarely exposed to the kind of thoughtful material Chambers sought to introduce in his coursework programs. With accounting now firmly established as an important business discipline, management teachers would do well to heed his call for less 'training' in favour of more 'education.' We show in chapter 9 that Chambers' post-retirement accounting education articles lamented this was not occurring.

Interestingly, as discussed later, some financial accounting research has also regressed with its emphasis on capital markets research and critical accounting research. Whittington has suggested to the authors that it is difficult to identify an accounting component in some of that capital markets research.[43]

Notes

1. Chapter epigraph:
   Chambers' letter upon his retirement to contemporary, U.S. accounting critic Abraham Briloff, P202 #7682, 17/02/1983.
   Chambers' letter to colleague and contemporary accounting critic, Professor Tom Lee, P202, #7197, 01/08/1990.
2. Chambers (2000, 'Aide Memoire,' Section 9—Articles) provides full details.
3. Chambers (1991a, 103). Interestingly, several decades after Chambers' post-WWII experiences Johnson and Kaplan's *Relevance Lost* (1987) told a similar story.
4. He mentions numerous general decision-making uses (e.g., Chambers, 1948a, 1948b, 1950b); and in respect of specific uses, the role of accounting measurements (e.g., Chambers, 1949a; 1949b, 1950a).
5. As reported in P202, #27, 15/09/1948.
6. P202, #4982, 12/05/1976.
7. P202, #266, 01/03/1958.
8. P202, #627, 23/05/1960.
9. Chambers (1948b, 322).
10. Chambers (1948b, 324).
11. Chambers (1948b, 326).
12. Chambers (1948b, 327).
13. Chambers (1990, 144).
14. For more about these events, especially staffing and course development over this period, see Clarke *et al.* (2012, especially chapter 4) and Wolnizer and Dean (2000).

15. Reference details are to Edwards (1960), Garner (1954), Littleton (1933), Sprague (1907/17), Hatfield (1909), Paton (1922), Canning (1929), Sweeney (1936) and Gilman (1939).
16. For more about this curriculum, see Appendix II in Clarke *et al.* (2012).
17. Information is taken from P202, #179, 28/12/1956 and #1106, 19/08/1963.
18. Slater to Chambers, P202, #179, 28/12/1956.
19. For more about the establishment of the college, see Copland (1957).
20. P202, #645, 01/06/1960 and #646, 28/09/1960.
21. Chambers (1956, 74).
22. Chambers (1956, 74).
23. Chambers (1956, 76).
24. Chambers (1956, 80).
25. For more about the attitude towards such institutions in the United Kingdom, see Napier (1996).
26. For a complete list of institutions, see Appendix 14 in Chambers and Dean (2000e, and Chambers (2000e)).
27. For more about these events, see Salveson (1997).
28. P202, #124, 26/11/57.
29. Details about this are in the Chambers Archive correspondence, for example, P202, #176, 01/12/1955; #238, 06/12/1956; #121, 01/03/1957. Weinwurm was promoted to full professor in 1959.
30. P202, #124, 26/11/1957.
31. P202, #173, 25/08/1955.
32. Dean and Clarke (2010a) and also P202, #175, 20/10/1955 and #177, 01/12/1955.
33. P202, #498, 04/06/1959. This presentation was published as Chambers (1960a).
34. P202, #8175, 13/04/82 reflecting on the measurement and other debates in the early 1960s; and #6651, 25/01/1983.
35. Dean and Clarke (2010a, 14–15).
36. Around the time of this work, the ASA in conjunction with the universities and technical institutes were discussing the prospect of revisions to the necessary course requirements for tertiary accounting graduates to be able to qualify to undertake the admission examination. Chambers presumed the aim was to ensure 'that a comprehensive test of knowledge and understanding would result.' Chambers was integrally involved in those deliberations. An excellent summary of the pertinent issues is provided in an eleven A-4 page, single-spaced appendix to a letter that Chambers wrote to the relevant ASA Councillors and other members of the ASA in September1968—P202, #11257, 18/09/1968.
37. Chambers (1965b, 45).
38. Chambers (1965b, 46).
39. Chambers (1965b, 46).
40. Chambers (1965b, 49).
41. Extract from Chambers' published letter to the editor, 'Soft and Hard Management Training,' *AFR*, 2 March 1966, recorded in P202, #8658. The letter was written on 24/02/1966 in response to commentary on Australia's Martin Report on Management Education and similar U.S. reports in the late 1950s and early 1960s. He laments in the letter that little of the ideas of thoughtful people who have concerned themselves with the problems of education—such as, A.N. Whitehead, Jacques Barzun, Ortega y Gasset, Philipp Frank—has found its way into business education programs.
42. Clarke *et al.* (2012).
43. Whittington (1990/2007). Chambers' (1974a) and (1993) critiques of stock market-based accounting research are other examples. Endnote #s32, chapter 3, #10, chapter, 6 and related text discusses Chambers' reservations about critical accounting research.

6   Theoretician:

A New System of Accounting—CoCoA

Whether he believes it or not, Ray has made the future of CoCoA secure.
—Stamp, 1982

Living is full of arrangements and occasions by which we come to terms with our physical and social environments. We prefer peaceable, orderly arrangements. Things we can change, we change when necessary. We decide, we legislate. Things we cannot change we strive to understand. We research, which is just another way of saying we strive to refine and extend our understanding of the way things are and how they work. From elementary bits of knowledge, elaborate bodies of knowledge and powerful devices have been constructed—all from the conjunction, on the one hand, of what we observed to be the nature of and the relations between things observed and experienced, and, on the other hand, of decisions to exploit those natures and relations.
—Chambers, 'In Quest of a Framework,' 1995[1]

Chambers is best known for works as an accounting theorist. As the American Accounting Association's 1977 *Statement on Accounting Theory and Theory Acceptance* (*SATTA*) monograph acknowledges, developing his CoCoA system and related writings resulted in him being regarded by the SATTA committee and others as one of the 'golden age' accounting theorists.[2]

Throughout, this narrative reveals Chambers' pleas for a fundamental rethink of accounting thought and practice, stemming from a concern about accounting's parlous state. He observed in a letter to Tom Lee that his December 1991 *Accounting Horizons* article: 'should make it clear that all the debate in accounting has arisen through "internal definitions" that have little to do with commercial affairs; and that a whole, self-consistent theory and process can be derived from a few observations [and related economic propositions] constrained by logical and mathematical laws. Why that is not obvious to others is for them to say;

but so far, the excuses have all been piecemeal, not based on any systematic, self-consistent body of ideas.'[3]

In *Accounting, Evaluation and Economic Behavior* and other places Chambers argued that an accounting theory must entail a body of self-consistent propositions based on the observed wider (than accounting) domains of individual and group behaviour and economic organization. Further, accounting, like any instrument, has specific and limited functions. These ideas are illustrated in his hand-prepared lecture diagrams reproduced in Illustration 3.2 and Illustrations 6.1–6.6.

Chambers' pioneering theoretical works enquired into fundamentals, his 'premises or postulates.' Other theorists used different names: Moonitz described them simply as 'postulates,' Mattessich 'theorems,' and Ijiri 'axioms.' And they had differing ideas about the many fundamentals covered (for exposition below we will use postulates), such as adherence to measurement rules, regarding accounting as communication within an information system, and recognizing the dual functions of accounting, namely decision usefulness and accountability. Advocates of multiple postulates were in contrast to other contemporaries who advocated single postulates, such as Leonard Spacek's 'fairness,' David Solomons' 'accuracy,' Weinwurm's 'factual information,' and Briloff's 'integrity.' Irrespective of the number, calls persisted for more research into fundamentals, for more rigour in determining the profession's accounting postulates and principles that would underpin practice.

Chambers examined fundamental notions in many of his 1950s and '60s works. He later codified them in several places. As noted in chapter 3 this was especially so in *Foundations of Accounting*—his accounting conceptual framework. In examining further his ideas on the foundations of accounting and the development of CoCoA and his Sydney School, the influences of a number of forces (individuals and ideas) are noted—including several U.S. academics who provided the initial correspondence and, in time, U.S. and other networking opportunities, namely Professors Paton, Garner, Dixon, Martin Black, Moonitz, Mattessich, Zeff, and Weinwurm.[4] The Archive reveals many other academics corresponded with Chambers in the mid-to-late 1960s and beyond on foundational and other issues.

Specifically, in the price level accounting discussions, the notion of fair value and its drift into accounting are shown in chapter 8 to be a major influence on Chambers' thinking. Clarke (1980) argued those features were an example of the 'accidents of history' phenomenon. Importantly, as noted throughout the biography, Chambers distinguished fair value from his preferred notion of real exit value (value in exchange).

Considering financial and management matters as integrals, not isolates, underpinned Chambers' 1950s and later works that sought to resolve several problems simultaneously:

1. the measurement conundrum (as examined in debates with Moonitz, Ijiri, Mattessich, and discussions with others like Weinwurm and Sterling);
2. the accounting anomalies that arise in *unexpected* company failures—a subset of many asset and liability conundra in booms and busts (others also occur in takeover settings in economic boom periods); and
3. how to account systematically for the financial effects of price and price level changes.[5]

This perception of the problems being interconnected differentiated Chambers' ideas from those of most of his contemporaries. In response to an 'out of the blue' correspondence with John Hanks, a Melbourne mathematician, he observed that:

> It was only after wading through all the traditional accounting argument and related economic theory that I saw that the *whole* problem [i.e., the interconnectedness of the above problems] was soluble as a simple extension of a few mathematical principles and a few empirical propositions.[6]

Chambers' seminal *Towards a General Theory of Accounting* monograph of 1961 and its incorporation into *Accounting, Evaluation and Economic Behavior* are now examined.[7] A complex of normative and positive ideas is revealed as he sought accounting to be more scientifically based. Keen to distance himself from any attempts to divorce the normative from the positive in accounting research, he saw the empirical and analytical domains as inextricably linked. Trying to categorize things as either normative or positive was a fruitless, sterile exercise.[8]

This is most clearly seen in the criticisms by Chambers and others, including Sterling, of what became known in the 1970s and '80s as 'Positive Accounting Theory,' a set of ideas that emerged from one of the most cited articles in the accounting literature, 'Ball and Brown 1968' published in the *Journal of Accounting Research*.[9] Positivist accounting research was popularized in the 1970s in many of the Ross Watts and Jerry Zimmerman pieces, and codified in their 1986 book, *Positive Accounting Theory*. It has been noted that:

> Ball and Brown (1968) is "viewed as a prominent moment in the scientific transformation of accounting" (Reiter and Williams, 2002, 582, 592). In the same year Beaver (1968) helped form "the core of the capital markets paradigm, and spurred a growth industry in empirical-based accounting research" (Brown, 1996, 745).[10]

Assisting in understanding the early development of Chambers' theoretical ideas is his November 1971 submission pamphlet 'Accounting, Evaluation and Economic Behavior Explanatory Note,' prepared for examination by the University of Sydney of the award by publications of a DSc(Econ.). It describes *Accounting, Evaluation and Economic Behavior* as a system: 'of business accounting which [Chambers] later styled "continuously contemporary accounting [CoCoA]." Its principal elements are the use of market (selling) prices for the periodic valuation of business assets, and the use of price index adjustments for the measurement of periodical business income.'[11]

Interestingly, the second aspect is overlooked in most commentaries suggesting the features of CoCoA are similar to those of the fair value system. Several major differences exist. Contrary to CoCoA, fair value accounting: uses 'expectations' in determining 'level three fair values,' lacks a uniform measurement property for assets and liabilities and also lacks an inflation adjustment mechanism.

In the preface of the 1974 reprint of *Accounting Evaluation and Economic Behavior* Chambers observes that CoCoA 'is a lineal descendant of work begun some twenty years earlier. The first published indication of direction was "Blueprint for a Theory of Accounting" (*Accounting Research*, 1955). A more comprehensive development was offered in 1961 in *Towards a General Theory of Accounting*. These and others in the interval, and indeed the present volume, are to be considered as stages in the growth of an idea.'[12] Those other works included the late 1950s articles, 'A Scientific Pattern for Accounting Theory' and 'Detail for a Blueprint,' and the early 1960s articles, 'The Conditions of Research in Accounting,' 'Why Bother with Postulates,' 'Measurement in Accounting,' and 'The Role of Information Systems in Decision Making.'[13]

The pamphlet also fleshed-out the broad nature of the catalysts for developing his accounting system:

> The financial statements yielded by the [historical cost] system fail seriously to report on the financial states of companies and their results in terms of which are significant in day to day financial affairs. And they fail to satisfy the statutory principle that they should give a true and fair view of positions and results.
>
> As the financial information published by companies is widely used in the public securities markets and in private negotiations, the quality of that information has a significant bearing on the equity or fairness of stock market operations, and on the allocation of resources. The mode of accounting may influence the conclusions of observers, economists and public officials, based on the rates of profit earned by individual companies and by industrial groups of companies; indirectly it may influence relaxation of tariffs and the decisions of wages and

other tribunals. The traditional mode of accounting has been held by [Gottfried] Haberler and others to exacerbate swings in general business conditions by exaggerating the changes in the fortunes of business from year to year.[14]

With that backdrop, let's return to the practice and academic thought about accounting in the mid-to-late 1950s.

An Age of Experimentation, Discovery, and Innovation

Throughout the 1950s and '60s accounting research developed rapidly. Chambers' primary accounting theme was *decision usefulness*, and his primary moral focus was accounting's *accountability*—to tell it as it is, to provide reliable knowledge. Together with a few contemporaries he developed fundamentals as a way to overthrow the trendy metaphoric conventionsofaccountingpractices—namely,stewardshipandconservatism— known also at that time as doctrines. They had resulted in traditional accounting being the product of primarily historical cost-based allocations, conjectures, all part of what was known then as the process of 'matching' allocation-based costs and expenses with revenues. National standards setters for decades, and the international IFRS regime since 2005, have claimed that the matching process and related cost allocations are no longer dominant features of income determination and asset valuation in a fair value and impairment regime. We, and we believe would have Chambers, disagree.[15]

Returning to his search for premises, Chambers settled in his *Towards a General Theory* on four: (a) accounting entities are collaborative systems, (b) which are managed rationally,[16] (c) by recourse, inter alia, to accounting reports providing current and relevant financial information, and (d) the derivation of which is a service function. He then proposed forty postulates and twenty-one related principles. The title of an early 1960s article in New Zealand's *The Accountant's Journal*, 'Conventions, Doctrines and Commonsense,' captures what he perceived as the main issues. Although accounting was regarded by many as an accepted scientific discipline, Chambers viewed financial and management accounting practices as lacking common sense— a critical part of his understanding of what is scientific.

As discussed in the previous chapter, Chambers, unlike most other accountants, was moving in the circles of those in the broader management science area (especially Operations Research) and was corresponding with overseas academic founders of TIMS, such as William Cooper, Abraham Charnes, and Ernest Weinwurm.[17]

Chambers and other golden age theorists discussed the postulates and principles issues in many forums and papers. The present authors have published several accounts of their epistolary exchanges.[18] One, for example, considered the more than a hundred letters in the Chambers Archive over thirty years between Weinwurm and Chambers.[19] It showed how Chambers forged his ideas on measurement, theory development and decision, making; noting how an enduring, albeit sometimes tense, relationship between Chambers and Weinwurm produced subtle changes to the former's thoughts on measurement.

Another is the *Abacus* editorial review of thirty years of correspondence between Chambers and Briloff, 'Revisiting Chambers and Briloff on Accounting—Correspondence 1964–1993.' There, their views on matters of communication were shown to be quite different. Chambers focused on the faulty financial messages conveyed by the accounts, while Briloff centred on the misleading message provided by the words used in the audit opinion.[20]

Two other sets of exchanges from the Chambers Archive that have not been previously examined are now reviewed. The first, with Moonitz, concerns fifty-five letters between 1960 and 1965 (26 letters in 1961 and 15 in 1962); and the second, with Mattessich (thirty-seven between 1957 and 1995). Interestingly, Chambers visited many academics, *inter alios* Moonitz and Mattessich at University of California Berkeley on his first overseas sabbatical, not long after both had become familiar with Chambers' research works.[21]

Correspondence with Moonitz (AICPA Accounting Research Director at the time) began in April 1960 when he invited Chambers' 'untrammelled' comments on several AICPA Accounting Research Study (ARS) drafts.[22] Moonitz invited him to join the 1960–63 ARS program administered at the AICPA's New York office. Chambers agreed and corresponded often in 1961 and 1962 on ARS drafts; and he spent three months there in early 1962. Moonitz initially had been wary of such a lengthy stay, writing to Chambers: 'You are quite right in suspecting that I was a bit hesitant at first about committing myself to a longer period of time, but after seeing your draft on "General Theory" all hesitancy is gone.'[23]

Two extracts from letters to Moonitz are especially instructive about Chambers' concern with fundamentals. The first, in 1961, responding to a draft memorandum (antecedent) of the ARS1, *Basic Postulates*, monograph:

> On the exploration of the environment for postulates I agree. However, I do not think the exploration has been pushed back far enough, or into as many corners as are necessary. In particular, all accounting is done in the expectation of the use of its results by some person. The personal qualities of users of information seem to me to require some attention. True, you allude to rational decisions in several places (pp. 14, 38) but without reference to the underlying nature of economic action and without discussion of 'rational.'[24]

And later that year:

> Beneath my para. 2, p. 2 [in my letter of 27 January 1961], there is a fundamental uneasiness, a feeling that it is easy but not necessarily proper

to come closely to grips with currently accepted lore in the early stages of [your] inquiry. The emphasis on income measurement (found in official statements and followed by many writers) betrays a monistic view of accounting; I . . . take a pluralistic view as . . . there are several basic ideas of equal rank beneath any social study and beneath accounting in particular. Another facet of my uneasiness is the 'scheme' which the Special Committee adopted, the linkage of' postulates, principles and rules. That there is a relationship of this kind is admitted but there is a clear possibility that in the search for postulates existing rules may be so much in our minds that we see only those postulates which support the existing rules. The *priority* of the income statement is a piece of dogma at the moment. I have made some attempt to explode it in 'The Implications of Asset Revaluations and Bonus Share Issues' (*The Australian Accountant*, Nov. 1957 at pp. 513–14) and in 'The Function of the Balance Sheet' (*The Chartered Accountant in Australia*, April 1957, at pp. 565–7).

On expected exchanges (p. 40), my own ideas are not quite clear; hence my earlier questions [in previous letters]. If 'expected' is admitted, however, the propriety of subjective evaluations is admitted; expectation is subjective. 'Market price,' to refer to your example, is objective; but the choice of cost or market price is subjective, however widely the cost or market rule is accepted. My point about the historical record is that what has transpired can be assessed with more or less accuracy by competent observers. No one can *measure* the future; there is nothing to measure; one can only form expectations. Please understand my present ambivalence on the permissibility of expectations.[25] (emphasis added)

The letter (and subsequent ones) continues with specific observations on propositions in the draft research study. While Chambers' views differed in some areas, Moonitz was clearly keen to receive his observations.[26]

Contiguous with the publication in September 1961 of ARS1, Chambers mailed Moonitz (second class airmail—as money was never freely available at this time) his *Towards a General Theory* paper. It produced this response:

I am tremendously impressed by the manuscript. . . . It is a first-rate piece of work and it does clarify for me many of the points which you have been making in correspondence over the past year. The first part in particular does fill in the areas which I, in my study, skipped over or ignored.[27]

To flesh out some of those 'areas' and the need, as perceived by Chambers, to link postulates with principles, we visit his thoughts expressed in an early 1962 letter to Weinwurm in respect of the AICPA's ARS1 and ARS3:

The Special Committee of the Research Program had the right idea, in my opinion, in that principles would be derived from postulates.

My paper [*Towards a General Theory*] attempts to provide by cross-references the necessary linkage; but in the Sprouse and Moonitz [draft of the ARS3] paper apart from mentioning the Moonitz [ARS1] postulates there is no linkage of the principles with the postulates. I think that the Moonitz postulates, even if they were adequately differentiated and described, would be found inadequate to support the principles put forward. In this respect I disagree with the Special Committee's assumption that postulates would be few in number. For a "common-sense" general picture of accounting they may be few; but for any "scientific" picture they will necessarily be many, otherwise the deduced principles will lack precision and usefulness—in theoretical work or practice. I have redrafted the summary paragraphs of my paper to spell out about 40 postulates—a greater number than in the copy I sent you, but a greater number still than Moonitz identifies.[28]

Chambers really enjoyed his experiences at the AICPA as this extract from a 1962 letter to Moonitz indicates:

> May I again 'thank you' for the privilege and pleasure of working with you. The division seemed to possess a liveliness, an intense concern for and with the substantive problems of accounting, which one would hope to find in an accounting community but which few academic communities seem to possess in the same measure. It was most enjoyable.[29]

We now turn to the Chambers and Mattessich correspondence. It also examined the need for a fundamental rethink about accounting, again focusing on postulates. Mattessich wrote in 1957 commenting on Chambers' 'Blueprint' article. During 1957 and 1958 their correspondence continued.[30] In a biographical memoir, *Foundational Research in Accounting*, Mattessich reflected on their lengthy debates on postulates, measurement and related matters:

> Chambers (1966/75) presents a vast number of postulates and definitions without clearly indicating which are which. The processes of inductive inferences leading to the postulates, and of the deductive inferences leading to the many theorems thereby presented, cannot be traced. My own attempts to prove several of *his* theorems on the basis of the reference numbers given as hints by Chambers were a complete failure—this may be due to my own limitations.[31]

Earlier, again reflecting on their correspondence and published debates, Mattessich's (1980) 'Personal Account' in *Accounting and Business Research* challenged many of Chambers' ideas. After not corresponding with Mattessich for over two decades, but soon after the 'Personal Account' was published, Chambers was defiant and penned a letter away from the public spotlight, seeking to clarify the issues—in particular about postulates and related matters:

> We are both endowed with a liberal share of confidence in what we support. So, if there is a suspicion that one of us will not understand the other, the most congenial thing perhaps is to notice one another at a distance, in silence. . . . [But] [y]our 'Personal Account' in *ABR* prompts me to break the silence. . . . I recall that it was a pleasure to me in the mid-fifties to have a letter from you on the publication of the 'Blueprint' piece [USA P202, #245, 23/04/1957]. There were very few who were the least bit interested in analysis of the state of the game and the possibility of its reconstruction. But even that long ago there were differences between us. They can be illustrated by the differences between the content of my four premises of 1955 ['Blueprint'] and your eight theorems of 1957. ['Towards a General and Axiomatic Foundation of Accounting,' published in *Journal of Accounting Research*]
>
> My premises are descriptive of kinds of substantive action; your theorems relate to form only, without reference to function. My own style and predilection arose from a number of years experience in industry, commerce and government in which the relationship of information to substantive action became very plain. My concern with the matter was not simply a concern with logical or other formal elegance but with the springs of action in a workaday world. I was not so little concerned with generality as the emphasis on your own search for generality ('Account,' 164) suggests. My 'Scientific Pattern' (1955) pointed out the defects of excessive abstraction and generality, and suggested that there were at least four features of all conceivable entities that may require different specific accounting rules as between differently classified entities. If the greater part (but not all) of my work since then has been on business accounting, it was because it seemed to me impossible to deal with the problems (and existential difficulties) of accounting for all kinds of entities by recourse to one single set of ideas.
>
> You, on the other hand, chose to deal in general patterns but to leave the specifics blank (the 'place-holders' of *AAM* [*Accounting and Analytical Methods*]). That removed one potential burden from your shoulders—in the absence of specifics you could avoid the obligation to test the consequences. No one could prove you wrong, for you had prescribed nothing.
>
> That was my main complaint in the review article of [*AAM*] 1966.[32] I tried then to be as clinical and fair as possible. I did not anticipate that you would judge it to be 'devastating criticism'; for I expect those who pioneer to be shell-backed and hard-nosed. Much of what pioneers do is directly or implicitly critical of their contemporaries or their antecedents; and what they accomplish in the end is often the consequence of the 'hard-live' they have along the way, when others kick back. I rather

supposed you might have taken my criticism as a spur to fill the place-holders, even if only tentatively. But your response (*JAR* 1967) was entirely defensive. But enough was enough. Silence is the kindest thing sometimes.[33]

These debates show the keen interest of the golden age theorists to identify and discuss accounting fundamentals, like postulates; and how intense their debates became. There is still no resolution of these matters.

It is interesting to reflect on what it was like to be part of the action in those heady years. The Sydney School was a propitious development, for it brought together a group that was keen to learn, and whose members could contribute when given the opportunity. Foremost throughout the 1950s and '60s accounting debates was a focus on the history and development of ideas, their mutation, often their misuse.

It was truly an age of accounting discovery. The excitement and experimentation of the participants resemble similar periods in other areas, like the Impressionists and Modernist art movements with their influences from developments in disciplines such as music, fashion, theatre, and cinema. In the case of accounting those other disciplines included law, economics, mathematics, psychology, and communication. Experimentation and excitement flourished with the cross-fertilization of ideas. Chambers experimented with simplified frameworks (e.g., his 'transactionless' firm, a different balance sheet notation and a penchant for eclecticism), and drew widely on contemporary developments in those disciplines, in particular metrology, communication, and psychology.[34] His enthusiasm was contagious for his Sydney University associates, as he led by example in his pursuit of academic excellence. The evidence includes the number of his successful PhDs and professorial appointments noted in chapter 2.

That pursuit and breadth of scholarship rivalled two other contemporary schools of accounting—namely the London School of Economics (with the likes of 1930s theorists, Ronald S. Edwards and Ronald H. Coase, joined in the 1950s and '60s by others, including William Baxter, Harold Edey and David Solomons, Basil Yamey), and the Chicago School with, initially, Coase, who had moved from the LSE, and later others including Sidney Davidson, David Green, Charles Horngren, George Sorter, Bill Vatter (before he moved to University of California Berkeley), and Nicholas Dopuch.[35] The LSE was known for reconciling concepts of accounting and economic income, specifically advocating deprival value—as a variant of replacement cost accounting; Chicago was noted for its advocacy of 'free market'-based solutions rather than government intervention.

Another feature that characterized Chambers' academic work was his careful and meticulous use of language. As the photo of Chambers in his office (Figure 6.1) illustrates, he was immersed in various papers, books—his sources of evidence; and the surrounding shelves contained an array of dictionaries, books of synonyms and antonyms, thesauruses and other literary tools. His work was characterized by tight logic that he often demonstrated graphically (see pp. 123 and pp. 127–29), by the use of empirical data that was directly to the point being argued, and by conclusions that could clearly and exclusively be drawn from the preceding argument. Those techniques are demonstrated *par excellence* in *Accounting, Evaluation and Economic Behavior* and *An Accounting Thesaurus*.[36]

As Gaffikin has suggested: 'There is little doubt (and no evidence to suggest otherwise) that Chambers was the first in the English accounting literature to fully explicate such a rigorous scientific method and then consciously employ it in developing a theory.'[37]

We now return to matters raised earlier in this chapter.

Accounting Reform—the Method that Forged CoCoA

Chambers' continuously contemporary accounting is often criticized as being normatively based. In a sense the *normative* label suited Chambers as it implied he was a *thinker*. But, as alluded to earlier, it also irked him that 'normative' was intended by many in the post-1970s accounting research community to be derogatory, not merely categorical. To him research (drawing on, *inter alia*, the ideas of Simon, 1990, 663) was 'Thinking: That's research!'[38] Accordingly, he actively pursued methods that often enquired deeply into individual instances, individual observations of accounting practices, in need of explanation—in the pursuit of a deeper understanding. Works over nearly twenty-five years demonstrate this: 'Accounting and Shifting Price Levels,' 'Financial Practice and Fiscal Policy,' *Company Annual Reports: Function and Design*, 'The Implications of Asset Revaluations and Bonus Share Issues,' 'Financial Information and the Securities Market' and the codification of these in his 1973 *Securities and Obscurities: Reform of the Law of Company Accounts*. Our later discussion of other works supports this view.

In a 1993 letter to Moonitz he reflects on his approach and that of many others: 'All the number-crunching, bitty surveys, and sham experiments that seem to dominate the journals—all under the self-claimed rubric of "research"—seem to miss entirely the point that advances depend not on masses of data but on discriminating thought.'[39] Contrary to the often levelled criticism, Chambers' approach is thus defensibly empirical and, indeed, more closely related to the origins of science than are those techniques of enquiry employed by many declared positivists.

We should not lose sight of the notion of experience changing form (at least) from the time of Bacon's *novum organum* and being subsumed by the concept of facts—a notion of facts pushing to the backbenches theoretical imagination, speculation and inspired *guesswork*. Nor should we lose sight of the repetitive, recurring nature of many of the matters (real world problems) into which Chambers enquired. Roszak, for instance, noted that 'ideas precede evidential facts'—that is, ideas precede '*ceteris paribus* assumptions.' If there are no ideas, there is no reason to observe, and there

Figure 6.1 Ray in His Office in the 1980s

Chambers in his work office in the early 1980s; surrounded by the various papers, books—his sources of evidence. They would become the Chambers Archive.

are no *facts* to accumulate and analyse mathematically or indeed in any other way![40]

Chambers' ideas were perceived as novel and attracted much interest, including many critics of his CoCoA—such as the 1960s reviews by Larson and Shattke, Solomons, Wright, Baxter, Benston, Staubus, Iselin, and Leftwich.[41] Chambers responded to these at the time and in summary in *Abacus* articles, 'Second Thoughts on Continuously Contemporary Accounting,' 'Third Thoughts. . .' and in 'CoCoA: Misunderstandings and Misrepresentations.'[42]

Contrary to the popular opinion of his time, Chambers was not antagonistic to his detractors who often failed to think through problems in the rigorous (and importantly to Chambers, the unpoliticized) manner he so admired as the 'well-spring' of true scholarship. The following observations in a 1975 letter to an Australian university colleague commenting on a paper Chambers had just received capture his concerns about the lack of scholarship in the academy. It supports a similar point he made in the letter to Mattessich above[43]:

The most influential men of words are demagogues—and there are more of them and they are more vocal than scholars; that gives the

academic less and less chance. . . . In our own particular enclave—
academic accounting—these tendencies are particularly noticeable. As
I read you, you contemplate a commitment to what is the present best
and a search for better. But how many accountants in the universities
have a commitment to any line of thought in their field? There is so
much "on the one hand this, on the other that, on the other something
else," that they remind me of those many-handed eastern deities. If
academic work has become no more than airing alternatives without
any respect for what is best, if it has reached the low point of undisciplined chatter, if it is careless of choosing and standing up for what
one can firmly establish, I see little prospect of "satisfying achievement
and distinction."[44]

Gaffikin observed that Chambers is recognized as one of the earliest
accounting academics to impose methodological rigour in the 1950s articles
attempting to develop his theory of accounting.[45] Those articles provided
a breakthrough. Most accounting texts up to that time had been manuals of practice containing very little attempt to reason why those practices
should be used; and as Whittington opines, much of the effort to improve
external financial reporting practice was based on inductive empirical reasoning.[46] In theorizing, Chambers drew upon his observations of the way
accounting was influenced by its cognate fields and this provided his empirical domain (his *conceptual framework*) from which to draw the foundations
of accounting.

In the development of CoCoA the intertwining of the normative
method and the positive commercial domain is well summarized in
Chambers' supplementary DSc submission, which noted: 'periodical
financial information, as it was published, diverged in a great many
cases and by very great amounts from what should be expected from
the official and textbook doctrine. Practical exigencies, indeed, had
obliged companies to resort to numerous *ad hoc* and theoretically
unjustifiable devices to "rectify" the distortions arising through adherence to the "original cost" rule. It showed that investors and directors—even those who had access to expert advice—were misled on a
large scale by companies which had made use of the traditional rules.
It showed directors and managers were often embarrassed by, but also
often took advantage of, the inadequacy and looseness of the rules
avowed by the profession. The evidence pointed in the direction of
accounting in terms of the contemporary prices of assets. All was proposed within the context of accounting being understood to be a serviceable technology underpinning commercial transactions, corporate
financing and restructuring decisions, being the efficient and equitable
basis of taxation levies and the like.'[47]

Chambers argued that accounting's function is to provide information
that is *generally* relevant for the actions of many commercial parties. He

provides additional insights about what influenced his ideas on relevance and reliability in a letter to Tom Lee:

> Enough of that [discussion of experiences in teaching management, working for the Prices Commission]. I have long been an avid reader of accounts of investigation and discovery, in mathematics, chemistry, physics, biology, cosmology, archaeology, and what not. I have long toyed, for relaxation, with whodunnits and other kinds of logical and verbal puzzle. I had been a consultant to firms in a variety of trades and industries, an inquisitive reader of business histories and of the current business and financial press. In all these directions, dated actions proceeded from dated facts. And dated facts are, *ipso facto*, verifiable and therefore reliable. [Hence] the idea of relevance was to me just a commonplace. Going after the facts would relieve accounting of all the fumbling and guesswork that made its products neither fact nor fiction, but some indescribable mixture of the two. In terms of rationale or theory, going after the presently dated facts was simply doing what is done in all disciplined inquiry and systematic practice. [see the chapter 2 discussion on this point with the U.K. economist G.L.S. Shackle]
>
> I can pinpoint no prime source of the matrix of ideas that I encapsulated in [the notion of] relevance. Factuality, contemporaneity and verifiability had been among the features of accounting mentioned in discourse before my time; but they were in effect contradicted, discounted, nullified, by the rules and practices commonly taught and followed. If to the general matrix mentioned there are added the constraints of ordinary commercial and financial dealing and the rules of mathematical propriety, CoCoA follows.
>
> The fundamental difference between the stance of Sterling and me and the stances of others has been that we have focussed on the facts about an entity *regardless of the users of those facts*. It's a clinical stance, after the pattern of scientific inquiry and the management of all kinds of technically complex and technically constrained operations. It meant rejecting all forms of guesswork, allocations based on expectations, and all rules invented by accountants that have nothing to do with the firm *per se*. The rules of mathematics and plain logic are what save one from falling back on mere opinion. It's the business of investors and managers to form opinions about the future. But if they do not know what they have now at stake [i.e. an entity's fortune or net wealth], they cannot begin to imagine what they can do to shape the future. What is now at stake is relevant information specific to a firm that accountants can, and nobody else can or does, systematically produce.[48] (emphasis added)

That the conventional system embodied 'guesswork, allocations based on expectations,' was something Chambers railed against. Correspondence with the U.S. accounting academic Arthur Thomas shows that he had been asked by Thomas, and he was very keen to assist, in developing Thomas' arguments in the seminal works on cost allocations, namely the 1969 *SAR* #3, 'The Allocation Problem: In Financial Accounting Theory' and the 1974 *SAR* #9, 'The Allocation Problem: Part Two.' In the second of those studies, Thomas describes cost allocations as being "incorrigible" and suggests market price as the preferred form of asset valuation. The impact of Chambers' thinking on some of Thomas' ideas has not previously been discussed in the literature.[49] It, however, needs more exploration than possible here. As does Chambers' advocacy of the possibility of producing a normative accounting standard that can provide *generally* relevant information about an entity's financial indicators necessary for decision making by interested parties (see Illustration 6.3). Others, like U.S. academic Joel Demski, argued strongly in *The Accounting Review* that this is an impossibility. Chambers provided an equally strong rebuttal.[50]

Chambers' initial theoretical thoughts about the preferred system to supplant historical cost accounting appeared in his 'Blueprint for a Theory of Accounting.' They were further embellished in *Towards a General Theory of Accounting*.

'Blueprint' was a seminal piece in which he recognized that accounting theory, such as it stood at that time, was ill defined and poorly structured; that the fundamental premises of a theory lay outside the field of accounting proper. Some of the merits of his system were indicated, particularly in the direction of eliminating unsystematic teaching and practice. In the 1974 Foreword to the Scholars reprint of *Accounting, Evaluation and Economic Behavior* he reflected that 'Blueprint': was not simply a paper on method [of constructive criticism] . . . it set out four substantive propositions . . . premises . . . ideas [which had] emerged from my work in the teaching of management [as discussed in chapter 5]. They seemed to have little to do with accounting. But they were the basis of all my later work.

Earlier, in response to questions from Mattessich after the appearance of 'Blueprint,' Chambers had noted:

> It was in 1953 that I introduced to the [Sydney University] courses . . . the idea of the essential complementarity of the disciplines of economics and accounting; the better students in each of the accounting courses were exposed to discussions of theoretical, marginal and controversial questions in accounting which arose partly from observation of business practices and partly from the promptings of their contemporaneous studies in economics. All species of the genus "accounting" were brought under their observation. In 1954 it was decided to give to all students of economics, whether or not they were to do further studies in

accounting, an outline of accounting—again on a broad scale, uninterrupted by treatment of many of the common technicalities; its purpose was to indicate the relationship between the products of the accounting processes and economic behaviour.[51]

Chambers had used the 1961 'General Theory' lecture to develop his economic foundations, individual and social, of accounting. Some characteristics of action in a market economy, like the need for adaptation noted by Austrian economists like von Mises, and the kinds and qualities of required financial information, are stipulated. As well as the foundations, twenty-one derived principles are presented. The principles include 'relevance,' 'neutrality,' 'correspondence,' 'uniformity of valuation,' and 'current valuation' as well as those usually listed or implicit in statements of principle. The solution proposed to the problem of the instability of prices is the use, *in principle*, of replacement costs. The separation of monetary (M) and non-monetary assets (N), the analytical device of the transactionless interval, and the symbolic notation M, N, L (Liabilities), R (Residual Equity), p (Rate of Change in the General Level of Prices) for representing periodical positions and changes in position are introduced. The analytical device was later found to be unnecessary, the notation was improved and exit prices were adopted universally to overcome the instability of prices.[52]

We recall again Chambers' 1974 reflections:

> The adoption of [the use of a simplified, transactionless firm and the rejection of the old balance sheet notation of Assets = Liabilities + Proprietorship for a notation which distinguished monetary from non-monetary assets]—since used by many others—was an important step in my work; they enable me to experiment with a wide variety of combinations of variables.[53]

But he was not satisfied. He wanted to produce a theoretically tight, albeit workable, legally defensible, and practical set of reforms.

Criticisms, and importantly the constant promptings of Weinwurm to his ideas on measurement, caused Chambers to rethink several aspects of his theory such as his initial use of replacement price as the preferred measure for several, but not all, classes of assets. As the epigraph to chapter 4 suggests, with respect to asset measurement issues Chambers 1955 differed from Chambers 1974.[54] The mixed measurement rules he initially proposed—current cash equivalents (CCEs) or exit prices for some assets and liabilities and replacement prices for others, like durable/fixed assets— were reviewed in the early 1960s. Coupled to a desire for 'consistency' as one of his overarching principles, this resulted in the CCE measure being used for *all* assets and liabilities.

Barton's 2000 *Abacus* Festschrift article sought to reconcile the use of replacement (entry) price and CCE (exit) price accounting measures, as had Edwards and Bell in their 1961 classic. Using Marshall's basic microeconomic theory of the firm he demonstrated the complementarity of the two accounting measurement systems. He noted that replacement price accounting was essentially a *flow* approach that enabled management to consider the long run operation of the firm; while the *stocks* approach of Chambers' exit price accounting focused on the short run utilizing knowledge about the firm's existing stock of resources. Knowledge of a firm's stock of resources also was said to be critical in the management of financial investment portfolios and financial assets generally. Neither system was shown to be able to provide *all* of the information necessary for the firm's effective resource management. Recall that Chambers had claimed his system would produce the *generally* relevant information—not *all* of the required information—sufficient for any decision.

In the early 1970s Chambers had even resolved to his satisfaction measurement problems related to 'thin' or 'no markets.' Such dilemmas would re-emerge in the CCA debates in the mid-to-late 1970s and several decades on in the aftermath of the GFC. Chambers' solution was to retain his CCE measurement approach and adopt a form of double account with related disclosures (see chapter 4).

More insights about Chambers' approach are revealed in a response to a critic:

> Perhaps the attempt to produce something theoretically tighter than alternatives, and at the same time to propose something which approached the ideal but was workable, was over-ambitious. [But] I cannot regret trying to meet practical difficulties without too great a sacrifice of principle. . . . There is no principle known to men that is not relaxed somewhat in application.[55]

Recall Chambers' 1981 letter to Mattessich:

> You have not been the only one to think my 1955 premises were defective in some way. But almost everything that I have done in the intervening quarter century is an elaboration of those premises. And at every step on the way I have found additional evidence of the propriety of one or another of my theorems or conclusions, or prescriptions. I am therefore in a position to go back and say "thank you" to the critics who found me wrong (for I have been wrong at many points); and "thank you" to the critics who mistakenly thought me wrong (for they prompted me to clarify and seek evidence); but to be not especially thankful to many of those who seemed to agree with me, for they did little to polish up or prompt me to polish up what I had begun. Your

"Account" makes clear to me that I was *not* mistaken about and *did* understand, the drift of your work. You were concerned with methodological purity—not with current practical anomalies, maladies and solecisms. I too was concerned with methodological questions, but not to the neglect of observable defects and dilemmas (which in other fields have been the empirical spur to a vast number of advances in knowledge and art).[56]

Importantly, his development of CoCoA took place while major changes in prices and price levels were occurring in Australia and elsewhere. They reinforced his thinking.

Accounting for Price and Price Level Changes[57]

Following World War II, the upsurge in manufacturing was accompanied by inflation. In many respects this proved a boon to Chambers' research, for it meshed with his idea that what is needed is a system that accounts for both price and price level changes—for increases and decreases. Some of his works at the time included: 'Accounting for Shifting Price Levels,' 'Depreciation on Replacement Cost,' 'Accounting and Inflation,' and 'Effects of Inflation on Financial Strategy.'[58] As in many countries, in Britain, machinery which had been purchased pre-war was then worn out because of the war effort and fully depreciated for taxation purposes. This resulted in the ICAEW petitioning the British government for special depreciation to be levied on the current replacement price of plant. It was refused, being said to be a corporate budgeting matter, not something that governments should be involved in. Observers at the time noted that the ICAEW argument was that capital, rather than profit, was being taxed. Later research reveals conflict between the practising and industrial arms of the ICAEW on this matter.[59] Inflation was perceived to entail only rises in the prices of goods and services. But inflation is calculated as the net of both rises and falls in specific prices, where the former outstrips the latter.

In the U.S. a similar phenomenon occurred. With the general level of prices rising accountants turned their major attention to methods of accounting for 'changes in the purchasing power of money,' no doubt buoyed by the works of Henry Sweeney on stabilized accounting which had appeared several decades earlier in serial form in *The Accounting Review*.[60] The method had been exposed as part of the responses to the German (and wider European) hyperinflation of the early 1920s. Sweeney's PhD thesis referred to the German and later French solutions to accounting for hyperinflation (namely in German *Indexbuchführung* or *Goldmarkbilanz*). They entailed indexing the historical cost-based balance sheets and income accounts with numbers drawn from an index of the general level of prices so as to have them restated (respectively either forwards or backwards) in terms of the number representing the index at the opening 1914 (pre-war) balance date. The indexation method of stabilization adopted in some U.S. financial reports of the late 1940s restated forwards the entity's accounts in terms of the index number representing the general price level as at the balance date.[61]

As noted, in the meantime Chambers had been revisiting the measurement problem as he had been thinking about the foundations of accounting. By the early 1960s he felt he had settled the measurement issue—CoCoA was almost outlined in full. *All* the so-called non-monetary assets were to be stated in balance sheets at their current cash equivalent, best indicated by their current selling prices, thereby providing clear indications of financial position at declared date times. As such the net assets (residual equity or wealth) provided the respective entity's capacity for adaptation. Income was to be the net change in the opening and closing residual equity amounts in terms of end-of-period purchasing power—an all-inclusive system capturing both trading revenue and capital gains.

A more detailed account of methods proposed to account for price level changes is provided in chapter 8. But briefly, to help understand the mechanics of CoCoA, Table 6.1 assumes a firm with *no* monetary assets, and:

Table 6.1 CoCoA Example

	t_1	t_2
Total Physical (Non-monetary) Assets at their Selling Prices	220,000	280,000
Total Liabilities at the Amounts then Owing	70,000	60,000
The Residual Equity =	150,000	220,000
Index of the changes in the general level of prices 100 to 110 (i.e. 10% inflation)		
Residual Equity at t_1 in t_1	$t_1$150,000	
Residual Equity at t_1 in t_2	$t_2$165,000	
Net Change in Residual Equity in t_2 =	$t_2$55,000 (t_2 220,000—$t_2$165,000)	

Note the net change in the firm's residual equity ($t_2$55,000) is calculated after maintaining capital in possession (under Chambers' CoCoA this represents an entity's wealth or command over general purchasing power) at the beginning of the period t_1 to t_2. Strictly speaking, this adjustment represents a purchasing power loss on the entity's opening capital. It is a charge against income (in bookkeeping terms, namely a debit to the Income Account) and a credit to the Capital Maintenance Reserve (amounting to

$t_2 15,000$), part of the total Residual Equity. Chambers described this as a 'black-box adjustment'—a capital maintenance adjustment.[62] It ensured the proper measurement of the profit or loss for the period.

Excursions into understanding the implications for accounting of measurement principles had led him to the conclusion that the comparison of Residual Equity at t_1 in t_1 with Residual Equity at t_2 stated in t_2 was mathematically (or technically) impossible where the general price level index had changed because of inflation or deflation—the purchasing dimensions of the opening and closing Residual Equities differed.

The relatively simple capital maintenance adjustment (shown in principle in an overhead prepared for one of his lectures) meant that Chambers' CoCoA accounted for inflation without argument—it did so without

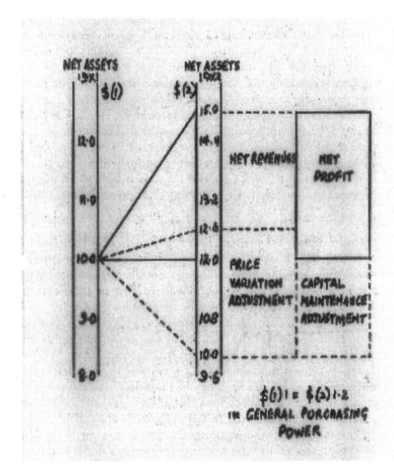

Illustration 6.1 General Purchasing Power Example

supplementary statements of the kind subsequently promoted in 1973 in the U.K.'s ED8, *Accounting for Changes in the Purchasing Power of Money*, without any departure from the double-entry system, without the distinction between monetary and non-monetary assets resurrected in 1974 by the U.K.'s Statement of Standard Accounting Practice No. 7 (SSAP7), without the adjustment of each item contestably making accounts meaningless, and without senseless explanation of why all items were assumed to be affected similarly by changing prices. It did so with one entry. Those mid-1970s professional, compromise responses had followed the economic disruptions from double-digit inflation. These and other proposed solutions to the so-called price level problem are discussed in chapter 8.

A few years after ED8's appearance came two Preliminary EDs issued by the Australian Accounting Standards Committee under the auspices of the Australian Accounting Research Foundation, *A Method of Accounting for Changes in the Purchasing Power of Money* (December, 1974) and *A Method of Current Value Accounting* (June, 1975). The latter's focus on current value accounting was unsurprising given the contiguous submission to the U.K. parliament for approval of the Sandilands Report, with its proposed current cost accounting (CCA); it was published in September 1975. The Australian profession's variant of current cost accounting would appear as a draft provisional standard, *Current Cost Accounting*, DPS 1.1 in October 1976. As usual, Chambers was quick to consider and comment on it in the press (see Table 7.5). This produced over six months later the 'out of the blue' three-page A4 letter from John Hanks and Chambers' response. They discuss the logical features of Chambers' inflation adjustment mechanism and the logical violations in the proposed CCA prescriptions. Hanks observes:

> Your strictures against the proposed current version of accounting for inflation [CCA] were reported in the press here. . . . Allow me to say that I thoroughly agree with you. Though not an accountant, I have had a long interest in the subject, with some reading on it, and as far as I can see your views and mine must be very close together. Like you I feel that inflation effects must be measured over all items in terms of money value changes so that the present ideas are lopsided and biased.
>
> Myself, I am a graduate in, *inter alia*, mathematics (from Sydney) and I therefore bring a mathematician's viewpoint to the question. It has long puzzled me that accountancy has not deeply consulted with mathematics on the validity of its procedures since all accounting statements are simple linear mathematical statements and of necessity need the underlying assumptions, the calculation methods, and the general processes all to meet the relevant criteria. If this had been done, some problems might not have arisen. I refer to several aspects below.

What follows in the letter are two A-4 single-spaced pages devoted to logical issues that had clearly been ignored by accounting practitioners over many years. Advocates of CCA were the latest to do so.[63] Chambers was clearly impressed and responded a week later:

> I was delighted to have your letter of 23 June. As you surmise, your views tally almost exactly with my own. That is the source of my delight; since, beyond the circle of people who have come to agree with me, there are few who have given the mathematical characteristics of accounting any thought whatever. And yet they are fundamental. It puzzles me too that, when most accountants confront mathematical or statistical problems, they tend to suppose they know all that needs to be known, without bothering to go back to experts in those fields to test their knowledge or for expert opinion. It's a kind of arrogance which I suspect we are all afflicted with in one way or another, unless we have developed the habit of re-examining what we think we know.
>
> But in learning accounting, according to the lore of the time, I (and all of my contemporaries) became so accustomed to the processes that I gave little attention to their mathematical validity, though those processes caused constant uneasiness. About 1962 I resolved to clear up the confusion, at least to my own satisfaction. I read extensively in the theory of measurement. The result was a 'theory of accounting' which was materially different from the then current theory and practice. I had to take account of the fact that the measurement unit (unlike the units of the natural sciences) is a perennially variant unit. After concentrated struggling with the problem for some three months in 1963 I found a solution and developed a notation which (after a few mutations) coped with all the relevant variables, including the variant dollar. It was only after wading through all the traditional accounting argument and related economic theory that I saw that the whole problem was soluble as a simple extension of a few mathematical principles and a few empirical propositions.[64]

Returning to 1975, in an exposure draft Chambers issued privately in September his particular inflation adjustment (the capital maintenance adjustment) and the individual exit price variation adjustments in respect of assets and liabilities were explained succinctly through a detailed example. Now a member of the N.S.W. Divisional Council and also of the General Council of the Australian Society of Accountants, Chambers' 'private ED' caused a sensation. He had offered the draft to the society requesting that it be published to augment the two other published 'official' preliminary exposure drafts neither of which claimed to account for inflation. Concern was expressed by some ASA members that Chambers was being disloyal to the ASA. Chambers disagreed. His thinking is revealed in this extract from a September 1975 letter written to Rex Thiele, then President of the ASA General Council. It followed conversations they had on this matter and in response to a 27 August 1975 letter from Thiele:

> I don't know whether you attach any importance to my own position in all this. I pointed out in my previous letter [18 August, 1975, USA P202, #4930] that the whole matter has been under my close examination for 20 years. I am known for it around the world, and it has sparked off a whole lot of new discussion. I have had my ideas published in a dozen countries and several languages, and I have tendered submissions (even sometimes by direct invitation) in a number of places. In the course of that work I have had to reject one or another of the various proposals (each of which I had held to be a "solution" before I found it to be faulty). I did not like to have to start all over again when I found that something I had supported wouldn't really work; but I did. My conclusions are not, therefore, the product of whim or fancy. They are the product of work done, laboriously and searchingly, over a far longer period than anyone associated with the present exposure drafts has even been vaguely interested in the matter. I do not like "puffing" in this fashion. But I do so with the object of pointing out that, whatever some Committee decides to adopt, it cannot be expected that I or anyone else will thereupon be bound by it if it offends common and practical good sense.[65]

The offer was rejected, so he went it alone. In a sense the ASA assisted him for he sent copies at his and the university's expense around the world to over 3,000 of his colleagues, not only to accountants but also to politicians, officers of companies, and those he thought ought to be interested. He thus most likely achieved a wider international circulation than he would have had the society accepted his offer. More discussion of this appears in chapter 8.[66]

Returning to the aspects of experimentation and novelty, we defer to Chambers' thoughts on these matters as outlined in the 1993 letter to Tom Lee:

> I am often in doubt about the provenance of an idea "of mine," so often have I found that it had been floating around long before I found use for it. The ideas of relevance and reliability are implicit in the relationship between bookkeeping and action posited in the manuals of five, four, three, two hundred years ago. The ideas got lost in the concentration of accountants on the mechanics of bookkeeping, on servitude to management, and on self protection over the last hundred years. When I turned my attention to the link with decision making, I thought I was doing something novel. So apparently did the authors

of [the 1977 AAA's] *SATTA* in attributing the decision-making drift to my work of the fifties and sixties. Only in the last twenty years have I found that I was simply unearthing (though, certainly, more thoroughly articulating) ideas of long ago. Every generation is the inheritor of the vast wisdom and the equally vast folly of the past. It seems to be hazardous indeed to attempt to separate from that inheritance the indubitable precursor of an apparently novel notion. As many of the historians of ideas have pointed out, novelty emerges often simply from the thoughtful and imaginative rearrangement of separate ideas that have long been current, from the mind as originator rather than from the mind as receptacle.[67]

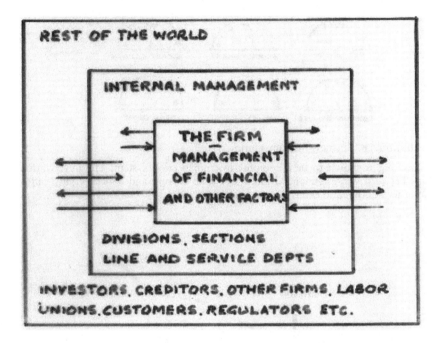

Illustration 6.2 The Context of Accounting

The above diagram and the illustrations on pages 128–29 were prepared by Chambers for seminar presentations. They depict respectively:

(i)   the context of accounting and the interactions of accounting with interested parties (investors, creditors, other firms, labour unions, customers, regulators, etc.) as those parties seek appropriate returns for their contributions to the firm. Managers clearly are at the nub of negotiations as they seek to coordinate operations;

(ii) accounting as a complex instrumentation system (Illustration 6.3);

(iii) the role of a manager in 'steering' (coordinating) an entity's affairs (Illustration 6.4); and

(iv) and (v) the role of accounting as a memory aid (Illustration 6.5) to assist those making financial business decisions (Illustration 6.6).

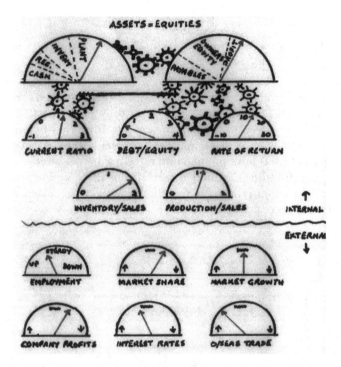

Illustration 6.3 Business Instrumentation

Accounting is shown to be a complex instrumentation system. The interrelationships between various financial indicators (like current and debt-to-equity ratios) and other internal and external factors are depicted.

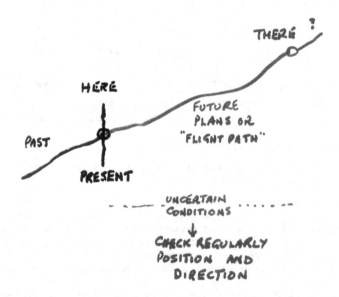

Illustration 6.4 Managing—Steersmanship

This diagram depicts the 'steersmanship' role of a manager in coordinating an entity's affairs. It highlights the importance of knowing an entity's present position, and its relationship to others.

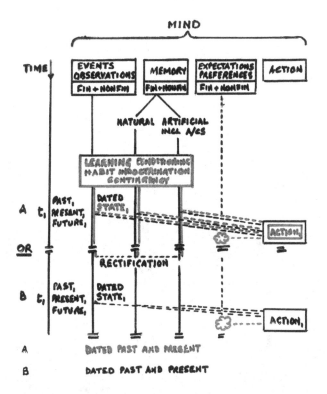

Illustration 6.5 Accounting as a Memory Aid

PAST	PRESENT	FUTURE
ACTUAL		
$S_{-1} + E_{-1} \rightarrow S_0$	$\rightarrow$	?
POSSIBLE		

$$S_{-1} \rightarrow \begin{matrix} E'_{-1} \\ E''_{-1} \\ E'''_{-1} \end{matrix} \rightarrow S_0 \dashrightarrow \begin{matrix} E'_{+1} \dashrightarrow S'_{+1} \\ E''_{+1} \dashrightarrow S''_{+1} \\ E'''_{+1} \dashrightarrow S'''_{+1} \end{matrix}$$

POSSIBLE DIAGNOSES POSSIBLE PROGNOSES

DECISION: SELECTED + KNOWN + PREFERRED
DIAGNOSIS STATE FUTURE STATE
$\longrightarrow$ PREFERRED ACTION E

S : A DATED STATE, FINANCIAL POSITION
E : FINANCIAL FEATURES OF EVENTS
S', E' : POSSIBLE STATES AND EVENTS

NOTE : KNOWLEDGE OF S_0 IS CRUCIAL

Illustration 6.6 Financial Statements and Decisions

Figure 6.2 Ray at the ASA Golden Jubilee National Congress in 1979

Above: Ray Chambers and the Premier of Western Australia, Sir Charles Court, at the ASA Golden Jubilee National Congress, Perth, June 1979.

Below: Ray Chambers with dignitaries and delegates (left to right of Chambers), Sir Charles Court, an unknown delegate and Bernard Wright at the ASA Golden Jubilee National Congress, Perth, June 1979.

Notes

1. Chapter epigraphs:
   Stamp's article in the *Abacus* December 1982 Festschrift 'Special Issue,' 187.
   Chambers, 'In Quest of a Framework' (1995b, 2).
2. Discussion of new age theorists appears in, *inter alia*, Nelson (1973) and Gaffikin (1988), SATTA (1977). See also the Prologue for the opinions of several colleagues and peers about Chambers' international reputation.

3. Chambers to Tom Lee, P202, #7403, 27/01/1993 in response to Lee's 13 January letter, P202, #7402.
4. Dean and Clarke (2010a), Persson (2013) and Gaffikin (1988).
5. For example, Chambers (1980b).
6. P202, #5196, 01/07/1977. A more detailed response is provided on pages 121–26 of our biography.
7. 'Towards' was originally presented as an ASA Research Lecture at the University of Adelaide, 2 August 1961, and published in June 1962 as an Australian Society of Accountants' booklet (48 pp). Later, Sidebotham (1965) reproduced an abridged version. Chambers (1974d) recalls the forces influencing the development and refinement of his ideas, culminating in their codification in *Accounting, Evaluation and Economic Behavior*.
8. For discussions on this see Chambers (1976b, 1980a, 1993), Chambers and Dean (1986c, Vol. 3), Sterling (1990), Dean and Clarke (2010c) and Edwards *et al.* (2013).
9. Ball and Brown (1968). Edwards *et al.* (2013) identify some others who were critical of that line of research.
10. Edwards *et al.* (2013, 369). Inter alios, Chambers (1974a, 1993) and Sterling (1990) provided critiques of this line of research. Interestingly, in 1975 Moonitz sent Chambers a letter strongly endorsing his 1974 "stock market prices and accounting research" paper observing among other things that it is a 'breath of fresh air in a stuffy room'; continuing that such research 'could not cast much light on the propriety of accounting practices and procedures, that, at best, their findings might be of use to an investor in informing him of the relative strength or weakness of published financial statements for his purpose in deciding whether or not to invest in certain securities' (P202, #4513, 16/01/1975).
11. Chambers (1971b, 7). Chambers' November 1971 pamphlet was submitted to the University of Sydney registrar in support of his DSc application. It is part of a collection of correspondence in P202, #10824. The recollections detailed in this pamphlet underpinned the introductory essay (Chambers, 1974d) included in the 1974 Scholars Reprint of *Accounting, Evaluation and Economic Behavior*. It is consistent also with a lengthy letter Chambers wrote to Tom Lee on 27 January 1993, P202, #7403, 27/01/1993, outlining the development and features of CoCoA.
12. Chambers (1974d, xxxv).
13. Reference details to Chambers' articles are 'The Conditions of Research in Accounting' (1960b), 'Why Bother with Postulates' (1962b), 'Measurement in Accounting' (1963a) and 'The Role of Information Systems in Decision Making' (1964c).
14. Chambers (1971b DSc. 'pamphlet,' 1–2).
15. This was elaborated in Clarke and Dean (2007, especially chapter 6). Nobes (2009, 2015) shows that in fact present-day conventional accounting is still primarily cost-based.
16. The question of what was meant by "managed rationally" produced debates between critics, for example Leftwich (1969) and Chambers 'Canons of Criticism' response to Leftwich. Chambers adopted the view of some Austrian economists, like von Mises in his *Human Action* (1949), that to act 'rationally' means everyone acts for what seem to him to be good reasons. Chambers' *Detail for a Blueprint* paper (1957b, 209) notes that for a manager of a business to act rationally would entail 'meeting the demands of the contributing parties [investors, employees, other interested parties] efficiently' as circumstances change. The corollary of this was the need for an information system that provides continuously up-to-date information. *A,E&EB* discusses this in detail in its first chapter, 'Individual thought and action.'

17. The introductory meetings and discussions between the OR researchers and Chambers on measurement, theory and decision-making issues are described in Dean and Clarke (2010a). Understanding the new ideas on metrology was critical as Chambers honed his CoCoA. Chambers' (1975d) unpublished Festschrift contribution notes Weinwurm's influence on his thoughts at this point: 'By 1961 I had examined critically most of the traditional ideas [in accounting] and had proposed modifications of some of them. In that I first attempted to set up a body of coherent ideas—in 'Towards a General Theory of Accounting . . . Was it proper to add an amount of cash to the replacement price of a non-cash asset? Did a replacement price represent, in respect of a particular asset, financial capacity for market action? I would have to turn to measurement theory and practice after all, as Weinwurm had been suggesting.' The change from replacement prices to exit price measures using a common measuring unit would be a major product.'

18. As well, other correspondence debates recorded in the Chambers Archive include those with the 'historical costers' like Robert Anthony, 'replacement costers' like Lawrence Revsine, Reg Gynther and William Paton, 'indexation advocates' like Henry Sweeney, 'cash flow proposers' like George Staubus and G. Lawson, 'present valuers' like Palle Hansen and 'deprival valuers' like David Solomons and Ken Wright.

    The Archive also retains correspondence with practitioners, like Bruce Marsden, and a former student, Peter Nelson, over the problems in valuing plant and equipment (and assets generally) at exit price. As discussed in the text and endnotes #63, chapter 6 and #64, chapter 6, Chambers asked another correspondent, practising mathematician John Hanks, to consider publishing his letter about the logic of Chambers' inflation accounting notation in an accounting practitioner journal. Chambers indicated he was willing to edit the letter to make it a suitable size for publication—P202, #5196, 01/07/1977. In another, he exchanged letters with John Barnes, a practitioner who had been inspired to send Chambers an article on ethics after reading Chambers' (1991b) 'Ethical Cringe' article—P202, #9676, 12 July 1991. Chambers seemingly was willing to carry on such discussions/debates with all comers no matter how busy he was.

19. Dean and Clarke (2010a).
20. Dean (2008).
21. For example, his 1955a and 1957b articles.
22. P202, #7688, 20/06/1960 and related letters, item #s7689–7710.
23. Moonitz to Chambers, P202, #7708, 23/10/1961. As well as commenting on ARS1, Chambers reviewed ARS3 'Postulates and Principles' study by Robert Sprouse and Moonitz. In the next few pages reference is made to the Special Committee on Research Program. In 1958 it recommended that the Committee on Accounting Procedure be replaced by a newly designated Accounting Principles Board, as well as recommending that the Board commission research studies on postulates and principles (see Zeff, 2001).
24. P202, #7689, 27/01/1961. Chambers' review of the Sprouse and Moonitz ARS3, 'Postulates and Principles' study was published in Zeff (1982). See also endnote #s16, 17, chapter 6.
25. P202, #7692, 26/04/1961.
26. The minutiae in these letters could be the basis of future academic research as all the correspondence is in the Chambers Archive.
27. Moonitz to Chambers, P202, #7703, 06/09/ 1961.
28. Chambers to Weinwurm, P202, #8129, 15/02/ 1962.
29. Chambers to Moonitz, P202, #7732, 19/12/1962.

30. Mattessich to Chambers, P202, #245, 23/04/1957.
31. Mattessich (1995, 50); and previously Mattessich (1970, 1971a, 1971b) and Chambers (1971c, 1971d).
32. Chambers' review article appeared in the Spring 1966 issue of the *Journal of Accounting Research*.
33. Chambers to Mattessich, P202, #6235, 09/01/1981.
34. Chambers (1991a, 1991c).
35. While other institutions, including the University of California at Berkeley, Stanford University, the University of Michigan and Ann Arbor had many leading accounting academics such as Moonitz, Sprouse, Vatter, Mattessich, and Paton, they were not known for any unifying school of accounting thought.
36. One of the present writers, Dean, was Chambers' research assistant from 1974 to 1976. He recalls on several occasions being asked to go to the Faculty of Economics' Wolstenholme Library to check in the larger *Oxford English Dictionary* the exact meaning of a word that Chambers was considering using. Words researched that Dean recalls caused some practitioners and other academics to wince, included 'otiose,' 'feckless,' 'brouhaha,' 'tergivisations,' 'floccinaucinihilipilification' and, later, 'corroborable' (see more discussion in chapter 2, 21–2). And there were also references to the broader literature, such as one met earlier, 'cleaning the muck from the Augean stables,' and to 'Janus, with two heads, and hence eyes that looked forwards and backwards.' They showed Chambers' breadth of reading, something later evidenced by his *Thesaurus* and his extensive library which is now part of the hard-copy Chambers Archive. Not all, however, were happy to see reference to that broader literature—in conversation with Dean Chambers recalled a referee's observation in respect of a 1970s submission to *The Accounting Review*. Referring to Chambers' Janus analogy to reject the view that accounting is both forward and backward looking, the referee observed: 'none of the current readers will be aware of the analogy.' Dean recalls Chambers' response to the editor, 'If this were so then this reflected more poorly on them than on my analogy.'
37. Gaffikin (2000, 228).
38. Chambers (1995b).
39. Chambers to Moonitz, dated 3 February 1993, unnumbered in the P202 archive.
40. Roszak (1986).
41. Larson and Shattke (1966), Solomons (1966), Wright (1967), Baxter (1966), Benston (1967), Staubus (1967), Iselin (1968) and Leftwich (1969).
42. Chambers (1970a, 1974b, 1976d).
43. Chambers to Mattessich, P202, #6235, 09/01/1981.
44. Chambers to Mr E. (Ted) McL Holmes, Department of Accounting, University of Melbourne, P202, #4465, 19/06/1975.
45. Gaffikin (1984, 1986, 1987, 1988, 2000). Later, in a personal reflection, Gaffikin (2012) is critical of Chambers for not recognizing the limitations of the type of method he had employed in his early theoretical works.
46. Whittington (1996, 6).
47. Chambers (1971b) pamphlet is part of a collection of correspondence in P202, namely #10824. Australia's largest company, BHP provides an early 1960s exemplar of the actions of some businessmen to circumvent the profession's 'historical cost' rule in the reporting of assets. Mr Geoff Bills, Manager, Research Department at BHP sought Chambers' advice as BHP continued to develop its fixed asset utilization reserve policy of valuing its fixed assets on a notional replacement cost basis—this was another means of recognizing in the accounts

the financial effects of price changes. See Bills' letter to Chambers P202, #823, 03/03/1961 and Chambers' response P202, #824, 09/03/1961.

48. Chambers to Tom Lee, P202, #7403, 27/01/1993.
49. P202, #s3191and 3193. In *SAR* #9 (51) Thomas notes that Sterling was perhaps the first in the Anglo-Saxon accounting literature to have used 'incorrigible' to refer to something that is impossible to verify or falsify.
50. Demski's (1973) 'impossibility theorem' generated Chambers' response (written in 1974 and published in 1976 in *The Accounting Review*). Hitz (2007) resurrected the debate in the *European Accounting Review*. Letters in the Archive between, Chambers, Sterling, Moonitz, Foster, and others are worthy of further analysis.
51. Chambers to Mattessich, P202 #246, 15/10/1957. This no doubt appealed to Mattessich, who, in 1956 had published 'The Constellation of Accounting and Economics.'
52. Chambers (1976d). Debates on this issue appeared in the early issues of the *Journal of Accounting Research*. Chambers (1970b) returned to the issue in a series of articles on inflation accounting methods in *The Accountant*.
53. Chambers (1974d, xii; and expanded in xiv-xix).
54. We noted earlier in chapter 4 that 'Chambers earlier' differs from 'Chambers later.' He revealed that a similar morphing of ideas occurred in respect of how to account for corporate groups. This aspect of Chambers' thinking is illustrated also in endnote #17, chapter 6, showing Weinwurm's influence on his views on measurement in particular.
55. Chambers (1968b, 247). This was primarily a response to Staubus' (1967) review and critique of the measurement aspects of Chambers' theory. The last part of the article is a short response to a review of Chambers' theory by Iselin (1968). The extract in the text responds to some of Iselin's concerns.
56. Chambers to Mattessich, P202, #6235, 09/01/1981.
57. This subsection draws on many of Chambers' price variation accounting articles from the late 1940s to the early 1980s. It also draws on Clarke's PhD, (1982), Tweedie and Whittington (1984) and several works by Zeff. A more detailed review of accounting for price and price level changes throughout the period beginning post-WWI and ending around 1980 is provided in our chapter 8. Other detailed accounts include Tweedie and Whittington (1984) and in several papers and monographs by Zeff.
58. Chambers: 'Accounting for Shifting Price Levels' (1949a), 'Depreciation on Replacement Cost' (1950a), 'Accounting and Inflation' (1952a) and 'Effects of Inflation on Financial Strategy' (1952c).
59. Lacey (1952). See also the Noguchi and Edwards (2004) account of the 1940–50s internal conflict within the ICAEW regarding the proposal in N15 to consider replacement cost accounting as a supplement to historical cost accounting.
60. These are described in Clarke (1976). They are also discussed in more detail in our chapter 8. The American Sweeney had studied the German hyperinflation following World War I and the stabilization or indexation methods (forwards restatements or *Indexbuchführung* and backwards restatements or *Goldmarkbilanz*) used to mitigate inflation's effect on accounts. The latter stabilization method included Mahlberg (1921) and Schmalenbach (1922)—for discussion of these see Clarke and Dean (1989a, 1989b), Graves (1989) and Holtfrerich (1986). Also, Tweedie and Whittington (1984, chapter 2) discusses these methods.
61. Jones (1955, 1956).
62. Chambers (1966, 251–3, 258–9).

63. Melbourne mathematician, John Hanks to Chambers, P202, #5195, 23/06/1977. The handwritten copy was retyped. Both are retained in the Archive.

64. Chambers to Hanks, P202, #5196, 01/07/1977.

65. Chambers to ASA President, Rex Thiele, P202, #4932, 04/09/1975. Thiele's letter is P202, #4931, 27/08/1975.

66. More discussion of this appears in Clarke *et al.* (2010, 2012, especially 44–51) and in our chapter 8.

67. Chambers to Lee, P202, #7403, 27/01/1993.

7 Practitioner:

Theoretician-Cum-Practitioner

J B Priestley[observed] 'Nobody in his senses would expect a born seer to do. That much is generally acknowledged. But it is equally ridiculous to suppose that a dashing and triumphant doer can really see.' In that little bit of philosophy lies the reason why practice and inquiry, in most learned professions, proceed in tandem, practitioners and investigators doing their own thing with their skills, each respecting the domain and the competences of the other.

—Chambers' response to induction to Accounting Hall of Fame, 1991

I have long been conscious of the fact that seldom did we exchange views on our separate deeply-held ideas about the ideal style of accounting. I have not been sure, for example, how closely the notion of fair value corresponds with market selling price. I did sense, for years, a great deal of argument and sentiment that was of the same spirit in our utterances—a concern for technical rectitude, for service to the clientele of the profession, and for professional excellence. I have been content to ride in parallel, with an experienced and thoughtful professional, rather than wishing to ride in tandem. For it seemed to me that working our own ways in our own branches of the profession may well be more fruitful than attempting openly to make a united stand against orthodoxy. So far, of course, I've not left noticeable marks on the beliefs of the academics; and I suspect you may have a similar opinion of your impact on the beliefs of practitioners. Nevertheless, I remain confident of the reliability of the foundations on which we have built; confident that things will change in that direction, perhaps within half a generation!

—Chambers to Spacek, 1983[1]

Theory and Practice

Whether accounting practice or theory was in focus, Chambers had few peers in the academy. But perceptions often differ from reality. There were many who viewed Chambers' new system of accounting (chapter 6) and his ideas on regulatory reform (chapter 8) with disdain, suggesting they were naive, impractical, costly, and far too theoretical. But there is ample evidence to rebut that. Contrary to the views of many, the evidence adduced in this biography, and in particular in this chapter, confirms that, through consultancy work, job experiences, and professional associations, Chambers understood practice extremely well and possessed all-round skills.

The formative period of Chambers' thinking about reform, the developments of CoCoA and the Sydney School of Accounting was one of substantial financial turbulence. As noted in the Prologue it was a period 'of substantial business growth, of conglomeration on a large scale by mergers and takeovers, of intense multinational corporate development, of increasing use of modes of organization and methods of financing that were novel at the beginning of the interval.'[2]

Reform was undertaken with the assistance of associates in practice and the academy. In the late 1950s and up to the end of the 1970s practitioners in Sydney, Melbourne and elsewhere like Spacek in the U.S. provided strong support for Chambers' moves to engender a strong town and gown relationship, and to have as a pre-requisite of admission to the profession that applicants must be university qualified. Consider the following extract from a 1958 letter from the president of the ICAA, R.A. (later Sir Ronald) Irish, who suggested presciently to Chambers:

> As you know, there are many in our profession who are pleased to see a closer relationship developing between the University and the Institute, and perhaps the time is not far distant when the academic training for our profession will become a wholly University function.[3]

Chambers had a continuing engagement with the practising arm of the profession for over forty years.

In the late 1950s the seed was sown for a closer relationship with practice, in his proposal to found the University of Sydney Pacioli Society. Irish and other practitioners like John P. Young were major supporters of this development by their attendance at the early meetings. The society endures, with meetings three times a year, as the only accounting town and gown society in Australia. And presently, less than a handful of such societies exist worldwide.[4]

That turbulent period was the backdrop of Chambers' school forging further commercial connections through involvement in conferences sponsored by bodies including the Sydney University and Appointments Board, the N.S.W. PARB, the Australian Institute of Management, the ASA; and through company-sponsored seminars (often discussing measurement problems) run by major Australian companies such as BHP, Qantas and CSR, and General Electric in the U.S.A. Connections were achieved also through lectures by Chambers and Sydney staff to accounting firms, and to organizations connected with business-linked organizations including the Royal Automobile Club, and Probus (a branch of Rotary) discussing business matters. He was also a Director of Nestlé Australia Ltd from

1967 until 1989. Further evidencing his desire to keep abreast of business practices was attendance for more than twenty years at the monthly city luncheon as a member of the General Management Group. The group comprised leading Sydney businessmen, and in 1983 (on the occasion of the twenty-fifth anniversary of the monthly meetings) Chambers was the only academic member.[5] At these meetings a member of the group would deliver a presentation. Chambers delivered two: 'Stereotypes—American and English Education,' August 1968 and 'The Future of Tertiary Education,' September 1981.[6] Chambers remarked to the present authors that he marvelled at the especially deep intellect of some members of that management group.

Further evidence of Chambers' business connections is an invitation to join the board of Melbourne-based management consultants, John P. Young & Associates Pty Ltd. in the late-1960s from its chairman, John Paul Young. It further confirms that practitioners regarded highly Chambers' views:

> I have read with great interest that you have joined the Board of the Nestlé Company. Now that you are becoming "commercially oriented," how would you feel about officially joining the Board of John P. Young & Associates (N.S.W.) Pty. Ltd.? I daresay you have a soft spot from the days when you started it and when you see how it has grown to what it is today.[7]

Chambers' response providing reasons for rejecting the board offer is also intriguing:

> I rather fear that you may regard my repeated expressions of inability as something of a sham. But it's not that. Like you I have become involved in a whole series of connections—almost all gratuitous for my part—in the last seven years. Between us, the Nestlé appointment was quite unexpected. I guess its origins date back many years, but the immediate occasion arose through acquiescence in the first place by the vicechancellor before I was approached. This is unusual and the circumstances make it almost impossible for me to go so soon with another similar request.[8]

Chambers had connections with the John P. Young firm much earlier. His 'Aide Memoire' notes that he had held a consultancy position with the firm from 1955–59, and a letter in the Archive indicates that he had received an offer from Young in 1956 to be a Regional (N.S.W.) Director of the firm.[9] The Archive is silent on whether this directorship was accepted.

The Nestlé directorship provided Chambers with opportunities to converse with national and international business leaders, augmenting opportunities already available from his CPA leadership positions and his later involvement with the General Management Group.[10]

The directorship and consultancy work also added to his finances. Table 7.2 shows that the yearly fees drawn from the Nestlé directorship ranged from around $300 (gross) in 1967 to around $3,000 in 1974, $4,000 in 1976, $6,000 in 1981 and, by 1986 it was $9,000. Those amounts were a reasonable proportion (but only occasionally more than 20%) of Chambers' annual university income. To put these figures in some perspective, in 1974 the yearly professorial remuneration at Sydney was in the order of A$25,000, and two years later following a review it had risen to $29,048. A research assistant's annual salary in 1974 was A$4,000, which in 2017 Australian dollar terms would be approximately $30,000.

Chambers viewed theory and practice as integrals. Drawing on the ideas of John Stuart Mill and others, he was well aware that behind every serviceable practice there is a theory (implied or explicitly stated), an explanation of how and why it works, an explanation of how and why it fits with other practices in the same field. He considered meta ideas unrelated to practice were unhelpful in solving practical problems. Consider the following quote from John Stuart Mill taken from Chambers' *Thesaurus* (*AAT*: s. 892, 850):

> Now, the reasons of a maxim of policy, or of any other rule or art, can be no other than the theorems of the corresponding science. . . . The art proposes to itself an end to be attained, defines the end, hands it over to the science. The science receives it, considers it as a phenomenon or effect to be studied, and having investigated its causes and conditions, sends it back to art with a theorem of the combination of circumstances by which it could be produced. Art then examines those combinations of circumstances, and according as any of them are or are not in human power, pronounces the end attainable or not. The only one of the premises, therefore, which art supplies is the original major premise which asserts that the attainment of the given end is desirable. Science then lends to art the proposition . . . that the performance of certain actions will attain the end. From these premises art concludes that the performance of these actions is desirable, and finding that it is also practicable, converts the theorem into a rule or principle.

This scientific understanding of the nature of things underpinned Chambers' theoretical and practical approaches to accounting. In contrast with many in the 1960s and today, he did not distinguish financial and managerial accounting—for him they necessarily coalesced. As illustrated on pp. 127–29, accounting, financing, and managing necessarily were seen as integrals in that, for there to be financial order in respect of a firm, they have to fit eventually with the past and present financial characteristics of how we sensibly analyse financial wellbeing. These characteristics include the idea of rates of return, of profits and losses, of revenues and expenses, of assets and liabilities and with the future financial characteristics from any proposed managerial action regarding capital investment. It follows that, whereas financial accounting for different industries focuses on different aspects of their financial wellbeing, ultimately they each rely on the same meta ideas underpinning the theory of money and the canons of financial calculation. These are the types of fundamentals noted in the Prologue that remain pervasive.

Chapter 1 revealed that Chambers' early commercial appointments all required an understanding of money and measurement, while the case vignettes in this chapter further illustrate the need to be cognisant of money's characteristics.

Accounting is a Matter of Reckoning—of Financial Measurement—of Wealth, and Changes in Wealth

Chambers' *Thesaurus* captures the essence of money with its myriad entries, such as: *Money and the money symbol*—6 entries (*AAT*: s. 110, pp. 97–8), *Money as a medium of exchange*—7 entries (*AAT*: s. 112, pp. 99–100), *Money as general purchasing power*—7 entries (*AAT*: s. 113, pp. 100), *The money unit as the common denominator of prices*—4 entries, (*AAT*: s. 114, p. 101), *The money unit as unit of account*—7 entries (*AAT*: s. 115, pp. 101–02); and of the purchasing power of money: *The dated purchasing power of money*—5 entries (*AAT*: s. 116, pp. 103–04), *A money unit of invariant purchasing power contemplated*—6 entries (*AAT*: s. 121, pp. 105), *A money unit of invariant dimension not essential*—6 entries (*AAT*: s. 122, pp. 105–06), *The variable purchasing power of the money unit*—9 entries (*AAT*: s. 123, pp. 106–07), *The value of money and the general price level reciprocally related*—7 entries (*AAT*: s. 124, p. 108), *Money not neutral in economic calculation and action*—8 entries (*AAT*: s. 126, pp. 110–11), *Differential impacts of changes in the purchasing power of money*—9 entries (*AAT*: s. 127, pp. 111–12), and, *The assumption of monetary stability*—9 entries (*AAT*: s. 129, pp. 115–16).

The content of the pieces from those mainly book extracts supported the proposition that accounting is intended to depict the financial position of an organization, and generally report to stakeholders the components of its wealth at particular times of reckoning and the changes in them since the previous reckoning (see also *AAT*: s. 161–83, pp. 144–46). Later the *Thesaurus* captures both aspects in extracts defining financial position (*AAT*: s. 400–99, pp. 397–485). Importantly, this confirms that financial calculation needs to accord with the known canons of measurement.

Reviewing accounting and cognate literatures indicates that measurement and valuation are two of the most used and abused terms in accounting—not the least by accountants. We touched on this in chapter 3 when reviewing Chambers' analysis of the work of John Bennet Canning, and again in chapters 5 and 6. Measurement is accounting's focus, as frequently there is reference to the measurement of assets, the measurement of expenses, the measurement of liabilities, the measurement of income, the measurement of rate of return, the measurement of financial position, and the like, describing the supposed end-product of accounting, without regard for the rules of measurement:

> Most philosophers and many scientists regard measurement as a simple look-and-see procedure. . . . In doing so they ignore the number obtained, its reference to something that has to be measured, and its physical dimension. . . [measurement] involves the use of certain rules of correspondence with performed theoretical constructs which greatly complicate the meaning of measurement. (Margenau, *AAT*: s. 243, 222).

Margenau alludes there to 'rules' such that the numbers can be subjected to the ordinary rules of mathematics, that they can be manipulated (added, subtracted, divided and multiplied) to yield aggregative and other similar useful totals of the thing, the property, that is being measured. Likewise the Stevens entry (*AAT*: s. 243, 223–24) notes: 'Measurement is the process of assigning numbers to represent qualities; the object of measurement is to enable the powerful weapon of mathematical analysis to be applied to the subject matter of science.'

Chapters 5 and 6 showed that Chambers drew heavily on and codified these general measurement rules when formulating CoCoA in *Accounting, Evaluation and Economic Behavior* (especially its chapter 4). This had followed a paper on 'Measurement and Misrepresentation' presented at a 1959 conference of TIMS in Chicago and published in 1960 in *Management Science*, as well as seminal works, the 1964 *Accounting Review* article, 'Measurement and Objectivity in Accounting,' and the 1965 *Journal of Accounting Research* article, 'Measurement in Accounting.'

In a lengthy review piece (referred to in chapter 5) Dean and Clarke unravelled how those ideas on measurement had been forged, showing in particular how a World War II-displaced Austrian Ernest Weinwurm (PhD, University of Vienna, 1920) in his post-war professorial position at De Paul University had cajoled Chambers to understand better the principles of measurement and to integrate them formally into his ideas on accounting theory development.[11]

Chambers' understanding was premised on the process of measurement being a scientific one—a process of identifying a common attribute of the objects subjected to the calculation—a unit of measure, and calculating and assigning the extent of the attribute each possesses on the same scale, so that comparisons can be made. In particular, that the total of the attributes can be added to each other and indeed are subject to all mathematical procedures properly, in an orderly manner, to yield meaningful and understandable totals. As Jones (*AAT*: s. 249, 229) observes:

> Now the order found to exist among those economic things the economist calls goods, services and money arises out of those things themselves. Our problem is to find what known form of mathematical order best describes the order of such things from an economic viewpoint.

And later (*AAT*: s. 253, 235), he proposes that: 'The dollar, the pound, the franc or other monetary unit must be used as a common denominator to permit land, buildings, and machinery to be added to inventories, accounts receivable, patents and goodwill.' Similarly, Broderick (*AAT*: s. 249, 229–30) notes: 'Counting yields measurement only when things are classified by some common property.' Thus Chambers argued that nobody measured assets—but that one could quite properly measure the attributes of assets, of expenses, of liabilities, of income, etc., and that the common financial attribute was current general purchasing power. Further, that the scale in this case is the ratio scale.[12] For, as Stevens (*AAT*: s. 249, 230) had noted, 'foremost among the ratio scales is the scale number itself—the cardinal number—the scale we use when we count such things as eggs, pennies and apples. . . [its use] is so basic and common that it is ordinarily not even mentioned in discussions of measurement.'

Likewise, one could express the increase in the common attribute over a period, and the common attribute of the components of financial position in it, with mathematical propriety.

Theory and Practice Exemplars—Pricing, Measuring, Valuing

Immersed in the practice of accounting, it was revealed in chapter 6 that Chambers was critical of those who drew a distinction between the practice and the theory of accounting. He found comfort in developing a *theory* from ideas based on his observations of practical situations. This process underpinned the practical solutions he presented in consultancy reports and professional and governmental submissions, and eventually in *Accounting, Evaluation and Economic Behavior*. This is evidenced, broadly in our two chapter 4 illustrations. For example, his use of the double account system to report properly the risk attendant with long-life assets; and thereby assist in resolving the energy pricing issues associated with a monopoly utility operation and the funding of the replacement of its generating capacity. The analysis was grounded in the theoretical underpinnings of his CoCoA. His group accounting model was also designed to overcome solecisms in the conventional consolidation form of group accounting. Further, some consultancy particulars below demonstrate this recourse to theory when resolving practical issues. As before, extracts only are reproduced—with the full details being available in the Chambers Archive.

Before examining several of those consultancies a brief account is provided of the early business and related experiences that influenced his accumulated theoretical and practical ideas about prices, measures and values. These were touched upon in chapters 1, 4 and 5. Following the path provided in 'An Academic Apprenticeship,' the story begins with Chambers' economics degree classes in the evenings at Sydney University and contemporaneous daytime positions 'as a junior clerk in the state public service and as stock clerk in a large company manufacturing and distributing petroleum products. Then followed two years as a materials control supervisor and statistical officer' and wartime employment at the Prices Commission. While suggesting in the apprenticeship article that the first three positions had no 'obvious association with matters financial,' which is something we question below, elsewhere he reflected that his work with a petroleum company revealed the importance of a ratio scale in such a measurement exercise—it would have an analogue in accounting—to ensure one added or subtracted like with like.[13] His petroleum-refining experiences revealed that when measuring the change in volume of petrol in a tank (by taking two volumetric readings at different times), it was critical that the temperature of the tank was held constant. In financial terms this equated to the need to ensure that there was a constant dollar across time, otherwise there would be no 'like with like' numbers. One is reminded of Fisher's observations about the 'money illusion' and the 'dance of the dollar' in his 1927 *Stabilization of the Dollar* and his 1911 *Purchasing Power of Money*, as well as Sweeney's 1936 'the dollar is a liar.' This matter is discussed in more detail in the preceding and following chapters.

Chambers' experiences at the Prices Commission appear to us, contrary to his published comments generally, to link the managerial with 'matters financial.' He described those experiences in several places, including the 1971 DSc (Ec) pamphlet mentioned in chapter 6, the 1974 introductory essay to the reprint of *Accounting, Evaluation and Economic Behavior*, and a 1993 private letter to Tom Lee. They were summarized in his 'Apprenticeship' article:

> A wide range of products and processes came under observation; price regulation was geared to costs of production [based on acquisition prices of materials, labour overheads] as well as the aggregate results of firms and industries; and the whole of the exercise had a reasonably clear object [to determine whether price gouging was evident. Were excess profits, rates of return being earned?].

Chambers does note here that 'financial statement analysis was an important part of the monitoring process.'[14]

Those experiences equipped Chambers for many government inquiries and consultancy briefs in areas of mining generally and the petroleum industry in particular, as well as specific price inquiries such as in respect of the electricity industry, the Sugar Millers' Association's request for advice about asset valuation and depreciation 'as a cost,' and, in the mid-1970s, the more general Prices Justification Tribunal (PJT) inquiries.

From those experiences Chambers observed that accounting was integral to many aspects of economic and social affairs. Those early working observations reinforced a desire to seek theoretical underpinnings to effective practices that recognized accounting's social and technical aspects; this was especially so when he was asked to provide an expert opinion about measurement and valuation matters.

Consultancies, Litigation, Expert Evidence, and Professional Advice

Chambers provided professional assistance or advice for plaintiff companies in several Australian commercial disputes—such as the seminal 1950s Arthur Murray taxation case where accounting and commercial notions of income and revenue were considered, and in several prominent Australian audit negligence cases including the 1960s cause célèbre *Pacific Acceptance Corporation Ltd v Forsyth and others* (1970) 92WN NSW 29 and the related *Simonius Vischer & Co v Holt & Thompson* [1979] 2 NSWLR 322. Both cases were adjudicated by Justice P. Moffitt.

While copies of the expert evidence provided are not publicly available (as is customary, the Chambers Archives reveal that copies of expert evidence were returned to the person or body seeking his expert opinion), the Archive does provide some assistance. Some material exists in respect of the Pacific Acceptance Corporation (PAC) case where Chambers provided assistance and advice to the plaintiff, PAC.[15]

There is reference to Chambers' expert evidence in the 1970 Second Interim Judgment by Moffitt J, who describes his reliance on Chambers' evidence in preference to some others.[16] But the Archive correspondence indicates that deciding whether to give expert evidence for PAC was apparently difficult for him.

PAC was a finance company operating in Melbourne. It lent money in tranches usually in excess of $10,000, upon the security of real estate. The matters that were the subject of dispute, the vouching of mortgage loans and all things related, covered the financial reports of PAC for the audit years 1958–60. The submissions and interim and final judgements canvassed broad areas of accounting and auditing, including an auditor's legal liabilities, questions of duty of care and skill, internal control systems, relevance of professional standards, an auditor's reliance on assertions by management and third parties, and the causal link between breach of duty and loss. Moffitt J's judgement found that the audit firm (Flack and Flack, a part of the franchise Australian Price Waterhouse & Co. since 1946) negligent and awarded damages against it. The case was a major one with many precedents for auditing (and nearly fifty years later the issues raised are still pertinent). The case began in February 1968 and extended over 214 sitting days, involving 7,500 pages of transcript and 1,600 exhibits which comprised perhaps five or more times that number of documents.

Together with several lawyers and other accountants, Chambers was asked by McCaw, Johnson and Co. (solicitors for PAC) in a December 1967 letter to provide 'professional advice.' Some preliminary reading matter was provided. He agreed. The rate of fees listed in that letter is of historical interest—fees were agreed at: '$12.00 per hour for preliminary work, involving reading, etc and $20.00 in respect of expert advice, conferences and evidence.'[17] A conference held between the plaintiffs and Chambers was noted in a letter from the solicitors the following January. Then, a 21 February letter from the PAC solicitors to Chambers suggested he had declined to give formal expert evidence. But the solicitors persisted. A letter from them dated 7 May suggests there was ongoing professional advice from Chambers to the plaintiffs. It refers to a request for him to consider an article by Donovan, published in the 1955 issue of the *Australian Law Journal*, in the light of 'the opinion which you have already expressed.' Other material in the Chambers Archive (included in Table 7.2) indicates fees were received from the PAC case in December 1967—March 1968 amounting to $420, and from November—December 1968 amounting to $180.

Clearly Chambers not only provided professional advice, but his expert evidence was relied upon in court. An indication of what it *may* have entailed is provided in the hard-copy Chambers Archive—specifically: a November 1969 letter to Chambers from Frank Edmonds, PAC Official Manager, and Chambers' reply, coupled to the existence of an undated (but most likely written in early 1968) eight-page typed manuscript titled 'Opinions on questions raised in connection with Pacific Acceptance.'

Further, Chambers' reply to Edmonds (which followed preliminary findings by Moffitt J in favour of the plaintiff) notes: 'Thank you very much for the transcript of the [Moffitt] interim judgement. I trust the final outcome will be no less satisfying—if one can use that term in respect of years of difficulty.'[18]

Chambers' undated 'Opinions on Questions' is strong on both matters of principle and observed practice in the areas covered. It conclusively supports our contention that he was acutely aware of the relevant commercial, accounting and auditing practices. The document gives approximately equal space (about two pages) on each of the four areas, and in our summary below we retain the underlining of the main issues used in the opinion.

(1) *The duty of an auditor to vouch and verify the existence of [in this case the mortgage] security.* Chambers was particularly keen to stress the need to sight the original documents, not to rely on managers' or others' assertions about their existence. (2) *General duty of an auditor to vouch and verify the receipt of the proceeds of a cheque.* Here Chambers again highlighted the need to delve rather than accept assurances from management about whether monies were received. He also noted an elementary audit principle, the need to consider an entity's internal controls, in particular the separation of duties. He further observed: 'in the circumstances cited [presumably based on the documents in the Archive which were provided to him by the plaintiff] the auditor's examination

of his client's records would have indicated the intention and grounds of any payment made.' (3) *General duties of an auditor with respect to the adequacy of provisions for bad and doubtful debts.* Chambers stressed the need to obtain information about the specific debt, and, generally, not to rely on past experiences of debts. (4) *General duty of an auditor to vouch and verify the declaration of a dividend declared by a subsidiary.* As explained below (and in chapter 4) Chambers had strong views about adherence to the separate legal entity doctrine in respect of subsidiary/holding company relationships—separate entity perspectives dominated his reasoning in respect of accounting for, and the auditing of, corporate groups.

In sum, Chambers' 'Opinions' document expressed strongly the need for auditors to extend their investigations generally—they were required to do more than just an annual audit, they needed to go beyond their client's books of account, reviewing management's assertions about things, in particular, about an entity's stock and the provision for bad debts.

Moffitt J was favourably disposed to Chambers' evidence. His second Interim Judgment (pp. 194ff.) noted:

> Professor Chambers was a helpful expert witness . . . well qualified to give evidence on audit theory. It was put that his evidence should be discarded because of his lack of practical experience and because he dealt rather with ideal standards. . . . Making due allowance for these considerations, Professor Chambers' evidence was useful and acceptable as a complement to other evidence of practice and the opinions of men with practical experience.

In discussing the defendant's evidence presented by a partner of Spry and Walker, Mr P.J. Davidson, Moffitt J noted that Davidson: 'is a man of considerable practical experience, and some of his evidence was helpful and acceptable. However, at many points it was in conflict with that of Cameron [a partner of Hungerfoord, Spooner & Kirkthorpe, one of the plaintiff's experts] and other acceptable views, and *on the whole I prefer the evidence of Cameron and Professor Chambers.*' (emphasis added)

There are many instances of the use of Chambers' practical knowledge. His 'Aide-Memoire' (see also Tables 7.1 and 7.2) indicates that he provided advice to the plaintiff, Simonius Vischer, in the 1970s audit negligence case, *Simonius Vischer & Co v Holt & Thompson.* While an empty folder exists in the Chambers Archive, none of the pertinent Chambers' correspondence in respect of that case is available. Presumably, as with the PAC case, it was returned to the client.

Briefly, the plaintiff was a wool company one of whose departments was alleged to be excessively buying wool without authority, losing $200,000 in the process. The auditor was sued. Failure to alert the head office to the operations of the department was alleged. *Simonius Vischer* confirmed the precedent in Pacific Acceptance of the need for auditors to extend their investigations generally—to do more than just an annual audit, to go beyond their client's books of account, reviewing management's assertions about things, in particular an entity's stock and the provision for bad debts. The traditional 'auditor as a watchdog' view was being extended to an 'auditor being a bloodhound.'

As well as being asked to provide advice on many commercial issues, such as work for the Department of Prime Minister and Cabinet's BHP inquiry (1972, 1973), Commonwealth Crown Solicitor (1972) and the N.S.W. State Crown Solicitor (1974–6), Chambers' opinion was sought by the practising arm of the profession. This included requests for his opinion from major law firms, amongst them Allen, Allen and Hemsley (1975) and Stephen, Jacques & Stephen (1980) and the management consulting firm John P. Young & Associates (1950s and 1960s).[19]

His work for associations such as the N.S.W. Institute of Launderers, the Oil Industry of N.S.W., the Australian Stevedoring Industry Board, and companies such as Civil and Civic (1958), CSR Ltd (1961), and BHP (1960s and 1970s) shows he was clearly highly respected for knowledge of pricing, valuation and other commercial matters. Consider also his general assistance for the PJT including in Ampol's 1975 pricing justification case. In another PJT hearing in 1973, while reluctant to appear as an expert witness for BHP, Chambers saw no problems in assisting BHP prepare a draft report about the legitimacy of their fixed asset utilization accounting policy. He had provided advice on this policy to BHP as early as 1961.[20] Clearly, his expert advice was sought by all the protagonists before the PJT. It certainly gives further credence to our claim that he was well versed in business affairs and their regulation.

The few instances where correspondence material from court cases or government inquiries has survived, including even some extracts from his opinions, provide evidence of Chambers' consultancy work and skills set, and sometimes the amount of fees paid. They again confirm he was equally at ease in the practical and theoretical domains.

For a busy academic, Table 7.1 clearly shows he was able to manage his time to enable the undertaking of a range of consultancy work over more than four decades. It reveals a commercial understanding across several industries—sugar cane, steel, oil and gas, stevedoring, construction, property—as well as in respect of myriad management (legal, financial and accounting) matters such as pricing, dividend constraints, revenue recognition, valuation of property, and auditor negligence issues. The all-rounder tag certainly sits well.

Research for this chapter revealed some unexpected data on income from several consultancies (Table 7.2). The Archive shows individual consultancy income sources like the £59 received in respect of the July 1960 Oil Industry

Table 7.1 Consultancies

N.S.W. Institute of Launderers (1947–53)
N.S.W. Public Accountants Registration Board (1952)
Australian Stevedoring Industry Board (1953)
J.P. Young & Associates (1955–59)
Arthur Murray litigation (1957)
Civil and Civic (1958)
General Electric consultancy and lecture on his overseas travel (U.S.A., 1959)
Oil Industry of N.S.W. (1960)
Colonial Sugar Refining Company Ltd (1961)
AICPA Accounting Research Division (working with Moonitz)
Pacific Acceptance litigation (1969–70)
Commonwealth Solicitor General (1972)
Proprietary Sugar Millers (1973)
PJT (1974, 1977)
Allen, Allen and Hemsley (1975)
State Crown Solicitor (1974–76)
Broken Hill Proprietary Ltd (1976)
Stephen, Jacques & Stephen (1980)

Source: Chambers on Accounting (Vol. VI), section 7 of Chambers 'Aide Memoire' (p. 11)

Table 7.2 Chambers' Summary of His Miscellaneous Income and Consultancies

N.S.W. Institute of Launderers (1947–53)	na*
N.S.W. Public Accountants Registration Board (1952–72)	na
Australian Stevedoring Industry Board (1953)	na
J.P. Young & Associates (1955–59)—see endnotes #9, chapter 7 and #21, chapter 7	na
Arthur Murray litigation (1957)—payment in September 1961	£84
ASA Chief Examiner/Marking Fees—622 papers (December 1957)[1]	£227
ASA Chief Examiner/Marking Fees—613 papers (December 1958). These continued for several years (1961–62, 1970) totalling	£228 £610
PARB Chief Examiner/Marking Fees (1961, 1965–69; 1971–74); average p.a.	$200
Civil and Civic (1958)	£142
General Electric consultancy and lecture on his overseas travel (U.S.A., 1959)	na
Oil Industry of N.S.W. (1960)	£59
Australian Accountants Research Services Foundation—Report On Draft Recommendations on Accounting Principles (February 1961)	£105
Colonial Sugar Refining Company Ltd (March 1961)	£240
AICPA Accounting Research Division (with Moonitz, 1962)	na
Arthur Murray—1966 High Court appeal	na
Pacific Acceptance litigation	
(December 1967 to March 1968)	$492
(April—December 1968)	$180
Department of Prime Minister and Cabinet—BHP Steel Prices Inquiry	
1972–7 hours; and September 1973–35 hours	$450

Commonwealth Solicitor General (1972)—*Heavy Minerals*	$250
Proprietary Sugar Millers (1973)	na
Prices Justification Tribunal (1974, 1975)	
BHP inquiry	$520
Ampol Inquiry (7–14 March 1975)	$352
Allen, Allen and Hemsley (April 1975)—two private company cases	na
State Crown Solicitor (1974–76)	
Dominance, N.L. and Kimberley Minerals cases,	na
Simonius Vischer case (27/8–6/11 1976)	$968
N.S.W. Corporate Affairs Commission (June 1978)—13 1/2 day meetings	$650
Stephen, Jacques & Stephen (April-June 1980),The *AFR* and Argus & Ors	na
Nestlé Directorship Fees (1967–86)—details of yearly fees on p. 139	$300—$9,000

Sources: Chambers on Accounting (Vol. 6), section 7 of Chambers 'Aide Memoire' (p. 11); augmented by extracts from an undated handwritten summary of miscellaneous income, etc from consultancies during 1947–86; an unnumbered part of the USA P202, Chambers Archive. Individual letters in the Archive also provide further data.

na* means data are not available.

of N.S.W. request to assist with their submission into the Land Valuation Act.[21] Particularly revealing is the folder (albeit, not noted in the Archive's official listing) containing handwritten summaries of Chambers' non-university consultancies and related income from 1947–86—a period prior to being appointed as a senior lecturer at Sydney University until a few years after his retirement. The summaries include fees paid annually during the late 1950s and throughout the 1960s for examination and marking that Chambers did for the PARB and the ASA. The handwriting is unmistakeably Chambers.' It is not stated (or otherwise known) the purpose for which this list was prepared—it is also undated—but the entries suggest it was most likely prepared around the end of 1986 or early 1987.

For comparative purposes a University of Sydney associate professor's salary in 1957 was £2,350.

We have slightly rearranged the handwritten listing to 'fit' the Table 7.1 consultancy listings, with appropriate additions.

Particulars from two 1970s commercial disputes are examined in some detail below as they are consistent with what was demonstrated in the Pacific Acceptance saga, namely Chambers' use of practical and theoretical lenses to examine commerce and related disputes. They are chosen because materials exist in the Archive to reconstruct the reports tendered, thereby enabling an analysis of the brief and of Chambers' thinking. The cases are the Proprietary Sugar Millers (1973) and the Commonwealth Solicitor General (1972) consultancies.

The first involves a request in early 1973 from the Queensland Proprietary Cane Growers and Sugar Millers' Association covering the broad question of 'Asset Valuation in the Sugar Growing and Milling Industry.'[22] Chambers' brief stated:

> We confirm that we would be pleased to receive from you in writing your opinion on (a) the best manner of valuing assets of growers and millers in a closed industry in an inflationary climate knowing that the valuations form a basis for the division of sugar monies, and (b) the treatment of the resultant depreciation as a cost.

Whereas Chambers' report to the Association is unavailable, the comments from the association's general secretary, John Desmarchelier, upon receipt of the report provide insights about what was contained in it.

The implied particulars of the report suggest that Chambers was influenced by his Prices Commission wartime and 1940s business experiences, coupled to his early education tasks covering the fields of management and finance. He was familiar with the relationships between prices and costs and the need in time of war and beyond to ensure rates of return (meshing financial and managerial accounting notions, namely, profits, costs, and rates of return) were understood properly, not viewed as isolates. The report illustrated how the valuation of assets impinged upon the notion of depreciation 'as a cost' and the relevant depreciation amount. In this and the second vignette Chambers' argument is interspersed with our comments. The underlining emphasis is as per the original.

This account is based on the general secretary's letter thanking him for his eighteen-page draft report, and noting his independence, something regarded by judges as critical in expert opinions. It was a characteristic commented upon by Stamp in the epigraph to chapter 2. That letter sought some minor presentation changes to Chambers' draft report:

> Could I therefore make some suggestions for the alteration in the presentation of pages 14–18 of your report. I would like to see your Summary stand independently and incorporate the work from the second paragraph of page14 onwards. The first section of the Summary could involve your statement of the present procedures (middle paragraph on page 14) followed by your comments and criticisms (bottom of page 14 and top of page 15). These comments could be spelled out 1, 2, 3. . . . While they are not all favourable to the present practice of mills, they do call into account the questionable procedures 'accepted' by the Central Board and this will be a key part of our overall submission to the Board. In the second paragraph on page 15 ('The frequency. . .') we would like to suggest a strengthening of the emphasis on the difference between land and depreciating assets.

> We understand from our discussions with you that you view assigned land (over 60% of the growers' assets) in a different light to other assets:

- all usable coastal land in Australia is subject to inflation;
- the value of assigned land reflects the profitability of cane farming and is therefore self-inflationary; and
- land is regarded as 'low risk' compared with other forms of investment.

You are correct to point out in the last paragraph of page 15 that no account has been taken of working capital in the past. Its inclusion may be adverse for mills, but we do not suggest deletion of this paragraph. Also, as you suggest, credit for growers, including progress payments from mills, is adequate. Could I now suggest some change in emphasis to the Summary items on page 16?

Item 1. Our interest is in 'assets employed' by millers and growers rather than 'sums invested' or 'currently in use.'

Item 2. The above comment applies to Item 2 to the extent that the two are connected.

Item 3. Again a comment that 'funds invested' may be expressed as 'assets.' If your whole report had to be summarized in one paragraph it is this one. It is a regulated, specialized industry, with a restricted market for assets and it is continuous.

Item 4. I think it follows from your earlier comments that, the sugar industry being a regulated one, a special index is more appropriate in current value accounting for the sugar industry. Indeed there may be two separate indices—for land and other assets.

Item 5. Your comments are correct. However, the mill panel does not alter. All information is available to the Board, but the only index they examine is the C.P.I.

Upon receipt of Chambers' final report the general secretary noted:

You are to be sincerely congratulated for grasping and understanding so quickly an area of activity which is complex even for those who have spent many years in the industry. As you have suggested your report has been written in a manner that is most suitable for submission to the Central Board as an Exhibit. Initially, of course, it will be submitted to our Counsel who are at present preparing the form of presentation of argument to the Central Board. Your report will be a source of enlightenment to them and your findings will be used by them. The use of Exhibits is subject to their advice. However, it is most likely that your report will be presented and particularly the summary part which will be more readily digestible by a basically non-accounting-orientated Board.

Responses to Chambers' consultancy reports indicate this response was not uncommon. Correspondence in this first case also provides another indication of Chambers' humour, with the concluding comments in his final letter to the general secretary observing:

> The sugar industry and I don't seem to get on very well. Harvesting and milling were washed out in Bundaberg; the Fiji mill workers went on strike for the whole of my visit! I've seen plenty of cane, but no sugar!

The second vignette covers a 1972 commercial consultancy for the Commonwealth Crown Solicitor, *Re Heavy Minerals Pty Ltd (In Liquidation)*. It relates to profit determination, asset revaluations, and dividend payments considering the prospect of any disadvantage to creditors relative to owners. Similar dilemmas with corporate group activities were shown in chapter 4 to have dogged commerce, the accounting profession and lawyers for many decades and Chambers' analyses and syntheses of the issues are revealing of his knowledge in this area. For instance, take this extract from the Commonwealth Crown Solicitor's letter of 5 July 1972 seeking advice and Chambers' response a week later:[23]

> The liquidator . . . Mr. J.R. Partridge has asked me to act on his behalf to recover an amount equal to that paid to the shareholders . . . by way of dividend on 30th April, 1960. Your advice is sought upon the form of the accounts of the company for the relevant period and in particular your opinion upon specific questions set out hereunder relating to the possibility that payment of the dividend was other than from available profits.

Chambers 13 July response:

> I refer to your letter of 5 July and the papers appended thereto. I give my opinion in paragraphs corresponding to the numbered questions in paragraph 21 of your letter.
>
> (i) *Did the Profit and Loss Appropriation Account shown in the Balance Sheet of the next preceding year disclose sufficient available profits for the declaration of the dividend on 30 April 1960?*

Yes. Disregarding the sums received in respect of the cancellation of contracts, there remained a sum of £112,532 of undistributed trading profits at 30 June 1959. The whole tax for the year ended 30 June 1959 was first assessed at £41,800 (your para. B); the liability to the Commissioner of Taxation at 30 June 1960 has been said to be £42,205 (letter of Mr. J.R. Partridge, 5 June 1972). Either way, there would have remained sufficient to meet the liability for taxation out of the balance of profits at 30 June 1959, after payment of the dividend of £60,088 in April 1960.

   (ii) *Is the capitalization of losses on realization of plant, machinery and rights to mine under the heading of 'Intangible Assets' in the amount of £445,123 a generally accepted and sound accounting practice?*

When the amount of any such loss is small (say, on the sale of a single machine at less than its book value), it is commonly charged against gross income in arriving at the profit of the year. Large losses, however, if treated in this way, would distort the 'pattern' or 'trend' of profits. They are not therefore charged against gross income in the year in which they occur by companies which intend to carry on their business. Like payments for formation expenses and goodwill, they are carried in the accounts with the intention that they will be written off when sufficient profits have been earned to offset them, partially or wholly. The different treatments in practice of small losses and large losses suggest that there is no generally accepted principle at issue.

It is my personal belief that all such losses and payments (for formation expenses and security issue costs, for example) which do not give rise to tangible assets, should be written off forthwith. The money so laid out has gone. But it is widely held in the accountancy profession that to carry forward these balances, properly described, serves as explanation of what has happened to the total tangible assets which formerly were shown to be at the disposal of the company and its directors. It is curious to describe a heavy loss as an 'intangible asset'; it would be less curious to show it separately on the assets side of the balance sheet, since both assets and losses are represented by "debit" balances. But when described as a loss, it is misleading to no one, however it appears. On this view the practice of the company would not be considered unsound. The question refers to 'capitalization of losses.' The term is, I think, confusing. The capitalization of expected profits, as when the company revalued the original mining rights by £250,000, gives rise to a debit balance. The capitalization of losses cannot mean something analogous to this, since it also gives rise to a debit balance. I take the term to signify only that the losses are not immediately written off against past profits or subscribed capital. It is not necessarily implied that it is to be regarded as a 'capital loss' or a 'loss of capital'; it has no different effect from a sustained series of trading losses.

More generally, this view continued to underpin Chambers' academic and educational ideas about an entity's 'performance' (colloquially its periodic profit or loss), something that is well described in *Accounting, Evaluation and Economic Behavior* and *Securities and Obscurities* and summarized in our chapter 6. In brief, it is generally accepted that business is undertaken by sole traders, companies, or other entities with the aim of increasing the funds (wealth) contributed to those business activities. Any increase in wealth may arise from various sources—related to what in earlier times were described as either 'fixed' or 'circulating' capital (components of wealth), terms used in the consultancy report above. Whether that increase was due to trading gains or holding (capital) gains from those sources of capital is not seen as critical by Chambers.

> *(iii) If not [a generally accepted and sound accounting practice], what is the more appropriate method?*

I have said that the method used by the company is curious but not misleading. As the loss has already fallen on the amount of the shareholders' interest, it would be better to bring together the amounts representing the aggregate interests of shareholders; in summary form as at 30 June 1960, thus:

	£	£
Subscribed capital		253,004
Profit and Loss Appropriation Account		57,334
		310,338
Less Loss on realization of assets	(445,123)	
Capital reserves	220,985	(224,138)
Net shareholders' equity		86,200

To show the net interest in this, which preserves the distinctive character of each contributory item while showing the net financial effect.

> *(iv) If the company had profits available, was it prevented from distributing such profits by the capital losses suffered by it?*

The conventional meaning of 'capital loss' is a loss sustained on the sale of so-called fixed assets at less than their book value. A 'loss of capital' on the other hand, has occurred when assets exceed liabilities by less than the amount of the subscribed capital. A capital loss in the above sense does not necessarily entail a loss of capital; its amount may be less than the profits of any given year, or less than the total amount of undistributed profit. On the other hand, a loss of capital in the above sense does not necessarily arise from a capital loss; it may arise through a series of trading losses.

In the present case the capital loss was so large that its consequence was a loss of capital.

But did the loss stand in the way of distribution? Any part of the undistributed profit could have been distributed at any time prior to 30 April 1960. It is well established that a balance of profits does not lose its character as profit available for dividend unless and until it is converted, by explicit resolution, into a dividend payable or an increase in share capital, or unless and until it is reduced by subsequent trading losses. It is also established that where a company's fixed assets have depreciated in value (declined in aggregate money's worth) it is not necessary first to make good that depreciation before a dividend may be paid; it is sufficient that the 'current receipts' shall exceed the 'current payments.'

(Lee v. Neuchatel Asphalte Co. Ltd.)[24]

If, as may be the case, this question (iv) has in contemplation the notion of 'loss of capital,' the point may be argued from a different direction.

It will be recalled that the directors in 1956 revalued the mining rights by £250,000 and made a bonus issue of shares out of the resulting surplus. This revaluation may properly be described as the capitalization of *expected* profits. There was therefore no real substance in the addition of £250,000 to the subscribed capital, such as there is when, for example, the land and buildings of a company are written up to approximate a current market value and a bonus issue is made out of the resulting surplus. It is a personal view that no such capitalization of expected profits should occur, since it results in the mixing, under 'subscribed capital,' of money funds contributed, or deemed to be contributed, by shareholders, and of a mere speculative expectation. Nevertheless the practice is an accepted practice.

. . .

On these grounds it seems permissible to disregard what amount to mere book entries, by deleting the sum of £250,000 both from the intangible assets (and subsequently the realized loss) and from the 'subscribed' capital. The balance sheets of the three years of interest would then appear thus:

	30 June	*1958*	*1959*	*1960*
		£.	£.	£.
Assets—	Current assets	39,896	85,177	30,852
	Investments	154	154	154
	Fixed assets	182,862	177,414	
	Mine development	25,825	25,618	
	Intangibles	6,454	71,600	65,224
		225,191	359,963	96,230

(Continued)

(Continued)

30 June		1958	1959	1960
		£.	£.	£.
Equities—	Current liabilities	83,343	15,941	10,030
	Secured creditors	1,332		
	Deferred liabilities	72,922	7,500	
	Subscribed capital	3,004	3,004	3,004
	P&L Appropriation	94,590	112,532	57,334
	Capital reserve		220,986	220,985
	Realized loss			(195,123)
		255,191	359,963	96,230

The representation of the *realized* loss in the amount of £195,123 is consistent with the substantive facts, since the amount of £250,000 shown among 'mining rights' was never a sum paid out, and its inclusion in the total amount of realized loss in the accounts does violence to the usual understanding of realization. The figures now show . . . no loss of capital in any substantive sense, since the realized loss falls short of the amount of the profits represented by the Profit and Loss Appropriation Account balance and the Capital reserve.

On both the grounds considered, it does not seem that the company was prevented from distributing the profits by the loss it suffered.

> (v) Is the loss on realization of plant, machinery and mining rights at actual cost a charge against available profits for the year ended 30 June 1960?

No. Following *Lee v. Neuchatel* etc., the directors were at liberty to treat it otherwise than as a charge against the profits otherwise determined for the year.

It should be noted that the relevant 1880s company law precedent held that there was a clear distinction between 'fixed' and 'circulating' capital. Only reductions in the latter were to be charged against the profits before determining whether a dividend might be paid. This was subject always to there being sufficient in total capital (i.e., the entity was solvent) to pay a dividend without disadvantaging creditors.

> (vi) Was it necessary . . . to consider the loss of £445,123 . . . when the dividend was paid . . .?

The precedents are not clear. In *Verner v. The General and Commercial Investment Trust*, [*Verner v General & Commercial Investment Trust* [1894] 2 Ch 239. . .] it was said that 'fixed capital may be sunk and lost, and yet . . . the excess of current receipts over current payments may be divided.' This relates, it seems, to the excess of receipts over payments of a 'current' year in which or before which the fixed capital was sunk or lost. It does not seem to relate to a division in one year of profits made in prior years. The dictum in *Lee v. Neuchatel*, etc. also seems to apply to profits earned subsequently to or during the year in which the loss of value occurred.

But the question in the present case is whether profits earned *prior* to a capital loss may be carried forward as a distributable profit notwithstanding the loss. The position is made clear in the 1963 *Glenville Pastoral* case (*Glenville Pastoral Co Pty Ltd v FCT* 109 CLR 1999). It was held that the directors may, 'by a positive and final decision, apply distributable profit to make good lost share capital.' But in the absence of any such decision, profits ascertained for a given year or carried forward from previous years continue to be distributable.

It does not therefore seem to have been necessary to take into account the loss on realization when considering the payment of the dividend on 30 April 1960.

Paras vii—xi of Chambers' report are not reproduced; they continue the analysis of the revaluation, profit, and dividend issues from a practical/theoretical lens.[25]

The commercial issues raised in this consultative report especially in respect to solvency have ongoing relevance. Similar matters emerged in several Australian financial affairs and related investigations in the late 1980s and early '90s, including in the Bond Corporation case, with its dealings with the Bell Group in particular, and the Adelaide Steamship case,[26] as well as the financial fiascos of the 2000s at Allco, Macquarie Bank, and Babcock and Brown.[27] Briefly, each of those affairs involved complex economic entities—they had intertwined corporate structures, with equally complicated financing arrangements that proved problematic for many parties to unravel when the groups either collapsed or were in financial difficulties. Overlaying this complexity were accounting questions pertaining to whether asset revaluations by subsidiary companies could be used as part of reported profits, thereby enabling dividends to be dispersed in other parts of the economic group.[28] The reported profits/dividends test is less relevant in the second decade of the new millennium in Anglo-American countries, but its replacement by the solvency test means that much of what Chambers discussed in this consultancy still has indirect relevance.

The succinctness with which Chambers unravelled the issues in his brief, his summary of the legal and accounting precedents and the infusion of his personal with conventional approaches reinforces appreciation of his range of skills, in particular his theoretical and practical understandings of such matters.

Financial Press

In economics a several-centuries-old tradition exists of philosophers, professionals, and lobbyists using the press to influence public policy by exposing to the public and the government proposed reforms.[29] Early twentieth-century examples of this in the U.K. include Sidney and Beatrice Webb's efforts to promote the Fabian Society and their press and other attempts to pave the way for increased welfare arrangements in Britain. Consider also the Keynesian and Hayekian economic proposals after World War I and after the Depression.[30]

In accounting, such actions are not as common. However, unlike most accounting academics of his time, Chambers and his colleagues, in the U.K. Eddie Stamp and in the U.S. Abe Briloff, were persistent contributors to the financial press following corporate episodes where accounting was perceived to be inadequate—namely periods of takeover excesses, inflationary periods and when large companies unexpectedly collapsed. Table 7.3 presents a compilation based on Chambers' 'Aide Memoire' of his press publications (and unsuccessful press submissions), as well as articles in professional journals covering nearly forty years.

Chambers' range of practical and theoretical knowledge is evidenced by the breadth of areas covered: technical accounting topics, like asset valuation, depreciation, inflation accounting and accounting for deferred taxation, auditing, education, standards setting, general regulatory issues, as well as discussions in the broad covering accounting, finance and management.

Professional Service

Chambers' consultancy and press experiences were augmented by many decades of service on a number of professional and governmental committees. He was an ad hoc member of ASA Research Committee on various issues; an Examiner of the Board of Directors of ASA 1955–64; a N.S.W. Divisional Councillor 1965–79; N.S.W. State President 1975–76; an ASA National Councillor 1972–79; and National President 1977–78.

Table 7.4 is reproduced from the 'Membership' section of Chambers' 'Aide Memoire'; it reveals much about his major contributions from the length and seniority of positions held. It discloses also that attempts to be involved in practical matters extended to presentations at what he labelled 'Social Clubs.' While 'socializing' outside the academy, he never missed an opportunity to tell his story about the inadequacies in the 'conventionally prepared and audited accounts' of corporates, with the concomitant inefficiencies for businesses and inequities they created for shareholders, creditors, and other market participants.

He was always keen to test his ideas about accounting's products with those who use them. Copies of his many lectures and related correspondence of those Rotary, Probus, Sydney Legacy, Chamber of Commerce,

Table 7.3 Chambers' Letters to the General Press and Professional Journals

1954	'Tax allowance inquiry' (plea for a new basis of tax assessment), *Sydney Morning Herald*, October 1, 2.
1962	'University education in accounting in Australia,' *The Accountant*, March 10.
	'Advertiser case,' *SMH*, June 23, 8.
1963	'Reviewing investment techniques,' *Australian Financial Review*, January 31, 2.
	'Stock exchanges and company reports,' *SMH*, March 19, unpublished.
	'Under the law of the jungle. . .' (on stock exchanges and company accounts), *AFR*, May 28, 2.
	'More on financial reporting' (response to E.J. Green), *AFR*, June 11, 2.
	'Financial information and the securities market' (under the caption—'Professor Chambers replies' this is a response to letter of E. York Seymour to *AFR*, October 15), *AFR*, October 29, 2.
1966	'Soft and hard management training,' *AFR*, March 2, 3.
	'Accounting should move into the space age' (comment on article of John Lloyd, 'Accountants should change their ways in the space age'), *The Australian*, March 28, 6.
1967	'Education for management,' published as 'Wrong approach to education for business?' *AFR*, April 27, 3.
	'How do our businessmen rate?,' *The Australian*, May 16, 10.
	'Auditors and accounting,' published as 'Need for watch on company statements of fact,' *AFR*, June 8, 3.
	'Accountants and mathematics,' published as 'More exact accounting,' *AFR*, October 11, 3.
1968	'Consolidated statements' (reply to letter of R.C. Dalton on Chambers' article on this topic in *The Australian Accountant*, February), *The Australian Accountant*, April, 231–32; reprinted in Thomas Burns and H.S. Hendrickson (Eds), *The Accounting Sampler*, second edition, McGraw-Hill, New York, 1972.
1969	To the editor, *The Australian Accountant*, on some gaffes and infelicities in contents of the journal, January 29, unpublished.
	Response to letter of R.M. Trueblood on personal and business accounting, *Journal of Accountancy*, January; *Journal of Accountancy*, August, 26–28.
	Response to letter of L.S. Leask on balance sheets, *Journal of Accountancy*, February 1969, *Journal of Accountancy*, October, 32, 34.
	Letter about Morris on current value accounting, *AFR*, unpublished.
1970	'Deferred tax accounting,' published as 'Top accountants called to account,' *AFR*, February 17, 3.
	'Future of management education,' published as 'Learning the business,' *AFR*, February 25, 3.
	'Replacement price accounting,' response to letter of Professor Amey of 11 June 1970 same journal, *The Accountant*, September 24, 420.

(Continued)

Table 7.3 (Continued)

1971	'On the failure of accounting to eliminate misdirection and the need for some fresh devices,' *AFR*, unpublished.
	'On the appropriateness of the SEC as a model for Australia,' *AFR*, unpublished.
1972	'The audit of accounting' (response to articles of Ashley McKeon), *AFR*, July, 7pp. unpublished.
	'The other side of the account' (on the inquiries of Professor S.A. Zeff), *Australian Financial Review*, December 12, 3.
1973	'On the relevance of cash equivalents' (response to letter of A. Robinson, *The Chartered Accountant in Australia*, January), *The Chartered Accountant in Australia*, March, 45–46.
	'On financial position' (response to letter of A. Robinson, *The Chartered Accountant in Australia*, March 1973), *The Chartered Accountant in Australia*, May, 36, 38.
	'Simple reforms in accounting,' (response to letter of G.S. Kirk, May 9, *Australian Financial Review* on Chambers' address to Pacioli Society, May 9) *AFR*, June 13, 3.
	'On income and other matters' (response to letters of A. Robinson and C. Warrell), *The Chartered Accountant in Australia*, June, 47–48.
1974	'MBA is not a mish-mash' (response to A J Hamilton on University of Sydney MBA proposal, *AFR*, January 31), *AFR*, February 6, 3.
	'Accounting and valuing' (comment on W. R. Mason, 'The separate and distinct philosophies of accounting and valuing,' *The Chartered Accountant in Australia*, November 1973), *The Chartered Accountant in Australia*, March 1974, 48.
	'Accounting standards: objectives, problems, achievements' (comment on article of B. Feller under this title, *The Australian Accountant*, August), *The Australian Accountant*, October, 569.
1975	'A company fraud cure,' *AFR*, January 8, 2.
	'On accounting for inflation'; letter of March 12 to *Sydney Morning Herald*, in response to a series of articles on the matter; unpublished.
	'Accounting for inflation,' *Accountants' Journal*, September, 299–300.
	'Company report shows flaws in CPP accounting theories,' *AFR*, May 30, 16–17.
	Response to letter of I.A.A. Vassie ('CVA accounting has flaws too,' *AFR*, June 10), submitted to editor June 17, unpublished.
	'Another method of coping with inflation,' *SMH* August 7, 22.
1976	'Correcting an impression' (D. C. Bell, letter, *Accountants' Journal*, November 1975) that Chambers' proposal is a variety of replacement price accounting, *Accountants' Journal*, March.
	'Accounting for inflation; a reply to Popoff,' *Accountants' Journal*, April, 92–94, response to Boris Popoff, 'Accounting for inflation: Chambers and CCA,' *Accountants' Journal*, February 1976.

'Nails will not help tax case' (criticism of an article on the Mathews Committee proposals on income taxation, *The Australian*, July 7), *The Australian*, August 3, 12.

'Accounting for inflation' (comment on a letter by Okai responding to Chambers' article in *The Accountant's Magazine*, March), *The Accountant's Magazine*, August, 306–07.

'Accounting for inflation' (comment on a review of Chambers, *Accounting for Inflation*, 1975), *The Australian Accountant*, September, 514.

1977	'What does it [CoCoA] stand for?,' *The Accountant's Magazine*, August.
1978	'CCA: criticisms of some comments,' *The Chartered Accountant in Australia*, July, 88–90.
	'Unanswered questions,' *The Chartered Accountant in Australia*, November, 4.
1979	'Comment on an editorial on the Report of the ASRC,' *Law Society Journal*, Vol 17, April, 145–51.
1980	'A Christmas present indeed' (on a financial reporting standard, FASB33, promulgated by the U.S. FASB), *The Chartered Accountant in Australia*, February, 2.
1984	'The new AUP3—is the emphasis misplaced?,' *The Australian Accountant*, July, 411.
	'Financial position and results defined,' *The Australian Accountant*, November, 807.
1992	'Rubbery figures stretch assets,' *The Australian*, June 2, 12.
	'Accounting standards—a fatal flaw,' submitted to *Business Review Weekly* June 15, unpublished.
	'When the assets indicator sticks,' *The Australian*, June 19, 12.

Source: Chambers on Accounting (Vol. 6), section 12 of Chambers 'Aide Memoire' (pp. 35–7)

Table 7.4 Memberships—Technical and Professional Associations

1941–99	Australian Society of Certified Practising Accountants (formerly, Commonwealth Institute of Accountants, and later, ASA); life member, 1979
1941–79	Institute of Chartered Secretaries and Administrators (formerly Australasian Institute of Secretaries)
1943–66	Australasian Institute of Cost Accountants (amalgamated with ASA, 1966)
1944–76	Economic Society of Australia and New Zealand
1946–55	Institute of Industrial Administration (U.K.)
1951–55	Australian Institute of Management
1957–99	AAA
1960–69	BACA (committee, company secretary roles)
1960–71	International University Contact for Management Education
1960–99	Accounting Association of Australia and New Zealand (formerly Australasian Association of University Teachers of Accounting); foundation president; life member, 1983
1961–71	TIMS
1962,1968–99	Sydney University Pacioli Society (foundation president; president, 1992)
1966–99	Academy of the Social Sciences in Australia (formerly Social Sciences Research Council of Australia)
1974–99	ARIA
1974–99	Academy of Accounting Historians
1976–99	Beta Alpha Psi (U.S. National Accounting Fraternity)
1980–99	Accademia Italiana di Economia Aziendale
1987–99	IAAER
1997–99	Societa Italiana di Storia della Ragioneria

Social clubs

1935–99	University of Sydney Union
1953–61	The Accountants Club (foundation committee)
1960–87	University of Sydney Staff Club (president, 1961–62, official opening, 21 July 1961)
1961–71	Sydney Rotary Club
1966–99	General Management (monthly luncheon) Group
1972–9	Royal Automobile Club of N.S.W.
1986–99	Sydney Probus Club

Source: Chambers on Accounting (Vol. 6), section 5 of the 'Aide Memoire' (p. 8)

Bankers' Institute of Australia, Institution of Engineers of Australia, N.S.W. Computer Society, Beta Alpha Psi and Sydney University Society meetings (Economics Society, and Kabeiori), lectures to professional and other business communities, along with addresses to company-organized meetings, such as at BHP and Qantas, are available in the Chambers Archive.[31] In a letter related to his Probus talk, 'Life on the Fringe,' the president of the Sydney branch sent an account of the talk to the members remarking on Chambers' passion and engagement:

> At our well attended March meeting our own Member Prof. Ray Chambers treated us to a dissertation about "Life on the Fringe." In a most interesting address Ray outlined some of the problems which are encountered by those who attempt to push out the "fringes" of knowledge; challenge the accepted view and seek to bring about change and improvement in the fields of accounting and accountability. A well earned vote of thanks was moved by Ian Matheson [at the time Managing Director of one of Australia's largest banks, Westpac] and strongly supported by those present.[32]

Submissions to Professional and Governmental Enquiries

Chambers undertook numerous submissions over a period of nearly thirty years as listed in Table 7.5. The data imply evidence of enduring energy—through submissions to accounting profession exposure drafts and regulatory inquiries both nationally and internationally. Breadth and persistence again best describe the areas covered and the number of submissions. Matters examined include: disclosure, national and international 'principles,' then 'standards,' reforms to accounting education, changes to companies' legislation primarily in respect of asset valuation and the true and fair view override issues, price and price level accounting reforms, especially during the 1960s and '70s inflation accounting debates. Those submissions underpinned the 1978 N.S.W. ASRC Report (analysed chapter 8).

Internationalization of Accounting

Chambers had some limited influence in pursuing the need for accounting matters to be considered from an international perspective. Especially prominent are his efforts in the 1960s and the early '70s. For example, his correspondence with Sir Henry Benson (who in 1973 became the first chairman of the International Accounting Standards Committee) stressing the need for an international accounting authority prior to the IASC being formed, and his exhaustive efforts in the founding of *Abacus*.[33] The correspondence reveals that Chambers founded *Abacus* because of a perceived lack of quality accounting journals devoted to international issues.[34] Other

Table 7.5 Submissions to Public and Professional Bodies

Year	Submission
1960	Report to the Chairman, N.S.W. PARB, on investigation (1959) of steps taken in England and the United States to ensure adequate disclosure of financial information in published company reports, March, 5 pp.
1961	Comments on draft recommendations of ICAA, prepared at the request of the Institute, 1961, 26 pp. Chambers (convenor) with L. Goldberg and R.L. Mathews, Report of the Advisory Panel to the Committee of Review on educational standards and examinations of ICAA, April, 60 pp. mimeograph
1962	Comments on research studies for Accounting Research Division, AICPA, New York, August—September: Perry Mason, 'Cash flow analysis and the funds statement,' 6 pp.; 'The price level study,' 16 pp. A Wyatt, 'Accounting for business combinations,' 15pp; 'Accounting for non-profit organizations,' 9 pp.
1963	'Higher education for management,' opinion on a draft report for the Martin Committee on tertiary education, 12 pp.
1964	Chambers (convenor) with L. Goldberg and R.L. Mathews, (Second) Report of the Advisory Panel to the Committee of Review on educational standards and examinations of ICAA, October, 20 pp.
1966	'Suggested amendments to the Companies Act,' submission to N.S.W. Registrar of Companies, January 19, 16 pp. Notes on Accounting Research Study No. 6 and the price level opinion, to Director of the Accounting Research Division, the AICPA, New York, August, 10 pp. with tables (this and next item written while working in the AICPA Research Division). 'Concepts and principles,' draft notes as suggestion for proposed statement by the Accounting Principles Board of AICPA, September, 40 pp.
1967	Submission to the Chairman of the Accounting and Auditing Research Committee of the AARF, critical of a proposed questionnaire on the function of published financial statements, September, 5 pp. 'Suggested amendments to the Companies Act,' submission to the (Commonwealth) Company Law Advisory Committee (Eggleston Committee), October 27, 34 pp.
1968	'Horizons for a Profession—some jottings,' notes on Roy and McNeill's book of that title, prompted by W. Bruschi, Director of Examinations, AICPA, on the occasion of his visit, August, 11 pp.
1969	'Limited professional liability,' a note of March 6 on limited liability proposals, to Divisional Council, ASA, per C.M. Orr.
1970	Report to the Chairman of the N.S.W. PARB on the style and substance of examinations of the ASA under new oversight arrangements, November 16, 10 pp.
1971	'Some aspects of an efficient securities market,' submission to Select Committee on Securities and Exchange, Australian Senate, April, 33 pp. 'The objectives of accounting,' submission to Accounting Objectives Study Group of AICPA, December, 11 pp. 'Inflation and accounts,' critique of the English Institutes' price-level adjusted accounting proposals, submitted to Technical Officer of ICAEW, December, 12 pp.

1973	Comment on exposure draft, 'The concept of materiality,' submitted to ICAA and ASA, January, 5 pp.
	Comment on exposure draft, 'Accounting for the extractive industries,' submitted to ICAA and ASA, March, 5 pp.
	Comment on exposure draft, 'The use of the equity method in accounting for investments in subsidiaries and associated companies,' submitted to Australian Joint Accounting Standards Committee, November.
	Comment on exposure draft, 'Translation of amounts in foreign currencies,' submitted to Australian Joint Accounting Standards Committee, December 28, 6 pp.
1974	Memorandum on Statement DS5, 'Depreciation of non-current assets,' submitted to Executive Director, ASA, January 15, 7 pp.
	Memorandum to Australian Attorney-General's Department on proposed changes to Ninth Schedule of Companies Act, March 29, 3 pp.
	Submission to the U.K. Government Committee of Inquiry into Inflation and Company Accounts, April 23, 31 pp. and 7 appendices.
	'Research activities of the Society,' working paper submitted to General Council of the ASA, May, 15 pp.
	Notes on 'Commentary on the Statements of international accounting standards,' submitted to IASC Sub-Committee, Melbourne, July 5, 3 pp.
	Notes on IASC Exposure Draft No. 1, 'Disclosure of accounting policies,' submitted to IASC Sub-Committee, Melbourne, July 8, 7 pp.
	Response to U.S. Financial Accounting Standards Board Discussion Memorandum on the objectives of financial statements, September, 15 pp.
1975	Memorandum for Australian PJT, 'Accounting for the effects of inflation,' March 7, 6 pp.
	Submission and Supplementary Memorandum to Australian Government Committee of Inquiry into inflation and taxation (Mathews Committee), March 14, 11pp; April 3, 8 pp.
	Submission on accounting for inflation to Australian Government Committee to advise on policies for manufacturing industry, March 24, 13 pp.
1976	Submission to the Education and Membership Committees, ASA, 'Admission and Advancement Qualifications,' January, 15 pp.
	'Accounting for changing prices,' presentation to hearings of a Review Committee set up by the Australian Accounting Standards Committee, on methods of inflation accounting, March
	Open letter to the Chairman of the Australian Accounting Standards Committee (on fair judgement as between inflation accounting proposals),June, 7 pp. + appendices; copies to members of the Executives of the ASA and the ICAA and the Australian Accounting Standards Committee
1977	Submission to ASA (and later to the Integration Committee of the Society and ICAA) on 'An Institute of Specialist Accounting Colleges,' (a development of the submission of January 1976, see above), 15 pp.
	Submission to Inflation Accounting Steering Group (U.K.) on Exposure Draft No. 18, 'Current cost accounting,' May, 9 pp.
	Submission to Joint Standing Committee of Australian Professional Bodies, 'The progress of CCA,' May, 9 pp.
	Submissions to U.S. Financial Accounting Standards Board on 'Tentative conclusions on objectives of financial statements of business enterprises' and on memorandum 'Conceptual framework for financial accounting and reporting,' June, 22 pp. + 2 appendices
	Submission to CICA on Discussion Paper 'Current value accounting' of the Accounting Research Committee of the Institute, June, 15 pp.

(Continued)

Table 7.5 (Continued)

1978	Response to invitation of the Education Review Committee of the ICAA to comment on professional education for and professional qualification in accounting (with M.C. Wells), January, 3 pp.
	'Some Comments on Budgeting and Planning for Development in Developing Countries,' submission to Economic and Social Affairs Secretariat, United Nations, New York, January, 4 pp.
	Proposal and proposed constitution of an International Association for the Advancement of Accounting Education, addressed to Louis Perridon (France), Seigo Nakajima (Japan), Adolf Enthoven, Maurice Moonitz, Gerry Mueller, David Solomons (U.S.A.), 5 pp.
	Submission to Australian Accounting Research Foundation on exposure draft (July 1978) on gains and losses on holding monetary resources, December, 10 pp.
1979	Submission to Australian Financial System Inquiry (Australian Government; the Campbell Inquiry), March, 12 pp.
	Submission to CICA Accountants on Accounting Research Committee paper, 'Financial reporting and changing prices,' May, 10 pp.
	Comment on U.S. Financial Accounting Standards Board exposure draft (December 1978) on 'Financial accounting and changing prices,' June, 9 pp.
	Comment on exposure draft (September 1979) of AARF on asset revaluations, September, 4 pp.
	'Suggested amendments to the accounts and audit provisions, including the Fourteenth (accounts) Schedule, of the Companies Act of Sri Lanka,' submitted to the Registrar of Companies, Sri Lanka, November, 34 pp.
1980	Submission to the Research Manager, CICA on an exposure draft on current cost accounting, February, 4 pp.
1982	Submission to National Companies and Securities Commission on a proposal to establish an Accounting Standards Review Board, March, 8 pp.
	Submission to Accounting Standards Board of Australian Accounting Research Foundation, on 'objectives' of accounting, June, 3 pp. plus his 'The functions of published financial statements' (1976).
1985	'A True and Fair View,' submission to National Companies and Securities Commission, February, 6 pp.
1991	Submission to Research Committee of The Institute of Chartered Accountants of Scotland on 'Making Company Reports Valuable— Melody plc,' March, 9 pp.
1994	Letter to President, ASCPA, on professional aspirations and performance (no response).

Source: Chambers on Accounting (Vol. 6), section 13 of the 'Aide Memoire' (pp. 38–41)

examples include Chambers' pursuit of an international 'think-tank' of academics and the related participation in the elite accounting society ARIA,[35] his involvements in several world accounting congresses as a speaker and Congress organizer, and his, together with others,' efforts in the 1970s that resulted in the 1984 formation of the IAAER.

ARIA

In early 1974 several so-called golden age U.S. accounting theorists—Sterling, Staubus, Ijiri and Thomas—were concerned about developments in accounting and jointly created an elite organization, ARIA. Membership was by invitation only and Sterling clearly was the driving force. Chambers was one of the first to be invited as a member in September 1974.[36] With Sterling serving as its first president its initial aim was: 'to protect and advance normative-based research [and to have members as a] . . . well-recognized, dedicated group of scholars [who] would create an environment in which individual differences would wilt under the pressure of scholarship. . . . The early members also shared a mutual zeal for effectual progress and a common passion to rid accounting practices of its defects.'[37]

Correspondence suggests Chambers was an enthusiastic recruit initially but soon became frustrated with the lack of reform action by ARIA.

The irony of the exercise was that, in failing to recognize fully the implications of the empirical revolution that was increasingly prevalent in post-1960s research in accounting in the U.S., ARIA adopted the very tactics of which it had accused the rampant empiricists—recruiting 'the very individuals whose choice of degree school and scholarly pursuits labelled them as academics committed to superseding within the academy the type of scholarship and values that the early members espoused.'[38]

International Accounting Initiatives—Think Tanks and the IAAER

The mid-to-late 1960s and early 1970s was a propitious time to prosecute an international focus in accounting education and research. The proliferation of multinational companies had accompanied trade globalization. 'Big 8' accounting firms, as they were known then, facilitated this by setting up branches globally; and national (and then international) accounting standards setters like the IASC, stock exchange commissions and other regulatory mechanisms either sought to adopt 'international' rules or tried to standardize rules across countries. Other related international accounting organizations had their genesis in the late 1970s—IAFC, IAAER, and Accounting Historians.

While an International Congress of Accountants had been meeting every five years since 1904, in the early 1960s several academics were pressing for a separate international conference on accounting education (ICAE), including Paul Garner, Hanns-Martin Schoenfeld, and Vernon Zimmerman. The first ICAE was held in 1962 in Urbana–Champaign, Illinois. Chambers attended those early conferences which were held every five years, presenting papers at several. He convened the third ICAE held in Sydney in 1972.

Edwards *et al.* is apposite regarding Chambers' views about the need for an international accounting focus: 'Soon after his admission to ARIA, Chambers returned to his think-tank idea and suggested that the internationalization of academic engagement might be a role for ARIA to pursue,'[39] particularly given that it was an area neglected by the leading American academic accounting association, the AAA. Chambers favoured a meeting confined to idealists committed to 'change' and to the development of a program capable of achieving change: 'What we need is an integration of ideas rather than continued aggressive assertion. I could just hope that people dedicated to cleaning up the Augean stables might agree on a point or two.'[40] Barring the 1970s 'Taxi Symposium' discussed in Edwards *et al.*,[41] there was little action in this regard by ARIA. Although Chambers had high expectations he was extremely disappointed in the symposium's outcome, as this extract from a letter to Stamp attests:

> The [ARIA] Taxicab problem was a genuine attempt to focus attention [of a group of like-minded researchers] on a "specimen," as is the manner of scientists. The experience showed that the "focussing" was not effective. Some other mode of focussing might be more fruitful. If I ever have time, I propose to give it a try.[42]

This presaged late 1970s and early 1980s survey work undertaken by Chambers in several countries (with different co-authors).[43]

The Chambers Archive reveals that Chambers had raised the idea of an international-based forum (a 'think-tank') of accounting teachers and researchers several times, in the late 1950s with Moonitz, Mattessich, and Weinwurm. He continued to pursue this proposal in the 1960s.

December 1974 correspondence with Sterling shows that, over a year before the 9th World Accounting Congress of accounting practitioners was to be held in Paris in 1967, Chambers had suggested to Congress President, François-Maurice Richard, that there should be an international association like the International Economic Association. Its membership ought to be limited to about fifty, with a meeting to be held every few years:

> I would therefore like to see established an international accounting association or academy the members of which would be people having a thorough knowledge of their local practices and theoretical developments and a strong sense of the importance of international collaboration and continuous exchanges of ideas. As you will appreciate, in social affairs the opportunity for experimentation is limited, and

developments of social institutions are very much a matter of choosing the advantageous elements of other observable institutions. International cross comparison is a critical process in the promotion of advantageous changes.

I have long been dismayed by the absence of serious appreciation of this. But beside it runs the naive belief that each country can generate 'the best' ideas without needing to draw on the inventiveness and acumen of the members of another. No such belief is held in the sciences or indeed in most of the cultural and industrial arts. The freedom from political barriers is one of the great sources of vitality in those fields, a vitality which I venture to think accounting cannot claim.

You will know that there are international associations of many kinds. The kind I have in mind is an association of individual members, not representatives of associations, or even of countries. Ideally they would be people who have made some significant contribution to the practice or literature of accounting, and who would be willing seriously to propose ideas, or to criticize the ideas of others, or to feed in particular examples, background material, experiences and so on as tests or supporting evidence of the ideas of others. No balance as between membership from different areas, or as between say practitioners and teachers, is envisaged. I think only of a group wholeheartedly concerned with the advancement of accounting, that is all.[44]

Richard responded, albeit over eighteen months later, that:

Your letter of 11th January 1966 developed many interesting recommendations regarding the establishment of an international accounting association of some sort. I have received a number of requests from various Institutes to bring up officially the subject of the establishment of a permanent secretariat during the 9th Congress. This question will be discussed at the general meeting of Institute Presidents on Tuesday 12th September 1967.[45]

Chambers replied promptly:

Could you tell me whether anything emerged from the discussion? . . . I did not think a representative committee, merely representing the official associations, would procure the object I sought. From my observations of professional organizations in English-speaking countries, there seems to be a great reluctance to take a firm line on matters of principle, largely I suppose because their memberships embrace many people with widely divergent but firmly held views.[46]

Richard did not respond. Chambers lamented to Sterling that as nothing came of the late 1960s think-tank proposal 'a couple of years ago

[May 1972] I made another suggestion to Leonard Spacek, 'that perhaps the FASB might consider funding a conference of international researchers, together with members of the Board, say every two years.'[47] The May 1972 letter had followed publication in the *Journal of Accountancy* of Chambers' 'Anguish of Accountants,' and the AICPA's 1972 'Wheat Report' disclosure of the proposed U.S.$500,000 annual research budget of the (replacement) FASB research division. It also provides further thoughts on the international 'think-tank' idea:

> The Report of that Study [Wheat Report] leaves me with the curious feeling that people believe that money is the cure for whatever ills beset the profession. I refer only to the proposed budget for research—$500,000 or more per year. I am only a small fish, and likely to be staggered by such a figure. But I would really like to know whether any serious thought has been given to what can fruitfully be done with so much money every year. . . . The mere mention of all that money recalled to mind a project I have often thought about. Progress depends, I believe, not on the more or less random association of people with different viewpoints, but on the association of people with some kind of passion for substantive improvement. Less debate and more concerted effort to construct anew is what is needed. I have envisaged the bringing together of people from a number of countries who have worked for some time on the analysis or clarification of principles. Let them meet, for, say a month each year for several years, to participate in the presentation and discussion of argument and evidence. Let them discuss the pros and cons of all the main schemes which have been suggested as the hard-core ideas of accounting. Let them be a forum, not a committee commissioned to prepare a report. Let the necessity of reporting emerge when they are sufficiently convinced of the soundness of any conclusions they reach. Let them work freely over all the proposals which have been put up, with the object of finding the best, the scheme best supported by the evidence they can bring together.[48]

Again, nothing came of this. This must have frustrated Chambers; he had discussed this in principle now for over two decades. The formation of ARIA may have given Chambers hope that some form of think-tank of interested academics was nigh. But that hope faded quickly as he became frustrated with the lack of actions at ARIA.

Undeterred, on the last day of the October 1977 Berlin International Conference of Accounting Education, where Chambers had been a major organizer of the speakers, he raised publicly the idea of an international association of accounting teachers and researchers. His earlier think-tank version was put to the sideline. He referred to the prospect of forming a confederation of academic accounting associations of teachers and researchers, similar in basic style to the just formed International Federation of Accountants (IFAC). But other delegates had different views about the form and scope of such an international body.

After the conference a working group was formed, comprising Adolf Enthoven, Louis Perridon and Chambers. Other delegates such as David Solomons, Gerhard Mueller, Moonitz and Seigo Nakajima were carbon copied on group correspondence. The differences within the group are evident in post-conference draft proposals and comments between those academics. In November Enthoven distributed a draft constitution to the working group for their consideration and comments. By mid-December 1977, having received comments, he circulated a revised draft. The proposed body was now much grander, involving amongst other things fee-paying individuals and association members. Other, extended and mainly co-ordination features are captured in the revised draft association's major aims: (1) to foster closer ties between accounting educators throughout the world, exchange information, research efforts and know-how, and spur by mutual effort post-secondary school accounting education and training in both developed and developing nations of the world, in order to make accountancy more relevant and useful in the socio-economic process of nations; (2) to aid accounting educational bodies, and/or educators/institutions in third-world countries/regions in their efforts to improve accounting education, know-how, research and development, and practices.[49]

Material in the Archive suggests that Chambers was unhappy with what might eventuate. Solomons expressed similar concerns. They had wanted the confederation idea to be considered thoroughly. Not rushed.

Chambers' suggested that the much more elaborate scope of the latest draft could lead to just another dues-paying international association! He had hoped for a much simpler confederation of local associations that would 'assist' the activities of national associations and 'foster' international issues—a body that would operate as a clearing house for national associations operating in parallel with IFAC whose interests were primarily related to practical accounting and auditing issues.[50]

In May1978 after correspondence by others, Chambers returned to the issue. He responded to Enthoven's December draft with several letters. He explained that the hiatus on his part was due to an extremely taxing workload during the last few months of 1977 and early months of 1978. His letters discussed a lengthy proposal and an accompanying draft constitution in which he continued to advocate a much simpler organization, with the view to letting it grow naturally, thereby making less of a demand on educators.[51] He put forward a 'Proposal and proposed constitution of an International Association for the Advancement of Accounting Education,' addressed to Enthoven, Moonitz, Mueller, Nakajima, Perridon, and Solomons. The first six clauses of his proposed constitution are reproduced in full; clauses 7–13 pertaining to administrative procedural issues about meetings and committees are omitted:

Name and Objects

1. There shall be an association entitled, the 'International Association for the Advancement of Accounting Education.'

2. The Association shall be an association of national or regional bodies of accountants whose members are principally persons engaged as teachers or researchers in universities and equivalent institutions.

3. The objects of the Association shall include:

    (a) to foster the dissemination among members of the member-associations of information relating to activities of the Association and its member-associations.

    (b) to seek the collaboration of national and regional journals in giving publicity to activities of the Association and generally of matters which are of more than regional interest.

    (c) to assist in the dissemination of information relating to employment and research opportunities.

    (d) to explore the possibility of exchanges of faculty personnel and students.

    (e) to seek to collaborate with and to foster the collaboration of member-associations with international and regional associations of accountants in practice and in commerce, industry and government, on educational matters and on accounting research.

    (f) to assist in the organizing and conduct of periodical international conferences on accounting education.

    (g) to foster and to assist in the establishment of national or regional associations having aims and objects similar to those of member-associations.

    (h) to assist in securing sponsorship or financing for the translation of significant books or articles on matters of interest to the Association.

    (i) to do such other things as are necessary to advance these objects.

Membership

4. The member-associations shall in the first instance be (here insert such associations as signify their wish to be named in this clause, provided they satisfy clause 5).

5. Member-associations shall be associations of the kind described in clause 2, provided they have a membership of not less than 50 individual members.

6. Associations of the kind described in clause 2 which have fewer than 50 individual members shall be eligible to be corresponding

members, and shall have all the privileges of members other than provided by clause 8.[52]

Those efforts to form a new international association of accounting educators (teachers and researchers) then stalled.

Interestingly, only two immediate post-1978 Chambers Archive items about the proposal were located. Chambers wrote in May 1979 asking Moonitz:

> What has happened about the "international association of academic societies"? Since I sent off some comments before the 1978 AAA meeting on Adolf's draft, I've heard nothing more about it whatever. Has it died, or is it incubating somewhere?

Moonitz replied:

> Adolf has been busy . . . [writing and circulating overseas, especially among the developing countries] the report of his AAA Committee on International Accounting Operations and Education.[53]

Attached to the Report as an appendix was the December 1977 Enthoven draft mentioned above, with revisions. Moonitz summarized that its emphasis was still on a dual (organizations and individuals) fee-paying membership. There were to be: 'two types of membership: Full and individual. Full members are professional organizations, and associations of teachers in post-secondary institutions. Individual membership has undergone a metamorphosis, and now leans in your direction, if memory serves me right. "Individuals" are defined as: (a) academic and other post-secondary accounting educational institutions; (b) groupings of individual educators and practitioners . . . *where no national entities exist;* and (c) international, regional and local development agencies, foundations and other interested bodies.'

It took nearly four years before there were any firm moves to form what would ultimately be the IAAER. Needles and Olmsted's account of the history of the IAAER records that Norlin Rueschhoff, Chairman of the Monterrey 1982 Fifth Conference on Accounting Education played a prominent role in reactivating the push for the new international association. Interestingly, the Chambers Archive confirms that Rueschhoff wrote to Chambers in September 1982 seeking his views about the previous work in this area. Chambers' response included a summary of events, concluding:

> When it was put [in 1978] the form of the proposal became another association of individual members, with all the trappings of such an association—not a confederation of the style I advanced. . . . My antipathy to the full-blown, individual membership scheme [proposed by Enthoven] was no doubt apparent. Gradually the interchanges ceased. That was that.[54]

Post-1982 correspondence between Nakajima, Chambers, Mueller, Enthoven, and others is revealing. It suggests another major catalyst was the urging of Nakajima who had been asked by the Organizing Committee at the Monterrey Conference to help administer the Sixth Conference on Accounting Education to be held in Tokyo in 1987. Necessity seems to have been critical. The Japanese Accounting Association had been invited to oversee the 1987 Conference but, through Nakajima, it informed Chambers, Mueller, and Enthoven that a formal letter from an international association of accounting educators and researchers was needed before it would be able to obtain financial support from the Science Council of Japan for the proposed Conference. The following extract from a letter Nakajima wrote to Chambers on 21 December 1983 is instructive:

> In order to secure a financial support from the above-mentioned Council for 1987, it is necessary to receive *a formal letter from an international academic organization on accounting*, requesting the Japan Accounting Association to sponsor the 1987 Conference in Japan, *by February, 1984*. The letter should be written by a non-Japanese and should be mailed from outside Japan. Since we do not yet have any formal, permanent, international and academic organization on accounting on a global basis, the above-mentioned formal letter is hardly available. The Special Committee of [the] Japan Accounting Association requested me to contact such eminent persons as you so as to organize urgently an international organization of such a nature and to secure such a letter as would satisfy our Science Council for this purpose. In our preliminary discussion, it was judged that, because of the very tight restriction on time, forming a federation of existing national academic or regional organizations would be difficult to realize, because this would need longer time to secure approval of respective governing bodies.

Nakajima put forward a necessary, but temporary proposal:

(1) To organize *International Association on Accounting Education and Research* with voluntary individuals from Canada, U.S.A., U.K., West Germany, Australia, Netherland and Japan.

(2) To accept those on the attached list and others who are recommended by them, who expressed their wish to join this Association, as *founder members*.

(3) To collect *ten U.S. dollars* from each member as the membership fee for the years 1984 and 1985.

(4) To nominate *a president tentatively from senior U.S.A. members*, based on ballots among U.S.A. members.

(5) To arrange a formal opportunity to examine, and approve constitution and by-laws, and to appoint officers as early as practicable.[55]

Chambers was quick to respond on 19 January 1984:

> I agree with the proposal of your letter of December 21. There was a proposal in 1977 to form an international organization as a confederation of academic associations. But it lapsed. The limited time you now have for action makes your proposal the only presently feasible arrangement. I enclose my cheque for $13 Aust. which I judge will more than cover the membership fee. I hope the scheme turns out to be satisfactory.[56]

Letters were sent by Nakajima to numerous international accounting academics. With many paying the individual membership fee the IAAER was thus formed. Paul Garner was elected its first President on 1 June 1984. A few months later John Brennan was announced as its first Secretary-treasurer.

The association's primary task was to be a relatively simple one. It was to assist Nakajima and the Japanese Accounting Association organize the Sixth Conference on Accounting Education. As Needles and Olmsted observe the minimalist form would change after the Tokyo Conference with the selection of an Executive Committee of prominent academic historians and teachers. Reflecting some of Chambers' earlier ideas, subsequent amendments over the next few years (see endnote #52, chapter 7) produced a confederation-style association of fee-paying individuals and association-members; but with an extended scope.

Chambers' other international involvements included his participation in international congresses in the 1970s and '80s held in Sydney. He was a major organizer (with Australia's leading auditing practitioner Sir Ronald Irish) of the 1972 Tenth World Congress of Accounting practitioners, and together with Murray Wells he organized the 1988 University of Sydney-sponsored World Congress of Accounting Historians. The conferences were extremely successful, drawing large numbers. Support from both academic and practitioner associates is another indicator of Chambers' strong standing in the profession as he approached, and later in, retirement.

Summing Up

The above reveals several underappreciated aspects of Chambers' career. While chapter 8 provides evidence of his understanding of the political process of regulatory change this chapter shows that he sought reforms at national and international levels in various ways, not simply by arguing that his preferred approach was logically based. He advocated on several occasions, unsuccessfully, for the formation of an international think-tank to drive an improvement in accounting. Accepting the need for some means of achieving international consideration of accounting research and practice he put aside the think-tank idea and argued for a confederation of national associations of accounting educators and researchers. This ultimately saw the formation of the IAAER in 1984.

He remained, however, convinced that, to be effective long-term, accounting reforms had to be underpinned by logical reasoning and be grounded in practice. The latter required a familiarity with commercial fundamentals and how accounting meshed with them. His consultancies, employment experiences, and professional activities assisted in that regard and they underpinned his theoretical ideas. Although often described as such, in the terminology of many of the 1960s and 1970s academics, Chambers was thus far from being simply a 'normative' theorist.

Notes

1. Chapter epigraphs:
   Chambers' response, induction to The U.S. Ohio State University Accounting Hall of Fame, 13 August, 1991 (held in Nashville, Tennessee), P202, #7357, 13/08/1991.
      Chambers to Leonard Spacek, Arthur Andersen Partner, P202, #6653, 25/01/1983. Spacek was a U.S. practitioner and long-time friend of Chambers who convinced his firm, Arthur Andersen and Co. to sponsor the publication in 1969 of a collection of Chambers' articles, titled, *Accounting, Finance and Management*.
2. Chambers and Dean (eds) (1986a, General Preface).
3. Practitioner and friend, Sir Ronald Irish to Chambers, P202, #327, 29/09/1958. Irish was inducted into the University of Melbourne AAHoF in 2015. With Chambers in the 1950s they prepared a structure for accounting degrees acceptable to Sydney University and the ICAA.
4. Clarke, Dean and Wells (2010, 2012, especially Chapter 8) provides more details about the Society.
5. Regarding one BHP executives course correspondence from P.E. Rossell to Chambers, P202, #751, 24/02/1961 records: 'It was generally agreed by those who attended and the observers that your contribution was particularly valuable; I would go as far as to say it largely determined the success of the course.' See P202, #6597, 01/07/1983 which lists attendees at the 25th anniversary meeting of the General Management Group and the Management Group's 'ode.'
6. Archive entries, P202, #2425, 08/03/1968 and P202, #6206, 17/08/1981.
7. John P. Young to Chambers, P202, #2274, 05/05/1967.
8. Chambers to John P. Young, P202, #2275, 19/05/1967.
9. John P. Young to Chambers, P202, #165, 02/08/1956.
10. P202, #s2214, 2222 provide congratulatory comments from business colleagues about Chambers' appointment.
11. Dean and Clarke (2010a).
12. Chambers' *Accounting, Evaluation and Economic Behavior*, 94–5.
13. Chambers' 'An Academic Apprenticeship' (1991a, especially 102).
14. Chambers' 'An Academic Apprenticeship' (1991a, especially 102).
15. The authors were unable definitively to locate Chambers' expert evidence through searches of the public record. What appears to be a copy was located in an unnumbered box file in the hard-copy Chambers Archive, labelled 'Pacific Acceptance.'
16. PAC Second Interim Judgment by Moffitt, J. (194*ff.*).
17. Professional charges have increased significantly in the last fifty years.
18. Chambers to Frank Edmonds, P202, is available in the unnumbered box file labelled 'Pacific Acceptance' (Burren Street Library).

19. While not discussed in detail here Chambers' consultancy reports detailed in P202, #11255, 15/04/1975 (for Allen, Allen and Hemsley) and #11256, 18/06/1980 (for Stephen, Jacques & Stephen) show his extensive finance, management, legal, accounting and auditing skills coupled to his report writing skills.

20. Letter from Chambers to W(Bill). Hunter (BHP), P202, #11253, 17/10/1973. See also endnote #47, chapter 6.

21. P202, #616, 27/07/1960. Amounts received in respect of some other consultancies are available in the Archive, like the 1958 Civil and Civic request for advice about the 'buy versus lease' decision: P202, #269, 23/04/1958 and related £141.15.0 fees, USA. P202, #376, 04/11/1958 and the 1955 John P. Young & Associates-requested report for Chas Steele and Co. Chambers received payment of 1.5 guineas per hour for his 38 hours work, P202, #82, 04/04/1955. Another major consultancy was the 1973 request from Department of Prime Minister and Cabinet for advice in respect of the inquiry into the proposed BHP Steel Price Increase—P202, #11252, 27/02/1973. A summary of several consultancies from 1947–86 appears in Table 7.2.

22. Several in the Chambers Archive provide the basis of the case summary and our analysis, including: P202, #11243, 03/04/1973 regarding the Price Decisions (Cane Growing) for 1959–66, and the subsequent ones in 1973, P202, #11244–46, covering the request to Chambers for his views on the valuation of the assets of cane growers and sugar millers and the treatment of depreciation as a cost, and Chambers' response.

23. Correspondence with Chambers and Commonwealth Crown Solicitor, documents and Chambers' opinion on the questions regarding *Heavy Minerals Pty Ltd (in liquidation)*—Chambers Archive, P202, #11247, 13/07/1972. The letters contain all the relevant details necessary for Chambers to analyse the transactions and provide a detailed report.

24. *Lee v Neuchatel Asphalte Co.* (1889) 41 Ch D 1 . . . 415.

25. They are available at P202, #11247, 13/07/1972.

26. Clarke and Dean (2007, chapter 5).

27. Clarke and Dean (2007) and Lawrence and Stapledon (2008).

28. Lawrence and Stapledon (2008).

29. Muller (2002) provides an account of many well-known public policy advocates of different aspects of capitalism in modern European thought. Nassar (2011, 91–138) discusses the actions of Beatrice and Sidney Webb.

30. Earlier U.S.A examples seeking to influence public policy were press activities by leading economists like Irving Fisher and Friedrich Hayek. More recent examples seeking to influence public policy in the U.S.A., by both left- and right-wing advocates, include popular press articles and paperback books by, respectively, Paul Krugman and Niall Ferguson.

31. They provide the flavour and energy that Chambers brought to those meetings. He was always well prepared, with detailed notes, tailor-made overheads, and often handwritten copies of the talks surviving as part of the Chambers Archive.

32. *Probus Bulletin* #111 thanking Chambers for his presentation, P202, #10865, April 1992.

33. Wells (2000).

34. Consider also, Edwards *et al.* (2013, especially, 369–70).

35. For example, see the Edwards *et al.* (2013) account of the twenty-year life of this elite accounting society, extracts from which appear immediately below.

36. Sterling's acknowledgement of Chambers' all-round skills provides a likely reason for inviting him to join ARIA; see Sterling's letter to Chambers, P202, #2329, 23/04/1968: 'I was completely unaware of your work in the Australian Journals [in the 1940s, 1950s and early 1960s] and but of course I know that *Accounting, Evaluation* . . . has gone much beyond my manuscript. . . .

However, you put your finger on the problem. How do I handle the publication of a work which is so similar to yours? I had come to the same conclusion as you did: A note in the preface indicating that we arrived at the same conclusions independently, giving the date of my copyright, admitting my ignorance of your work in the foreign (non-U.S.) journals, paying homage to the superiority of your *Evaluation* but saying something about the simplicity of my model permitting easier handling of the problem and a sharper focus on the different valuation methods, and so forth. I'd like for you to see and comment on such a preface before it was printed but the above ought to give you a general idea of what I had intended.' Two similar letters by Sterling are available in the Archive: P202, #1975, 23/02/1966 and P202, #1836, 07/10/1966. They reveal Sterling had similar ideas as Chambers during the early- to mid-1960s. His major work was not published till 1970.

37. Edwards *et al.* (2013, 365).
38. Edwards *et al.* (2013, 365). Chambers to Sterling, P202, #7361, 20/09/1991 bemoans the activities of ARIA: 'Now and then I have entertained the notion of an International Accounting Reform Club. Perhaps that was your intention. But, as a group, ARIA is more argumentative than discriminating, more concerned with the periphery than with the guts of accounting—fiddling while Rome burns.'
39. Edwards *et al.* (2013, 369), based on Chambers to Sterling, P202, #7518, 08/12/1974.
40. Chambers to Sterling, P202, #7520, 31/12/1974.
41. Edwards *et al.* (2013, 369–70).
42. Chambers to Stamp, P202, #5395, 25/08/1978; a similar idea appeared in an earlier letter to Sterling, P202, #9501, 13/06/1978.
43. Chambers (and several co-authors) undertook surveys in five countries, beginning with Chambers' (1980c) Australian survey; others were undertaken in South Africa by Chambers and Maguire (1982, 1983), in the U.S.A. Chambers, Hopwood and McKeown (1984), in Canada Chambers and Falk (1985) and in Singapore Chambers, Ma, Hopkins and Kasiraja (1987).
44. Chambers to Richard, P202, #2172, 11/01/1966. International gatherings of leading scientists, economists, and other professionals had been occurring for many years. Although the idea was not revolutionary, no separate body of international accounting academics existed. The IAAER was formed in 1984 (see endnotes #s 38, 45–48 in chapter 7).
45. Richard to Chambers, P202, #2173, 22/08/1967.
46. Chambers to Richard, P202, #2174, 20/11/1967.
47. Chambers to Sterling, P202, #7518, 08/12/1974.
48. Chambers to Sterling, P202, #9017, 12/05/1972. 'Chambers' 1972 'Anguish' article suggests the work of the AICPA had produced little progress since Chambers had written of the prospect for improvement in his 1960 'Conditions of Research in Accounting' article.
49. P202, #s5111, 5114, 5117, 5118, 5375–79 and 5383.
50. Chambers to Solomons, P202, #5376, 07/12/1977.
51. Chambers to several people, P202, #s5385–88.
52. Chambers 'Proposal. . .,' P202, #5383, 7/07/1978; Enthoven response to Chambers, P202, #5385, 27/07/1978. Clarke *et al.* (2012, 119–20) show that another 'Sydney Schooler,' Murray Wells was one of several instrumental in forming the IAAER in 1984. He was its second President in 1987, and in that year, argued successfully for broadening the body to be a federation of associations of accounting educators and researchers. Another 'Sydney Schooler,' Sid Gray was appointed as the third President and continued the federation-type

aims of the association in the early 1990s. He sought greater prominence for research. He organized the 1994 IAAER Conference on Accounting Education held in Paris. Needles and Olmsted (2004) provide a history of the formative years at the IAAER, albeit only beginning their narrative just prior to 1984. Dean, Persson and Clarke (2018) examine the 1960s through to the 1990s to better understand the genesis of the IAAER. Someya (1996) describes the early International Conferences on Accounting Education (identifying dates, topics, and speakers since the first Conference in 1962).

53. Chambers to Moonitz, P202, #5799, 08/05/1979 and Moonitz's response, P202, #5801, 21/05/1979.
54. Chambers to Rueschhoff, P202, #6476, 23/09/1982 in response to Rueschhoff's letter, P202, #6475, 10/09/1982.
55. Nakajima to Chambers, P202, #6742, 21/12/1983.
56. Chambers to Nakajima, P202, #6744, 19/01/1984.

8 Reformer of Corporate Financial Reporting

I resigned recently [from the Australian Accounting Standards Board], out of a conviction that nothing was likely to emerge from the Board's processes that was free of the stamp of reactionary inertia or immaturity. I'm content to let history be the judge of things—and I'm increasingly confident that someday there'll be a switch from conventionalism to a more tightly reasoned body of rules.

—Chambers letter to Briloff, 1982

As for myself, I have given up trying to influence the profession and the legislators and standards bodies. I suspect it will take almost another generation (the present generation of students, perhaps) to make a dent in the carapace of inertia with which official and other bodies shield themselves.

—Chambers letter to Manchester Business
School's Edmond Grace, 1983[1]

Chambers was a reformer with a missionary zeal. It was evident in many areas. But not all academics or practitioners agreed with what they perceived to be his direct, holistic approach. He had also for many years showed similar determination in advocating accounting as a tertiary discipline, with entry to the accounting profession being graduate based. With several other Australian colleagues, practitioners, and academics, he fought hard for accounting to be recognized alongside other university disciplines.

Two regulatory reform areas specifically highlight that resolve. They provide insights as to whether his approach to reform was, as some have suggested, naive.

First, as noted in chapters 3 and 6, for decades Chambers documented defects in the law and practice of corporate financial reporting. It led him to pursue related regulatory reforms in many ways. Broadly, he sought evidence to support what he had for years perceived as a watering down of the financial publicity regulations relating to corporations. He regarded this as the product of compromise in reconciling the conflicting urges of the legislature for more publicity, and of businessmen for continued privacy.

Several of his books, articles in practitioner and scholarly outlets, and newspaper pieces provided the evidence of the need for reform. They documented across several jurisdictions many hundreds of instances of flaws in the information provided to the stock market. Related to seeking that better understanding, little, however, has been written of the strong contacts Chambers made with practitioners, politicians, and corporate regulators over many decades. These included correspondence and meetings with: SEC Chief Accountant Andrew Barr and the SEC Commissioner 'Manny' Cohen in the early and middle 1960s; with SEC Chief Accountants, John ('Sandy') Burton during the mid-1970s and Walter Schuetze in the 1990s. Also pertinent was Moonitz's commissioning of Chambers to work at the APB on their postulates series; discussions with Australian regulators, like Frank Ryan, the N.S.W.'s Registrar of Companies in the 1960s and N.S.W.'s Corporate Affairs Commissioner in the 1970s, and later, with heads of Australia's national regulator, the NCSC; as well as through submissions to formal inquiries by various attorneys-general. Perhaps because much of that has remained undisclosed, some commentators have claimed Chambers was naive in the way he sought reforms.

Second, Chambers was in the thick of the accounting profession's moves to respond to changing prices and price levels. Augmenting the post-World War II professional initiatives worldwide, the universal standards-setting brouhaha that began in the late 1960s and continued throughout the 1970s led to proposals in the form of accounting profession exposure drafts and standards. These were initially to supplement and then to supplant historic cost accounting—namely the professionally endorsed CPP and CCA Preliminary EDs of the 1970s—and eventually (as noted in chapter 6) to Chambers producing and distributing in September 1975 his own ED.

These two broad areas of reform, clearly interconnected, are now dealt with.

Our review presumes that successful reforms require more than a well-advocated case. Political forces, and as Tweedie and Whittington and others have noted, the way ideas are transmitted, influence the effectiveness of any reform proposals.[2] Steve Zeff argued in many places that political forces as much as technical argument lead to the 'forging' of any changes to corporate financial reporting in the short-term.[3] The review here suggests that Chambers was aware of this. But he felt strongly that effective, longer term corporate regulatory changes required also that more attention be given to the logical validity and economic reasoning underlying the prescriptions. As revealed in Chambers' works on education discussed in chapter 5, equally important was the need for greater interdisciplinary study by academics leading to accounting being better located in a disciplinary sense in educational courses. Were this to occur students could reasonably be expected to have less multidisciplinary knowledge, but an understanding of how accounting connected to cognate disciplines. The *differentia specifica*

of accounting, including an understanding of the economic and social reper-
cussions of accounting, ought to be paramount.

Understanding and Reforming the Co-regulatory Regime

Background—'Publicity' and 'Truth and Fairness'

Underpinning the reforms pervading many of Chambers' papers and
addresses in the early 1960s and beyond was a desire to seek truth and
fairness in commercial negotiations through reforms to accounting. This
presumably was due to many factors, including his historical readings about
the need for trust in commercial dealings, the role of information in engen-
dering it, and his moral convictions (likely influenced by his religious beliefs)
about the need for truthful accounts to ensure a level playing field.

Before reviewing this proposition briefly, we provide his son Kevin's
observations in correspondence to the writers:

> He was very strict in terms of behaviour in the household and could
> become very irate if things were not done correctly. I am sure he always
> considered himself to be very fair and I remember asking him about his
> work from time to time to try and get a handle on what he was doing.
> One of the, (I thought) telling examples he gave—was it fair that some
> people ("insider" executives) would know the true value of a company
> if it was a public company owned by many other "outsiders," and that
> those other "outside" shareholders did not know the value as well as
> the executives did? He thought that was very unfair and was one of the
> things that he kept pursuing, he did not have any objection to people
> furthering their own good fortune so long as it was done fairly and
> everyone was on a level playing field.

This view is supported by his daughters' recollections:

> Honesty was always very important at home as we grew up. We were
> held to account for our actions and were expected to be able to defend
> our opinions. As we grew up issues of fairness became great discussion
> points around the dinner table. We used to have many debates at home
> and Dad could become very passionate on issues of public or private
> policy, justice, morality and integrity.

Chambers' religious convictions influenced his strong concerns about
'truth and fairness' that implicitly underpinned some of his early-to-mid-
1950s works, like his 1951 Sixth Commonwealth Institute of Accountants
Annual Research Lecture, 'Accounting and Business Finance,'[4] and the
monograph *Company Annual Reports: Function and Design*.[5] Our reviews
suggest that, while the phrase 'truth and fairness' did not appear in those

works, 'publicity' in the form of 'disclosure' as a 'condition of incorporation' and the accompanying 'limited liability' notions did. Explicit reference
to truth and fairness first appears in the 1957 ASA Research Lecture, published in 1958 as 'Asset Revaluations and Dividends.'[6] It was followed soon
after by works such as a commissioned 'Report in March 1960 (5 pp.) to the
Chairman of the N.S.W. PARB' detailing recent reforms to ensure adequate
corporate financial disclosures in England and the U.S.A.; a March 1960
ASA Seminar on 'A True and Fair View' of accounting in the U.K. and
the U.S.A.; a series of financial press articles published in 1963 discussing
flaws in financial reporting practices in Australia and elsewhere—including
a May 1963 *AFR* article, 'Under the Law of the Jungle'[7] discussing stock
exchanges and company accounts; a four-part, July 1963 *AFR* newspaper
series, 'Traps for the Unwary Investor,'[8] detailing defects of the law and
practice of corporate financial reporting; a September 1963 ASA Endowed
Lecture, 'Financial Information and the Securities Market' delivered at the
University of Sydney; and a December 1963 ABC radio interview on company losses and anachronistic accounting. Handwritten notes for this interview in the Chambers Archive indicate clearly that his preferred solution
in the early 1960s 'lies in the development of a system of financial record-
ing and reporting which simultaneously serves both management and those
having financial interests in companies.'[9]

Hence, what would later appear as CoCoA and the importance of truth
and fairness to that system were never far from his thinking in the many
areas he was addressing from the early 1950s. The more recent of the above
items were completed while Chambers was finalizing *Accounting, Evaluation and Economic Behavior*. Significantly, a major section of that work
concerned the nature of the corporation and the importance and accessibility of information about it. He refers (p. 345) to a public benefit from
incorporation being 'traded' for a public obligation to provide adequate
information publicity. He accepted the proposition that the trade-off arose
in the mid-nineteenth century U.K. because legislators sought to balance
the desire of businessmen for secrecy and the need of investors (suppliers of
funds such as creditors and shareholders) for sufficient information to assess
risk and return prospects properly. That prescribed information should be
truthful and fair. Concerns about misleading information being provided to
investors and how this could be mitigated were crucial in Chambers developing a more reliable form of accounting.

At about that time and following the observed misinformation evident in
the post-mortems in the 1950s and 1960s of several large Australian corporate failures Chambers provided the lead article in the inaugural issue
of *Abacus* 'Financial Information and the Securities Market'—a slightly
revised form of a mimeo developed for the 1963 ASA Endowed Lecture.[10]
Its importance is evidenced by Chambers' claim that accounting fails as a
language because the looseness of its rules produces anarchy in financial
reporting. He observes that under the accounting recommendations and

principles of the time there are 'A million sets of mutually exclusive rules each giving a true and fair view of a company's state of affairs and its profits, That is absurd!'[11] Also, an article covering similar ground appeared in the October 1964 *Current Affairs Bulletin*, 'Company Losses—Safeguarding the Investor,'[12] and familiar ideas appeared in the 1967 Berkeley Symposium paper, 'The Foundations of Financial Accounting.'[13] That looseness endures in the 2000s. This has occurred, notwithstanding legislation in many countries prescribing the use of international accounting standards. That legislation had the stated *intention* of achieving greater comparability through minimising opportunities for the use of differing accounting treatments.[14]

Chambers was not averse to seeking assistance from friends in higher places through informal means. Archive correspondence with Frank Ryan, then N.S.W. Registrar of Companies, shows that in January 1966 Chambers made a nineteen-page submission on the proposed amendments to the Accounts and Audit provisions of the Companies Act which Ryan agreed to discuss with other state registrars at an upcoming forum. Ryan wrote to Chambers on 22 February 1966 that he was disappointed the other state registrars were: 'not prepared to consider your suggestions in detail as they had not received a copy prior to the meeting. Nevertheless, I did have an opportunity to attempt to put across to them your views as to the desirability of a balance sheet representing the contemporary state of affairs of the company. I was disappointed that they were lukewarm towards the proposal not, I think, because of any belief that the proposals were undesirable but by reason of the difficulty they foresee in persuading the Ministers to adopt them.'[15]

Several related works followed from 1967 to 1975. The first was 'Suggested Amendments to the Companies Act,' a thirty-four-page submission to the Australian (Commonwealth) Company Law Advisory [the Eggleston] Committee, in October 1967.[16] In 1968 an article considered in some detail in chapter 4, 'Consolidated Statements Are Not Really Necessary' was published in a *The Australian Accountant*.[17] During 1971–73 Chambers was a member of the N.S.W. Government Corporate Advisory Committee. This appointment coincided with the preparation of an unpublished paper, 'The Companies Amendment Act, 1971—Accounts and Audit,' that was a revised, much longer version of the submission to the Eggleston Committee. In 1973 he revisited his views in this area in a major article 'Accounting Principles and the Law' which was published in the *Australian Business Law Review*. His reputation in this area was growing and it was not long before he was commissioned to prepare a section on 'true and fair' for the *Butterworths Corporation Law Bulletin*, a national loose-leaf update publication. In late 1977 Chambers' university colleague, commercial lawyer T. Sri Ramanathan responded to an inquiry from George Venturi, Legal Adviser to Frank Walker's Attorney-General's Department whether the N.S.W. Supreme Court could make a declaration, if requested by an applicant, that the accounts of a company comply-ing with accounting standards but which did not provide a true and fair view, did not comply with the provisions of the Companies Act. Ramana-than responded supplying legal reasoning that such a declaration could be made.[18] This was consistent with a view that Chambers had held for some time.

Those ideas in published and unpublished works were codified in the 1973 book, *Securities and Obscurities: Reform of the Law of Company Accounts* Also, they were summarized in Chambers' 1978 'Chairman's Preface' to the Report of the N.S.W. ASRC, *Company Accounting Standards*. Particulars of the formation and product of that Committee are discussed below.

Chambers' efforts regarding reforms to the operationalization of true and fair continued. He sought 'true and fair' to be recognized as an overrid-ing criterion to the presentation of the accounts, a principle to which the accounts must adhere. During the mid-to-late 1970s Chambers was invited to make submissions to State and Federal legislative inquiries into corpo-rate law and to the 1979 Campbell Inquiry into Australia's financial system (Table 7.3). His lengthy submission to the latter reiterates the flaws in the legislatively mandated corporate accounts provisions and summarizes his solutions.[19] In 1985 he made a six-page submission on the NCSC consulta-tive document 'A "True and Fair View" and the Reporting Obligations of Directors and Auditors.'[20] He returned to the issue in an interview with Linda English, editor of the *Australian Accounting Review* in 1990,[21] and again in two publications co-authored with Wolnizer in the early 1990s (discussed in chapter 3). He sent copies of those publications to regulators, including the chairmen of the NCSC, Henry Bosch, and of the ASC, Tony Hartnell. During January 1991 over twenty-five interested associates were also sent the papers. Responses are recorded in the Archive, but most are like that of Tony Minchin, Assistant to the Auditor General, who noted the concerns but, without providing reasoning, was mostly lukewarm to the proposals.[22] The noted observation made twenty years earlier by Frank Ryan about ministers being resistant to major corporate regulatory reforms was indeed prescient.

Chambers also made detailed submissions to various attorneys-general and to the royal commissioners leading the early 1990s inquiries into the collapses of major financial institutions, Rothwells and Tricontinen-tal. A similar submission two decades earlier was sent to Senator Robert Rae, Chair of the Rae Committee of Inquiry into Australian Securities Markets.[23]

Augmenting those publications, formal submissions to professional and government inquiries and interviews, Chambers used other means of poten-tial influence. He pursued numerous contacts with politicians, academics, and practitioners associated with professional bodies; as noted in chapter 6 he accepted a commissioned work in 1961–62 at the APB with the respected accounting academic Maurice Moonitz; undertook discussions (see below) with the N.S.W. Corporate Affairs Commissioners, then with the National Companies and Securities Commissioners; made similar contacts with SEC Chief Accountants and Commissioners; accepted an offer from the N.S.W. Attorney-General Frank Walker to Chair the 1977–78 N.S.W. ASRC which would produce in May 1978, *Company Accounting Standards*; and also, in response to an advertisement in late 1979, he applied to be either a full- or part-time member of the newly created National Companies and Securities Commission. His application letter contains a 'Statement of Interest.' The following extract is instructive about his suitability for this position due to his experiences and observations in related areas:

> Over thirty years I have observed the growth, amalgamations, take-overs, reconstructions, disputes and failures of companies and the litigation that has arisen from alleged misdemeanours—in Australia, the United Kingdom and the United States. That difficulties and mis-demeanours persist in spite of varied attempts to tighten the laws and regulations seems evidence of the difficulty of securing a fair market in securities while the information made available on companies is out-of-date and unreliable, even when it is not intentionally false or fraudu-lent. My book, *Securities and Obscurities*, is a catalogue of hundreds of instances of misleading information and its consequences, and I have written extensively on the matter elsewhere.
>
> I have not been concerned with these matters simply as an accounting technician, but for the effects they have on the economic efficiency of companies, on the fairness of the securities market to those who deal in it, on the efficiency of the market as a discriminating capital-rationing device, and on the capacity of regulatory bodies to oversee the conduct of corporate business in the public interest. My views, developed by reference to the conduct of particular companies, and the emergence of remedial changes in statutes and regulations, have been made known to the Rae Committee, the Campbell Committee and in numerous other publications, including the Report of the ASRC.[24]

Instructive also is how the decision to appoint the NCSC members was conveyed to Chambers and the 'head-hunter' administering the reviews of potential appointees. Both were initially informed that Ministerial Coun-cil decisions about the full-time members had been made at their 8 Janu-ary 1980 meeting, but decisions about the part-time members were to be deferred till the next meeting in March. Surprisingly, even to the consultants according to the letter Chambers received from them, the Council reversed this decision a week later and all appointees were announced in the press on 16 January. Chambers was not offered either of the two part-time positions.

In 1982 Chambers received much more positive news. He was invited to join the Australian Accounting Standards Board. However, as the epi-graph to this chapter shows, eight months into the appointment, due to disappointment and frustration in the overly political process of reviewing standards, he resigned. This would be his last professional or government appointment.

Several earlier chapters have revealed Chambers to have been a passionate theorist, including chapter 7 which described how his theoretical ideas were honed from observing the affairs of businesses and regulators through his decades of consultancies, professional, and government relationships and appointments. An understanding of financial management and the corporate regulatory system was essential for his development of an effective long-term reform of accounting.

General Discussion of Attempts to Better Understand the Regulatory System

Explanations follow of what underpinned many of Chambers' works covering the broader area of regulatory reform. They provide additional particulars to enable assessment of the criticism by some observers that he was naive in the way he sought to reform corporate reporting practice. The substance of the reforms has been described above and is well covered in *Securities and Obscurities* and the ASRC's *Accounting Standards* (of which Chambers was the Chair). Little of the detail in the former is repeated here, but some related matters are.

Securities and Obscurities illustrates the breadth of his knowledge of corporate financial reporting regulations worldwide. From the mid-1950s till the early 1970s he had inquired of regulatory agencies about their regulatory regimes, and purchased actual regulations such as the SEC's reporting requirements in its 10-K forms, and the various U.K. Companies Acts in the nineteenth and twentieth centuries. Further, the Chambers Archive reveals early 1960s correspondence with academics and regulators in the U.K., Europe (especially Germany and Holland), the U.S.A., Australia and elsewhere. He was seeking information about the publicity obligations of corporations in respect of financial statements, namely the override criterion, the English and some European countries' 'true and fair view' and the North American 'fairly presents.' This all shows a desire to be fully aware of the regulatory matters being examined.

An early example was Chambers' 1959 request to LSE Professor Harold Edey and other U.K. accounting academics to provide a summary of the U.K. reporting obligations for corporations. A request followed in 1963 to Welsh economists, E. Victor Morgan and W.A. Thomas, who had published their seminal *History of the Stock Exchange*,[25] to write for the proposed *Abacus* journal a piece on the London Stock Exchange's reporting obligations of their listed companies. While this request was unsuccessful, Chambers maintained the correspondence, resulting in Morgan doing some voluntary 'research assistance' about the London Stock Exchange's publicity obligations.[26]

Other examples a few years later are revealed in this extract from a 1966 letter to Professor Leopold Illetschko, Hochschule für Welthandel:

> I shall be visiting Europe this summer to make some inquiries into the present status, background and prospects of the financial publicity required of companies under the corporation codes and rules of the stock exchanges and regulatory bodies. Professor Heinz Burgstaller, who is presently visiting Illinois, kindly gave your name and that of [your colleague] Professor Erich Loitlsberger as academic persons who might be able to help me when I visit Vienna. I have also been referred to Dr Franz Heissenberger, of the Creditanstalt-Bankverim, of whom I have asked whether I could obtain copies of statutes, regulations, and statements by professional bodies on the keeping of accounts, the appointment of auditors and obligations to have published statements audited.[27]

A similarly worded letter was sent to University of Frankfurt am Main accounting academic Peter Swoboda, who had also been introduced by Burgstaller.[28] In time, meetings were arranged with each as part of Chambers' European travels.[29]

Chambers continued to search for many more years for what underpinned his perceived 'universal' corporate financial publicity obligations in market economies. In the mid-1960s he wrote several times to the SEC Chief Accountant Andrew Barr, in particular seeking knowledge of specific SEC-prescribed publicity obligations under the Regulation S-X and Form 10-K requirements; on another occasion requesting examples of SEC-filed annual reports;[30] and on another requesting to meet the SEC Chairman Manny Cohen during his scheduled visit to the U.S. Barr's responses were cordial and helpful. Barr introduced him to Cohen, with Chambers sending a letter detailing his concerns about the lack of specificity in accounting prescribed in legislatures in the Anglo-American jurisdictions and requesting a meeting as part of his travels. Cohen responded promptly, agreeing to meet with Chambers and noting:

> Thank you very much for your letter of November 24 and the several papers in which you discuss the problems of financial reporting and the securities markets. While I have not had an opportunity to read these papers, Mr. Barr reports that he has done so with considerable interest.[31]

There is no record in the Archive of what occurred at the 1966 meeting. Interestingly, while Chambers and Barr maintained contact, there is no record in the Archive of Barr having responded to another of Chambers' requests several years later seeking 'any reasons' why his 'arguments and conclusions were not valid.'[32]

Over the next two decades, Chambers engaged in correspondence with three other SEC Chief Accountants: Sandy Burton, A. Clarence Sampson, and Walter Schuetze. He first contacted Burton in 1969 in his capacity as professor of accounting at Columbia University in the City of New York, and kept abreast of Burton's thoughts on the U.S. override 'fairly presents' through reading his February 1975 Emanuel Saxe Distinguished Accounting Lecture, 'Fair Presentation: Another View.' Chambers made a submission directly through a letter to Burton on the SEC's 1976 'Replacement Cost' proposal in ASR190.[33]

In the late 1980s and early '90s Chambers maintained personal acquaintance with Schuetze, who was introduced to him by Sydney School colleague Peter Wolnizer. In 2001 Schuetze delivered the R.J. Chambers Memorial Lecture, in which he mirrored Chambers' views on the need for a market (exit) price system to replace the (primarily historic cost-based) accounting system.

Regulatory correspondence and meetings also occurred with Australian regulators during those four decades. First, Chambers corresponded quite often with the 1960s Registrar of Companies in N.S.W. (and Corporate Affairs Commissioner 1971–78), Frank Ryan[34]; and also with the 1970s and '80s NCSC chairmen, Leigh Masel and Henry Bosch. Both delivered Pacioli Society addresses in the early-to-mid 1980s. And he corresponded over several years with the inaugural chairman of the Australian Law Reform Commission (1975–83), Michael Kirby.

Ryan (1967) contributed an article on true and fair view in one of the early issues of *Abacus*. The closeness of their relationship is evident in their correspondence.

In 1980 and 1981 Chambers and Masel corresponded on several occasions.[35] Their relationship was professional. Not long after the NCSC had been founded (with Masel as its founding chairman) Chambers wrote:

My interest in the adequate oversight of the conduct of corporate affairs—by all who may have interests in them—prompts me to write to you. I know it is early days in the life of the N.C.S.C. and that currently occurring matters will make immediate demands on the attention of the Commission.

I first served on professional committees concerned with those matters some thirty years ago, and more recently I served a number of years on the senior executive committees of the accountancy profession. I have also corresponded for many years with the officers of overseas professional bodies. I think I may claim to be well aware of the extent to which the conclusions and edicts of those committees are conditioned by conventional practices; and aware of the difficulty of bringing under consideration, by those committees, the financial information by which investors, creditors, regulatory bodies and others may fairly judge what has occurred. There seems to be only one way of breaking through that impasse—and that is to specify more clearly in the Companies Act, or in regulations under that or other Acts, the kind of information that is demonstrably serviceable.

There have, over the years, been many amendments to the accounts sections and the relevant schedules of the Companies Acts, intended to supplant less satisfactory provisions or to secure the giving of information deemed to be necessary. But there has been no general examination of the *quality* of the information required or given. The emphasis has been on *quantity*, rather than on *quality*. I am of the opinion that this has led to the disclosure of more information of questionable utility, not to improvement in the utility of the information. From time to time I have suggested to professional bodies that great service could be done if they would re-draft the Ninth Schedule (for example) in the light of what the financial and commercial community needs to know in the interest of fair negotiation and fair dealing in securities. But without effect.[36] (emphasis added)

This letter generated a request from Masel for Chambers to travel to Melbourne to discuss his ideas with members of the Commission. Chambers accepted but, due to travelling overseas, he could not arrange an immediate meeting. The Archive is silent on whether a meeting ever occurred.

As well, Chambers exchanged letters with commercial and securities lawyers around the world including Harvard University's Law School Professor, Louis Loss and New York University's Professor of Commercial Law Homer Kripke. Of especial note are some matters raised with Kripke. Extracts from several letters between these two are provided.[37]

In August 1972 Chambers corresponded that he had great sympathy with the concerns raised in Kripke's 1970 article, 'The SEC and the Accountants, Some Myths and Some Realities,' observing:

As far as I can recall, yours is the only well-argued stand by a legal scholar for something better, in almost a generation. . . . [And, in conclusion] There seems to be only one way of defeating the present inertia, and that is by keeping up the attack on the traditional mode on as wide a front as possible. I hope there will be an increasing number of articles like those of yours.

In a lengthy handwritten response Kripke indicated a detailed awareness of Chambers' writings, suggesting they had similar concerns about the lack of investor protections in the U.S. securities acts and in legislation in other countries.[38]

They corresponded for eighteen months. A letter from Kripke and Chambers' response reveal that, while they were as one in proposing market prices rather than costs being reported in a company's accounts, differences appeared in respect of which market prices—exit (selling prices) or entry (replacement) prices. A further difference was Kripke's advocation of forecasted data, possibly even being included in the accounts.[39] Chapter 6 reveals that reporting forecasted data in accounts was anathema to Chambers.

Another set of correspondence discussed the issue of whether valuation issues should be directed at the whole firm or at the individual asset level. Kripke had raised the issue in the context of a lengthy railroad company example where major infrastructure costs had to be accounted for. He noted such issues applied to large companies like the Penn Central Railroad.[40] As usual Chambers was adamant that individual (in the normal business sense) assets should be the focus of accounting.

What Chambers gained from these sources corroborated the corporate particulars he had documented over many decades (assisted by his long-time research assistant Dorothy Simons, whom he appointed in the mid-1960s). Those research efforts had unearthed what Chambers viewed as a mass of corporate anomalies—in respect of inventory valuation methods, corporate takeovers, random asset revaluations, bonus issues, corporate profits and losses, creative accounting, and generally, the inability of conventional accounting to account systematically for price and price level changes.[41]

All of this activity and searching preceded Chambers chairing of the N.S.W. ASRC.

N.S.W. Accounting Standards Review Committee[42]

Presumably because of Chambers' regulatory contacts, his accumulated knowledge about true and fair view and his interest generally in corporate reporting matters, in November 1977 he was invited by Attorney-General Frank Walker to chair the N.S.W. Labor government's Review Committee. The early part of the 1970s saw historically high price levels in many countries, and companies faced financial pressures culminating in many large, often unexpected, corporate collapses. Governments around the world set up inquiries into many aspects of regulating, financing, managing, accounting, and auditing of those companies. In the U.S., for example, the Big 8 accounting firms, as the largest international accounting firms were known then, came under close scrutiny with the 1975 Moss and 1976 Metcalf Committee enquiries of the U.S. House and Senate respectively,[43] as did the profession's standards setting and enforcement practices.

Australia was no exception. The ASRC was set up in November 1977 to examine the accounting standards which have been promulgated either in their final form or at the exposure stage by the accountancy profession and any other standards coming to the attention of the committee which should be considered in the interest of parties who use the published accounting information.[44]

The Committee initially was intended to comprise two members chosen by Chambers and one from each of the ICAA and ASA. This did not eventuate. When it reported in May 1978 the Committee comprised only Ray Chambers, along with two University of Sydney staff, commercial lawyer and former Sri Lankan United Nations delegate T. Sri Ramanathan, and accounting academic Harry Rappaport. After considerable prevarication the ICAA had declined a formal invitation for one of its members to participate and the ASA had withdrawn its nominated member. In a curious twist, the professional bodies unwittingly gave Chambers' claims for accounting reform an unfettered public forum in which to expose its ideas and to do it with a relatively free hand.

Frank Walker's committee had emerged against a background in which several of the 1967–1970 mining-boom companies with clean audit reports unexpectedly collapsed. Then the real estate property boom and bust in the first half of the 1970s, coupled to several years of increasing audit qualifications in respect of failure to comply with accounting standards, had also prompted extensive public concern.[45]

Like their counterparts in the early 1960s, corporate and accounting anomalies in the 1970s cases, including Mineral Securities, Mainline Corporation, Cambridge Credit Corporation, and Gollins Holdings, put pressure on Australia's corporate regulators to reassess the utility of existing regulatory mechanisms—in particular, the serviceability of the professionally prescribed accounting and auditing practices.

The issue of non-compliance in the 1970s, as now (four decades on), was a major problem for the profession and regulators. Non-compliance with the approved standards was, and is still seen in all cases to be deviant, non-professional behaviour. There continues to be a push by the regulatory bodies for compliance of a voluminous set of the initially professionally, and more recently, regulatory or legislatively mandated rules. These included, for example, providing for depreciation on buildings when the overall market price of property (including the buildings) was increasing, the reporting of asset valuations on a cost-allocated basis, providing for future income tax and booking 'future income tax benefits' and 'provisioning' without the immediate existence of or any definite prospect that the supposed assets or liabilities would materialize. In late 1990s Australia the nebulous FITB assisted a financially distressed HIH insurance company being able to be presumed 'solvent' on an audited net-asset basis according to its 2000 balance sheet. A similar issue had emerged a decade earlier in the unravelling of the Bond Corporation collapse. Bond at the time was one of Australia's largest listed companies.[46] Its audited financial accounts for several years before the collapse had not disclosed the worsening financial position.

Whereas the ultimate response by the professional bodies to the 1978 ASRC Report would be low-key and rather secretive, the profession's early involvement was more positive. At the June 1977 National Congress of the ASA Frank Walker had signalled a desire to pursue company law and accounting reforms. Chambers Archive correspondence indicates that he was concerned about the failure of the Crown to prosecute successfully individuals who were operating 'on the fringe' because of the difficulty in defining 'proper' accounting practices, as well as a concern about the concentration of the large accounting firms. This mirrored contemporary concerns expressed in the U.S. Moss and Metcalf inquiries.[47]

Walker referred to the need for an Accounting Standards Review Board in the 1977 Congress paper and in several letters in the Chambers Archive. After receiving a letter also containing a copy of Walker's paper from his long-time friend Frank Ryan, Chambers responded giving his personal opinion about the review board proposal.[48] He wrote to the Attorney-General in mid-August, outlining his approval of the proposal.[49] Writing to Ryan, Chambers especially noted the significance of recent large losses suffered by creditors in unexpected corporate failures:

> There is one matter which stands out quite clearly: In none of the argument or the product [of the standard-setting operations of the profession] has the least attention been given to the relevance of the proposed kind of information to creditors. It is a matter of historical fact that the publication of financial information by companies was instituted as a "quid pro quo," by which creditors could protect themselves by information on the assets and liabilities of companies, in lieu of the right to sue proprietors directly (that is, where liability was unlimited). And as companies still depend heavily on creditors, that form of protection is still pertinent and (obviously, from many of the cases of the last 20 years) necessary. Further, the kind of information pertinent to creditors is equally pertinent to shareholders. For if a company is running into difficulties with its creditors, trouble lies ahead also for its shareholders, since their rank is subordinate.

Stung by major company failures in the 1970s, it came as little surprise on 17 November 1977 when Walker acted. But rather than announcing a 'review board,' a he created a Review Committee. A letter to Chambers from a partner of Arthur Andersen indicates that this was probably not a surprise to some in the profession. It reveals that representatives of the profession had met three months earlier with Frank Walker on 17 August to discuss the 'review board' and 'review committee' ideas.[50] What may have caused surprise, however, was the proposed composition of the five-member review or steering committee; and that the draft terms of reference of the proposed 'Review Committee' provided the powers to initiate, rather than just review, standards.

Correspondence between the N.S.W. Society President, Ron Waldron, and National President of the Institute, Phillip Cox, suggests that, from the beginning, neither was pleased with the committee's composition. Indeed, they had quickly met with the Attorney-General the day following the public announcement of the committee's structure. Their understanding of the committee and how it was to function differed from what they considered to be implied in the public announcement of its creation, and in advertisements inviting submissions to it. Correspondence reveals that they explained their misgivings to the Attorney-General, complaining that the committee had been referred to as a 'steering committee' and not the 'review board' the Attorney-General had been talking of establishing; that it did not comprise the normal cross-section of people 'concerned with accounting standards and their practical application as to give [it] an acceptance in the professional and commercial community,' and that its membership ought to include representatives of the Institute of Directors, stock exchange and small business.[51]

Nonetheless, the Society nominated an appointee but the ICAA held off doing so.

Having now lost out on the composition of the ASRC, the strategy adopted appears to have been to ignore it, starve it of legitimacy and play a neater game with the proposed review board.

But behind the scenes there was action. On the eve of the Society's Trevor Russell's resignation from the ASRC Geoff Vincent authored a paper 'The Current Position of the N.S.W. Accounting Standards Review Board.' It contained the understatement of the year—that the review committee had become *political*. There was a hint that Chambers has placed the ASA in an embarrassing position, concern about the technical ability of members of the committee and the fact that the committee was unbalanced—with those accepting nomination being dominated by the Sydney University staff members, pro-Chambers in outlook. There was also a strong hint of 'playing the man' in the Institute's unwillingness to participate with the whiff of the idea that, as both the National President of the Society and chair of the Committee, the Society would be seen to favour Chambers' views. The paper expressed the view that the ASRC Report would be derogatory of the profession's standards.

The ASRC completed its inquiries and its report appeared in May 1978; and although not mentioned by name CoCoA was the template for its 'General Standard' to replace the then current batch of professionally endorsed standards. Although this was a major change, what few realized was that Chambers had been working for many years in this area, as evident in *Securities and Obscurities*. He had explored much of the early report chapters on the Companies Act provisions, ideas on the functions of accounting standards, his all-inclusive income, capital maintenance, financial position, and financial performance notions, and indeed he had reviewed the raft of questionable practices of companies that had either unexpectedly failed or were in financial distress and the concomitant machinations of the legal advisers with their notions of what was meant by profit and loss. He had worked over such things for the best part of forty years. His dissatisfaction with the current systems in Australia and indeed elsewhere was not a matter of whim, but rather a well thought through case with all the evidence he believed one would need to convince people of goodwill. CoCoA had had a long and thorough gestation period and although it had its detractors none had come forward to question the depth of his analysis, as he had invited them to do in 1967 at the Berkeley Symposium where he put up a grid comparing the alternative systems.[52]

Behind the Report's general standard was the idea that the preparation of accounts was subject to an explicit overriding principle, namely that they shall provide a true and fair view of an entity's financial position and performance. In such a setting it mattered little how accounting firms went about their work, provided the mandatory financial reporting principles were adhered to. Common practices—'standards'—that would ensure accounting data were serviceable, would evolve.

Overall, the financial press appeared to hold a view that the committee had undertaken the task in a manner that recommended a norm for companies to account sensibly for their periodic wealth and progress. It seemed to make common sense to them. And many suggested, like the *Australian Financial Review's* Chanticleer that historical cost accounting had been dealt a death blow.

But the Institute and the Society met the Report's publication with what Chambers viewed as a contemptuous public silence—indeed in the Presidents' jointly signed communication with Attorney-General Walker on 25 January 1980 they stated that the delayed response was to enable them to consult widely, especially to survey and analyse views from executives of the Group of 100 major Australian companies. They also stated without reasoning we do not consider: 'it appropriate to comment in detail on all the matters raised in the Report. . . . We have, therefore, confined our response to . . . the more important issues raised. . . . We believe, however, that much of the critical comment contained in the report regarding the content of individual standards developed . . . largely through its research arm, the Australian Accounting Research Foundation, is not justified . . . that detailed comments on various aspects of the report of the Committee would serve no useful purpose.'[53]

In the interregnum, however, behind the scenes they were busy trying to gather support to scuttle the ASRC Report.

The Report's critique of conventional accounting, augmented concerns expressed in the ASA General Council White Paper in the mid-1960s.[54] As noted, prior to the ASRC Report's release the N.S.W. Attorney-General had threatened State intervention in the Accounting Standards-setting process unless the accountancy profession issued sensible and enforceable directives. For whatever reason, however, little direct action resulted from the ASRC report and those threats. Many years later Chambers observed

publicly on the "boycott" of the profession in ensuring a lack of any legislative response:

> But the boycott held, the profession closed ranks; neither body deigned
> officially to notice our report! And whether the Attorney-General had
> been got at we do not know; but no action whatever, except publica-
> tion, was taken consequent upon the inquiry.[55]

By the early 1980s the N.S.W. Labor government was gone, voted out of
office, and the report went with it.

Setting up the ASRC was a politically shrewd response by the government
to the public outcry at the circumstances in which companies with clean
audit reports collapsed suddenly; and in other cases audit qualifications for
non-compliance over technical accounting matters were rife. But because
of inaction the losers were the investors (shareholders and creditors). More
than twenty-five years after the 1966 ASA White Paper, this time in the U.K.
another professional inquiry occurred, the *Pratten Report*. It was commissioned after another spate of unexpected corporate collapses.[56] But fundamental accounting changes were again absent.

Upon retirement Chambers was disappointed. He was disillusioned with
the lack of effective regulatory reform, as indicated in the following extract
from a letter to long-time colleague, Zeff:

> It seems to me that the ferment has exhausted itself and that the
> profession—practising and academic alike—has reconciled itself to a
> libation of flat, stale dregs. After years of working on the sidelines,
> I was at last (1982) invited to spend a term on the local [Austra-
> lian] Standards Board. Eight months of striving to accustom myself
> to endorsing or seeing others endorse questionable or baseless conten-
> tions, I gave it up.[57]

And in another letter, this time to Briloff, he suggests some reforms are,
however, inevitable:

> I have been continually amazed, even amused, by the frequency and
> persistence of sloppy arguments, lacunae, solecisms and unsupported
> assertions in the past history of accounting thought. It can only get bet-
> ter, but it will be after my time, I suspect.[58]

Reforms to Account for Changing Prices and Price Levels[59]

This was another major reform area related to practice. Our account shows
that on several occasions Chambers put forward his ideas on the "so-called
price level problem." He argued that accounting for both price and price
level changes should be adopted by practitioners. Failing this, professional

and other regulatory bodies should prescribe them. Beginning in the late 1940s with several articles in Australian professional accounting journals this reform campaign continued into the early 1980s.[60]

Chambers summarized the context and the arguments in his early thoughts on inflation accounting proposals in the 1965 *Journal of Accounting Research* article 'The Price Level Problem and Some Intellectual Grooves':

> Almost all the writing on this subject in the decade 1946–55 was against the background of rising prices of capital goods, a pent-up demand for such goods both for expansion and replacement, and high rates of taxation on business incomes. [A proposed new accounting paradigm] could be challenged on two grounds at least: they could be said to be special pleading [by interested parties], or they could be said to be of ephemeral interest, interest which would wane as prices tended to become more stable.

Chambers continued: 'To be of any lasting consequence as an intellectual question, the *so-called price level problem* had to be seen as an integral part of accounting and not a mere appendage' (emphasis added).[61] This was the catalyst for his search, as outlined in chapter 6, for a general set of ideas based on logic, scientific method, some economic notions and the need to comply with the rules of mathematics.

Continuing the context of his ideas, fast forward to the early 1970s after inflation had spiked. Interest in the price-level problem quickly regained momentum in many countries. The U.K. professional accounting bodies, for example, responded with the January 1973 ED8 proposal for supplementary information to be provided in a form of stabilized accounting known as CPP accounting. But, as in earlier decades, the government soon became involved as arguments for taxation relief for companies emerged.

In June 1974 the British Chancellor of the Exchequer (Anthony Barber) and the Secretary of State for Trade (Peter Walker) appointed Sir Francis Sandilands to be chair of its committee to enquire into inflation accounting (see chapter four for details). Sandilands was an insurance executive without an accounting reputation (in either academic or professional accounting). It seemed to some a strange, albeit a somewhat independent, choice. Indeed, the committee's report was criticized by Chambers just after its release and later, by amongst others the Sydney schooler, Frank Clarke. The main concerns were that its conclusions, perhaps due to compromise, failed to account properly (i.e. systematically) for the price and price level change features of inflation.[62] Its suggested reforms did not reflect the financial experience during inflationary periods over many centuries, namely that changes in individual asset prices varied—some rose, some actually fell and still others remained steady, and that those that rose or fell did so at different rates.

The Report published in September 1975 dismissed the case for Continuously Contemporary Accounting (CCA) to be accepted as the method of accounting for inflation. Also, not only did Chairman Sandilands reject CCA as described in Chambers' lengthy submission, but he expropriated the label for the recommended Current Cost Accounting proposal.

Not to be outdone Chambers quickly adopted the CoCoA label. Also, by then he had dropped the use of replacement price as an approximation of the current cash equivalent of assets other than cash and receivables from its 1966 book-length exposition. As noted in chapter 6, adhering to his 'consistency and measurement principles,' he now reported *all* assets at their current cash equivalent.

Although the Sydney School was highly critical of the attempts over several decades by professional bodies to produce recommendations or standards on how to account for inflation, in the early 1970s it was on good terms with practitioners due to Chambers building those connections. The Department of Accounting at Sydney hosted the Chartered Institute hierarchy for lunch several times a year. In those days smoking after lunch was common. In late 1975 it was suggested that to embellish the luncheon table we might place thereon match folders and coasters with an advertisement, 'Try CoCoA'—just to show that although somewhat down at that moment Chambers was 'not out.' The department was still smarting at the drubbing Chambers had received by Sandilands. And after all, it was the first meeting of the parties since the report's release. Chambers agreed to the proposal. When the guests saw the match folders and coasters they jumped to the conclusion that Chambers had had thousands printed and had already posted them around the country and overseas. Nobody disabused them, and Chambers rapidly made sure their presumption was correct. Delighted with the outcome, he quickly took on the new spelling.

In a curious way Sandilands' action in expropriating CCA set in motion a number of events that arguably did more to promote CoCoA than would otherwise have occurred. It intensified the impetus for the CoCoA label and the circumstances that led to its form. And, not long afterwards Chambers and other members of the Sydney School were asked to present Professional Development courses for the ASA on 'inflation accounting,' which they did until the end of the decade.

Those courses, which gained added importance in the explanation of Chambers' system, provided a valuable promotional platform that unquestionably enhanced its general visibility, and most likely motivated Chambers' recourse to political means.

But, as alluded to at the beginning of this section, price and price level accounting had had a long genesis, to which we now turn briefly. We include in this brief account some of Chambers' responses to ideas emerging from those lengthy academic and practitioner deliberations. We mentioned Chambers had sought throughout his career to influence not only the theory but the practice of accounting for price and price level changes through his writings and submissions to inquiries by professional bodies and various governments. Addressing the practical accounting problems created by price and price level changes was critical in developing his theoretical reforms

Figure 8.1 CoCoA is My Cup of Tea

more generally, especially as they related to measurement and reform of the law of company accounts.

Prior Literature

Archive materials and entries from literature in his *Thesaurus* show that Chambers was well aware of much of the literature described here. Also, Chambers' research assistant Dorothy Simons facilitated greatly his understanding of the European business economics literature covering the first half of the twentieth century. This was through her commissioned (by Chambers) translations in the late 1960s and '70s of 'classics' by well-known Italian, Dutch, and German authors including Pietro Onida, Theodore Limperg, and Fritz Schmidt.[63] They cover some of the post-World War I European attempts to account for the changing prices and price levels of the ensuing hyperinflation, such as: Schmidt's 1921 *Die organise Tageswertbilanz*, Mahlberg's 1921 *Bilanztechnik und Bewertung bei schwankender Waehrung*, and Eugen Schmalenbach's 1922 *Goldmarkbilanz*. Such works and early 1920s articles appearing in German business trade journals had prompted the American Henry Sweeney to write the series of articles in *The Accounting Review* in the late 1920s and early 1930s—these were augmented by the publication of his 1936 classic, *Stabilized Accounting*.[64]

During the 1960s and early 1970s Chambers sought manuscript submissions for the early issues of *Abacus* from European scholars with knowledge of business economics (*Economia Aziendale* in Italy, *Bedrijfseconomie* in the Netherlands and *Betriebswirtschaft* in Germany). Contributions that were published include: Mey ('Theodore Limperg and his Theory of Values and Cost'), Kohler and Matz ('Swiss Financial Reporting and Audit Practices'), Vos ('Replacement Value Accounting'), Hansen ('An Operational Cost Information Model'), and Burgert ('Reservations about "Replacement Value" in the Netherlands').

Debates in Anglo-American countries after World War I have been shown to have drawn heavily on those European business economists' ideas.[65] Chambers' notion of the theory of the firm certainly drew on them.

Debate over how to account for inflation followed quickly after World War II, much as it had following World War I. Indeed, it gave Chambers' push to reform corporate accounting in *Accounting, Evaluation and Economic Behavior* another point of focus, for during inflation the defects in general everyday accounting are exaggerated. In particular, academic discussion and practitioner and regulatory actions reinforced his notion that accounting standard setters had it wrong regarding the measurement of the relevant property of a firm's assets and the need for a standard unit of measure. This was evidenced by the dysfunctional use of the rule of addition in preparing balance sheets. Aggregate balances of assets and liabilities with different purchasing powers were combined, money in possession was added to money long gone and to monetary amounts never possessed by a company. Further, capital as part of the balance sheet was not maintained in a purchasing power sense. All of these matters, examined in more detail below, helped fine tune Chambers' reform ideas in respect of the function of accounting and what was meant by financial position and all-inclusive income and related measurement issues.

'The Price Level Problem and Some Intellectual Grooves' contained Chambers' preliminary thinking on matters that had appeared in several articles in the late 1940s and early 1950s. We noted those pieces included a preference for reporting fixed assets at replacement prices. Data in Tables 7.3 and 7.5 show that Chambers continued for several decades to write articles and books about price and price level accounting as well as make related submissions to professional and regulatory inquiries. As well as distributing internationally his private ED on accounting for inflation Chambers had made submissions to all the major mid-to-late 1970s national and international professional and government enquiries into accounting for price and price level changes. By then, as Chapter 6 revealed, Chambers had seen the need for a consistent measurement basis for all assets and had settled on his capital maintenance adjustment to account for changes in the general level of prices. He also noted that attempts by academics, practitioners, and regulators had failed to resolve the accounting problems created by price and price level changes.

Protracted deliberations due to inflationary disruptions invariably feature switches in opinion and in emphasis as changes occur in the political and socio-economic contexts in which they continue, as old participants leave and new ones enter. Although the problems noted below are somewhat related, they certainly are not the same. Nor are all of them accounting problems, even though each has financial (hence accounting) implications.

Chambers noted in several works prior to the 1970s CCA debates that price regulation or rate fixing is not peculiar to either inflationary or deflationary conditions. It is a quasi-financial problem. Also, the imposition of taxation rates can be such that payments on that account are high irrespective of whether prices fluctuate. Calculations required for taxation purposes involve a highly specific contextual application of accounting techniques which need not bear any relationship to the techniques of external financial reporting. The problem of funding asset replacements or repairs to existing assets so that physical capital may be maintained is a financial management matter, not an accounting reporting one. The financial consequences of inflation may well make rate fixing more difficult, taxation payments more burdensome and asset replacement more costly. But that does not mean that accounting to incorporate the financial effects of inflation needs to pay any particular attention to those problems. In fact, however, it did. The origins of many of the arguments for making replacement price adjustments in accounts are glossed over too often in the eagerness to use them as methods of incorporating the effects of inflation. The issues change, and so do the grounds for argument. Chambers' 1976 ICRA monograph, *Current Cost Accounting—A Critique of the Sandilands Report* and his 1980 *Price Variation and Inflation Accounting* demonstrated that the CCA debate, whether to adopt replacement prices, is no different.

Elsewhere Clarke has shown how the relevant prior literature can be dissected into distinct phases.[66] In the first, the setting was mainly utility pricing. Germain Boer traced the development of the arguments for calculating depreciation charges on the basis of current replacement prices of assets in the context of the utility rate fixing in the U.S.A. from the turn of the century to the late 1930s.[67] The dominant themes were how depreciation was argued to be a necessity to provide funds for the replacement of the productive capacity of essentially non-adaptive private water and electricity companies during the 1920s that had been granted monopolies by the government, and how this notion drifted into the external accounting domain, namely in determining the profits and losses of ordinary companies. In the second, the setting was taxation, and a similar argument, that depreciation created a fund for the replacement of assets, was pursued by lobbyists for post-World War II taxation reform. In the first decade of the third, the setting was the proposed supplementation of historical cost-based accounts to incorporate adjustments for changes in the general level of prices, *only*. The next decade considered differential price adjustment proposals. We show that the replacement price argument was met by Chambers' CoCoA head-on. Space considerations mean that only a portion of the academic arguments and professional proposals in those phases are discussed.

Phase I: 1930s Regulated Pricing and the Capital Replacement of Utilities

The managerial problem facing the utilities was the need to provide finance for the periodic replacement of plant of the same general kind they currently had in use to 'maintain productive capacity' in their utility operations. In those circumstances continued concern over the provision of finance to enable reinvestment in plant similar *in function* to that currently in use was entirely consistent with the non-adaptive nature of the utility companies and the continuation of their operations. Generally, those non-adaptive utilities were incorporated to provide a particular monopoly service and not to do anything else. The push for replacement costs was also consistent with social economic theory requiring the continued existence of a unit providing a socially necessary service, but not necessarily consistent with the theory of private economic enterprise.

The utilities were thus a special case. They had a particular problem because of their non-adaptive character. However, the notions of necessary replacements and continuous reinvestment in like assets (and related deprecation backlog arguments) are presented often in the later literature as if they were necessary patterns of activity also for *adaptive* enterprises, not locked in to any one line of activity.

Fast forward several decades to Chambers' thinking. His 1977 *Financial Analysts Journal* article 'Delusions of Replacement Cost Accounting' responding to a July-August 1976 article by Vancil and Weil 'Current Replacement Cost Accounting: Depreciable Assets, and Distributable Income' addressed the matter directly, even though the context was several decades later.[68] He noted with numerical examples 'that the view often proposed 'that by reinvesting the amount of the depreciation each year the amount of the backlog can be made good,' was fallacious. In other works, such as his ICRA *A Critique of the Sandilands Report* and *Price Variation and Inflation Accounting*, Chambers observes that the context of the depreciation problem for the utilities differs from the private sector. In the former depreciation calculations were intended, primarily, for the *internal* purposes of determining acceptable cost structure and adequate rates of return, as part of utility operators' negotiations with government authorities regarding the setting of rates.

Although the effects of agreed rates filtered through into the utilities' published accounts, contrary to the 1970s inflation accounting proposals the 1920s and 1930s, calculations were not primarily designed for the purposes of *external* reporting. Indeed, the utilities were rigidly controlled in respect of their external reports. They adhered to a strict regime of historical cost in the preparation of their published accounts.[69]

Phase I also witnessed the quasi-reorganizations effected through the asset revaluations of the Roaring '20s and devaluations in the Depression of the 1930s. There also was the development of the arguments for *base stock* or *last-in-first-out* (LIFO) inventory valuations pursued by many, such as Nickerson, and Arthur.[70] In contrast with the utility price fixing episodes, the latter were directly related to the problems of external reporting. Even so, the special pleading element evident in the utility cases was present in the growing pressure for LIFO to be accepted for taxation purposes; and also it underlies the description of the LIFO movement by many commentators.

Phase II: Hiatus Before Replacement Costs and Indexation Re-Emerge

Notwithstanding what appeared to be settlement of the utility depreciation issue in the late 1930s, bar Henry Sweeney's 1936 classic there is little evidence in the American literature up to the appearance in 1961 of Edwards and Bell's *The Theory and Measurement of Business Income* of any consensus regarding the use of replacement prices for either depreciation calculations or for calculating cost of goods sold. The latter, however, provides a useful overview of the 1950s arguments about replacement cost accounting proposals. Furthermore, the attention in much of the 1940s and 1950s literature was directed almost entirely on the calculation of income, without much regard to the basis upon which assets were stated in balance sheets.

Opposition in phase II to replacement prices as a basis for asset valuation was consistent with the trends emerging in both the general journal literature and the official publications of the American accountancy bodies. Calls for some form of monetary stabilization technique which would take into account the purchasing power variations accompanying inflation were strengthening.

Along with all the academic debate, there was some practitioner action. In the United States in 1946–47 the Crane Company, Du Pont de Nemours, U.S. Steel, and Libbey-Owens-Ford Glass took the initiative. Crane appropriated profits to a reserve for replacements, the others provided for the cost of current construction with credits to a 'reserve for revaluation.' The editorial in a 1947 issue of the *Journal of Accountancy* reporting on those moves hit out at the 'unreliable' practice, noting: 'It is difficult enough to estimate the useful life of plants. . . . How much more difficult to foresee the cost of replacing them years in the future.'[71] The controversy created by this form of accounting was commented upon in the latter part of 1947 in several presentations by Earle C. King, Chief Accountant to the SEC.

Table 8.1 lists some of the major initiatives in the U.S.A. and the U.K. during Phase II.

Selected commentary on those initiatives follows.

The 1948 *Revision of Accounting Concepts and Standards Underlying Corporate Financial Statements*, issued by the AAA, noted that 'a marked,

Table 8.1 Phase II—1945–1956 Selected Individual, Professional, and Regulatory Initiatives

U.S.A.	
1947	AIA, ARB 33, 'Depreciation and High Costs' (December)
1948	AAA, *Revision of Accounting Concepts and Standards Underlying Corporate Financial Statements*
1950	AIA, *Five Monographs on Business Income*
1951	AAA, *Supplementary Statement No. 2*, 'Price Level Changes and Financial Statements'
1953	AAA, *Supplementary Statement No. 6*, 'Inventory Pricing and Changes in Price Level'
1955	AAA sponsored study by R.C. Jones, *Price Level Changes and Financial Statements: Case Studies of Four Companies*
1956	AAA sponsored study by R.C. Jones, *Effects of Price Level Changes on Business Income, Capital and Taxes*
1956	AAA sponsored study by P. Mason, *Price Level Changes and Financial Statements*

U.K.	
1949	U.K. Government, Millard Tucker (Chairman), *Interim Report of the Committee on Taxation of Trading Profits; the Final Report* was published in 1951
1949	ICAEW, Recommendation N12, 'Rising Price Levels in Relation to Accounts' (January)
1951	ICAEW and National Institute of Economic and Social Research Joint Exploratory Committee, *Some Accounting Terms and Concepts*
1952	ICWA, *The Accountancy of Changing Price Levels*
1952	ICAEW Recommendation N15, 'Accounting in Relation to the Purchasing Power of Money' (May)
1955	U.K. Government, *Royal Commission on the Taxation of Profits and Income*
1956	U.K. Government, *Report of Inquiry into the Electrical Supply Industry*

permanent change in price levels might impair the usefulness of statements reporting asset costs.' The AAA's Committee on Concepts and Standards issued its *Supplementary Statement No. 2* ('Price Level Changes and Financial Statements') in August 1951 and reinforced the sentiments expressed in the 1948 *Revision of Accounting Concepts*. It concluded that information on the effect of the 'changing value of the dollar upon financial position and operating results may be useful' and that 'the accounting effects of the changing value of the dollar should be made the subject of intensive research and experimentation.'[72] Emphasis was clearly upon the financial consequences of inflation in general, and on purchasing power changes in particular. Jones' 'nine steel companies' study had already appeared in 1949. This theme was carried over into his 1955 and 1956 monographs sponsored by the AAA. The substantive empirical work up to that time, therefore, had used the forward indexation method of adjusting for purchasing power changes. The AAA also sponsored in 1956 Mason's *Price Level Changes and Financial Statements* monograph on indexation techniques. Sponsorship of Jones and Mason in those exercises was consistent with the trend and with the AAA practising what it preached at the time.

Despite some dissent by individual members, the consensus of the 1951 Study Group on Business Income was that the 'replacement fund theory' which underlay the push for replacement cost depreciation 'does not work . . . [and was] born of confusion between financial requirements and income determination.' Wilcox on behalf of the Study Group explained: 'the [replacement] proposal is, in short, that we stop keeping track of things in terms of money and start keeping track of money in terms of things.'

Over the period immediately after World War II until the end of the 1950s the English literature was marginally more sympathetic to replacement price techniques. Primarily this was due to the efforts of those lobbying for taxation relief. This was so, even though the ICAEW exhibited the same trends for adjusting conventionally prepared accounts for purchasing power changes that the American Institute and the AAA had displayed. The pressure during the late 1940s and early '50s for some kind of taxation relief gave the replacement price cause in the United Kingdom a shot in the arm. Essential plant was physically exhausted by the war effort and fully depreciated, generally having been purchased prior to the war. Like the rate fixing episode in the U.S., the quest for taxation reform in the U.K. was a case of special pleading with, as argued in the introduction to this section, no necessary relationship to questions on the vagaries of accounting. There was no good reason, then, why the special (taxation) case should have been taken into the context of external financing and financial reporting.[73]

The U.K. 'Committee on Taxation of Trading Profits' (Millard Tucker Chairman) had been set up in 1949 to enquire into the computation of trading profits for taxation purposes. The inquiry attracted strong lobbying for replacement prices to be used as the basis of taxation depreciation charges and inventory costs. An Interim Report which appeared in 1949 did not support that push. Contiguously, the ICAEW's N12 (*Rising Price Levels in Relation to Accounts*), dismissed the replacement price arguments and recommended profit appropriations to meet any shortfall between depreciation charges and ultimate replacement costs. That approach was consistent with both the special statement issued by the American Institute in 1947 and with ARB33. Millard Tucker's Committee did nothing to disturb the status quo. It recommended that tax accounting methods be left as they were, but that a system of 'initial allowances' as lump sum deductions of plant costs in the year of purchase be introduced to provide some relief. N12 came under attack in 1952 for its 'orthodoxy' in the Association of Certified and Corporate Accountants' *Accounting for Inflation*. The Association's Taxation and Research Committee responsible for the publication carried on the lobby for taxation relief with the familiar replacement cost arguments. Although it identified post-war inflation as the cause of the financial strain British industry was experiencing in meeting both taxation payments and capital replacement, curiously, the possibility that attention be given to maintaining purchasing power was swept aside.

The notion that plant *had* to be renewed also ran through Lacey's 1952 *Profit Measurement and Price Changes*, as it had two years earlier in *The Accountancy of Changing Prices* by the Research and Technical Committee of the ICWA. Generally, the depreciation backlog issue was avoided by arguments that the continuous reinvestment of depreciation charges based on replacement prices would produce an accumulated fund sufficient to finance replacement. We noted that two decades later Chambers (1976a, 1977 and 1980b) suggested this claim was an old accounting and finance chestnut—as depreciation *charges* do not necessarily provide cash that can be reinvested in anything. Furthermore, the connection between the renewal or replacement of assets and depreciation charges had already been discredited in numerous initiatives. Despite the taxation lobby, the ICAEW reinforced the 'appropriations' recommendation previously set out in N12 by restating it in N15. The new statement, *Accounting in Relation to the Purchasing Power of Money*, was directed more at the effect the changing purchasing power of money could have on 'the affairs of the business.'

On the political front, replacement cost adjustments for taxation purposes were rejected in the U.K. 1951 *Final Report of the Committee on the Taxation of Profits*, though not without criticism. This continued after the 1955 Royal Commission reported. Walker is representative, complaining that the Commission was guilty of 'ambiguity and incompleteness [in] its treatment of the problems of inflation and replacement cost accounting.'[74] Chairman of the LSE, Sir John Braithwaite, likewise spoke out in favour of replacement price adjustments. Replacement costs were advocated also in the 1956 *Report of the Committee of Inquiry into the Electrical Supply Industry*, but notably it referred to what were non-adaptive enterprises and thus it was another instance of special pleading.

Phase III—1960s and Beyond

A few academics proposed integrating both individual and general price changes into the accounts. Edwards and Bell's in his 1961 classic and Chambers' 1961 *General Theory* paper did so. By 1963 Chambers had proposed a general notation for price and price level accounting.

Zeff's 1962 state-of-the-art paper[75] refers to the general confusion in the literature up to the early 1960s over the nature of prices and price level changes and how to account for them. And, that confusion continued throughout the 1960s and 1970s as distinctions drawn in the literature between monetary and physical capital were ambiguous. The tendency was to treat capital as an amorphous thing, monetary in nature if that suited the argument, and as a physical quantum if that better fitted the line of reasoning.

Participation in the 1960s and early 1970s debates by the U.K. and U.S. accountancy bodies was almost entirely directed at methods of supplementing conventionally prepared accounts to incorporate adjustments for changes in the general level of prices, only. In retrospect, such a preoccupation was unusual. Chambers' submissions to the relevant U.S. and U.K. inquiries during that period (see Table 7.5) noted among other things this partial feature; as did his 1976a ICRA *A Critique of Sandilands Report* and the 1980 *Price Variation and Inflation Accounting* monograph.

Edwards and Bell's 1961 *The Theory and Measurement of Business Income* and in the same year Chambers' *Towards a General Theory of Accounting* should have removed the cause for further dispute about the differential behaviour of prices and the related aggregate price levels during inflationary conditions. The need to account for changes in both specific prices and the general level of prices was prompted again by Chambers in *Accounting, Evaluation and Economic Behavior*. Its argument for reporting of assets at their current cash equivalents (usually their selling prices) caused many to reassess the pervading concern up to that time for the use of replacement prices. Similar arguments appeared in Sterling's 1970 *The Theory of the Measurement of Enterprise Income*.

Meanwhile, the Phase 1 and II arguments for taking account of differential price variations, namely replacement prices re-appeared. It appeared in Gynther's 1962 and 1966 publications and in the AAA's 1966 *A Statement of Basic Accounting Theory*. The monograph was written by a committee of the AAA but it did not purport to be an expression of the AAA's collective view.

The U.S.A. accountancy bodies' consideration of indexing accounts data to reflect changes in the general level of prices received further impetus in 1963 from the AICPA's *Reporting the Financial Effects of Price Level Changes* (ARS6). In a more detailed manner than the comparable phase II publications, it illustrated and encouraged use of some of the stabilization techniques that the Henry Sweeney had presented thirty-five years earlier in his *Accounting Review* articles; those techniques were summarized and extended in his 1936 *Stabilized Accounting*. Interestingly it was reissued in 1964 with new Forewords by Zeff and Paton. Sweeney also provided a new introductory article, 'Forty Years After: Or Stabilized Accounting Revisited.' Stabilization was clearly still deemed relevant.

Importantly for future developments, contrary to Sweeney's preferred approach, ARS6 stated explicitly that the use of replacement (specific) prices and the indexation techniques were directed at unrelated problems. It thereby was perpetuating the illusion that specific price changes could be ignored in attempts to account for the effects of inflation, the very point which the literature at the time was strongly disputing.[76]

Chambers 1967 'A Study of a Price Level Study' argued that ARS6 was an enigma in many ways. Its juxtaposition with the academic and some of the professional literature on differential price variation effects during inflation might be explained by the fact that the study had been commissioned in the latter part of phase II.[77] Other matters are not so easily explained. ARS6 ignored Sweeney's (and many of the 1920s German *Betriebswirtschaft* theorists,' like Fritz Schmidt's) preference for a replacement or reproductive cost-based form of stabilized accounting. Edwards and Bell's classic, which discussed entry and exit price changes as well as general price level changes, had also not long been in print.

The notation Chambers developed in his 1961 *Towards a General Theory* paper was used in ARS6 to help explain the notion of a 'gain or loss of purchasing power on monetary items.' This is not surprising, given Chambers time at Berkeley and the AICPA Research Division in the late 1950s and early 1960s with Moonitz. Yet ARS6 failed to consider the effect on the purchasing power of a firm if specific prices changed other than in line with the general level. Chambers' notation was not limited in that way in its 1961 context and in his subsequent revisions to that notation.

The influence of ARS6 on subsequent events is a matter for conjecture. As Table 8.2 reveals, it is significant, though, that during the following twelve years accountancy authorities in the U.S., U.K., Canada, Australia, and New Zealand issued publications on the method that ARS6 had illustrated. ARS6 appears not only to have been a catalyst for those actions by the national accountancy bodies, but also the general template for the various exposure drafts, discussion papers, and provisional statements that ensued.

Chambers noted in several places that the 1960s and '70s exhibited regression in the debate about accounting for inflation. Partial solutions continued with an emphasis now on specific (replacement) prices. Augmenting discussion in chapters 4 and 6 about the effects of the inflation spike in 1973 we note that Australia's second exposure draft, *A Method of Current Value Accounting*, was followed in September 1975 by the publication of the Sandilands Report in the U.K., and the supplementary replacement cost disclosure proposals in ARS190 in the U.S. in March 1976. In August 1976 the CICA Research Committee also produced a discussion paper on *Current Value Accounting* and was still pursuing its enquiries in that direction.

The Australian current value draft appeared with approval from some sections of industry, particularly manufacturing. It came in the wake of the mid-1970s Federal government-sponsored Mathews inquiry, *Inflation and Taxation* with its proposed replacement price-based depreciation and stock adjustments, reminiscent of ideas in the early 1950s. Table 7.5 shows that Chambers had provided a submission and supplementary memorandum to the Mathews inquiry.[78] He noted therein several objections to taxes being based on replacement prices, concluding that much of his reasoning was consistent with the push to account for the differential price movements which were a feature of inflation.

Based on the 1975 CCA provisional ED, the issuing by AARF's Current Cost Accounting Committee of a draft provisional standard on CCA (DPS1.1) in October 1976 was an unusual step. It contained no indexation

Table 8.2 Phase III—1961–1980 Selected Individual, Professional, and Regulatory Initiatives

U.S.A, *Australia, New Zealand.*

1961	Edwards and Bell, *The Theory and Measurement of Business Income*
1962	Chambers, *Towards a General Theory of Accounting*
1963	AICPA, ARS 6, *Reporting the Financial Effects of Price Level Changes*
1966	Chambers, *Accounting, Evaluation and Economic Behavior*
1966	AAA *A Statement of Basic Accounting Theory*
1969	APB, Statement No 3, (APB3), 'Financial Statements Restated for General Price Level Changes' (June).
1974	FASB, Exposure Draft, 'Financial Reporting in Units of General Purchasing Power'
1974	AARF, Australian Accounting Standards Committee, Preliminary Exposure Draft, 'A Method of Accounting for the Purchasing Power of Money' (December)
1979	Australian Government-sponsored, *Report of the Committee of Inquiry into Inflation and Taxation* (Russell Mathews as Chairman), *Inflation and Taxation* (May)
1975	AARF, Australian Accounting Standards Committee, Preliminary Exposure Draft, 'A Method of 'Current Value Accounting'' (June)
1979	CICA, *Discussion Paper: Current Value Accounting* (August)
1975	Chambers, Private Exposure Draft, 'Accounting For Inflation' (September)
1975	SEC, Accounting Series Release No. 190, 'Notice of Adoption of Amendments to Regulation S-X Requiring Disclosure of Certain Replacement Cost Data' (23 March)
1976	AARF, Australian Accounting Standards Committee, Statement of Provisional Accounting Standard, 'Current Cost Accounting,' DPS 1.1 (October)
1976	NZ Government (Richardson Chairman), *Report of the Committee of Inquiry into Inflation Accounting* (September)
1976	AARF, Current Cost Accounting Committee, Exposure Draft, 'The Recognition of Gains and Losses on Holding Monetary Items in the Context of Current Cost Accounting' (July)
1980	FASB, Financial Accounting Standards 33, 'Financial Reporting and Changing Prices' (September)
	AARF Current Cost Accounting Committee, Revised Exposure Draft, 'The Recognition of Gains and Losses on Holding Monetary Items in the Context of Current Cost Accounting' (August)
	Chambers, *Price Variation and Inflation Accounting*

(Continued)

Table 8.2 (Continued)

U.K.	
1968	ICAEW, Research Committee, *Accounting for Stewardship in a Period of Inflation*
1973	Accounting Standards Steering Committee, Exposure Draft 8, 'Accounting for Changes in the Purchasing Power of Money' (January)
1974	Accounting Standards Committee, Provisional Statement of Accounting Standards No. 7 (PSSAP7), 'Accounting for Changes in the Purchasing Power of Money' (May)
1974–5	Inflation Accounting Committee (F.E.P. Sandilands Chairman), *Inflation Accounting: Report of the Inflation Accounting Committee* (September, 1975)
1975	CCAB, *Initial Reactions to the Report of the Inflation Accounting Committee* (November)
1976	ICAEW, Accounting Standards Committee (Morpeth Chairman), Exposure Draft 18, 'Current Cost Accounting,' (November)
1980	ICAEW, Accounting Standards Committee SSAP16, 'Current Cost Accounting' (March)

mechanism, and it was against the tenor of current discussion in the U.K. and elsewhere in the English-speaking countries.

The 'new' 1975 CCA proposals, had essentially required that *only* movements in *specific* (mostly replacement) prices be accounted for. Although both Australia's current value draft (and subsequent provisional standard) and Sandilands' current cost prescription contained some exceptions, each used the old continuity-necessary asset replacement (or renewal) dicta, the 'matching/costs attaching' arguments familiar in the LIFO debate appeared again in support of the cost-of-goods-sold adjustments, and the old conundrum whether to account for purchasing power gains and losses on monetary items was aired once again in later professional proposals. The issues raised, the questions and suggested 'alternative' answers were the same. As in phase II *no conclusion* was forthcoming. As Sterling so presciently observed, accounting problems had been recycled, not resolved.[79]

The Richardson Committee in New Zealand had finalized its report in mid-1976, with strong hints appearing in the press that some kind of purchasing power adjustment (either the 'gearing' or 'working capital' adjustment) was likely to be proposed, as was likely in the U.K. where ED18 was being forged. The 1976–77 deliberations of the Morpeth Committee resulted in the move to combine Current Purchasing Power Accounting and Sandilands' CCA in the manner suggested in ED18. Table 7.5 reveals that, as well as providing submissions to Sandilands, Richardson and the Australian CPP, CCA preliminary EDs and related inquiries, Chambers had provided a submission to Morpeth, which was to be read in conjunction with his 1976 ICRA monograph. His criticisms are evident in the section headers: 'ED18 does not represent an inflation accounting system,' 'Financial position is not defined,' 'Value to the business" is ambiguous and misleading,' 'CCA balance sheets [and CCA Profits] are fallacious and misleading,' 'The CCA provision for "backlog depreciation" is ineffectual.' 'The piecemeal proposals of ED18 are unnecessarily complex and inconsistent with the financial features of the firm as a whole.'[80]

He suggested that ED18 was little more than an attempt to preserve the purchasing power maintenance concept supposed to underlie CPP accounting. Instead, the ED18 proposal produced a form of CCA/CPP prescription with partial adjustments (namely the 'gearing'—the proportion of an entity's loan to capital—and 'working capital' type adjustments). Chambers critically observed in the concluding section of his Morpeth submission: 'The proposal for showing the effect of the change in the value of money is technically incorrect and in a practical sense unjust.'

Further, ED18 contained some of the features of the methods outlined in the 1960s in Edwards and Bell, the AAA's *A Statement of Basic Accounting Theory* and the AICPA's ARS3. It also was closer to Sweeney's preferred stabilization method than the advocates of CPP accounting seem to have realized. These purchasing power adjustments, in principle, sought to recognize a loss in purchasing power in respect of the opening capital (value) of the business. Sydney Schoolers Chambers and Clarke were critical that the notion of value was not defined and then consistently used. If it were to be defined as general purchasing power, then the adjustments had technical propriety. However, Sandilands, the 1975 *Initial Reactions* of the CCAB and hence the compromised CCA/CPP type adjustment in ED18 as well as in the Hyde-type gearing adjustment, did not use value in that sense. Their adjustments technically could not achieve what they set out to do.[81]

Similarly, the SEC's supplementary replacement cost disclosure proposals in ASR190 were subjected to substantial criticism in the U.S. because they failed to account for general price level changes. Three and a half years later the SEC's Accounting Series Release No. 271, 'Deletion of Requirement to Disclose Replacement Cost Information' meant it had deferred to the FASB which, a month earlier, had released FAS33, 'Financial Reporting and Changing Prices.' Accounting for changing prices remained unresolved.

Summing Up

Chambers often lamented to the present authors that he was frustrated that more of his ideas had not been accepted by regulators or accounting standards setters. Yet, the Prologue (xxviii) notes that while disappointed, he did have some successes. At a general level his decision usefulness ideas were adopted by the profession; as had been, in principle, his inflation accounting notation and ideas on the conceptual framework hierarchy.[82] There was also some limited movement away from historic costs to a form of market price measures for certain assets, like financial instruments and durable assets.

He continued to attack accounting's role in not forewarning early enough corporate dilemmas, especially asset valuation anomalies in settings of unexpected company failures and in takeover sagas involving asset-stripping. Thus, although accounting for inflation was in focus at various times it was a complete overhaul of corporate accounting that he had in his sights. But given the intensity of the 1970s inflation debates, he returned to that inflation focus. A 1976 book *Accounting for Inflation* (to pick up on the fact that during inflationary periods corporates experienced some price movements in their asset and liability portfolios both up and down) and four years later, *Price Variation and Inflation Accounting* (to illustrate where the dominant price movement was upwards, CoCoA captured those changes too). The latter followed his privately issued Exposure Draft of *Accounting for Inflation* and the 1978 ASRC Report, *Company Accounting Standards*.

The 1970s had been an exceedingly busy and frustrating period for Chambers, as is captured in Tables 7.3 and 7.5. Around the time of the publication of the ASRC Report he wrote to Stamp noting this, but also a determination to continue to fight for change:

I have found the whole business [in recent times] like walking a tight-rope. I have known (from observation of past experiences of the profession over its history) that this or that is bound to fail. But no one learns from history, I'm told. I have found it necessary to bite my tongue; to encourage people to try, even when I "knew" they would fail; to keep down my propensity for frontal attack in many cases and to seek my own ways around obstruction. All of that is very demanding on one's patience, ingenuity, tolerance, and so on; so demanding that there is often little energy (nervous or any other kind) for skirmishing with others, for compassion with the struggles of others, and for more than the occasional outburst of irritation. It has been thus especially over the last couple of years. Concurrently with a rather gruelling year as [National] President of the Society, I ran the enquiry I mentioned earlier on accounting standards.[83]

Chambers' pursuit and exposure of what was meant by the prescribed publicity obligations, especially the true and fair view override, the 1966 publication of *Accounting, Evaluation and Economic Behavior*, the international distribution of his inflation accounting exposure draft a decade later, his involvement in the ASRC and contributions to the price and price level debates worldwide in the 1970s show that there was a growing national and international recognition that Chambers and the Sydney School provided ideas to be considered by regulators, especially that accounting is critical for corporate decision making.

Chambers' and his Sydney School had an opportunity to influence regulation. Chambers had chaired the ASRC and he had been appointed in 1982 to the Australian Accounting Standards Board, the federal government-initiated agency given the brief of developing a conceptual framework of accounting—in the absence of a similar project produced by the accounting profession. Exasperated with the overly politicized process of the Board's deliberations, he resigned eight months later.

Also in 1982, another notable Sydney Schooler, Bob Walker (then holding a chair in Accounting at the University of New South Wales), was appointed a member of the Accounting Standards Review Board (ASRB). Walker soon drafted a 'Criteria for the Evaluation of Accounting Standards' (published in 1985 as ASRB Release 100) setting out a series of 'preliminary assumptions' about the purpose (function) of financial reporting, and the concepts of reporting entity, asset, liability, residual equity, contributions, distributions, revenues, and expenses. The ASRB also produced a document concerning principles of accounting measurement. Consistent with the ideas of the Sydney School, it argued that 'in principle' accounting was not concerned with valuing a business but the assets of a business, so that values should be assigned to the non-current assets that were individually saleable. In 1983, the National Companies and Securities Commission had undertaken a review of the disclosure requirements in the then Companies Act and Codes. Contiguously, an NCSC Green Paper (also largely drafted by Walker), *Financial Reporting Requirements of the Companies Act and Codes*, reflected many of Chambers' and the Sydney School's ideas.

In contrast to the ASRC's immediate, radical reforms the Green Paper proposed the provision of supplementary information. It proposed also an incremental approach, allowing for several options. Notably, the document not only drew on the history of disclosure rules in British and Australian legislation, but also it principally advanced the decision usefulness theme so prominent in Chambers' works.[84] That stands in stark contrast with contributions from bodies like the Eggleston Committee of 1967–70 which had rejected proposals for modest disclosure reforms on the basis that its brief was to consider measures that would 'protect' shareholders rather than 'inform' them.

Chambers has been criticized for being naive in having pushed for too holistic a change, based on the rules of mathematics, a few economic propositions, and plain logic, when incremental changes with fewer constraints may have been more politically acceptable. Evidence is presented contesting the naivety claims. Many factors influenced his reforms, including his religious belief in a desire for a level playing field, and that his often direct, personal approach was much more nuanced, heavily evidence-based, than generally acknowledged.

His push for a more serviceable accounting, some form of market price-based accounting, seems irreversible. Were this to occur, Chambers would rightly be viewed as a major Anglo-American contender for the father of such a change, along with Paton, Canning, Sweeney, MacNeal, Edwards and Bell, Sterling, and Baxter.

Notes

1. Chapter epigraph:
   Chambers letter to Briloff, P202, #7680, 12/10/1982.
   Chambers letter to Manchester Business School academic Edmond Grace on 'true and fair view,' P202, #6731, 9/12/1983. The Archive reveals that Chambers corresponded with Grace on various accounting issues for more than two decades.
2. Tweedie and Whittington (1984)—see also Persson and Napier (2014).
3. Zeff (1971, 1972).
4. Chambers (1952b).
5. Chambers (1955c).
6. Chambers (1958).
7. Chambers (1963b).
8. Chambers (1963c).
9. Chambers' detailed handwritten notes, P202, #1119, 12/12/1963 for interview on 13/12/1963.
10. The biography reveals, especially when considering the impact of European ideas on inflation accounting ideas (endnotes #60, chapter 6 and page 121), and elsewhere more generally (Clarke *et al.*, 2012), how Chambers used *Abacus* as an outlet for reproducing ideas that had international relevance. It appears to have been part of his learning process.
11. Chambers (1965a, 16).
12. Chambers (1964d).
13. Chambers (1967).
14. Walker and Oliver (2005) and Oliver and Walker (2006) provide examples in the context of reporting for software. They conclude that the looseness endures as the standards permit over a million ways to account for software.

15. N.S.W. Companies Office Registrar, Frank Ryan to Chambers, P202, #8665, 22/02/1966.
16. Chambers 15 October 1971 submission to the Eggleston Committee, 'Some Aspects of an Efficient Securities Market,' USAP 202, unnumbered folder containing various submissions. A listing of his submissions appears as Table 7.5.
17. Chambers (1968a).
18. Sri Ramanathan to George Venturi, Legal Adviser to the N.S.W. Attorney-General's Office, P202, #11196, 21/11/1977.
19. P202, #s 9504, 9505, 27/03/1979. For several decades after the phrase true and fair view first appeared in Australia in the 1961 Uniform Companies Act it was problematic whether it was an override criterion relative to professionally prescribed accounting rules. Similar uncertainty existed in the UK and elsewhere. Clarke and Dean (2014, chapter 2) suggest this uncertainty endures, but argue the phrase is, and should be, an override.
20. P202, #9582, 07/02/1985.
21. Chambers (1989b).
22. Chambers sent several individuals two papers (see P202, #9650, an undated typed and handwritten list of names and addresses of local and international persons). Responses are recorded in P202, #9657, 08/02/1990; but most responded like Tony Minchin, Assistant to the Auditor General, P202, #9684, 09/12/1991.
23. Submissions to the early 1990s Rothwells and Tricontinental Royal Commission inquiries (respectively: P202, #9637 and #9638, 23/01/1991), and two decades earlier following the 1967–70 mining boom, to Senator Rae, Chair of the *Rae Committee of Inquiry into Australian Securities Markets*, P202, #4254, 24/08/1974. A listing of his submissions appears as Table 7.5.
24. Chambers to Geoffrey Luck, Principal, Spencer and Stuart Consultants, P202, #10827, 20/09/1979.
25. Morgan and Thomas (1962).
26. P202, #10513, 06/05/1963.
27. Chambers to Professor Illetschko, P202, #2062, 14/03/1966.
28. Chambers to Professor Swoboda, P202, #1767, 21/03/1966.
29. Chambers' draft 1966 travel itinerary is outlined in P202, #1875; undated, it was most likely composed in early 1966.
30. These are discussed in two letters—P202, #1160, 10/04/1963; P202, #1819, 24/11/1965. By the mid-1970s Chambers had collected and catalogued thousands of annual reports from Australian, U.S.A., U.K. and European listed companies.
31. Chambers to the SEC Chairman, Manuel F. Cohen, P202, #1820, 24/11/1965 and Cohen's response, P202, #1821, 03/12/1965. Chambers corresponded with SEC Commissioner H.M. Williams in 1977, sending him copies of several of his books and articles—P202 #9500, 18/08/1977.
32. Chambers to Barr, P202, #8781, 17/06/1969.
33. Chambers to the SEC's Chief Accountant Sandy Burton, P202, #12035x, 23/07/1976; and letter from SEC Chief Accountant A. Clarence Sampson to Chambers, P202, #9500, 29/08/1977, asking Chambers to send copies of the material he supplied to the SEC Chairman Williams (endnote #31, chapter 8).
34. During the 1960s and 1970s Chambers and Ryan corresponded often, P202, #s5292, 5293, 5476, 5479, 5480, 8264, 8665.
35. Chambers' and Masel's 1980s correspondence, P202, #s6118–6120, #10698, and #11981 29/03/1992.
36. Chambers to Masel, P202, #6118, 30/06/1980.
37. Surviving Archive correspondence between Chambers and contemporary U.S. commercial academic lawyer Homer Kripke are #s9172–80. They cover the 1972–73 period.

38. Chambers to Kripke, P202, #9172, 04/08/1972; and a lengthy handwritten response by Kripke, P202, #9173, 21/08/1972.
39. Kripke to Chambers, P202, #9175, 20/09/1972 responding to Chambers, P202, #9174, 05/09/1972. In his December 1971 submission to the AICPA's Accounting Objectives Study group (see Table 7.5 for details; and also see P202, #9038, 14/12/1991) Chambers had expressed those concerns clearly: 'Suggestions that published corporate reports should include [various projections] . . . I regard with alarm.' He continues noting Edward Angly's 1931 book *Oh Yeah?* with its collection of numerous U.S. instances of such faulty corporate projections—and concluding that: 'There could be no form of protection against the publication of forecasts or projections of dubious value; for the forecaster could always claim their projections were made in good faith.'
40. A letter from Kripke to Chambers,P202, #9178, 20/12/1972 and Chambers' equally detailed response, P202, #9179, 11/10/1973. Recall also the discussion in chapter 4 on reporting infrastructure costs.
41. Chambers (1973a, 1973b) documents these anomalies.
42. The following subsection draws on material first published by Clarke and Dean (2007, 106–27); and reproduced in Clarke *et al.* (2012, especially 51–62).
43. Moss (1976) and Metcalf (1977).
44. ASRC (1978, no page number; letter accompanying submission to the Honorable the Attorney-General, dated 19 May, 1978.).
45. Articles on these matters included Birkett and Walker (1974), Birkett and Walker (1971), and several of Chambers' articles already discussed.
46. Owen (2003) discusses HIH's failure; while Clarke, Dean, and Oliver (1997, chapter 13) discusses the rise and fall of the Bond Corporation.
47. Endnote #43, chapter 8 for details.
48. Chambers' letter to Ryan on 29 July, P202, #11181, 29/07/1977. He observes: 'Perhaps you know of some suggestions of mine on possible ways of tightening the relevant provisions of the Act—given in the last chapter of *Securities and Obscurities*. Perhaps you have some opinions on them. . . . I am convinced—from the history of the matter in the U.K., the U.S.A. and Australia, over the last 30 or more years—that the things that bedevil investors and creditors (and the regulatory bodies) will not be reduced or eliminated without a tightening of the accounts provisions of the statute.'
49. Chambers' letter to Frank Walker, P202, #11182,16/08/1977
50. Letter from Philip Pearce to Chambers, in correspondence about the ASRC in P202, #11183, 18/08/1977.
51. As we have shown this 'groupthink' notion was anathema to Chambers.
52. The proceedings of the 1967 Berkeley Symposium were published in Vance (1967).
53. ASA and ICAA Presidents' jointly signed letter to Frank Walker, P202, #9491, 25/01/1980. This letter forms part of related 1979–81correspondence between Chambers, the Australian professional bodies and Walker. Interestingly, while declining to comment on many aspects they did raise the BHP blast furnace example to reject the Report's General Standard (see discussion on reporting infrastructure costs) above.
54. ASA General Council (1966).
55. Chambers (2000b, 324).
56. Pratten (1991).
57. Chambers to Zeff, P202, #6982, 16/06/1986.
58. Chambers to Briloff, P202, #7680, 12/10/1982.
59. This subsection draws extensively on the ideas first published in Clarke's 'CCA—Progress or Regress?' (1977); and the related section of his 1982 PhD

thesis, *The Tangled Web*. . . . Tweedie and Whittington (1984) also provide a comprehensive account of the issues and the periods covered here.

60. Chambers (1986d, Volume IV, *Price Variation Accounting*) provides a 333-page collection of his articles and some other papers on the issue. Also, Table 7.5 provides a listing of his professional and regulatory submissions to related professional and regulatory inquiries.

61. Chambers (1965d, 242).

62. Chambers (1976a) and Clarke (1982).

63. Those, as well as commissioned translations by other 'Sydney Schoolers,' are available in the Chambers Archive. The translated material is held in University of Sydney Burren Street library and some is also available in digitized form at P202, #s10953–60. One feature of the Anglo-American literature is the introduction of the 'gearing' adjustment (the gain on purchasing power associated with the proportion of loan to equity capital) to augment the basic replacement (current) cost accounting proposals. This idea had appeared in the writings of Fritz Schmidt in the early 1920s. It is discussed further below—see endnote #81, chapter 8.

64. For details see endnote #60, chapter 6. It was the custom for such pre-publication of thesis chapters in those times.

65. See, for example, Clarke and Dean (1990) and Küpper and Mattessich (2005).

66. Clarke (1976). This work is extended in Clarke (1982). The accounting expert may wish to by-pass this subsection and move to the 'Summing Up.' Non-accountants who wish to examine numerical examples to better understand the technical material should review the various Tables and related text in Clarke (1982) detailing many price-level accounting mechanisms, or the relevant discussion in Tweedie and Whittington (1984).

67. Boer (1966).

68. Vancil and Weil (1976) and Chambers (1977c). Chambers (1977d) repeated the arguments in his submission to ED18 (see endnote #80, chapter 8). This had been discussed also in his ICRA review of the Sandilands Report (Chambers, 1976a).

69. Clarke (1982). In the 1980s in the UK, Australia and elsewhere those ideas would resurface quite properly in public sector infrastructure accounting debates—for example, the UK Byatt Report (1986).

70. Nickerson (1937) and Arthur (1938).

71. The Editorial in the January 1947 issue of *Journal of Accountancy*. The issue was equally problematic in the 1970s, and in the second decade of the present century.

72. The AAA's Committee on Concepts and Standards issued its *Supplementary Statement No. 2* ('Price Level Changes and Financial Statements') in August 1951, 24.

73. Wiles (1951) emphasized forcibly that 'bad effects of taxation, to repeat, are logically separable from the finer points of accountancy,' even though on balance he could be taken to have had more sympathy for the use of replacement prices in calculations for taxation purposes.

74. Walker (1955)

75. Zeff (1962).

76. Whittington emailed the authors (28 July 2017) that, notwithstanding its rejection of replacement cost stabilization, Sweeney wrote a very supportive review of ARS6. Whittington suggested a possible reason for this: 'Sweeney (like Chambers) drew a very clear distinction between the measurement process (historic cost or a current value) and the measurement unit issue (inflation).' Zeff (14 November 2017) also emailed the authors recalling he had introduced Chambers to Sweeney in 1962. Zeff invited Chambers to accompany him to

downtown Manhattan where they met Sweeney in his office. Later Chambers corresponded with Sweeney on several occasions, once to thank him for sending an inscribed copy of the 1964 reissue of *Stabilized Accounting*. ((P202, #1350, 02/02/1965). He noted: 'Your introductory note fills in splendidly some gaps in our understanding of the origins and fortunes of the book; to one who is interested in the development of ideas it gives the setting as only you would know it, and as otherwise we could not understand it now.' For those interested in more details about the 1970s CCA and CCA/CPP professional deliberations and related debates in the literature Tweedie and Whittington (1984) and Clarke (1982) provide lengthy accounts.

77. Chambers (1967b).
78. Chambers eleven-page submission to the Mathews Committee of Inquiry, P202, #9330, 14/03/1975 and supplementary memorandum, P202, #9332, 03/04/1975.
79. Sterling (1975).
80. Chambers' submission to ED18, 'Current cost accounting,' P202, #9458, 26/05/1977.
81. Clarke (1982/2006, chapter 13) examined 'adding' to the basic current cost measurement process a purchasing power adjustment, either the 'gearing' or 'working capital' adjustment. He concluded (344): 'In terms of what they were intended to achieve [namely that no profit could arise until the 'operating capacity' of an entity had been maintained], the changes in the adjustments were cosmetic.'
82. These matters are discussed in Chambers (1978) and Staunton (2007).
83. Chambers to Stamp, P202, #5395, 25/08/1978.
84. We thank Bob Walker for providing information by email about some of the NCSC's activities during the early 1980s.

9   Unfinished Business

There have always been two strands at least to my work. One is analytical, a kind of 'reculer pour mieux salter,' not merely critical for the sake of criticism. The other is constructive and expository—and it arises from the former . . . I have . . . given more time to developing different angles or facets of a position first stated than to straight out response. Nowhere has indifference and disregard of what I have said and done been more apparent than over the period of 15 years I have served on the councils of a professional body. I have a fat wad of submissions, suggestions, memoranda etc made internally to that body, which have provoked little more than polite acknowledgement, and often not even that. I have seen years of time wasted on matters for which I had already provided 'solutions' or 'proposals'—and the passage of time has only proved . . . that I was right. One can grieve over the waste; but grief is not productive. The only thing is to strike out again, and again, and again.

—Chambers' letter to Stamp, 1978

The prospect of laying firmer foundations for accounting than mere convention was exciting, and I guess both of us faced it with unabashed hope. The uninteresting style and flimsy basis of much exposition, the widespread allegiance to existent doctrine, the antipathy of the world of practice to innovation, the well-intentioned but fumbling steps of the professional bodies to advance their standing and the expertise of the members—these and like things could be faced with little else than hope . . . Perhaps after 30 years we have left a few marks on the state of our art; improved a little the relationships between town and gown; had some influence, for good or ill, on hundreds of students. But looking around the literature now, I've some sense of having seen its like before. There are many new words and phrases, but there are identifiable instances of all the fallacies, solecisms and non-sequiturs of years ago. However, if as Keynes remarked, few are able or willing to embrace a new idea beyond the age of thirty, progress must be slow. There is still a lot of work ahead for the hopeful.

—Chambers' letter to Mathews, 1983[1]

Chambers' frustration is evident in both epigraphs. Inertia, conservatism by practitioners, and antipathy to innovation, as well resistance based on privacy grounds by business to market price accounting proposals by

Chambers and other contemporary reformers has mitigated any effective change. The many other cited letter extracts, as well as comments in uncited letters in the Chambers Archive during the mid-to-late 1970s and beyond, confirm this and justify his feelings of frustration and disappointment. Consider a letter to Stamp where, as well as noting the lack of official responses regarding his 1976 AAA Distinguished Lecturer tour and the lack of any visible acceptances of the arguments by professional bodies in his numerous submissions, he laments:

> I submitted a response to EDI8; but I'm almost sure, from the outset, that it does not a bit of good. The countless hours I've put into submissions to Australian, New Zealand, Canadian, U.K. and U.S. committees are a write-off, so far; and I see no prospect of change.[2]

Fast forward over fifteen years. A letter to Maurice Moonitz in February 1993 and two earlier letters to Bob Sterling are particularly revealing—especially the comment to Sterling about his 'shabby treatment' in retirement.[3] In those letters he also expresses concerns about the undergraduate, postgraduate, and PhD programs that he and the Sydney School had built up being unwound; and he laments that the Sydney School 'has become just another of the indistinguishable and undistinguished schools that comprise the accounting landscape'; that his journal may change its focus and that there is no longer a desire, probably due to a lack of a sufficient mass of like-minded academics at Sydney, to continue the reform agenda.

But those frustrations failed to dampen his desire to press ahead with ways of promoting his reforms. He continued to publish in academic and professional outlets, make submissions to professional enquiries (Table 7.5), submit letters to the press, and undertake interviews (Table 7.3). However, for the five decades and more he lived on the fringe academically he was not completely alone. There were other fringe dwellers. He was buoyed by many letters of support for his ideas, some of which were discussed earlier. Some came from his Sydney School members, from Australasian colleagues like Allan Barton, Russell Mathews, Lou Goldberg, Ronald Ma, Wal Nichols, Roy Sidebotham, while others were from local practitioners, lawyers, regulators, other professionals, mathematicians, engineers.

He was further buoyed to see similar ideas and support generally being proffered by overseas academics. Support was to be found during the 1960s—80s, in the work of North American academics and practitioners such as William Paton, Bill Vatter, Robert Dixon, Leonard Spacek, Paul Garner, Ernest Weinwurm, Maurice Moonitz, Norton Bedford, George Staubus, Thomas Burns, Arthur Thomas, Steve Zeff, and Abe Briloff. In the 1990s and beyond academics, including Paul Rosenfield, John Boersema, James McKeown, Haim Falk, and Gary Previts, were supportive. In the U.K. supporters included Eddie Stamp, Ron Brooker (who joined the Sydney School in 1963), Bob Parker, Tom Lee, Geoffrey Whittington, and Michael Bromwich. Also mitigating his frustrations was the release of the 1977 Annual report of NZ Challenge Corporation. This was the first listed company to adopt and implement CoCoA. Others soon followed as a consequence of their involvement in the inflation accounting research project, known as the Waikato Project.[4] The project sought to determine the feasibility and costs of implementing the various proposals. As Chambers had often suggested, operationalizing CoCoA was shown to be feasible, at minimal extra cost. The Chambers Archive has copies of all these reports, so Chambers was well aware of them.

Heartening also was the official imprimatur of his system in the 1988 Scottish Institute's Report, *Making Corporate Reports Valuable*, and to a lesser extent information in letters provided by colleagues such as one from his former masters' student and who was then Professor of Accounting and Finance at Glasgow University, Sid Gray, showing that Norway's Bergesen d.y. Group had included in its 1989 Annual Report a supplementary income statement and balance sheet, a form of value-added statement based on market prices.[5] In Australia three years later an official federal government publication, *Company Law and Economic Reform Program, No. 1*, endorsed the need for a form of market price accounting.

But those, and the other positives previously recounted, did not satisfy him and, as he observes in a June 1984 letter to former colleague Peter Standish, there is always more to be done: 'To advance, to err, to change direction, to stumble are features of . . . making progress, in all fields. The journey may be exasperating . . . may be fun; but . . . finished it will never be.'[6] Undeniably Chambers was still seeking to influence the development of accounting ideas when fate struck in early September 1999.

Chambers, Sterling, Paton, Sweeney, MacNeal, Spacek, Briloff, and Baxter were among those who have railed against traditional accounting for nearly three-quarters of a century. Yet, as this biography goes to press the majority of conventional accounting endures, warts and all. This is evident in the accounting criticisms in the aftermath of the GFC. Thus, effective reform remains a major 'unfinished business.'

The enduring accounting disarray provides the platform to canvass what Chambers observed still needed to be done to produce a better, more serviceable accounting.

Well into retirement, in late 1990, around the time of his first letter to Sterling expressing his frustrations, Chambers felt compelled, as he suggested to one of the writers, to 'get on the soapbox' again—to deliver an address to the University of Sydney Pacioli Society, 'Accounting and Corporate Morality—Ethical Cringe.' It was delivered on 1 May 1991, around the time Chambers was publishing works drawing on his knowledge of the history of ideas (as discussed in chapters 3, 4, 6 and 8) to reflect on many accounting issues—including: the two 'True and fair view' papers and 'Historical Cost—a Tale of a False Creed.'

The Pacioli Society address suggested things had changed little. It was underpinned by frustrations that many of his reforms had not been implemented—they had been effectively challenged. Chambers reiterated the need for any future accounting reforms to curb corporate immorality, and to bring the notions of equity, trustworthiness, fair dealing to the forefront of people discussing corporate and accounting abuses. His use of analogy and of extreme examples as well as a call for a major set of reforms are evident in this observation:

> Piece-meal *patching* can never make a worm-eaten craft sea worthy; neither will piece-meal *tinkering* of individuals, boards and committees make cost-based valuations trustworthy—as the *unexpected* company collapses, bankruptcies, official investigations and prosecutions of the past four decades should surely have demonstrated. (emphasis added)[7]

He noted also that equity and fairness are ethical norms, lamenting that 'commonly we tend to shy away from the words ethical and moral when dealing with business and corporate affairs. That is what I mean by "the ethical cringe." '[8] One would imagine his recourse to ethics would resonate with many in the tertiary (especially the business) sector today.[9]

Ideas in Chambers' address and the articles discussed below about his proposed accounting education reforms were similar to those undergirding his major unfinished business, a proposed book-length exercise—*Wisdom of Accounting*.

Chambers' felt his academic apprenticeship was completed with the finalization of his *Thesaurus*. He had the evidence needed to compose *Wisdom*. While the book had been scoped, he had made only minimal advances with its text. Analysis below of the retrieved archive materials shows what he had planned and what he may have accomplished, as he continued to seek solutions to the two puzzles that we noted in chapter 3, puzzles that had bedevilled him for years. He had alluded to them in the concluding paragraph of his *Towards a General Theory of Accounting* paper. And, over thirty years later, they are explicitly outlined in 'Historical Cost—a Tale of a False Creed':

> how to devise a form of accounting that would yield the necessary information on the component and aggregate amounts of property and debt from time to time, and how to explain the emergence and survival of a body of universally endorsed accounting rules that did not yield information of that kind.[10]

A comment in a September 1961 letter from Moonitz in response to Chambers' proposals in his *Towards a General Theory of Accounting* analyses the puzzles and the related riddle of the money illusion:

> Even If I accept your 'synthetic' approach of constructing an accounting framework out of the basic elements you have set forth, one major

puzzle remains, where did these "actors" [interested parties in an entity's affairs] go astray? Why haven't they been using "stabilized" accounting of one sort or another in their monetary calculations which guide their actions in the world of markets? Who or what or where is the villain of the piece? Your type of analysis would lead me to expect an insistent demand from the "actors" themselves for adjusted accounting data. Instead I detect no ground swell from them, but observe that the drive for stabilized accounting comes from the specialists (economists [like Irving Fisher], accountants [like Sweeney, MacNeal, Chambers and Edwards and Bell]). If you or I or anyone else can solve the riddle of the "money illusion" we will have accomplished a tremendous feat.[11]

Chambers' response reveals his thinking about those puzzles and an in principle way to resolve them:

Your penultimate paragraph poses a problem which may well seem to be a knockout. I have long been aware that it lies halfway along the road of deductive analysis. A complete deductive theory of accounting will build up an ideal system from concepts having correlates in reality; but it must go on to explain also why the real arose when the ideal should have arisen. I have already laid the foundation—in para. 55 [of *Towards*; there he discusses the quality of accounting information], for example. And para. 119 provides further clues to my explanation of the questions you raise.'

In fact para. 119 states that conventional accounting 'has survived simply because of the enormous richness of informal flows of information [financial and physical information] in an around business and other organizations . . . which helps men to manage in spite of the flaws in conventional accounting.'

A second, related unfinished business was the need to reinforce the belief in several of his published articles (reproduced in *Chambers on Accounting*, Volumes 2 and 6) that accounting's educational place as a university discipline should never be taken for granted.

For accounting to be viewed as an equal with their university brethren is not a right, it requires constant attention. Chambers had suggested this in two pieces in the mid-to-early 1960s, and he would return to it in later decades. In 1961 a sixty-page 'report' of the Advisory Panel to the Committee of Review on Educational Standards and Examinations of the ICAA was prepared by Australian professorial associates, Lou Goldberg and Russell Mathews, with Chambers as convenor. It proposed a revolutionary idea, namely that the basic educational preparation should be a university degree course. It was followed in 1964 by a second, twenty-page report (see Table 7.5 for details). Then in August 1964, informed by the work of that advisory panel, he prepared a five-page seminar paper on the 'Role of Universities in Administrative Education' in which he proposed a much broader

role for accounting. His *Auto-Bibliography* summarized the paper's enduring controversial contents:

> Administration requires an integrated breadth of view. The traditional
> division of knowledge [in university courses] into fields is a pedagogi-
> cal convenience. But the greater the growth in specialized knowledge,
> the greater is the need to integrate and interrelate specialist principles
> and practices. The proliferation of subjects in curricula of adminis-
> trative studies [nowadays described as commerce or business studies]
> and the recourse to case studies threatens to produce not disciplined
> minds, but those adept at superficial ad-hocery. What is required is less
> multi-disciplinary study by students and more interdisciplinary study
> by academics.[12]

Based on correspondence we believe Chambers would claim that those
concerns persist. In a letter to Briloff in 1982, he had noted the significant
hurdles that needed to be overcome:

> Academics are as pig-headed as any other class. I thought they would
> be able to see useless addition and faulty syntax and twisted argument
> without too much aid. That was a mistake on my part. But I continue
> to hope.[13]

The lament is repeated about two years later in the letter to a 1960s University of Sydney and department colleague, the prominent 1980s company
lawyer, Bob Baxt: 'The prospects of reform we then entertained with some
optimism are still, in large measure, only prospects. The educational adventure yields its fruits slowly against inertia and conservatism.'[14]
But this did not deter Chambers continuing to argue his case for reform.

Wisdom of Accounting

Chambers often used analogy to argue a case. It is unsurprising then that
Chambers' final, unfinished book had 'wisdom' in its title—separating wisdom from folly had been a lifelong exercise for him, as it had been for
Hanbury Brown in his analyses of how science developed. Wisdom could
be in observing practices of any applied discipline. The folly of the past he
felt could be seen by wise observers. But he was well aware that experience
and observing are not the same—perhaps many have had all the experience
(and potentially wisdom), but not had the privilege of making the necessary
observations to learn from their mistakes.
The Chambers Archive provides some snippets about the content of
that proposed book. One source is a writing pad with several pages of text
detailing what were draft ideas for a manuscript. In close proximity are
other loose pages. These provide an overview of the proposed chapters and

a brief synopsis of each. They also note that the materials to be drawn upon were the common references to those areas assembled in his *Thesaurus*. The prospect of *Wisdom of Accounting* advancing in this way had been conveyed by Chambers to two of the authors (Clarke and Dean) and another colleague (Peter Wolnizer).

The October 2000 *Abacus* article, 'Early Beginnings,' which was drawn upon in our chapter 1, was to be included as the introductory chapter of *Wisdom*. When located in the Archive it was to have the same title as the proposed book. When published posthumously as 'Early Beginnings: An introduction to *Wisdom of Accounting*' it carried with it an editor's note: 'Incomplete manuscript found in Ray Chambers' home study after his death by his daughter Rosemary [Pearce].'[15]

The full list of *Wisdom*'s proposed chapter headings, augmented in brackets with what we deduce could have been the relevant sections ('the evidence') in his *An Accounting Thesaurus*, are: 'The Wisdom of Accounting' (*AAT*: ss. 100s and 200s), 'Truth in Accounting' (*AAT*: ss. 207, 812), 'Accounting as Communication' (*AAT*: ss. 038, 234–39), 'Accounting as Measurement,' *AAT*: ss. 250, 320), 'Accounting as Instrumentation' (*AAT*: ss. 054, 055), 'Accounting as History' (*AAT*: s. 311), 'Money, Wealth and Income' (*AAT*: ss. 031, 151). Related materials: 'Accounting as Vocation' and 'Modern Accounting Thought,' because of the subject matter and their placing in the archive, suggest they were likely to be subsections of *Wisdom*.

Undated papers in a folder labelled 'M.A.T.' that were found in the Archive near the *Wisdom* draft material suggest Chambers had likely contemplated years earlier a similar book—*Modern Accounting Thought*. References in these notes indicate the material was prepared around 1980–81, immediately before his retirement. The structure of each chapter of *Modern* is given in that folder—as is a detailed text of several sections. Given the likelihood that the two projects covered similar territory, we examine the *Modern* draft materials to augment our earlier thoughts on *Wisdom*.

In the folder those draft chapters were listed under three categories:

I. *Introductory*—covering 'Practice, Thought and Theory,' and 'The Nature of Accounting'—covering arithmetical, financial, economic, legal communications.

II. *Elements*—covering 'basic formal notions' like Historicity, Stewardship, Accrual, Consistency, Going Concern, Double-Entry;

'Accounting and Decision Making' discussing functions or objectives, uniformity;
'Financial Position and Capital'—discussing solvency and leverage;
'Income, Rates of Return';
'Valuation and Measurement'—discussing issues of aggregation;
'The Object of an Accounting'—discussing the accounting entity;

'Money and Prices';
'Price Variations';
'The Regulatory Control of Accounting'—discussing disclosure, materiality;
'Group Accounting.'

III. Systems—discussing systems proposed by authors like Paton, Sweeney, Sanders, Hatfield and Moore, GAAP, etc.

While the outlines of *Wisdom* and of *Modern* cover similar terrain, in the years between their preparation Chambers had prepared and published his *Thesaurus*. By the late 1990s he was surer than ever of the need for the proposed reforms that had coalesced during the 1960s and early '70s but that had not been implemented.[16] The brief extracts reveal again his concern for better understanding of accounting fundamentals.

Two extracts from *Modern* are reproduced almost as they appeared in Chambers' files. The first, 'A Review and Critique,' is essentially a prologue, and the second, 'Practice, Thought and Theory,' an early chapter.

Modern Accounting Thought: A Review and Critique

This work is a study of modern accounting thought as it has found expression in the English language literature.[17] . . .

By 'modern accounting thought' I mean, generally, those ideas which have from time to time been advanced by practitioners, researchers or theorists as the ideas which they consider to underlie the practice of accounting. By 'modern,' I mean generally the ideas which have been held or which have emerged during some part of the late nineteenth century up to the present time [early 1980s].

Accounting ideas and practices have been traced by some to remote antiquity. But the corpus of present ideas and practices can reasonably be said, I believe, to be a product of the past century. I may have occasion to refer to some earlier work, but it will be occasional only. It is tolerably certain that the literature in languages other than English will have contained ideas of a kind not to be considered. But in the light of the widespread practice of what has been described as traditional [or conventional] accounting, those differences are not likely to be substantial; and in any case, to tap them is beyond my competence.

'Modern accounting thought' has been chosen rather than 'modern accounting theory' for a number of reasons. Ideally 'theory' relates to a systematic and self-consistent set of ideas or 'thoughts.' But scarcely at all in the century under discussion has there been any set of ideas, advanced or adopted as the basis of practice, that was systematic and self-consistent. Ideally, also, 'theory' relates to a systematic set of ideas that have a demonstrable connection with the elements of experience. But, quite generally, the sets of ideas which have been developed as the basis of practice have only partial connections with the elements of experience; and many of the ideas that have been advanced as alternative bases of practice have likewise had only partial connections with the elements of experience.

Faced with the diverse ideas and the diverse expressions of ideas and the diverse associations of ideas over a century, the method I have adopted is initially atomistic. I have sought out the occurrence and the persistence of specific notions, the elementary bricks out of which more complex propositions have been built. I have sought to discover what these specific notions entail, whether that is implicit, as it often is, or explicit. It emerges that there is a significant body of ideas that emerge through the literature, and which may therefore be considered the core of modern accounting thought. It emerges also, however, that many ideas that are potentially serviceable have been combined in exposition in a manner that confuses the outcome, leading to doctrines or rules that are unjustifiable, logically or practically. Thus, although I begin with atomistic analysis, the work proceeds to the analysis of 'compounds,' propositions intended to be conclusions from stated or implied premises and intended to be prescriptive of practices. The raw material of the study is 'the literature' . . . major works of the period—in a loose sense, 'the classics'. . . . A selection of textbooks and articles, spread though not evenly over the century, has been used. . . .

Use has also been made of other literatures which deal with matters of common concern to accounting and other disciplines. The accounting literature is spiced, but lightly, with reference to other literatures. The practice has sometimes led to the elucidation of an idea, sometimes to misconstruction, and sometimes to confusion.

. . .

To understand a matter—a body of practices, a 'subject,' a field of discourse—is more than merely knowing the present, overt form of it. The links of its present form with the past and with the thoughts of others who have put the matter under scrutiny enrich the understanding, and therefore the capacity to make informed judgements about it. To promote that understanding is the object of this book.

Practice, Thought, and Theory

. . . .

Knowledge of the proper usages of symbols and of the characteristics of natural phenomena are both cultural artefacts. The propositions that express what men believe to be the case may be found to be dependable over long periods of time, and while believed to be dependable they are described as 'knowledge.' But if the knowledge of one age is found to be unreliable or less serviceable in another, it is supplanted by new knowledge.

There are three kinds of knowledge, knowing *what* is the case, knowing *how* it comes to be the case, and knowing *why* it is the case. Plant biologists know that the seeds of certain plants are oily, and that some seeds yield more fats and oils than others. They know this by simple observation. They also know how, by cross-breeding and cultivation, to increase the yields of certain kinds of plants. They have discovered this by observation and experimentation. All of this knowledge has been accumulated without knowing why the seeds in question are oil-bearing in the first place. Indeed, the 'why' of many things has for centuries been deemed to be beyond the realm of scientific inquiry and to be, instead, part of the realm of speculative philosophy.

The case is different in respect of wholly invented technologies or artefacts. Writing may have been devised for the pleasure of self-expression, or to convey messages to others, or as an aid to memory, or for other purposes. These objects or functions are expressions of human desire, wish or intention. Commonly we learn *how* to write without any conscious understanding of *why* writing is done. But no explanation of writing can be given that makes no reference to human desire and intention. And no explanation of a change or 'improvement' in a writing technology can be given without a similar reference. In particular, the reading and writing and arithmetic that are specific to accounting are inexplicable without reference to aims, desires and intentions. *Why* men write what they do determines—or should determine—what they write.

Wish, desire, and intention are the products of thinking. And how we shall give effect to wishes, desires, and intentions, by recourse to external means or objects is likewise the product of thinking. So also is the invention and improvement of technical devices for that purpose. Thinking of the latter kind may range from the loose association of a few ideas, tossing them around in one's head to see what may happen—to the deliberate association of many ideas in the form of an argument. The history of invention is full of instances of both. But whether or not thinking is fruitful turns not on the thinking process solely, for we may have overlooked or set aside some features of the problem which engages attention. It turns on the effectiveness in use of the tool, device, or programme that is the outcome of thinking. The practical inventor seeks, then, to test the product of his thinking in a practical setting, to see whether it 'works.' He tinkers with it, adding a new element here, eliminating an element there, simplifying an element elsewhere, making such variations as he thinks will make his invention work or work better. The process is commonly described as 'trial and error.' A better description is 'trial and error elimination,' for the object is not simply to find one's errors but, having found them, to put something better in their place.

A simple device designed to do one job is readily testable. Whether it is 'strong' enough to do the job and whether it does the job at all are easily discoverable. But there may be years or decades between the conception of an idea and the discovery of a means of turning it into a serviceable device. Even such an everyday article as a zip fastener was thought of years before a way of making it was developed. A complex device that is expected to be serviceable in a variety of settings is not so readily testable. Each of its components must be devised so that as a whole they "work together," and as a whole the device must stand the test of a battery of settings.

Accounting falls into this class of complex devices. It has many technical 'parts'—original records, ledger accounts, periodical adjustments and periodical summaries—all of which are intended to interlock in a systematic fashion. And these parts are expected to work together in such a fashion that a variety of ends is served. Those 'ends' have been variously specified; and with varying degrees of precision. Generally they have been related to the provision of assistance to managers and investors and creditors and others. Ideally, it might be expected that the many parts and the whole would be so constructed that specific ends (even though varied) would be served. But, like all other complex practical devices, faults have shown up from time to time in the serviceability of parts of accounting, either in the processes or in the products of those processes. In the manner of 'trial and error,' a variety of suggestions has been made which their authors have considered as ameliorative.

Given an agreed way of testing the serviceability of the end-products of accounting, every input and process, and every newly suggested input and process, could be subjected to test; for inputs and processes contributing to an end-product cannot be at odds with the function of the end-product. Deficient inputs and processes could be replaced with better. 'Trial and error-elimination' could be expected to yield increasingly serviceable end-products.

However, if an accountant (or his client or the chief executive of the firm he serves) has reason to believe that an accounting rule of his choice yields information no less serviceable than any other rule, there is no reason why he should test it. Beliefs of that kind have dominated decades of thought. They have been propped up by a further belief to the effect that faulty rules are bound to be 'found out,' and the corollary, that the prevailing rules at any time are the best that have been so far devised. These notions stand squarely in the path of any attempt to test actual or proposed practices or rules. Error-elimination is inconceivable, for nothing can be shown to be in error if nothing is tested.

The less naive may be disposed to treat rules as tentative directives awaiting trial or testing of their fruitfulness, or superiority over other rules. It is not difficult to treat an innovative variation of or substitute for an old rule as tentative. A new rule will not have had time to settle itself into the matrix of thinking, to become 'accepted,' as it is said. However, every newly proposed rule will have some justification in the opinion of its proponent. Its claim to general endorsement must then rest on the relative merits of the justifications of the old and the new rules. In that setting an old rule has a clear advantage, for the product of its use will often be deemed to be the criterion for testing the new rule. That apart, every rule may be treated as having been a new rule at some time. We may therefore consider in general the possibility of putting any rule under *test*. (emphasis added)

There is no better way of putting a rule under test than by reference to the utility, in a practical setting, of the product of its use. But not only is accounting itself a complex device; the settings in which its products are used and the classes of person who make use of them are diverse. Further, those products are used in conjunction with a diverse array of other kinds of information. If a certain judgement or decision arises in part from the use of some accounting information, therefore, it is difficult to assert with confidence what impact the accounting information may have had on the judgement or decision. If it were possible to associate a specific rule with a certain outcome over a number of trials in which all or most of the other situational variables were constant, the utility of the rule could be appraised. But that kind of testing is not available in a practical setting. The user of accounting information may be differentially influenced from instance to instance by his own temporal exigencies; or if we consider a number of users, each will be influenced differently from others by his own wishes and exigencies. The environmental contexts of different singular trials may differ, in a host of particulars.

The likelihood of reaching any confident conclusion about the merits of any rule from the casually observed outcomes of instances of its practical use seems remote indeed. Yet until the mid-twentieth century, casual observation (as by practitioners or textbook writers) was the dominant source of whatever confidence was placed in prevalent accounting rules. Rules survived not because they had been shown 'to work,' but because they were believed to work and had not yet been shown to produce a notable mischief or nuisance. In that setting, error-elimination is not inconceivable, but it is unlikely. That is one reason, if not the principal reason, for the persistence of so many variant and often conflicting rules. The development of the corpus of accounting rules has been not so much a process of trial and error-elimination as of trial and error-accumulation.

Chambers was disappointed at what passed for 'testing' the quality of accounting information. He had rejected in the mid-1970s the use of regression association studies of share price returns and EBITDA, EBITA, and EBIT. In chapter 6 we noted that in his 1974a and 1993 *Abacus* articles he viewed this approach as futile; as had others, including Sterling in his 1990 article in *Abacus* and Cooper and Zeff in their 1992 *Critical Perspectives on Accounting* article. This approach, however, has persisted into the 2000s causing Dyckman and Zeff in 2014 to express similar concerns in an article in *Accounting Horizons*.[18] We noted in chapter 8 (see endnote #52, chapter 8) that as well as being critical, constructively Chambers had proposed a test grid to compare alternative accounting systems using the criterion of how serviceable were the products of each system.

Accounting Educational Reforms

Given Chambers' thoughts on how best to achieve long-term regulatory reform, unsurprisingly, his other major unfinished business relates to the continuing need for educational reform. The chapter's epigraphs reveal high hopes of major changes to accounting when setting out on his academic career. In the 1960s and early '70s he continued to advocate for a move away from dogma, from the prevalent indoctrination asserting that there are many equally valid ways to prepare accounts. He sought a more reliable, serviceable form of accounting, systematically constructed on a body of scientific knowledge.[19]

But by 1980 those hopes for change had been dashed. In correspondence with Briloff Chambers observed:

> I believe several generations of teachers are to blame (though the fault lies not only there) . . . every man may clothe his utterances in words of his own choice. But communication rests on cognitions shared by the speaker and his audience; if he *is* to convey any message, his freedom of choice is thus restricted, disciplined, by what his audience can grasp. When a magician saws a young lady in half, we know he is doing something else altogether; we (the audience) know it is illusion. But, when an accountant adds up numbers which auditors make some noises [either positive or negative opinions] about, we do not expect the result to be, or intended to be, an illusion. The accountant and the auditor do not think it is an illusion, because they have been taught that it is a quite proper thing to do. And yet it is, if the aggregation is logically improper. . . . Until accountants have established the linkages between specific kinds of information and their specific uses (separately or in combination), it cannot be claimed that their processes are "disciplined," and the prospect of weeds over-running the garden will persist.[20]

Yet, he still held out hope of change in the future.

In retirement he wrote two articles outlining the malaise in accounting education and possible ways forward—'Accounting Education in the 21st Century' and 'The Poverty of Accounting Discourse' as well as delivering an occasional address, 'An Educational Scandal.'

Chambers' views on teaching had changed little in principle since his early writings discussed in chapter 5—where he stressed the need for students to be provided an 'education,' and not simply a 'training,' in accounting. This required examination of matters of principle, more so than simply indoctrinating students as to what the Recommendations (then) or mandatory Standards (later) required. Inculcating matters of principle would stand students in good stead as they grappled later in their career with ever-changing business structures, complex financial instruments, and the inevitable (due to lobbying and political compromises) changing accounting standards. He was not, however, suggesting students should not be immersed in practice—to the contrary.

The *Sydney School of Accounting* monograph provides evidence of the curricula developed by Chambers and his followers at Sydney. Letters in the Chambers Archive from the early 1950s reveal his ideas regarding the shape of a university curriculum in accounting and hinted at how the Sydney curriculum should develop over the next thirty years. Of particular note is the relevance of key ideas to contemporary problems. His focus was to inject accounting curricula with the nuances of financial economics, and social and public interest aspects of accounting were always to the fore. He lamented that accountants and economists tended to disregard the advances made in the related commercial disciplines. This was so even when fundamental ideas in accounting were less than settled themselves. He also sought to include in the curriculum how accounting ideas, that had developed and become entrenched over time, reflected the general ignorance of the history of ideas and accounting ideas in particular. Chambers challenged the questionable mores and theories of related business disciplines and pursued curricula in which accounting was directed to be serviceable in its ordinary, everyday functions.

Extracts from letters show a clear and unique thinking on such matters. A mid-1960s proposal for an honours program in accounting (embracing private, public and social accounting covering empirical and analytical studies) augmented an equally unorthodox undergraduate program where the accounting course was supplemented by studies of the assumptions on which accounting techniques are based, and of the alternative hypothetical techniques. Much earlier in his 1952 senior lectureship application he had detailed a three-year undergraduate program, noting:

> It is possible to develop a course in accounting along theoretical lines, rather than on purely technical lines. In a three-year course there would be ample opportunity for training in the techniques of accounting, for developing a theory of accounting and for encouraging a critical attitude towards theory and practice. . . . An understanding of the economic and social repercussions of accounting should be, in a University course, of equal importance to the development of technical expertness in manipulating numerical abstraction.[21]

That program was implemented.

Pursuing curricula within an applied setting that recognizes corporate financial successes and failures was essential. This was achieved by drawing upon the roles of accounting and auditing in notable past events: for example, the World War I and post-1920s U.K. Royal Mail fiasco and contemporary anomalies at New York Stock Exchange-listed firms run by the likes of Ivar Kreuger and Samuel Insull; attempts by 1920s U.S. accounting academics, among them Paton and Sweeney, to ensure accounting mechanisms incorporated the effects of the post-war hyperinflation; regulatory developments in accounting rule setting following the New Deal; and incursions into accounting theory development by the likes of U.S. scholars Paton, Canning, MacNeal, Sanders, Hatfield, and Moore during the 1920s, 1930s, and 1940s.

Regarding the dominant issues after World War II, courses also considered how accounting performed under stress, namely how had accountants grappled with inflation, especially the so-called taxation of inflation-created *false profits* discussed in chapter 8; the introduction of professional agitation for research funding; consequences of compulsory accounting standards in a professional discipline; and auditing being viewed as a practice worthy of serious theoretical enquiry, as suggested by (say) Mautz and Sharaf's 1961 auditing classic. The golden age accounting monograph literature during the 1960s and (then) the 1970s–80s was also examined to understand the myriad notions of accounting fundamentals: assets, liabilities and residual equity, revenues and expenses, capital maintenance, income and loss, financial performance, and financial position. How well those notions performed was questioned, bearing in mind contemporary incidents of corporate finagling. Also canvassed was how the previous methods to inject accounts with the financial effects of inflationary and hyperinflationary price and price-level changes in the 1920s were being promoted (in particular, again by the profession) to handle the accounting distortions caused by the inflation of the 1960s through the 1970s.

Whereas like-minded individuals pursued aspects of those matters, few did so in anything like the ordered and enthusiastic way in which Chambers guided his staff. None attempted to design a curriculum which addressed that material in such an organized way. He also sought advice from practitioners like Irish and Spacek (see endnote #3, chapter 7)

It meant that graduates from the Sydney School during those days, particularly those who undertook the honours program, entered business, the profession, or academe with a perspective of accounting underpinned by a clear understanding of the functions of that technology, what various scholars over time had said its functions ought to be, and the critical historical and contemporary means for evaluating how present practices were to be measured against both. Ordinary undergraduates indirectly, honours degree and postgraduates directly, had exposure to matters of practice and theory, of historical and contemporary incidents which few others in private practice or commercial employment experienced.

Interestingly, more than fifty years later in Australia a major enquiry by the Australian Federal government sought to determine the 'Threshold Learning Outcomes' of accounting and other professional degree programs (undergraduate and postgraduate) offered by universities and other service providers in Australia. Chambers' prescience on that score should be a template for those making ongoing enquiries.[22] The focus on enquiry, constructive criticism, and the inclusion of an understanding of the history of accounting and connected disciplines are necessary features of such degree offerings if the graduates are to be capable of moving the accounting discipline away from dogma and being captive to the rules of custom that have either facilitated or at least not mitigated, most recently, the financial mayhem of the GFC.

But those education program developments may have been transitory even at Sydney University. For upon retirement and with new teaching staff Chambers became frustrated and disappointed that his innovatory program was languishing. Correspondence with Sterling in the early 1990s highlights this, as well as his annoyance with the Faculty of Economics' treatment of him as an emeritus professor. Consider this 1990 letter to Sterling:

> but as I told you before, I have tried to keep my nose out of the running of anything since I retired. If my help would have been welcome I'd have been glad to give it. But, for at least five years I've had the blunt end of neglect, if not rejection. I believe I'm not a dull lecturer, and over those years I have written several papers which I would class among my better. I've been asked to give only three or four lectures here [at Sydney] over that time. When, perhaps a couple of years ago, I heard that getting *Abacus* edited was troublesome, I offered to pitch in. But, I heard no more of it. In any case, it is trying enough to be around to see the sand castle I spent 30 years abuilding get washed away by the raging tide of ignorant egotism.[23]

The importance to Chambers of changing the education program at Sydney to achieve effective reform of accounting practice is further evident in correspondence with Briloff:

> I've become quite weary of city antics. They only survive at all because accounting is so inept. It's an ineptitude that reaches to its roots. It seems a rather cute division of labour, then, that while you attack its malformed flowers [accounts and audit opinion] I attack its roots [logic and postulates]. I have despaired of making my presence felt through the city's affairs. Company officers, professional accountants, lawyers, and so on, have an established status that permits them to laugh off such pricks and prods as I can muster. My own conclusion, long ago, was that reform is slow; it proceeds through the educational processes in civilizations organized like ours; and one way of stimulating the rejection of what is parasitic is therefore to force educators themselves to recognize it.[24]

Chambers felt that other tertiary institutions had not progressed in accounting education terms since the 1950s. This caused him to write the 1987 *Abacus* article, 'Accounting in the 21st Century,' which canvassed many of his perceived flaws in accounting education. The concern was that textbooks and curricula paid no attention to the fundamental task of accounting (its function), namely to provide reliable knowledge. The abstract notes textbooks and curricula:

> perpetuate processes that had their origins in the desire to conceal rather than to disclose. Recurrent criticisms of the products of practice [such

as occurred twenty years later following the GFC] may only be averted if the educational establishment gives greater attention to the nature of money and prices, the conditions of valid measurement, the logic of choice, the regulation of complex processes, and the consequences of misdirected thought and misleading practices.

In his hometown, Newcastle, Chambers felt compelled to repeat that 1987 call to arms in a 1991 address, 'An Educational Scandal.' He reflected on over forty years of teaching—much of it at the University of Sydney. He referred to the undisciplined, shoddy state of accounting education which had escaped being an educational scandal by reason of the esoteric and unintelligible mumbo jumbo in which teaching practice has been clothed. Two fallacies were noted: the aggregation of unlike amounts and the mistaken belief in the utility of out of date information, concluding that these are a recipe for disorder. Further, he observed that the accounting educational establishment should know better for it rubs shoulders with teachers and researchers in other fields whose respect for mathematical logic and observable facts is unquestionable. The late 1980s government-sponsored inquiry which led to the three-volume *Accounting in Higher Education* report (Mathews Report, 1990) had been asked to review the discipline, identify areas of concern, and make recommendations. It contains much about the length of degree programs, class sizes, teaching methods, teaching loads, and funding, but Chambers suggests there is minimal discussion on the intellectual content, logical rigour, or the practical utility of what is taught.

The impotence of countless standards committees or boards has failed to stamp out the misrepresentation of business affairs. The Newcastle address concluded that if an educational establishment fails to discriminate between what is fundamental and recurring and what is superficial and incidental, or to teach the few fundamental principles, it's an issue of prime neglect, perhaps culpable neglect—an educational scandal.

He revisited and extended his ideas on education in a 1992 'Poverty in Accounting Discourse' seminar paper (published seven years later, just prior to his death). It began by looking at the only principle of conventional accounting, the double-entry bookkeeping equation, noting it has a built-in safeguard against errors in record-keeping, but not against errors in the amounts entering the record. 'If the inputs are false or imaginary, the outputs cannot be factual, and useful, as fact, in making judgments about the past or decisions about the future. . . . But things are seldom what they seem.'[25]

'Poverty' examined the fallacies suggested in 'Accounting in the 21st Century.' Accountants would have preserved themselves and their art from recurring criticism by recourse to any number of well-known systems of ideas. First, there is arithmetical propriety, the dominant rule of which is that only like quantities may be added and subtracted if the result is to be of the same class or kind as the components. Yet, nowhere in manuals of a few hundred years ago or in the vast textbook literature that serves today's novices is that principle enunciated or followed. Second are the related ideas of wealth being dated general purchasing power, income being the periodical increment in current general purchasing power, and asset value being value in exchange— approximated by the dated selling prices of property in possession. Third, law and order have long required that true accounts be kept and that true representations of wealth and income be given in the financial statements of companies. Yet, as it happens, dated financial statements are described as 'true' notwithstanding that they comprise compounds of past facts, present guesses, managerial opinions, accounting conventions, and faulty arithmetic. Fourth, despite allusions to accounting information about the past and to decisions about the future, conventional accounting's disregard for changes in the prices of property, and changes in the general purchasing power of money, means that corporate reports cannot fulfil the necessary information needs that underpin commercial judgement and choice. Fifth, the canons of language and understanding are offended by financial statements that purport to be a true and fair view of a company's wealth and progress but are no such thing. As intelligible communications, financial statements are a delusion. Sixth, in common accounting discourse, measure and measurement are the most common terms. Yet, as noted in principle 1 above, accounting does not conform to the rules of simple arithmetic. Scarcely ever is the vast literature on measurement outside of the accounting discipline referred to in the standard textbooks on accounting. Seventh, though the vagaries of politics and ethics enter the behaviour of individuals in commerce, the literature on accounting alludes to such matters but with little conviction. 'Poverty' concludes by suggesting that those seven fields of disciplined enquiry— mathematics, economics, law, judgement and choice, language and communication, metrology, and politics and ethics—support a form of continually and realistic up-to-date accounting. It notes that in existing accounting thought and practice, dogma has replaced reliable knowledge.

Around the time 'Poverty' was being composed Chambers made the following comments in response to Bob Baxt's address at a July 1991 Sydney University dinner to recognize his upcoming induction into The Ohio State University U.S. AHoF:

> But seeing that dramatists, philosophers, and mathematicians favourably would notice bookkeeping among the useful arts of men, perhaps its mid-20th century corpus of fallacious and contradictory rules could be disciplined by basic universal knowledge as are the other arts that flourish in the atmosphere of universities. To make it so was, to me, an ambition, though to others I cautiously made it appear as a dream.[26]

Chambers' papers suggested much still needed to be accomplished. It is incontestable, as was argued in the *Accounting Education* special issue on 'Poverty,' that in the twenty-odd years since those articles appeared little in the way of effective change has occurred in accounting educa- tion, in Australia and elsewhere.[27] In a commentary Lee observes pre- sciently: 'The surprising thing about this situation is not that it takes place. Instead, it is that the reporting scam has not been exposed fully and the right of accountants to be called professionals challenged.' The fault (as Chambers suggests, 251) is with the occupants of the 'palaces of the profession' and the 'halls of learning.' Lee continues: 'academics . . . must be prepared to teach about a system of accounting that corresponds to the economics of the corporation. Every student of accounting should be locked in a room with Chambers' paper until he or she commits to a lifetime's effort to bring about the Copernican revolution that Chambers calls for in accounting.'

Peroration

Clearly, there is much 'unfinished business,' as Chambers' two 'puzzles' remain unsolved. Commercial disorder remains.

This biographical study was described in a pre-publication review by Geoff Whittington as a 'sympathetic portrait of one of the outstanding accounting thinkers of the twentieth century, offering new insights, from original sources, into his astonishingly varied interests and activities.'[28] It uses appreciative inquiry to review, amongst other evidentiary sources, the Chambers Archive. It acknowledges Chambers' achievements, his perspi- cacity, his long hours of dedicated work with practitioners, business, and regulators in pursuit of a better accounting. The recently discovered mate- rials from the proposed *Wisdom of Accounting* reveal that, while frus- trated, he was unfazed by the persistence and strength of the challenges to his reforms. He was convinced that for effective long-term reform, there remains a need to educate the accounting educators. His pursuit of reform remained a work-in-progress up to his death.

Our analysis suggests that initial concerns advanced by academics and practitioners about the general relevance of CoCoA to business decision making and the excessive cost of implementing it, persist; but they are no longer pervasive. There is some evidence of the recourse to market (essen- tially exit) prices in several past and recently promulgated accounting stan- dards. However, this development still only affects a small proportion of the total number of IFRSs. Regarding one area affected, Bedford commented in his 1982 *Abacus* Festschrift article about the impact of Chambers on the scope of accounting, especially his pioneering valuation reforms. While one should not ascribe too much to the influence of one person Chambers': 'emphasis on the importance of liquidity, may explain, in part, the emphasis financial analysts and accounting standards setting bodies are giving to vari- ous types of cash flow accounting reports. . . . [and] the budding shifts in thinking of investors, financial analysts, managements, and others suggests that much of the future accounting practice will be traced back to Chambers' proposals.'[29]

But other concerns reflecting what Chambers described as the 'dead hand of orthodoxy,'[30] have endured since Bedford made those observations. Resistance from inertia, antipathy to accounting innovation, a penchant for conservatism, and political forces have changed little since the 1950s. Those running businesses generally prefer secrecy to disclosure. Practitioners, standards setters, and educators are generally unconvinced about the net decision making benefits of the main features of Chambers' reforms—namely, that provision of market price information in respect of *all* of an entity's assets and liabilities, albeit with estimation error, is preferable to supposedly less error in respect of the primarily conventional cost-based information reported in accounts.

But there is some support for Chambers' ideas. U.K. economist and financial commentator John Kay's *Other People's Money* (2016) critiques present accounting, financial, and other regulatory interventions, saying they are too rules-based and generally add more of the same types of rules after each crisis. This has occurred since the 1930s SEC disclosure regime. Kay proposes, like Chambers and interestingly as does the Bank of England's Andrew Haldane, a simpler, more nuanced regulatory system.

Again, recall the view of Kay, who is sceptical of the use of the profession's fair value accounting, especially its mark-to-model form. Chambers was also consistently critical of the type of forecasts that underpin the reported asset and liability amounts under that form of accounting. He was particularly concerned that the resulting data were unverifiable, a critical shortcoming in his search for commercial order. His view, as noted in chapters 4 and 6, is that where no present market price exists, either due to no or thin markets, then a zero amount should be reported in the accounts using the double account method with a twist, with an explanation in the Notes.

Further, Chambers' sceptics remain unconvinced of the need for an accounts adjustment to reflect changes in the general level of prices. An adjustment, along the lines of Chambers' capital maintenance adjustment (chapters 4 and 6) was explored by professional bodies worldwide in their 1970s and early '80s CCA/CPP solutions (chapters 6 and 8). But the decline in inflation worldwide removed the catalyst for fundamental change, just as had occurred in the mid-to-late 1920s after the hyperinflation in Europe, and in the years following the post-World War II inflation.

Further obstacles to change include the ongoing focus of accounting practitioners and standards setters on users, rather than accounting's uses, recourse to committees to resolve accounting technology problems, the proliferation of expectations in financial reporting data, the acceptance of conservatism (nowadays described often as prudence) and the acceptance of management discretion (often described as 'earnings management' and 'income smoothing').

Formative experiences from a strong religious background, as well as from practical engagements in business, government, and the profession, were augmented by consultancies in the 1960s and 1970s across those sectors. They underpinned Chambers' resolve to pursue change. He maintained a belief in the legislative true and fair view override, an ethical code, and for it to be more effectively enforced.

His goal was that accounting data would be perceived as being rigorously prepared, and concomitantly, that they would be viewed as being trustworthy. Were this to be achieved, accounting would again be held in high esteem, as it was by Luca Pacioli and his Renaissance associates over five centuries ago.

Chambers' failure to achieve substantial reforms has been said to be because of a focus naively on ideas, not special interests, always seeking 'truth in accounting.' This raises the question of whether an alternative way of producing change is required. There is no doubt, however, that without change accounting cannot be the serviceable technology suggested in Goethe's *Wilhelm Meister's Years of Apprenticeship* (1795–96), approvingly quoted in Chambers (1961 and 1983), where accounting is described as 'one of the finest inventions of the human mind,' or, the similar approbation expressed around hundred years later by William Cayley, Cambridge professor of mathematics, who wrote that the theory of double-entry bookkeeping 'is in fact like Euclid's theory of ratios an absolutely perfect one, and it is only its extreme simplicity which prevents it from being as interesting as it could otherwise be.'[31]

Chambers had suggested presciently in 'Poverty' that a GFC-type crisis was possible without a major reform of accounting. Given the post-GFC response by albeit well-intentioned accounting profession committees—with more tinkering and boondoggling—it is likely that Chambers would hold a similar view today. Namely, no matter what approach is adopted, if those seeking effective change to the present instrumentation system are unsuccessful, then the existing misinformed, rudderless commercial system may again produce a financial meltdown.

Chambers' search for order in commerce, through an improved financial reporting mechanism that reports systematically *all* price changes and addresses the 'riddle of the money illusion,' remains an imperative for educators, practitioners, and regulators.

Notes

1. Chambers to Eddie Stamp, P202, #5395, 25/08/1978 and Chambers to Russell Mathews, P202, #6555, 07/02/1983.
2. Chambers to Stamp, P202, #8062, 01/07/1977.
3. Chambers to Moonitz, dated 3 February 1993, unnumbered in P202; and Chambers to Sterling, P202, #7662, 12/03/1990 and #7668, 18/03/1991.
4. Discussion of the University of Waikato inflation accounting research project appears in Clarke *et al.* (2012, 27). For resource details see http://trove.nia.gov.au/people/1271221?c=people.
5. Sid Gray to Chambers, P202, #7377, 20/01/1992.
6. Chambers to Peter Standish, P202, #6569, June 1984.
7. Chambers (1991b, 19).

8. Chambers (1991b, 10).
9. Clarke, Dean and Oliver (1997, especially chapter 18).
10. Chambers (1994, 77).
11. Moonitz's response to Chambers' proposals in *Towards a General Theory . . .*, P202, #7703, 06/09/1961. Chambers response (see extract in text)—P202, #7704, 12/09/1961. Interestingly, in para 119 of *Towards* Chambers also observes the importance of modern accounting: 'Goethe had one of his characters describe double entry as one of the finest inventions of the human mind, because it enables one to see clearly the whole without becoming confused with details.' He would return to this point in Chambers (1983); as we do in the chapter 9 'Peroration.'
12. Chambers' *Auto-Bibliography* (1977a, 14). See also endnote #14, Prologue and related text, as well as chapter 5.
13. Chambers to Briloff, P202, #7682, 17/02/1983.
14. Chambers to Baxt, P202, #6579, June 1984.
15. Editors' Note in Chambers (2000a, 313).
16. Chambers (1974d, Introduction to the Scholars Book release of *A,E&EB*) and related matters discussed in chapters 6 and 8.
17. A loose page found in the *MAT* folder contains draft text discussing Chambers' understanding of what is meant by the word 'thought': 'For three reasons the present work deals with "modern accounting thought." That "the wish is father to the thought" is not only characteristic of Henry IV. It is common to many who have sought to improve, to simplify, to explain, to demonstrate, to win an argument, to preserve the status quo, and so on. The potentially mixed parentage and lineage of thoughts is seldom realized. However, there appears to be ample evidence of it in the period denoted by "modern" and in that part of the thought that is "accounting thought." '
18. Dyckman and Zeff (2014), and endnotes #s10, chapter 2, 51, chapter 3, 43, chapter 5.
19. An excellent example is 2 June 1973 address to ICAA (N.S.W. branch twentieth annual congress), 'What should tomorrow's accountants be taught' (Chambers, 1973d). The address is summarized in an article in the *AFR*, which is available also at P202, #9159, 04/06/1973.
20. Chambers to Briloff, #5788, 22/03/1979.
21. Chambers' 1952 Senior Lectureship application, P202, #10770, 22/07/1952. Extracts in Clarke *et al.* (2012, 83–6 and Appendix II). He was appointed in 1953.
22. Clarke, Dean and Edwards (2010).
23. Chambers to Sterling, P202, #7662, 12/03/1990.
24. Chambers' post-retirement reflections in a letter to Briloff, P202, #7682, 17/02/1983.
25. Chambers (1999, 242).
26. Chambers' response to Bob Baxt's address, at a 27 July 1991 Sydney University Dinner, P202, #7336, 27/07/1991.
27. Clarke, Dean and Wolnizer (2005) is a rejoinder to special issue commentaries on Chambers' 'Poverty of Accounting Discourse' by Amernic (2005), Lee (2005), Mattessich (2005) and Tinker (2005).
28. Comments provided by Whittington in an email to the authors.
29. Bedford (1982, 117).
30. Chambers to Sterling, P202, #742, 23/11/1993.
31. Cayley (1894, Preface).

Bibliography

Accounting Standards Committee, 1976, ED18, *Current Cost Accounting*, London: Accounting Standards Committee.

————, 1980, Statement of Standard Accounting Practice No. 16, *Current Cost Accounting*, London: Accounting Standards Committee.

Accounting Standards Review Committee (ASRC; Chairman R.J. Chambers), 1978, *Company Accounting Standards*, Sydney: NS.W. Government Printer.

Accounting Standards Steering Committee (ASSC), 1973, ED8, *Accounting for Changes in the Purchasing Power of Money*, London: ASSC.

————, 1974, Provisional Statement of Standard Accounting Practice No. 7 (PSSAP7), *Accounting for Changes in the Purchasing Power of Money*, London: ASSC.

Al-Hogail, A.A., and Previts, G.J., 2003, 'Raymond John Chambers' Contribution to the Development of Accounting Thought,' *The Accounting Historians Journal*, 28:2, 1–30.

American Accounting Association (AAA), 1936, A Tentative Statement of Accounting Principles Underlying Corporate Financial Statements, reproduced in AAA, 1957, 59–64.

————, 1941, A Tentative Statement of Accounting Principles Underlying Corporate Financial Statements, reproduced in AAA, 1957, 51–68.

————, 1948, Accounting Concepts and Standards Underlying Corporate Financial Statements: Revision and Supplementary Statements Nos 1–8, reproduced in AAA, 1957, 13–50.

————, 1951, Supplementary Statement No. 2, *Price Level Changes and Financial Statements*, Wisconsin: American Accounting Association.

————, 1953, Supplementary Statement No. 6, *Inventory Pricing and Changes in Price Level*, Wisconsin: American Accounting Association.

————, 1957, *Accounting and Reporting Standards for Corporate Financial Statements and Preceding Statements and Supplements*, Wisconsin: American Accounting Association.

————, 1966, *A Statement of Basic Accounting Theory*, Wisconsin: American Accounting Association.

————, 1977, *Statement on Accounting Theory and Theory Acceptance*, Sarasota, FL: American Accounting Association.

American Institute of Accountants (AIA), Accounting Research Bulletin 33, 1947, *Depreciation and High Costs*, December, New York: AIA.

——, Study Group on Business Income, 1950, *Five Monographs on Business Income*, New York: AIA.
American Institute of Certified Public Accountants (AICPA), Committee on Accounting Procedure, 1957, *Accounting Terminology Bulletin No. 4*, New York: AICPA.
——, 1959, ARB 51, *Consolidated Financial Statements*, New York: AICPA.
——, Accounting Principles Board (APB), APB3, 1969, *Financial Statements Restated for General Price-Level Changes*, New York: AICPA.
——, 1972, Establishing Financial Accounting Standards (The Wheat Report), *Report of the Study on Establishment of Accounting Principles*, New York: AICPA.
Amernic, J., 2005, 'A Legacy for Accounting Education: A Commentary on Professor Chambers' 1999 Paper "The Poverty of Accounting Discourse,"' *Accounting Education*, 14:1, 19–24.
Angly, E., 1931, *Oh Yeah?*, New York: Viking Press.
Arthur, H.B., 1938, 'Inventory Profits in the Business Cycle,' *The American Economic Review*, 28:March, 27–40.
ASRB, 1985, Release 100, *Criteria for the Evaluation of Accounting Standards*, reproduced in *Accounting Handbook*, 1999, Sydney: John Wiley & Sons.
Australian Accounting Research Foundation (AARF), Australian Accounting Standards Committee, 1974, Preliminary Exposure Draft, *A Method of Accounting for Changes in the Purchasing Power of Money*, December, Melbourne: AARF.
——, 1975, Preliminary Exposure Draft, *A Method of Current Cost Accounting*, June, Melbourne: AARF.
——, Current Cost Accounting Committee, 1978, Exposure Draft, *The Recognition of Gains and Losses on Holding Monetary Items in the Context of Current Cost Accounting*, July, Melbourne: AARF.
——, 1979, Revised Exposure Draft, *The Recognition of Gains and Losses on Holding Monetary Items in the Context of Current Cost Accounting*, August, Melbourne: AARF.
Ball, R., and Brown, 1968, 'An Empirical Evaluation of Accounting Income Numbers,' *Journal of Accounting Research*, 6:2, 159–78.
Barton, A., 2000, 'Reflections of an Australian Contemporary: The Complementarity of Entry and Exit Price Current Value Accounting Systems,' *Abacus*, 36:3, 298–312.
Baxter, W.T., 1966, 'Accounting Values: Sales Price Versus Replacement Cost,' *Journal of Accounting Research*, 4:2, 208–14.
Beaver, W.H., 1968, 'The Information Content of Annual Earnings Announcements,' *Journal of Accounting Research*, 6:(Supplement), 67–92.
Bedford, N., 1982, 'The Impact of Chambers on the Scope of Accounting: Extension and Analysis,' *Abacus*, 18:2, 112–8.
Benston, G.J., 1967, 'Book Review [A,E&EB],' *American Economic Review*, 63:March, 297–9.
Birkett, W.P., and Walker, R.G., 1971, 'Response of the Australian Accounting Profession to Company Failures in the 1960s,' *Abacus*, 7:1, 97–136.
Birkett, W.P., and Walker, R.G., 1974, 'Accounting: A Source of Market Imperfection,' *Journal of Business Finance and Accounting*, 1:2, 171–193.
Bloom, M., 2008, *Double Accounting for Goodwill: A Problem Revisited*, London: Routledge.

Boer, G., 1966, 'Replacement Cost: A Historical Look,' *The Accounting Review*, 41:1, 92–7.

Brief, R.P., 1966, 'The Origin and Evolution of Nineteenth-Century Asset Accounting,' *Business History Review*, 40:1, 1–23.

Briloff, A.J., 1958, 'Price Level Changes and Financial Statements: A Critical Appraisal,' *The Accounting Review*, 33:3, 380–8.

————, 1972, *Unaccountable Accounting*, New York: Harper & Row.

————, 1976, *More Debits Than Credits: The Burnt Investor's Guide to Financial Statements*, New York: Harper & Row.

————, 1982, *Truth About Accounting*, New York: Harper & Row.

Brown, H., 1986, *The Wisdom of Science: Its Relevance to Culture and Religion*, Cambridge: CUP.

Brown, L.D., 1996, 'Influential Accounting Articles, Individuals, Ph.D. Granting Institutions and Faculties: A Citational Analysis,' *Accounting, Organizations and Society*, 21:7–8, 723–54.

Brown, R.S., 1962, 'Accountancy Teaching in the University of Sydney,' *AAUTA News Bulletin*, 2:2, 19–23.

————, 1982, 'Raymond John Chambers: A Biography,' *Abacus*, 18:2, 99–105.

Burgert, R., 1972, 'Reservations About "Replacement Value" Accounting in the Netherlands,' *Abacus*, 8:2, 111–26.

Butlin, N., 1978, 'Fraternal Farewell: Tribute to S J Butlin,' *Australian Economic History Review*, 18:September, 99–118.

Byatt, I. (Chairman), 1986, *Accounting for Economic Costs and Changing Prices*, Report of His Majesty's Treasury working group, London: HMSO.

Byrne, P., 2009, *Mad World: Evelyn Waugh and the Secrets of Brideshead*, London: Harper Press.

Cadbury, Adrian (Chairman), 1992, *Financial Aspects of Corporate Governance*, London: Gee & Co.

CAMAC (Corporate and Markets Advisory Committee), 2000, *Corporate Groups Final Report*, available at www.camac.gov.au/camac/camac.nsf/0/3DD84175EFB AD69CCA256B6C007FD4E8?opendocument, accessed 27 November 2012.

Canadian Institute of Chartered Accountants (CICA), (1976), *Discussion Paper: Current Value Accounting*, August, Toronto: CICA.

Canning, J.B., 1929, *The Economics of Accountancy: A Critical Analysis of Accounting Theory*, New York: The Ronald Press Company.

Carnegie, G.D., and Napier, C.J., 1996, 'Critical and Interpretive Histories: Insights into Accounting's Present and Future Through its Past,' *Accounting, Auditing and Accountability Journal*, 9:3, 7–39.

Carnegie, G.D., and Williams, B.G., 2001, 'The First Professors of Accounting in Australia,' *Accounting History NS*, 6:1, 103–15.

Cayley, A., 1894, *The Principles of Bookkeeping by Double Entry*, Cambridge: CUP.

Chambers, R.J., 1947, *Financial Management*, Sydney: Law Book Company.

————, 1948a, 'Business Finance and the Analysis of Financial Statements,' *The Australian Accountant*, 18:8, 253–65.

————, 1948b, 'The Training of Accountants,' *The Australian Accountant*, 18:9, 321–8.

————, 1948c, 'Accounting and Management,' *The Australian Accountant*, 18:12, 417–20.

———, 1949a, 'Accounting and Shifting Price Levels,' *The Australian Accountant*, 19:9, 313–20.

———, 1949b, 'The Spice of Accounting,' *The Australian Accountant*, 19:11, 398–401.

———, 1950a, 'Depreciation on Replacement Cost,' *The Australian Accountant*, 20:2, 68–70.

———, 1950b, 'The Relationship Between Accounting and Financial Management,' *The Australian Accountant*, 20:9, 333–58.

———, 1952a, 'Accounting and Inflation,' *The Australian Accountant*, 22:2, 14–23.

———, 1952b, 'Accounting and Business Finance,' *The Australian Accountant*, 22:7, 213–30.

———, 1952c, 'Effects of Inflation on Financial Strategy,' *The Australian Accountant*, 22:9, 304–11.

———, 1955a, 'Blueprint for a Theory of Accounting,' *Accounting Research*, 6:1, 17–25.

———, 1955b, 'A Scientific Pattern of Accounting Theory,' *The Australian Accountant*, 25:2, 73–80.

———, 1955c, *Company Annual Reports: Function and Design*, Sydney: Law Book Company.

———, 1956, 'Educational Policy: A Suggestion,' *The Australian Accountant*, 26:2, 73–80.

———, 1957a, *Accounting and Action*, Sydney: Law Book Company.

———, 1957b, 'Detail for a Blueprint,' *The Accounting Review*, 32:2, 206–15.

———, 1958, 'Asset Revaluations and Stock Dividends,' *The Journal of Accountancy*, 106:2, 55–68.

———, 1960a, 'Measurement and Misrepresentation,' *Management Science*, 1:1, 141–8.

———, 1960b, 'The Conditions of Research in Accounting,' *The Journal of Accountancy*, 110:6, 33–9.

Chambers, R.J., 1961, 'Towards a General Theory of Accounting,' ASA Annual Research Lecture, University of Adelaide, 2 August, published as a booklet, 30 June, 48 pp.

———, 1962a, 'The Resolution of Some Paradoxes in Accounting,' ASA Annual Research Lecture, University of Tasmania, April 30. Published as Occasional Paper No. 2, Faculty of Commerce and Business Administration, University of British Columbia, 1963.

———, 1962b, 'Why Bother with Postulates,' *Journal of Accounting Research*, 1:4, 3–15.

———, 1963a, 'Measurement in Accounting,' 48 page mimeo for personal circulation; later revised and published as Chambers (1965c).

———, 1963b, 'Under the Law of the Jungle,' *Australian Financial Review*, 28 May, 2.

———, 1963c, 'Traps for the Unwary Investor: On Defects of the Law and Practice of Corporate Financial Reporting,' four-part series, *Australian Financial Review*, 4:9, 2 July, 11.

———, 1964a, 'Conventions, Doctrines and Common Sense,' *The Accountants Journal (N.Z.)*, 42:2, 182–7.

———, 1964b, 'Measurement and Objectivity in Accounting,' *The Accounting Review*, 39:2, 264–74.

————, 1964c, 'The Role of Information Systems in Decision Making,' *Management Technology*, 4:1, 15–25.

————, 1964d, 'Company Losses—Safeguarding the Investor,' *Current Affairs Bulletin*, 34:11, 162–70.

————, 1965a, 'Financial Information and the Securities Market,' *Abacus*, 1:1, 3–30.

————, 1965b, 'Professional Education,' based on an address, 'Professional Education and the Vatter Report,' presented at the Australasian Association of University Teachers of Accounting conference, May 1965, 31–49 in Chambers and Dean, *Chambers on Accounting*, 2, 1986.

————, 1965c, 'Measurement in Accounting,' *Journal of Accounting Research*, 3:1, 32–62.

————, 1965d, 'The Price Level Problem and Some Intellectual Grooves,' *Journal of Accounting Research*, 3:2, 242–52.

————, 1966, *Accounting, Evaluation and Economic Behavior*, Englewood Cliffs, NJ: Prentice Hall.

————, 1967a, 'Continuously Contemporary Accounting—Additivity and Action,' *The Accounting Review*, 42:3, 751–7.

————, 1967b, 'A Study of a Price Level Study,' *Abacus*, 3:2, 97–118.

————, 1968a, 'Consolidated Statements Are Not Really Necessary,' *The Australian Accountant*, 38:2, 89–92.

————, 1968b, 'Measure and Values—a Reply to Professor Staubus,' *The Accounting Review*, 43:2, 239–47.

————, 1969, 'The Canons of Criticism,' personal communication on a critique by Richard Leftwich (1969), first published in Chambers and Dean (1986e).

————, 1970a, 'Second Thoughts on Continuously Contemporary Accounting,' *Abacus*, 6:1, 39–55.

————, 1970b, 'Methods of Accounting—A Series,' *The Accountant*, 26 February, 299–303; 5 March, 341–5; 19 March, 408–13; 2 April, 483–6; 16 April, 551–5; 30 April, 643–7.

————, 1971a, 'Review Article—Income and Capital—Fisher's Legacy (on Irving Fisher, *The Nature of Capital and Income*, 1906),' *Journal of Accounting Research*, Spring, 9:1, 137–49.

————, 1971b, Submission Pamphlet, 'Accounting, Evaluation and Economic Behavior Explanatory Note,' prepared for examination of award by publications of a DSC(Econ) at the University of Sydney, November.

————, 1971c, 'Asset Measurement and Valuation,' *Cost and Management*, 45, March–April, 30–5.

————, 1971d, 'Measurement and Valuation Again,' *Cost and Management*, 45, July–August, 12–17.

————, 1972, 'The Anguish of Accountants,' *The Journal of Accountancy*, 122: March, 68–74; reprinted in *The Australian Accountant*, 42:2, 154–61.

————, 1973a, *Securities and Obscurities: A Case for Reform of the Law of Company Accounts*, Melbourne: Gower Press.

————, 1973b, 'Observation as a Method of Inquiry,' *Abacus*, 9:1, 156–75.

————, 1973c, 'Mining, Taxing and Accounting,' paper presented ASA Queensland State Convention, Mount Isa, 9 June.

——, 1973d, 'What Should Tomorrow's Accountants Be Taught,' address to the Institute of Chartered Accountants in Australia (N.S.W. branch), Surfers Paradise, 2 June.

——, 1974a, 'Stock Market Prices and Accounting Research,' *Abacus*, 10:1, 39–54.

——, 1974b, 'Third Thoughts,' *Abacus*, 10:2, 129–37.

——, 1974c, 'Trial and Error,' *Journal of Accounting Research*, 12:2, 341–7.

——, 1974d, 'The Development of the Theory,' Preface (v–xxvii) to the Scholars Book Co.; reprint of *Accounting, Evaluation and Economic Behavior*, Houston, TX: Scholars Book Co.

——, 1975a, Exposure Draft, *Accounting for Inflation*, September, Sydney: University of Sydney.

——, 1975b, *Accounting for Inflation: Methods and Problems*, Sydney: University of Sydney.

——, 1975c, 'Inflation Accounting and the Electricity Supply Industry,' paper presented at the Electricity Supply Association of Australia Conference, Hobart, 6–7 May.

——, 1975d, 'Accounting, Measurement and Mathematics,' unpublished proposed Festschrift article in honour of Ernest Weinwurm; located in Chambers Archive, USA P202, unnumbered.

——, 1976a, 'Current Cost Accounting—a Critique of the Sandilands Report,' ICRA Occasional Paper No. 11, International Centre for Research in Accounting, University of Lancaster, England.

——, 1976b, 'The Possibility of a Normative Accounting Standard,' *The Accounting Review*, Correspondence, 51:3, 646–52.

——, 1976c, 'The Functions of Published Financial Statements,' *Accounting and Business Research*, 6:22, 83–94.

——, 1976d, 'Continuously Contemporary Accounting: Misunderstandings and Misrepresentations,' *Abacus*, 12:2, 137–51.

——, 1977a, *An Auto-Bibliography*, ICRA Occasional Paper 15, International Centre for Research in Accounting, Lancaster University.

——, 1977b, 'The Integration of Managerial and Financial Accounting,' Shaoib Memorial Lecture, Institute of Cost and Management Accountants of Pakistan, Karachi, October, 26 pp.

——, 1977c, 'The Delusions of Replacement Cost Accounting,' *Financial Analysts Journal*, 33:4, 48–52.

——, 1977d, 'Submission on Exposure Draft 18 to the Inflation Accounting Steering Group,' Private submission to the U.K. Morpeth Committee, May.

——, 1978, 'The Use and Abuse of a Notation; A History of an Idea,' *Abacus*, 14:2, 122–44.

——, 1979a, 'Canning's *The Economics of Accountancy*—After 50 Years,' *The Accounting Review*, 54:3, 764–75.

——, 1979b, 'Usefulness—The Vanishing Premise in Accounting Standard Setting,' *Abacus*, 15:2, 71–92.

——, 1980a, 'The Myths and the Science of Accounting,' *Accounting, Organizations and Society*, 5:1, 167–80.

——, 1980b, *Price Variation and Inflation Accounting*, Sydney: McGraw-Hill.

——, 1980c, *The Design of Accounting Standards*, Sydney: University of Sydney.

——, 1981, 'The Search for System in Financial Calculation,' *Abacus*, 17:1, 78–82.

——, 1982, *The Design of Accounting Standards*, Monograph No. 1, Sydney: University of Sydney.

——, 1983, 'Accounting—"One of the Finest Inventions of the Human Spirit,"' Deloitte Haskins & Sells Distinguished Lecture in the University of Edinburgh, 451–72 in Chambers and Dean, 1986e.

——, 1989a, 'Time in Accounting,' *Abacus*, 25:1, 7–21.

——, 1989b, *Interview* by Linda Enlish, editor, *Australian Accounting Review*, December, 12–15.

——, 1991a, 'An Academic Apprenticeship,' *Accounting History*, 3:1, 91–111.

——, 1991b, 'The Ethical Cringe,' *Australian Journal of Corporate Law*, 1:1, 9–21; revision of same title published in *The Australian Accountant*, 61:July, 18–24.

——, 1991c, *Foundations of Accounting*, Geelong: Deakin University Press.

——, 1991d, 'Carpe Diem!' in Chambers R.J., and Dean, G.W. (Eds.), *Chambers on Accounting: Logic, Law, and Ethics*, New York and London: Routledge, 6, 144–6.

——, 1991e, 'Metrical and Empirical Laws in Accounting,' *Accounting Horizons*, 5:10, 1–15.

——, 1992, 'Poverty in Accounting Discourse,' *Abacus*, 28:2, 241–51; initially a Syme-Monash discussion paper same title, 2/1992. Republished *Accounting Education*, 1:1, March 2005, 1–16.

——, 1993, 'Positive Accounting Theory and the PA Cult,' *Abacus*, 29:1, 1–26.

——, 1994, 'Historical Cost—Tale of a False Creed,' *Accounting Horizons*, 8:1, 76–89.

——, 1995a, *An Accounting Thesaurus: 500 Years of Accounting*, Oxford: Pergamon.

——, 1995b, 'In Quest of a Framework,' *Asia—Pacific Journal of Accounting*, 1:1, December, 2–12.

——, 1996, 'Ends, Ways, Means and Conceptual Frameworks,' *Abacus*, 32:2, 119–32.

——, 2000a, 'Early Beginnings: Introduction to *Wisdom of Accounting*,' *Abacus*, 36:3, 313–20.

——, 2000b, 'Life on the Fringe—an Accounting Odyssey,' *Abacus*, 36:3, 321–6.

——, 2000c, 'Carpe Diem!' University of Sydney Dinner Address, Great Hall, 27 July 1991; reproduced in Chambers and Dean (2000a).

——, 2000d, 'Novocastrian Graduation,' Occasional address on admission to the degree of Doctor of Science *honoris causa*, at the University of Newcastle, 11 May 1990 in Chambers R.J., and Dean, G.W. (Eds.), *Chambers on Accounting: Logic, Law, and Ethics*, New York and London: Routledge, 6, 102–4.

Chambers, R.J., 2000e, 'Aide-Memoire,' *Abacus*, 36:3, 334–86.

Chambers, R.J., and Clarke, F.L., 1987, *Varieties and Uses of Financial Information*, Monograph No. 6, Sydney: University of Sydney.

Chambers, R.J., and Dean, G.W. (Eds.), 1986a, *Chambers on Accounting, Volume 1: Accounting, Management and Finance*, New York and London: Garland Publishing.

——, 1986b, *Chambers on Accounting, Volume 2: Accounting Practice and Education*, New York and London: Garland Publishing.

————, 1986c, *Chambers on Accounting, Volume 3: Continuously Contemporary Accounting*, New York and London: Garland Publishing.

————, 1986d, *Chambers on Accounting, Volume 4: Price Variation Accounting*, New York and London: Garland Publishing.

————, 1986e, *Chambers on Accounting, Volume 5: Continuously Contemporary Accounting 1986*; New York and London: Garland Publishing.

————, 2000, *Chambers on Accounting, Volume 6: Logic, Law and Ethics*, New York and London: Garland Publishing.

Chambers, R.J., and Falk, H., 1985, *The Serviceability of Financial Information: A Survey*, Vancouver: The Canadian Certified and General Accountants Research Foundation.

Chambers, R.J., Hopwood, W.S., and McKeown, J.C., 1984, 'The Relevance of Varieties of Accounting Information: A U.S.A. Survey,' *Abacus*, 20:2, 99–110.

Chambers, R.J., Ma, R., Hopkins, R., and Kasiraja, N., 1987, *Financial Information and Decision Making: A Singapore Survey*, SIM Research Monograph No. 2, Singapore: The Singapore Institute of Management.

Chambers, R.J., and Maguire, W.A.A., 1982, 'Responses to Financial Information: A South African Study,' *The South African Chartered Accountant*, December, 494–6.

————, 1983, 'Responses to Financial Information: A South African Study,' '*The South African Chartered Accountant*,' January, 2–5.

Chambers, R.J., and Wolnizer, P.W., 1990, 'A True and Fair View of Financial Position,' *Company and Securities Law Journal*, 8:December, 353–68.

————, 1991, 'A True and Fair View of Position and Results: The Historical Background,' *Accounting, Business and Financial History*, 1:2, 197–215.

Churchman, C.W., 1961, *Prediction and Optimal Decision: Philosophical Issues of a Science of Values*, Englewood Cliffs, NJ: Prentice Hall.

Clarke, F.L., 1976, 'A Closer Look at Sweeney's *Stabilized Accounting* Proposals,' *Accounting and Business Research*, 6:2, 264–75.

————, 1977, 'CCA—Progress or Regress?' reproduced in Dean and Wells, 1977.

————, 1980, 'Inflation Accounting and Accidents of History,' *Abacus*, 16:2, 79–99.

————, 1982, *The Tangled Web of Price Variation Accounting*, New York and London: Garland Publishing. This was reprinted in 2006 as part of the Sydney University Press Sydney Accounting Classics series.

————, 1996, 'A Treasury of Accounting Thought: R.J. Chambers, *An Accounting Thesaurus: 500 Years of Accounting*,' *Abacus*, 32:1, 111–7.

————, 2006, 'Introduction: True and Fair View—Anachronism or Quality Control par Excellence?' *Abacus*, 42:2, 129–31.

Clarke, F.L., and Dean, G.W., 1980, 'Schmidt's *Betriebswirtschaft* Theory,' *Abacus*, 22:2, 65–102.

————, 1989a, 'A Note: Graves, Sweeney and *Goldmarkbilanz*—Whither Sweeney and Schmidt's *Tageswertbilanz?*,' *The Accounting Historians Journal*, 16:1, 101–9.

————, 1989b, 'Conjectures on the Influence of 1920s German *Betriebswirtschaftslehre* on Sweeney's Stabilized Accounting,' *Accounting and Business Research*, 19, Autumn, 1–14.

————, 1990, *Contributions of Limperg and Schmidt to the Replacement Cost Debate in the 1920s*, New York: Garland Publishing.

————, 1993, 'Law and Accounting: The Separate Legal Entity Principle and Consolidation Accounting,' *Australian Business Law Review*, 21:4, 246–69.

———, 2007, *Indecent Disclosure: Gilding the Corporate Lily*, Melbourne: Cambridge University Press.

Clarke, F.L., Dean, G.W., and Edwards, J.R., 2013, 'Chambers and Others on Communication,' in Jack, L., Davison, J., and Craig, R. (Eds.), *Routledge Companion on Communication*, 2013, 26–41.

Clarke, F.L., Dean, G.W., and Egan, M., 2014, *The Unaccountable & Ungovernable Corporation: Companies' Use-by-Dates Close In*, London and New York: Routledge.

Clarke, F.L., Dean, G.W., and Graves, O.F., 1989, *Schmalenbach's Dynamic Accounting and Price-Level Adjustments*, New York: Garland Publishing.

———, 1990, *Replacement Costs and Accounting Reform in Post World War 1 Germany*, New York: Garland Publishing.

Clarke, F.L., Dean, G.W., and Houghton, E., 2002, 'Revitalizing Group Accounting: Improving Accountability,' *Australian Accounting Review*, 12:3, 58–72.

Clarke, F.L., Dean, G.W., and Oliver, K.G., 1997, *Corporate Collapse: Regulatory, Accounting and Ethical Failure*, Cambridge: Cambridge University Press.

———, 2003, *Corporate Collapse: Accounting, Regulatory and Ethical Failure*, 2nd rev. ed., Cambridge: Cambridge University Press.

Clarke, F.L., Dean, G.W., and Wells, M., 2010, *The Sydney School of Accounting: The Chambers Years*, Sydney: Sydney University Press; rev. ed., 2012.

Clarke, F.L., Dean, G.W., and Wolnizer, P.W., 2005, 'More Questions than Answers: A Rejoinder to the Commentaries on Professor Chambers' 1999 paper "The Poverty of Accounting Discourse,"' *Accounting Education*, 14:1, 39–51.

Clarke, F.L., Dean, G.W., and Edwards, P., 2010, *Submission on Accounting Threshold Learning Outcomes*, available University of Sydney Business School website: http://sydney.edu.au/business/data/assets/pdf_file/0004/77908/. Submission_on_ Accounting_Threshold_Learning_Outcomes.pdf, accessed 29 May 2016.

Clikeman, P.M., 2013, *Called to Account: Financial Frauds that Shaped the Accounting Profession*, 2nd ed., London and New York: Routledge.

Cobbin, P., Dean, G., Esselmont, C., Ferguson, P., Keneley, M., Potter, B., and West, B., 2013, 'The Accessibility of Accounting and Business Archives: The Role of Technology in Informing Research in Accounting and Business,' *Abacus*, 49:3, 396–422.

Committee of Inquiry into Inflation and Taxation (Russell Mathews Chairman), 1975, *Report: Inflation and Taxation*, Canberra: Australian Government Printer.

Consultative Committee of Accounting Bodies (U.K.), 1975, *Initial Reactions to the Report of the Inflation Accounting Committee*, November, London: CCAB.

Cooper, W., and Zeff, S.A., 1987, 'Kinney's Design for Accounting Research,' paper presented at the ARIA meeting, prior to August 1987, AAA Congress; eventually published with same title in the 'Critical Commentaries' section, *Critical Perspectives on Accounting*, March 1992, 87–92.

Cooperrider, D.L., Whitney, D., and Stavros, J., 2008, *The Appreciative Inquiry Handbook: For Leaders of Change*, Oakland, CA: Berret-Koehler Publishers.

Copland, D., 1957, 'The Australian Administrative Staff College,' *Australian Journal of Public Administration*, 16:2, 105–8.

Cork, Sir Kenneth (Chairman of the Cork Report), 1982, *Insolvency Law and Practice*, London: HMSO.

Crosby, A.W., 1997, *The Measure of Reality: Quantification and Western Society, 1250–1600*, Cambridge: Cambridge University Press.

CSR, 1950, *Capital Erosion and the Income Tax Assessment Act*, Colonial Sugar Refinery (CSR private publication), Sydney: CSR.

Dean, G.W., 2005, 'Editorial: "True and Fair" and "Fair Value"—Accounting and Legal Will-o'-the-Wisps,' *Abacus*, 41:2, i–vi.

———, 2008, 'Editorial, "Revisiting Chambers and Briloff on Accounting— Correspondence 1964–1993,"' *Abacus*, 44:1, i–v.

Dean, G.W., and Clarke, F.L., 2003a, 'An Evolving Conceptual Framework,' *Abacus*, 39:3, 279–97.

———, 2003b, 'Editorial,' *Abacus*, 39:1, i—v.

———, 2010a, 'Ray Chambers and Ernest Weinwurm—Scholars in Unison on Measurement in Accounting,' *The Accounting Historians Journal*, 37:2, 1–37.

———, 2010b, 'Commentary: Business Black Swans and the Use and Abuse of a Notion,' *Australian Accounting Review*, 20:2, 185–94.

———, 2010c, 'Unresolved Methodological Questions at the Cross-Section of Accounting and Finance,' *International Review of Business Research Papers*, 6:5, 20–32.

Dean, G.W., Clarke, F.L., and Capalbo, F., 2016, 'Pacioli's Double Entry—Part of an Intellectual and Social Movement,' *Accounting History Review*, 26:1, 5–24.

Dean, G.W., Clarke, F.L., and Wolnizer, P.W., 2006, 'The R.J. Chambers Collection: An Archivist's Revelations of 20th Century Accounting Thought and Practice,' *Accounting Historians Journal*, 33:2, 145–66.

Dean, G.W., Luckett, P., and Houghton, E., 1993, 'Notional Calculations in Liquidations Revisited: The Case of ASC Class Order Cross Guarantees,' *Company and Securities Law Journal*, 11:4, 204–26.

Dean, G.W., Persson, M., and Clarke, F.L., 2018, 'Note on the 'Antecedents of the IAAER—1966–1984,' *Working paper*.

Dean, G.W., and Wells, M.C., 1977, *Current Cost Accounting: Identifying the Issues*, Sydney: ICRA and Sydney University.

Demski, J., 1973, 'The General Impossibility of Normative Accounting Standards,' *The Accounting Review*, 48:4, 718–23.

Dyckman, T.R., and Zeff, S.A., 2014, 'Some Methodological Deficiencies in Empirical Research Articles in Accounting,' *Accounting Horizons*, 28:3, 695–712.

Edwards, E.O., 1954, 'Depreciation Policy Under Changing Price Levels,' *The Accounting Review*, 29:2, 267–80.

Edwards, E.O., and Bell, P.W., 1961, *The Theory and Measurement of Business Income*, Berkeley: University of California Press.

Edwards, J.D., 1960, *History of Public Accounting in the United States*, East Lansing, MI: Michigan State University.

Edwards, J.R., 1985, 'The Origins and Evolution of the Double Account System: An Example of Accounting Innovation,' *Abacus*, 21:1, 19–43.

Edwards, J.R., (Ed.), 1994, *Twentieth-Century Accounting Thinkers*, London and New York: Routledge.

Edwards, J.R., 2016, 'Asset Valuation, Profit Measurement and Path Dependence in Britain to 1800,' *British Accounting Review*, 48:1, 87–101.

Edwards, J.R., Dean, G.W., and Clarke, F.L., 2009, 'Merchants' Accounts, Performance Assessment and Decision Making in Mercantilist Britain,' *Accounting, Organizations and Society*, 34:4, 551–70.

Edwards, J.R., Dean, G.W., Clarke, F.L., and Wolnizer, P.W., 2013, 'Accounting Academic Elites: The Tale of ARIA,' *Accounting, Organizations and Society*, 38:5, 365–81.

Ern Malley (Ray Chambers' pseudonym), 1979a, 'Mind Your O.C.,' *Australian Accountant*, June, 310.

FASB, Financial Accounting Standards 33, 1979, *Financial Reporting and Changing Prices*, September, Stamford, CT: FASB.

Ferguson, C., 2012, *Inside Job: The Financiers Who Pulled off the Heist of the Century*, Oxford: One World.

Financial Accounting Standards Board (FASB), 1974, Exposure Draft, *Financial Reporting in Units of General Purchasing Power*, December, Stamford, CT: FASB.

Financial Stability Board (FSB), 2012, *Global Shadow Banking Monitoring Report 2012*, Financial Stability Board, 18 November.

Fisher, I., 1906, *The Nature of Capital and Income*, New York: The Macmillan Company.

Funnell, W., 1998, 'The Narrative and its Place in the New Accounting History: The Rise of the Counternarrative,' *Accounting, Auditing and Accountability Journal*, 1:2, 142–62.

Gaffikin, M.J.R. (Ed.), 1984, *Contemporary Accounting Thought: Essays in Honour of Raymond John Chambers*, Sydney: Prentice Hall Australia.

———, 1986, *Accounting Methodology and the Works of R.J. Chambers: A Critical Analysis of the Development of the Theory of Continuously Contemporary Accounting*, PhD thesis, University of Sydney.

———, 1987, 'Methodology of Early Accounting Theorists,' *Abacus*, 23:1, 17–30.

———, 1988, *Accounting Methodology and the Works of R.J. Chambers: A Critical Analysis of the Development of the Theory of Continuously Contemporary Accounting*, New York and London: Garland Publishing.

———, 2000, 'Chambers on Methods of Inquiry,' *Abacus*, 36:3, 285–97.

———, 2012, 'Raymond J. Chambers—a Personal Reflection,' *Accounting Education*, 21:1, 25–39.

Gaffikin, M.J.R., and Aitken, M., 1982, *Development of Accounting Thought*, New York and London: Garland Publishing.

Garner, P., 1954, *Evolution of Cost Accounting to 1925*, Tuscaloosa, AL: University of Alabama Press.

General Council of the Australian Society of Accountants, 1966, *Accounting Principles and Practices Discussed in Reports on Company Failures*, Melbourne; ASA.

Gilman, S., 1939, *Accounting Concepts of Profit*, New York: Ronald Press.

Gleick, J., 2011, *The Information: A History, a Theory, a Flood*, London: Fourth Estate.

Graves, O.F., 1989, 'Walter Mahlberg's Valuation Theory: An Anomaly in the Development of Inflation Accounting,' *Abacus*, 25:1, 22–38.

Griffiths, Sir P., 1974, *Licence to Trade: A History of the English Chartered Companies*, London: Ernest Benn Limited.

Gynther, R., 1962, 'Accounting for Price Level Changes: One General Index or Several Specific Indexes,' *Accountancy*, 73:July, 560–7.

———, 1966, *Accounting for Price Level Changes—Theory and Procedures*, Brisbane: Pergamon Press.

Hadden, T., 1992, 'The Regulation of Corporate Groups in Australia,' *University of New South Wales Law Journal*, 15:1, 61–85.

Hansen, P., 1970, 'An Operational Cost Information Model,' *Abacus*, 6:2, 154–68.

Hatfield, H.R., 1909, *Modern Accounting: Its Principles and Some of its Problems*, New York: D. Appleton and Co.

———, 1944, 'Replacement and Book Value,' *The Accounting Review*, 19:1, 66–7.

Hempel, C.G., 1964, *Fundamentals of Concept Formation in Empirical Sciences*, 7th ed., 2, Chicago and London: University of Chicago Press.

Herman, D., Jahn, M., and Ryan, M., 2013, *Routledge Encyclopedia of Narrative Theory*, New York and London: Routledge.

Hitz, J.M., 2007, 'The Decision Usefulness of Fair Value Accounting—a Theoretical Perspective,' *European Accounting Review*, 16:2, 323–62.

Holtfrerich, C.L., 1986, *The German Inflation 1914–1923*, Berlin: De Gruyter.

Houghton, E., Dean, G., and Luckett, P., 1999, 'Insolvent Corporate Groups with Cross Guarantees: A Forensic-LP Case Study in Liquidation,' *Journal of the Operational Research Society*, 50:May, 480–96.

Institute of Chartered Accountants in England and Wales (ICAEW), 1949, Recommendation N12, 'Rising Price Levels in Relation to Accounts,' London: ICAEW.

———, 1952, Recommendation N15, 'Accounting in Relation to the Purchasing Power of Money,' May, London: ICAEW.

Institute of Chartered Accountants in England and Wales and National Institute of Economic and Social Research Joint Exploratory Committee, 1951, *Some Accounting Terms and Concepts*, London: ICAEW.

Institute of Cost and Works Accountants (ICWA), Research and Technical Committee, 1952, *The Accountancy of Changing Prices*, London: ICWA.

Iselin, E., 1968, 'Chambers on Accounting Theory,' *The Accounting Review*, 43:2, 231–8.

Jack, L., Davison, J., and Craig, R., 2013, *The Routledge Companion on Communication*, London and New York: Routledge.

Janis, Irving L., 1972, *Victims of Groupthink: A Psychological Study of Foreign Policy Decisions and Fiascos*, Boston: Houghton Mifflin.

Johnson, H.T., and Kaplan, R.S., 1987, *Relevance Lost: The Rise and Fall of Management Accounting*, Cambridge: Harvard Business School Press.

Jones, M. (Ed.), 2011, *Creative Accounting, Fraud and International Accounting Standards*, Chichester: John Wiley & Sons.

Jones, R.C, 1949, 'Effects of Inflation on Capital and Profits: The Record of Nine Steel Companies,' *Journal of Accountancy*, January, 9–27.

———, 1955, *Price Level Changes and Financial Statements: Case Studies of Four Companies*, Sarasota, FL: American Accounting Association.

———, 1956, *Effects of Price Level Changes on Business Income, Capital and Taxes*, Sarasota, FL: American Accounting Association.

Jowitt, W.A., Jowitt, E., and Walsh, C., 1977, *Jowitt's Dictionary of English Law* (1), London: Sweet & Maxwell.

Kay, J., 2016, *Other People's Money: Masters of the Universe or Servants of the People?*, London: Profile Books.

Kearney, C.M., 1942, 'Letter,' *The Journal of Accountancy*, 121:5, 460–1.

Keenan, M.G., 1998, 'A Defence of "Traditional" Accounting History Research Methodology,' *Critical Perspectives on Accounting*, 9:6, 641–66.

Kohler, M.F., and Matz, A. '1968, 'Swiss Financial Reporting and Auditing Practices,' *Abacus*, 4:1, 3–16.

Kripke, H., 1972, 'The SEC and the Accountants, Some Myths and Some Realities,' *New York University Law Review*, 45:6, 1151–205.

Küpper, H.-U., and Mattessich, R., 2005, 'Twentieth Century Accounting Research in the German Language Area,' *Accounting, Business and Financial History*, 15:3, 345–410.

L.O.M. Bard (Ray Chambers' pseudonym), 1979a, 'Sonnet on my Blindness,' *Australian Accountant*, April, 157.

———, 1979b, 'Away with Inflation Accounting,' *Australian Accountant*, April, 169.

———, 1979c, 'Oh, C(al)C(cutt)A! or CCA!,' *Australian Accountant*, April, 169.

Lacey, K., 1952, *Profit Measurement and Price Changes*, London: Pitman.

Larrabee, H.A, 1945, *Reliable Knowledge*, Boston: Houghton Mifflin.

Larson, K., and Shattke, R.W., 1966, 'Current Cash Equivalent, Additivity and Financial Action,' *The Accounting Review*, 41:3, 634–41.

Laux, C., and Leuz, C., 2009, 'The Crisis of Fair-Value Accounting: Making Sense of the Recent Debate,' *Accounting, Organizations and Society*, 34:6/7, 826–34.

———, 2010, 'Did Fair Value Contribute to the Crisis?,' *Journal of Economic Perspectives*, 24:1, 93–118.

Lawrence, M., and Stapledon, G.P., 2008, *Infrastructure Funds: Creative Use of Corporate Structure and Law—But in Whose Interests?*, University of Melbourne Legal Studies Research paper, 314, February.

Lee, T., 2005, 'A Legacy for Accounting Education: A Commentary on Professor Chambers' 1999 Paper "The Poverty of Accounting Discourse,"' *Accounting Education Research*, 14:1, 19–24.

Leftwich, R., 1969, 'A Critical Analysis of Some Behavioral Assumptions Underlying R.J. Chambers' *Accounting, Evaluation and Economic Behavior*,' University of Queensland Papers, Queensland: University of Queensland Press, 1:7, August.

Leibler, M., 2002, Submission 50 and supplementary submissions 62 and 73 to JCPAA Inquiry, *Review of Independent Auditing by Registered Company Auditors*, AGPS, Canberra, available at www.aph.gov.au/Parliamentary_Business/Committees/House_of_Representatives_Committees?url=jcpaa/indepaudit/subs.htm, accessed 28 November 2012.

Littleton, A.C., 1933, *Accounting Evolution to 1900*, New York: American Institute of Accountants.

MacNeal, Kenneth, 1939, *Truth in Accounting*, Pennsylvania: University of Pennsylvania Press.

Madan, D., 1982, 'Resurrecting the Discounted Cash Equivalent Flow,' *Abacus*, 18:1, 83–90.

Magnan, M., and Makarian, G., 2011, 'Accounting, Governance and the Crisis: Is Risk the Missing Link?,' *European Accounting Review*, 20:2, 215–31.

Mahlberg, W., 1921, *Bilanztechnik und Bewertung bei schwankender Waehrung* [Accounting Technique and Valuation During Periods of Currency Fluctuation], Berlin: G.A. Gloeckner.

Margenau, H., 1950, *The Nature of Physical Reality: A Philosophy of Modern Physics*, London: McGraw Hill.

Mason, P., 1956, *Price Level Changes and Financial Statements*, Wisconsin: American Accounting Association.

Mathews, R., 1960, 'Inflation and Company Finance,' *The Accounting Review*, 5:1, 8–18.

———, 1982, 'Chambers and the Development of Accounting Theory: A Personal Reminiscence,' *Abacus*, 18:2, 175–8.

Mathews, R., (Chairman), 1990, *Accounting in Higher Education: Report of the Review of the Accounting Discipline in Higher Education*, Canberra: Australian Government Printer.

Mathews, R., and Grant, J.M., 1958, *Inflation and Company Finance*, Sydney: Law Book Company.

Mattessich, R., 1956, 'The Constellation of Accounting and Economics,' *The Accounting Review*, 31:4, 551–64.

——, 1957, 'Toward a General and Axiomatic Foundation of Accounting, with an Introduction to the Matrix Formulation of Accounting Systems,' *Accounting Research*, 8:4, 328–55.

——, 1964, *Accounting and Analytical Methods*, Homewood, IL: Richard D. Irwin Inc.

——, 1970, 'On the Perennial Misunderstandings of Asset "Measurements" by Means of "Present Values,"' *Cost and Management*, 45:March–April, 30–5.

——, 1971a, 'On Further Misunderstandings about "Measurement" and Valuation: A Rejoinder to Chambers' Article,' *Cost and Management*, 45:March–April, 36–42.

——, 1971b, 'Asset Measurement and Valuation—a Final Reply to Chambers,' *Cost and Management*, 45:July–August, 18–23.

——, 1980, 'Personal Account,' *Accounting and Business Research*, 37A:1, 158–73.

——, 1995, *Foundational Research in Accounting: Professional Memoirs and Beyond*, Tokyo: Chuo University Press.

——, 2005, 'On the Poverty and Richness of Accounting: A Commentary on Professor Chambers' 1999 paper "The Poverty of Accounting Discourse"—Illusion Versus Reality,' *Accounting Education Research*, 14:1, 29–33.

Mautz, R.K., and Sharaf, H.A., 1961, *The Philosophy of Auditing*, Monograph No. 6, Sarasota, FL: American Accounting Association.

Metcalf Committee (L. Metcalf, Chair), 1977, 'The Accounting Establishment,' Staff Study of U.S. Senate Subcommittee on Reports, Accounting and Management,' 95th Congress, 1st sess., Washington, DC: USGPO.

Mey, A., 1966, 'Theodore Limperg and His Theory of Values and Cost,' *Abacus*, 2:1, 3–23.

Meyer, P.E., 1973, 'The Accounting Entity,' *Abacus*, 9:2, 116–26.

Miller, P., Hopper, T., and Laughlin, R., 1991, 'The New Accounting History: An Introduction,' *Accounting, Organizations and Society*, 16:5/6, 395–403.

Moonitz, M., 1961, ARS1, *The Basic Postulates of Accounting*, New York: AICPA.

——, 1982, 'Chambers at the American Institute of Certified Public Accountants,' *Abacus*, 18:2, 106–11.

Morgan, E.V., and Thomas, W.A., 1962, *The History of The Stock Exchange: Its History and Functions*, London: Elek Books.

Moss Committee (E. Moss, Chair), 1976, 'Federal Regulation and Regulatory Reform,' Report of the U.S. Congress Subcommittee on Oversight and Investigation, Washington, DC: USGPO.

Muller, J.Z., 2002, *The Mind and the Market: Capitalism in Modern European Thought*, New York: Alfred A. Knopf.

Napier, C.J., 1996, 'Accounting and the Absence of a Business Economics Tradition in the United Kingdom,' *European Accounting Review*, 5:3, 449–81.

Napier, C.J., 1998, 'Giving an Account of Accounting History: A Reply to Keenan,' *Critical Perspectives on Accounting*, 9:6, 685–700.

Nassar, S., 2011, *Grand Pursuit: The Story of Economic Genius*, New York: Simon & Schuster.

NCSC 'Green Paper,' 1983, *Financial Reporting Requirements of the Companies Act and Codes*, Canberra: AGPS.

Needles, B., and Olmsted, L., 2004, 'A History of International Association for Accounting Education and Research (IAAER): 1984–2004,' paper presented at The St Louis Academy of Accounting Historians Conference, 3 August.

Nelson, C., 1973, 'A Priori Research in Accounting,' in Dopuch, N., and Revsine, L (Eds.), *Accounting Research 1960–1970: A Critical Evaluation*, Urbana, IL: Center for International, Education and Research in Accounting, 3–25.

Newman, J.H. (Cardinal), 1852/1996, *The Idea of a University*, New Haven, CT: Yale University Press.

Nickerson, C.B., 1937, 'Inventory Reserves as an Element of Inventory Policy,' *The Accounting Review*, 12:4, 345–54.

Niell, N., 1991, *Technically and Further: Sydney Technical College, 1891–1991*, Melbourne: Hale and Iremonger.

Nobes, C., 2009, 'The Importance of Being Fair—an Analysis of IFRS Regulation in Practice: A Comment,' *Accounting and Business Research*, 39:4, 415–27.

———, 'IFRSs Ten Years On: Has the IASB Improved Extensive Use of Fair Values? Has the EU Learnt to Have IFRS? And Does the Use of Fair Value Make IFRS Illegal in the EU?,' *Accounting in Europe*, 12:2, 153–70.

Noguchi, M., and Edwards, J.R., 2004, 'Accounting Principles, Internal Conflict and the State: The Case of the ICAEW, 1948–1966,' *Abacus*, 40:3, 280–320.

Oliver, G.R., and Walker, R.G., 2006, 'Reporting on Software Projects to Senior Managers on the Board,' *Abacus*, 42:1, 40–65.

Ortego y Gasset, J., 1946/63, *The Mission of a University*, translated and with an introduction by H.L. Nostrand, London: Kegan Paul, Trench, Trubner & Co.

Owen, N. (Royal Commissioner), 2003, *HIH Royal Commission*, Canberra: Australian Government Printer.

Pacioli, L., 1494, *La Summa de Arithmetica, Geometria, Proportioni et Proportionalità*, Tusculano: Paganino de Paganini (republished 1523); in English, *An Original Translation of the Treatise on Double-Entry Book-Keeping* (P. Crivelli, trans.), London: The Institute of Book-Keepers.

Pareto, V., 1916, *The Mind and Society*, translated by A. Bongiorno and A. Livingston, New York: Dover.

Parker, R., Wolnizer, P., and Nobes, C., 1996, *Readings in True and Fair*, New York: Garland Publishing.

Paton, W.A., 1922, *Accounting Theory*, Chicago: Accounting Studies Press Ltd.

Paton, W.A., and Littleton, A.C., 1940, *An Introduction to Corporate Accounting Standards*, Columbus: American Accounting Association.

Peasnell, K., 1979, 'Capital Budgeting and Discounted Cash Equivalents: Some Clarifying Comments,' *Abacus*, 15:2, 145–56.

———, 1981, 'On Capital Budgeting and Income Measurement,' *Abacus*, 17:1, 52–67.

Peliken, J., 1992, *The Idea of a University: A Re-Examination*, New York: Yale University Press.

Persson, M.E., 2013, *The Rise and Fall of Comprehensive Accounting Theories: R.J. Chambers and Continuously Contemporary Accounting* (PhD in Accounting), London: Royal Holloway University of London.

Persson, M.E., and Napier, C.J., 2014, 'The Australian Accounting Academic in the 1950s: R.J. Chambers and Networks of Accounting Research,' *Meditari Accountancy Research*, 22:1, 54–76.

Persson, M. E., and Napier, C.J., 2018, 'R. J. Chambers on Securities and Obscurities: Making a Case for the Reform of the Law of Company Accounts in the 1970s,' *Abacus*, 54:1, 36–65.

Potter, B., 2003, 'The Louis Goldberg Collection at Deakin University: Exploring a Rich Foundation for Historical Research,' *Accounting History, N.S*, 8:2, 9–34.

Pozsar, Z., Tobias, A., Ashcraft, A., and Boesky, H., 2010, *Shadow Banking*, NY: Federal Reserve Bank of New York Staff Report: 458, July (revised February 2012).

Pratten, C., 1991, *Company Failure*, London: ICAEW.

Previts, G.J., 1996, '*An Accounting Thesaurus: 500 Years of Accounting*: Review,' *The Accounting Historians' Journal*, 23:2, 114–6.

Previts, G.J., Parker, L.D., and Coffman, E.N., 1990a, 'An Accounting Historiography: Subject Matter and Methodology,' *Abacus*, 26:2, 136–58.

Previts, G.J., Parker, L.D., and Coffman, E.N., 1990b, 'Accounting History: Definition and Relevance,' *Abacus*, 26:1, 1–16.

Ramsay, I., and Stapledon, G., 1998, *Corporate Groups in Australia*, Melbourne: University of Melbourne, Centre for Corporate Law and Securities Regulation.

———, 2001, 'Corporate Groups in Australia,' *Australian Business Law Review*, 29:1, 7–32.

Reiter, S.A., and Williams, P.F., 2002, 'The Structure and Progressivity of Accounting Research: The Crisis in the Academy Revisited,' *Accounting, Organizations and Society*, 2:6, 575–607.

Report of the Committee of Inquiry into Inflation and Taxation in Australia (Mathews, R. Chairman), 1975, *Inflation and Taxation*, Canberra: Australian Government Printer, 22 May.

Richardson, I.L.M. (Chairman), 1976, 'Report of the Committee of Inquiry into Inflation,' presented to the House of Representatives by Leave, Wellington: New Zealand Government Printer, 28 September.

Rosen, S., 1976, 'Where Future Shock is Disputed,' *New York Times*, 18 June, 18.

Roszak, T., 1986, *The Cult of Information: The Folklore of Computers and the True Art of Thinking*, Cambridge: Lutterworth Press.

Ryan, F.J.O., 1967, 'A True and Fair View,' *Abacus*, 32:2, 95–108.

Salveson, M.E., 1997, 'The Institute of Management Sciences: A Prehistory and Commentary on the Occasion of TIMS' 40th Anniversary,' *Interfaces*, 27:3, 74–85.

Sanders, T.H., Hatfield, H.R., and Moore, U., 1938, *A Statement of Accounting Principles*, New York: American Institute of Accountants; reprinted in 1959, 1963, 1968 and 1974.

Sandilands, F.E.P. (Chairman), 1975, *Inflation Accounting: Report of the Inflation Accounting Committee*, London: HMSO, cmnd, 25 June; presented to Parliament, September.

Schmalenbach, E. 1922, *Goldmarkbilanz* [Goldmark Accounting], Berlin: Julius Springer.

Schmidt, F., 1921, *Die organische Bilanz in Rahmen der Wirtschaft* [Organic Accounting in the Framework of the Economy], Leipzig: G.A. Gloeckner.

Scott, W., 1944, *The Principles of Cost Accounting*, Sydney: Law Book Company.

SEC (United States of America Securities and Exchange Commission), 1976, *Accounting Series Release 190, Amendments to Regulation S-X Requiring Disclosure of Certain Replacement Cost Data*, Washington, DC: SEC.

———, 1979, Accounting Series Release No. 271, *Deletion of Requirement to Disclose Replacement Cost Information*, Washington, DC: SEC.

———, 2003, *Study Pursuant to Section 108(d) of the Sarbanes—Oxley Act of 2002 on the Adoption by the United States Financial Reporting System of a Principles-Based Accounting System*, Washington, DC:SEC, available at www.sec. gov/news/studies/principlesbasedstand.htm, accessed 28 November 2012.

———, 2008, *Report and Recommendations Pursuant to Section 133 of the Emergency Economic Stabilization Act of 2008: Study on Mark-To-Market Accounting*, December, Washington, DC: SEC, available at www.sec.gov/news/studies/2008/ marktomarket123008.pdf, accessed 16 July 2018.

Sidebotham, R. (Ed.), 1965, *Introduction to the Theory and Context of Accounting*, Oxford: Pergamon Press.

Simon, H.A., 1990, 'Information, Technologies and Organizations,' *The Accounting Review*, 65:3, 658–67.

Smith, A., 1776, *An Inquiry into the Nature and Causes of the Wealth of Nations*, London: Methuen & Co.

Solomons, D., 1966, 'Book Review [of A,E&EB],' *Abacus*, 2:2, 205–9.

Someya, K., 1996, *Japanese Accounting: A Historical Approach*, Oxford: Oxford University Press.

Sprague, C.E., 1907/17, *The Philosophy of Accounts*, New York: The Ronald Press Company.

Sprouse, R.T., and Moonitz, M., 1962, ARS3, *A Tentative Set of Broad Accounting Principles for Business Enterprises*, New York: AICPA.

Staff of the Research Division, AICPA, 1963, *ARS6, Reporting the Financial Effects of Price-Level Changes*, New York: AICPA.

Stamp, E., 1982, 'R.J. Chambers: Laudatio viri veritatis studentis,' *Abacus*, 18:2, 182–4.

Staubus, G.J., 1967, 'Current Cash Equivalent for Assets: A Dissent,' *The Accounting Review*, 42:4, 650–61.

———, 2003, 'An Accountant Education,' *Accounting Historians Journal*, 30:1, 155–96.

———, 2004, 'On Brian P. West's *Professionalism and Accounting Rules*,' *Abacus*, 40:2, 139–56.

Staunton, J.J., 2007, *Exiting Intellectual Grooves in the Reporting of Liabilities*, PhD thesis, Sydney: The University of Sydney, July.

Sterling, R.R., 1970, *Theory of the Measurement of Enterprise Income*, Lawrence: Kansas University Press.

———, 1975, 'Toward a Science of Accounting,' *Financial Analysts Journal*, 31:5, 28–36.

Sweeney, H., 1936, *Stabilized Accounting*, New York: Harper and Brothers.

———, 1964, *Stabilized Accounting*, New York: Holt, Rinehart and Winston.

Tett, G., 2009, *Fool's Gold: How the Bold Dream of a Small Tribe at J.P. Morgan was Corrupted by Wall Street Greed and Unleashed a Catastrophe*, London: Little Brown.

Thomas, A.L., 1969, *The Allocation Problem in Financial Accounting Theory*, Studies in Accounting Research No. 3, Sarasota, FL: American Accounting Association.

———, 1974, *The Allocation Problem: Part Two*, Studies in Accounting Research No. 9, Sarasota, FL: American Accounting Association.

Tinker, A., 2005, 'Rosemary's Baby: Neo-Classical Economics as Ray Chambers' Love Child: A Commentary on Professor Chambers' 1999 paper "The Poverty of Accounting Discourse,"' *Accounting Education Research*, 14:1, 19–24.

Tomlins, T.E., 1820, *The Law Dictionary*, London: Payne & Foss.

Tucker, P.M.W., 2010, *Shadow Banking: Financing Markets and Financial Stability*, Remarks by Paul Tucker, Deputy Governor, Financial Stability at the Bank of England, at BGG Partners Seminar, London, 21 January 2010, available at www.bankofengland.co.uk/publications/Documents/speeches/2010/speech420.pdf, accessed 28 November 2012.

Tucker, P.M.W., 2012, *Shadow Banking: Thoughts for a Possible Policy Agenda*, Speech by Paul Tucker, Deputy Governor, Financial Stability, Bank of England, at the European Commission High Level Conference, Brussels, 27 April 2012, available at www.bankofengland.co.uk/publications/Pages/speeches/2012/566.aspx, accessed 28 November 2012.

Tuite, L., 2013, *International Accounting Standards and Financial Stability*, PhD thesis, The University of Sydney.

Tweedie, D., and Whittington, G., 1984, *The Debate on Inflation Accounting*, London: Cambridge University Press.

U.K. Committee of Inquiry into the Electrical Supply Industry, 1956, *Report of Inquiry into the Electrical Supply Industry*, London: HMSO.

U.K. Royal Commission on the Taxation of Profits and Income, 1955, *Final Report. Royal Commission on the Taxation of Profits and Income*, London: HMSO, Cmd. 9474.

U.K. Committee on Taxation of Trading Profits (Tucker, Millard Chairman), 1949/1951, *Report of the Committee on the Taxation of Trading Profits, First Report, 1949; 2nd and Final Report*, 1951, London: HMSO.

Valukas, A.R., Examiner in Bankruptcy, 2010, *In re Lehman Brothers Holdings Inc*, New York: U.S. Bankruptcy Court, Southern District.

van der Laan, S., and Dean, G., 2010, 'Corporate Groups in Australia: State of Play,' *Australian Accounting Review*, 20:2, 121–33.

Vance, L. (Chairman), 1967, *Berkeley Symposium on the Foundation of Financial Accounting*, Berkeley: Schools of Business Administration, University of California.

Vancil, R.F., and Weil, R., 1976, 'Current Replacement Cost Accounting: Depreciable Assets, and Distributable Income,' *Financial Analysts Journal*, 32:4, 38–45.

Vatter, W.J., 1964, *Survey of Accountancy Education in Australia*, Melbourne: Ware Publishing.

Von Mises, L., 1949, *Human Action*, London: William Hodge and Company Limited.

Vos, J., 1970, 'Replacement Value Accounting,' *Abacus*, 6:2, 132–43.

Walker, D., 1955, 'The Royal Commission and Depreciation Allowances,' *Accounting Research*, 6:5, 369–81.

Walker, E.R., and Linford, R.J., 1942, 'War Time Price Control and Price Movements in an Open Economy: Australia 1914–1920 and 1939–1940,' *The Review of Economics and Statistics*, 24:2, 75–8.

Walker, R.G., 1976, 'An Evaluation of the Information Conveyed by Consolidated Statements,' *Abacus*, 12:2, 77–115.

———, 1978, *Consolidated Statements: A History and Analysis*, New York: Arno Press.

———, 1992, 'The SEC's Ban on Upward Asset Revaluations and the Disclosure of Current Values,' *Abacus*, 28:1, 3–35.

———, 2002, *Submission 41 to JCPAA Inquiry, Review of Independent Auditing by Registered Company Auditors*, available at www.aph.gov.au/Parliamentary_Business/ Committees/House_of_Representatives_Committees?url=jcpaa/indepaudit/subs. htm, accessed 28 November 2012.

———, 2007, 'Reporting Entity,' *Abacus*, 43:1, 49–75.

Walker, R.G., and Oliver, G.O., 2005, 'Accounting for Expenditure on Software Development for Internal Use,' *Abacus*, 41:1, 66–91.

Wells, M.C., 1976, 'A Revolution in Accounting Theory?' *The Accounting Review*, 51:3, 471–82.

———, 1984, *Current Cost Accounting and the Nationalised Industries: An Analysis and a Proposal*, Glasgow: University of Glasgow, School of Financial Studies.

Wells, M.C., 2000, 'Founding *Abacus*: Frustration to Fulfilment,' *Abacus*, 36:3, 255–66.

West, B.P., 2003, *Professionalism and Accounting Rules*, London and New York: Routledge.

Whitehead, A.N., 1929, *The Aims of Education and Other Essays*, New York: Free Press.

Whitley, R., 1986. 'The Transformation of Business Finance Into Financial Economics: The Roles of Academic Expansion and Changes in U.S. Capital Markets,' *Accounting, Organizations and Society*, 11:2, 171–92.

Whittington, G., 1980, 'Pioneers of Income Measurement and Price-Level Accounting: A Review Article,' *Accounting and Business Research*, 38, Spring, 232–41.

———, 1990, 'Is Accounting Becoming Too Interesting,' Sir Julian Hodge Lecture, Aberystwith: University of Wales; reproduced in Whittington (2007).

———, 2007, *Profitability, Accounting Theory and Methodology*, London and New York: Routledge.

Whittington, G., and Zeff, S.A., 2001, 'Mathews, Gynther and Chambers: Three Pioneering Australian Theorists,' *Accounting and Business Research*, 31:4, 203–34.

Wiles, P., 1951, 'Corporate Taxation Based on Replacement Cost,' *Accounting Research*, 2:1, 77–82.

Wolnizer, P.W., 1987, *Auditing as Independent Authentication*, Sydney: Sydney University Press.

Wolnizer, P.W., and Dean, G.W., 2000, 'Chambers as Educator and Mentor,' *Abacus*, 36:3, 243–54.

Wright, K., 1967, 'Capacity for Adaptation and Asset Measurement Problem,' *Abacus*, 3:1, 74–9.

Zeff, S.A., 1962, 'Replacement Cost—Member of the Family, Welcome Guest, or Intruder?' *The Accounting Review*, 37:4, 611–25.

———, 1972, *Forging Accounting Principles in Five Countries: A History and Analysis of Trends*, Champaign, IL: Stipes Publishing Company.

———, 1972, 'Chronology of Significant Developments in the Establishment of Accounting Principles in the United States, 1926–1972,' *Journal of Accounting Research*, 10:1, 217–27.

Zeff, S.A. (Compiler and Editor), 1982, *The Accounting Postulates and Principles Controversy of the 1960s*, New York: Garland Publishing.

————, 2000, 'John B. Canning: A View of His Academic Career,' *Abacus*, 36:1, 4–39.

————, 2001, 'The Work of the Special Committee on Research Program,' *Accounting Horizons*, 28:2, 141–86.

————, 2007, 'The Primacy of "Present Fairly" in the Auditor's Report,' *Accounting Perspectives*, 6:1, 1–20.

————, 2011, 'Review of *Sydney School of Accounting: The Chambers Years* (Sydney, Sydney University, The Accounting Foundation, November, 2010; co-authored by Graeme Dean, Frank Clarke and Murray Wells),' *The Accounting Review*, 86:3, 1484–5.

————, 2015, 'The Wheat Study on Establishment of Accounting Principles (1971–72): A Historical Study,' *Journal of Accounting and Public Policy*, 34:2, 146–74.

Index

Page numbers in **bold** indicate a table on the corresponding page

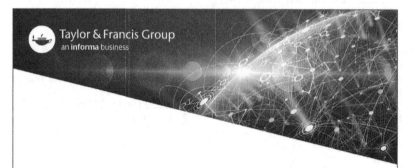

Printed in the United States
by Baker & Taylor Publisher Services